READINGS IN ECONOMICS

FROM FORTUNE

EDITED BY RICHARD E. MULCAHY

UNIVERSITY OF SAN FRANCISCO

REVISED EDITION

195

Readings in Economics

From FORTUNE

REVISED EDITION

Edited by RICHARD E. MULCAHY
University of San Francisco

HENRY HOLT AND COMPANY, NEW YORK

Cover design by Walter Allner

25890-0317

Printed in the United States of America

Preface to the Revised Edition

The very warm reception accorded the first edition of *Readings in Economics from Fortune* was most encouraging. The publication of the *Readings* was prompted originally by the idea that *Fortune* articles, resulting from the joint work of a staff of experts—economists, editors, reporters, and artists—are excellent material for the Economics Principles Course. The wide acceptance of the first edition appears to be a concrete confirmation of that idea. Students seem to appreciate the technical principles of economics served in such a readable style.

There was a temptation in this edition to make as few changes as possible, following that classical dictum in sports and cards, "Never change a winning game." Actually, however, the *Readings* has undergone major remodeling. There are fifteen new articles, sixteen of the original articles having been retained. It was easy to overcome the temptation to follow the *status quo* dictum because in the last three years *Fortune* has printed so many exceedingly valuable articles for the Principles course. Six famous series have been edited: The Changing American Market, The Dynamic Market for Capital Goods, The New Economy, The New Management, Financing the New Economy, and The New Goals—two of which have already appeared as separate books. Seven of the fifteen new articles have been chosen from these series. Excerpts from three others in the series have been used as long boxes limited to about a page. Here, as elsewhere, useful material had to be sacrificed in order to retain the original size of the *Readings* so that *Fortune's* articles could again be made available to students at a very low price.

The articles in the original edition usually presented a concrete description of some institution of economic life, such as the maze of tariff regulations, or offered a provocative discussion of a timely topic, as for instance the adequacy of America's natural resources. Additional current problems are discussed in the new articles: the astronomical rise in consumer debt, the need of tax reform, the gold question, mergers, currency convertibility, and automation.

However, a new type of article is prominent in this edition. In today's flourishing economy new trends are emerging which have been the subject of full-dress *Fortune* studies. The analyses of these major developments are found in the articles on population, productivity, income distribution, capital goods, management practices, and the stock market. The trends are identified and measured; their significance for the economic future of America is evaluated. Finally, there are two top historical studies on the Great Depression: why it happened and why it lasted so long.

A student survey helped decide which first-edition articles were to be retained in this edition. The results in some cases were quite surprising. A few articles I thought very interesting and useful appealed to the students hardly at all, and the criticisms they offered were penetrating and instructive. It might be of interest to know that the most popular article was the introductory 1940 survey of the U. S. economy; the second most popular, the story of the United Steelworkers of America.

As a result of the remodeling, all the articles are now from postwar *Fortune* except "The U.S.A." Two thirds of them were written in the 1950's and one half in the last three years. One new article is quite distinctive in that it was printed in April, 1948. It was not overlooked in the first edition but was omitted solely because the subject was covered by another article which was used for a dual purpose.

This revised edition of the *Readings* again offers selections for all the major topics normally treated in the Principles course. The *Readings* seems to have proved to be a suitable companion for any of the standard texts.

In keeping with the recent development in books of readings, articles of some length have been chosen on the whole. However, the articles have been cut somewhat to highlight the matter pertinent to Economic Principles and to enhance reading interest. Nothing has been added except a few stray footnotes dealing with facts and signed "Editor." Care was taken that the cutting did not affect the general tone or position of the article. The customary punctuation to indicate deletions was omitted in order to increase readability. Each article is prefaced by an introduction summarizing briefly the main ideas and highlighting the particular economic principle covered.

When the idea of the *Readings* was first conceived, it was thought that perhaps some professors might feel that the student would not receive a well-rounded picture because all the articles are from one source. The wide adoption of the first edition has dispelled this fear. However, it might be well to repeat here, for the benefit of the "newcomers," the reasons why it is believed that the student does not receive a one-sided picture but that actually the *Fortune* articles may contribute to a broader knowledge of economics and the American economy.

First of all, *Fortune's* outlook, especially in recent years, has been very well-balanced and, in particular, has shown an awareness of the social aspects of economic life. Secondly, as a general rule the policy articles present both sides, so that the student has available in one selection data gathered from many technical works and presented in a language he can understand clearly. An outstanding example of this is "Do Unions Raise Wages?"

Moreover, there is no reason why the student's outside readings should be confined to these selections. This work has been compiled as a core book of readings containing a limited number of selections which most professors would wish their students to read but which are difficult to obtain in quantity. Actually, this may have a tendency to increase the range of outside readings, since the professor has complete freedom to assign around this core whatever he feels best supplements it.

Perhaps it is almost unnecessary to say that these selections were chosen because it was my judgment that they were excellent reading material for the beginning economics student. They do not necessarily represent my views nor even those of the present editors of *Fortune*.

Many colleagues and friends contributed their services in the preparation of the original and revised edition of the *Readings*. I am indebted to them all. I

am especially grateful to the many economics professors who used the first edition in their classes and who aided this revised edition by their constructive criticism. Particular mention must be made of the competent assistance rendered by Miss Elizabeth A. Haggood who prepared the articles for the publisher and improved the manuscript by many valuable suggestions.

And, I am especially indebted to Time Inc., the publishers of *Fortune* magazine, who so kindly permitted the use of their copyrighted material and cooperated so generously in carrying out this work. Mr. Brooke Alexander, assistant to the publisher of *Fortune*, contributed to the original and this revised edition by his continual encouragement and assistance.

R. E. M.

University of San Francisco
December 8, 1956

Contents

1. THE ECONOMY: RESOURCES AND PEOPLE

1. The American Economy: THE U.S.A. 1
   Box: Industrialization in the South 3

2. Resources: THE CRISIS IN RAW MATERIALS 8

3. Population: SIXTY-SIX MILLION MORE AMERICANS 16

4. Productivity: THE ENGINE: RISING PRODUCTIVITY (by Gilbert Burck) 21

2. THE ECONOMY: INSTITUTIONS

5. The Labor Movement: THE U. S. LABOR MOVEMENT 27
   Box: Beyond the "Annual Wage" 31

6. Labor Unions: UNITED STEELWORKERS OF AMERICA 33
   Box: Communism in the C.I.O.? 36

7. The Corporation: THE AGE OF THE MANAGERS (by Herrymon Maurer) 38

8. Concentration: THE URGE TO MERGE (by William B. Harris) 44

9. Taxation: TAX REFORM: IT CAN HAPPEN 48

10. Money: GOLD: DOWN BUT NOT OUT (by Richard Austin Smith) 53

11. Federal Reserve: MANAGERS OF THE DOLLAR 58
    Box: Where Money Is Really Made 59

3. NATIONAL INCOME

12. Income Flows: THE HYDROSTATICS OF THE DOLLAR 62

13. Saving: WHY DO PEOPLE BUY? 65
    Box: The Old Saving Habit 66

14. Dissaving: THE COMING TURN IN CONSUMER CREDIT (by Gilbert Burck and
    Sanford Parker) 70
    Box: The Danger in Mortgage Debt 73

15. Investment: THE DYNAMIC MARKET FOR CAPITAL GOODS (by Gilbert Burck and
    Sanford Parker) 76

16. Cycles: WHAT CAUSED THE GREAT DEPRESSION (by Gilbert Burck and Charles
    E. Silberman) 82

17. Depression: WHY THE DEPRESSION LASTED SO LONG (by Gilbert Burck and Charles
    E. Silberman) 88

4. THE MARKET

18. The Consumer: THE NEW BUYING "HABITS" 95

19. Costs: HOW TO TELL WHERE YOU BREAK EVEN 97

20. Competition: THE NEW COMPETITION 99

21. Agriculture: FARM POLICY: A GREAT OPPORTUNITY 104
    Box: The Magnificent Decline 105
        The Apparatus of Farm Controls 108

22. Speculation: IS THE STOCK MARKET OBSOLETE? 110

5. INCOME DISTRIBUTION

23. Income Pattern: THE RICH MIDDLE-INCOME CLASS 115

24. Wages: DO UNIONS RAISE WAGES? (by Daniel Bell) 121

25. Profits: THE FUNCTION OF PROFITS (by Peter Drucker) 124

6. INTERNATIONAL ECONOMICS

26. Foreign Trade: "THE DOLLAR CRISIS IN NEW ENGLAND" (by J. K. Galbraith) . . 129

27. Tariff: U. S. TARIFF 131
    Box: Mr. Marx Vetoes Free Trade 131
        Waltham Watch Meets Swiss Competition 136

28. Foreign Exchange: CURRENCY CONVERTIBILITY—NOW (by Michael A. Heilperin) . 136

7. ECONOMIC SYSTEMS AND THE FUTURE

29. Communism: HOW BUSINESS GETS DONE IN RUSSIA 141

30. Capitalism: THE TRANSFORMATION OF AMERICAN CAPITALISM 147
    Box: The Average Stockholder's 19½ Shares 150

31. Automation: "AUTOMATION": NEWS BEHIND THE NOISE (by Herbert Solow) . . 152
    Box: Automation—Socially Desirable? 154

1. The Economy: Resources and People

1. THE AMERICAN ECONOMY

THE U. S. A.*

This introduction to the American economy describes its people, its resources, its material achievements, and its seven regional economies. The United States is great by reason of the integration of these divergent economies. What they grow, manufacture, and sell to each other reveals the complexity of America and the benefits of one vast market. Moreover, these seven shadowy nations exemplify the various species and stages of economic development: the man-versus-nature, the underdeveloped, the colonial, the frontier, the expanding, the balanced agricultural-industrial, and the mature creditor economies.

Less by definition than by achievement, the United States is the greatest nation on earth. Everybody knows it, everybody believes it, everybody says it—usually without quite knowing why. It isn't the greatest nation in size. Its continental area of 3,026,789 square miles is less than half the size of the Soviet Union, and smaller than Canada or Brazil. It is almost once and a half the size of Europe without the Soviet Union, but with all possessions it occupies only 7 per cent of the total land area of the world, whereas the British Empire sprawls across a third of the globe, Soviet Russia's chunk equals 14 per cent, and the French reservation another 8 per cent. The U.S. isn't the greatest nation by nose count. Its population of 130,085,000 is small compared to 450,000,000 Chinese, 353,000,000 Indians, and 170,000,000 Russians. Per square mile it has only forty-three inhabitants, and is more sparsely settled than any of the major nations with the exception of Soviet Russia; in contrast the 742 persons per square mile in England seems almost fantastic.

In spite of an unparalleled industrial civilization, the U.S. is not predominantly a manufacturing nation. Manufacturing accounts for less than a fifth of the country's total realized income, whereas in the United Kingdom and Japan over 30 per cent of national income is derived from factory trades; in Sweden 40 per cent. The U.S. has built the world's most fabulous cities, but it is not the most urbanized nation, even though the population of citified New York exceeds that of either Canada or Argentina, and though Pennsylvania has more inhabitants than Belgium or Hungary, citified Illinois more than Finland and Denmark together. But less than 30 per cent of U.S. citizens live in big cities. In England nearly 45 per cent of the people dwell in cities of 100,000 or more, and in Germany over 30 per cent. The U.S. is still predominantly small-town and rural; not metropolitan.

Commonly presumed to be wealthier in natural resources than any other nation, the U.S. in some respects

is probably equaled and in others exceeded by the British Empire and the Soviet Union, and its reserves may someday be equaled by those awaiting exploitation or discovery in South Africa, South America, and the hinterland of Asia. Furthermore, the U.S. has certain vital deficiencies. It consumes more than half the world's rubber crop, grows none. It drinks half the world's coffee, and again grows none. It uses three-fourths of the world's raw silk without cultivating any silkworms to speak of. It brings in (mainly from Argentina) 15 per cent of its hides. Its production of sugar, taken with that supplied by U.S. island possessions, is about 12 per cent of the world's total, but it consumes 20 per cent, and that 8 per cent difference amounts to 2,770,000 tons. It has virtually no tin, or platinum, or chromite, or antimony; precious little manganese, quicksilver, tungsten, and nickel. Granted that the superb U.S. technology could stop some of these gaps if war or other *force majeure* cut off imports, the fact remains that in a number of categories the U.S. is far from being independent of the outside world.

But in spite of all lacks and unfavorable comparisons the U.S. *is* the greatest nation on earth. Its actual greatness rests not on single assets, but on their combination. The greatness of the U.S. is the sum of a vast land area; a great, resourceful population of diverse origins and talents; a great agriculture of such richness that it embarrasses; a universal industry of cosmic dimensions; an enormous treasury of resources; a form of government that has stimulated the optimum development of all the components of the economy. It is the compounding of all these sources of greatness that makes the U.S. great.

And it is this compounding that has resulted in the creation of an American superman. For in a civilization based on energy and productivity the meaning and the effectiveness of every U.S. citizen are magnified and extended. Each has the largest per capita share of the world's coal and corn and iron ore and wheat and electricity and automobiles and bathtubs and radios and telephones and machines in general. It is as a nation of industrialized individuals who are

* From "The U.S.A.," February, 1940.

in effect supermen that the U.S. has attained wealth, productivity, and strength far beyond comparison with any other nation, or, for that matter, most combinations of nations.

THE REGIONS

But of course the overshadowing achievement of the American people—the achievement that is the foundation of the nation's greatness—has been the integration of the divergent economies of the U.S. Externally the nation looks like a compact, single economic unit, but a familiar inspection reveals that it is scarcely that. Indeed, it is a union composed of countless units, each with its own economy based upon its own sources of wealth, dominated by self-interest, and competing with every other unit. To take a *reductio ad absurdum,* each citizen is a complete unit, and essentially every worker is in competition with every other worker for the job he has, or a better one. At the other end of the scale there are certain vast and vague areas that have been traditionally divided against each other: the North versus the South, the East versus the West. The passions aroused by the conflicting interests of those areas have at times been intense. In politics these passions are known collectively as sectionalism.

Indeed, there are any number of ways of dividing the U.S., and concerning few of them do scholars agree. But they are most nearly in agreement on the relatively modern doctrine of regionalism, which is distinguished from sectionalism on a number of counts, but chiefly in the fact that, whereas the basis of sectionalism is often emotional and political, the basis of regionalism is truly economic, cultural, and social. In any event, a division of the U.S. into its regions provides the best opening to an understanding of its fundamental achievement.

Even regionally, however, there are a great number of ways of dividing the U.S. Few regions are crystallized; few correspond exactly to state borders. Yet for statistical purposes the regions must be built of whole states. *Fortune* has arbitrarily chosen the division illustrated by the map on this page: the Northeast, the Southeast, the Middle States, the Mountain and Plains States, the Southwest, the Pacific Northwest, and the Far West. While each of these regions contains subregions, this division would seem to be the most realistic one, on most counts, that students have devised.

THE NORTHEAST

Closest to Europe, and more nearly European than any other U.S. region, the Northeast has three tiers— New England; New York, New Jersey, Pennsylvania; Delaware, Maryland, West Virginia. Almost any snap characterization of this group of states is certain to be wrong. It has thirty-four cities of more than 100,000. Therefore it is a metropolitan region. Yet there is nothing so truly rural in the U.S. as the New England villages off the big highways radiating north from New York, where farming is still largely unmechanized and milch cows with bells around their necks are prodded down Main Street by towheaded youngsters, and sheep

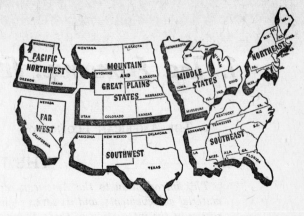

crop the green plots around the monuments to those who died at Cold Harbor and Bull Run. It is a metropolitan region with a population of over forty million occupying about 7 per cent of the nation's area. It is a highly civilized, highly educated, ultrasophisticated region, yet witchcraft flourishes in parts of southeastern Pennsylvania, where barns and houses wear cabalistic symbols designed to ward away the dreaded hex, and the pious Amish folk refuse to have their pictures taken. It is a calm, orderly, and settled region, but feuds still smolder and occasionally blaze among the mountain clans of West Virginia.

Economically the Northeast stands in relation to the U.S. about the way England stands in relation to the British Empire. The region is dependent on the rest of the country for its wheat and flour, and for a large part of its fresh meats, fruits, vegetables, and canned goods. It likewise is a heavy importer of lumber and allied products, newsprint, cotton, petroleum, although it supplies most of its own iron and coal.

To the U.S. the Northeast sells heavy machinery, coal, steel, railway equipment, paints, varnishes, glass, clothing and New England textiles, leather goods and shoes, paper, and tools. Again like England, the Northeast is the great concentration point of finance, ownership, and control. Of the national income the region draws nearly 40 per cent, and has 41 per cent of the nation's wealth. The value of its manufactures is 39 per cent of the nation's total; half the foreign imports of the U.S. clear through its ports.

Thus the Northeast draws financial tribute from every part of the U.S., and intellectual tribute as well. A common complaint throughout the country is, "All our smartest young people go east." They are drawn east, principally to New York and principally by the legendary glamour of the city that is the country's main source of information and entertainment. On a rock beside a river that is still one of the loveliest in the world the metropolis perches and its skyscrapers "lift their foggy plumes of stranded smoke out of a stony mouth." It is a phenomenon, but a typically American phenomenon. "Here, world, is a city," it seems to say. "Where but in America could you expect to find the like?"

From Pennsylvania on the south to New England on the north is a jump from a concentrated heavy-industry state to a section wherein industry is a small-scale, specialized operation. Only 2 per cent of the industrial plants in New England employ more than 500 workers, while in 88 per cent of the factories there are fewer than 100. The New England economy is a craft economy, reflecting the section's original isolation and its remoteness from the raw materials that make possible a mass-production economy. But the New Englander who first launched the craft economy had a native ingenuity that poverty sharpened. He put his eggs in as many baskets as possible, with the result that there are 200-odd different lines of manufacture in New England today, or about two-thirds of all the lines in the U.S. The section thus is virtually a "little nation" existing within the Northeast regional nation; economically indeed it is comparable to Switzerland. Its people are its chief asset, and its crafts its chief *raison d'être* in the U.S. economy. New England is preoccupied with its own problems, and they are sufficient to keep the New England mind firmly centered on New England. There is probably no more insular city on earth than Boston, and a perfect commentary on the Boston attitude is contained in the little anecdote about the Bostonian who planned to drive to California, and when asked which route he intended to take replied that he was "going by way of West Newton."

THE SOUTHEAST

The Southeast—Virginia, Kentucky, Tennessee, the Carolinas, Georgia, Alabama, Mississippi, Louisiana, Arkansas (which most Southerners consider more western than southern and pretty no-account anyway), and Florida (a freakish national phenomenon having little in common with the rest of the region)—has just entered the twentieth century. In a loose way it resembles the Northeast of the early days of the industrial revolution. The South begins in the Washington airport terminal where the signs on the two doors read "MEN (White Only)" and "WOMEN (White Only)." Across the Potomac lie Virginia's red-clay fields; to the southwest, the laurel-tangled mountains humping through Tennessee, Kentucky, and North Carolina; southward, the flatlands and thinly rooted pines of Georgia and South Carolina, the treeless, hard-baked vistas of Alabama and Mississippi, and the near-jungles of Florida and the lands along the Gulf. Down near latticed Charleston the Gullahs speak a primitive, liquid tongue, and bastard French is a useful language in the south Louisiana parishes. Mobile by night is hauntingly lovely, and Paris, Algiers, and Marseille converge beneath the wrought-iron balconies of New Orleans. To the west across the Huey Long Bridge the country is like a Rousseau painting, with pink flamingos toe-dancing across the black, green scummed bayous. In this romantic imagery, and indeed in almost every respect, the southeast is the precise opposite of the Northeast. It has more than twice as much land as the Northeast but only two-thirds as many people. Of these, 70 per cent are rural, and their per capita income is less than half that of the Northeast. Whereas the Northeast contains well over half of the 13,000,000 foreign-born U.S. white population, the Southeast has less than 2 per cent. Therefore it lays claim to being

"the most American region," even though 30 per cent of its people are black and unassimilable.

There is no occasion here to trace the history of the Southeast through feudal beginnings to the Civil War and the later Reconstruction, which failed to reconstruct. Slaves and cotton built the South, and the descendants of the slaves are today its greatest problem, and cotton its greatest curse. Among the U.S. regions it is the *enfant terrible*. Unlike New England, it is naturally rich, and if it is retarded, the blame rests squarely on the shoulders of the inhabitants, whose character, economy, and attitude are so different from New England's, and who thus far have displayed little of the Yankee's ingenuity in squeezing the best out of the land, and in developing appropriate regional industries.

However, precisely because it has been retarded, the industrial South appears to have the greatest growth potential of any region in the U.S. Today the value of southern manufactures is 10 per cent of the U.S. total, and almost four times the value of the agricultural

---

INDUSTRIALIZATION IN THE SOUTH

It was only thirteen years ago that Franklin Roosevelt could describe the South as "the Nation's No. 1 economic problem." Today it is doubtful whether the South could make anybody's list of the first ten economic problems of the U.S.

The Southern Association of Science and Industry recently noted that sales of southern manufacturers have increased more than 300 per cent since 1940. (Manufacturers' sales for the U.S. as a whole are 235 per cent above 1940.) Last year alone 12,000 new southern plants provided new industrial jobs for an estimated 339,000 workers. The great significance of these figures, according to the president of the association, Dr. Paul Chapman, who is associate dean of the agricultural college of the University of Georgia, is that the South has at last checked its "human erosion." Surplus labor freed by the very rapid mechanization of southern farming can find industrial employment in the South—frequently not more than a county or two away from the old farm.

—"Notes on the Permanent Revolution," August, 1951.

---

production of the region. It has 40 per cent of the U.S. forest land, accounts for 40 per cent of the total timber cut in the U.S., and has an investment of $225,000,000 in its pulp and paper industry. There is bauxite in Arkansas; there are oil, natural gas, and sulfur in Louisiana; phosphates in Florida, Tennessee, and South Carolina; marble, high-grade clays, and vast quantities of limestone. Around Birmingham coal crops up close to important iron deposits, and years ago the late Henry C. Frick predicted that by 1940 Birmingham would be a bigger steel city than Pittsburgh. It isn't—its capacity is only 3.4 per cent of the total U.S. steel capacity. But it could be.

The trouble with Birmingham—as the South sees it —is that it is owned by the North and, economically, that is the trouble with most southern industry. And as a tributary region this one is saddled with not only absentee industrialism, but also absentee farming, and northern hands take the dollars out of its pockets almost as rapidly as it puts them in. Thus its chronic depression will not be solved automatically by further industrialization by the North. And while dreamily contemplating the ivy twining higher around the crumbling white columns of a gracious, vanished southern past, the rest of the U.S. would do well to remember that if the per capita income of each Southerner were raised from its present $285 to the national average of $485 the nation would have captured a new market half again as big as the entire export trade, and be richer by billions.

THE MIDDLE STATES

If Hitler captured the Russian Ukraine and annexed it to the industrial Reich, the combination would produce an economy and a territory similar in many respects to the Middle States region, taking in Ohio, Indiana, Michigan, Illinois, Wisconsin, Minnesota, Iowa, and Missouri. Of all the regions, this one is most nearly independent of the others, could most easily drop out of the Union and survive as a separate nation. One of the world's greatest agricultural sections, it also ranks second only to the Northeast as an industrial region. It has few imports—coal, oil, lumber, and such —many exports, and its economy has been developed to a point where it processes its own raw materials and sells both commodities and finished goods. Since it has no reason for being jealous of any other region, it has few conflicts. And the conflicts that exist are chiefly social and political and cultural, rather than economic.

Settled originally by New Englanders and Southerners, followed by Germans and Scandinavians, the Middle States have a population of 35,000,000 dwelling on 15 per cent of the U.S. land. About two and a half millions of the people are farmers, and there are over four million workers in the industrial cities—those cities strung like beads of stone around the southern shores of the Lakes. The chief cities are not merely the national but the world headquarters of an industry— Detroit, Akron, Cleveland. Manufacture ranges from beer and soap and cash registers to steel and the heaviest of heavy machinery, and brings an income of four billion dollars to the middle-western economy.

The region is also second to the Northeast in the extent of urbanization. Yet it cannot by any stretch of imagination be called "urban." The urban Middle West is an arc from Cleveland to Milwaukee—close to the docks of the long, flat-topped freighters that carry through Sault Ste Marie locks more tonnage than clears the Suez or the Panama. Behind the cities of the Lakes lies a farming checkerboard, waving with yellow corn, black with plowed earth, and dotted loosely with fat red silos, magnificent barns, indifferent homes. Here—in addition to some 60 per cent of the nation's corn and a good 20 per cent of its wheat— are half the hogs and the greatest number of purebred, registered cattle in the U.S., producing (chiefly in Minnesota and Wisconsin) half of all the creamery

butter, 70 per cent of the factory cheese, more than 40 per cent of the milk. Here are also more than a third of the chickens laying nearly 40 per cent of the eggs.

In such lavish country a fundamental optimism is natural and infectious. The Middle West sees no confining horizons, is confident, boastful, scornful of penny pinching. Chicago is BIG—biggest hotel, biggest trading center, biggest crooks, biggest recreational waterfront. Detroit too is big—but Detroit is a renegade that constantly strives to have itself grouped with eastern rather than midwestern cities. And Cleveland has forgotten about bigness and pays more attention to cultural and intellectual niceties.

Outside of the cities the population is introspective rather than exuberant. Your typical farmer of the region is an individualist who will not be bossed, yet nowhere will you find a man more eager to be taught or more willing to make sacrifices for co-operative ventures. He knows soil chemistry, avidly follows the experimentation going on at his state agricultural college, and sits on his county agent's doorstep waiting for advice. He is rarely isolated, and almost never hidebound. The big cities he dislikes not so much on principle but because they represent—the eastern cities especially—the forces that are always trying to deprive him of political relief for the "farm problem"—i.e., the glut resulting from the application of his superior agricultural technology to his extraordinarily fertile land. No humble peasant, he has successfully used his political power time and again. He flocked to the Progressive party in Wisconsin, the Bull Moose standard back in 1912, created the Farmer-Labor party in Minnesota; and in Iowa and elsewhere oiled his shotgun and halted the wave of mortgage foreclosures in 1932 by the simple expedient of preventing bidding on foreclosed farms. He is probably the most completely democratic individual in the entire U.S., and he knows how to make democracy work for him.

THE MOUNTAINS AND THE PLAINS

West of the Mississippi you begin to find your pockets cluttered with round bits of white metal—mill pieces to pay the sales taxes—and west of the states bordering the river the last few vertebrae are ironed out of the land and the roads shoot westward like black arrows. To say that it is flat means nothing because flatness is only one dimension and here the sky closes in around your upraised hand, and the idea that the earth is round seems preposterous. Between the western Mississippi states and the foothills of the Rockies the only considerable break in the flatness occurs in the Black Hills of Wyoming and South Dakota, which loom up like a great island in a sea and then subside again in flatness. You drive across the plains at sixty, seventy, eighty—any speed. The ditches beside the road are dry and seem like gingerbread, and a rime of dust settles on your lips and on your windshield. Wheat stretches to the right of the road and to the left, and behind and ahead, and a few miles across the lonely flatness you see the combines spouting chaff. That treetop standing like a semaphore ten miles beyond your radiator cap means a farmhouse, and that gray smudge ten miles beyond the tree, a town. And when the wind blows hard, as it so often does, the tan dust eddies up above the tossing wheat and an iridescent curtain dims the sun.

There is no part of the American land that the men living on it do not love, but by all conventional standards the Northwest Plains states—Kansas, Nebraska, North and South Dakota—are the least attractive in the U.S. The plains run into the eastern halves of Wyoming, Montana, and Colorado, with the Rockies beyond running through Utah. These eight states cover 750,000 square miles—almost a quarter of the nation—and support a twentieth of the U.S. people. They were settled long after the Pacific states, in large part by a backwash of the Oregon and California migrations, and lately the settling process has been coming to a halt. The reason is simply that in spite of its great area the region is not productive enough to provide a living for its inhabitants. If the Middle West is an almost perfectly balanced economy, this region is entirely off balance, and it is certainly the least independent U.S. region. It is almost wholly agricultural, with only about 8 per cent of its $3,000,000,000 income coming from manufacturing, and it must import virtually all its finished goods, as well as many raw commodities. The region possesses enormous mineral resources—but these are largely low grade and unexploited, and the existing mining industry is controlled in large part by "foreign," i.e. eastern, capital, which draws the profits out of the region as fast as they are created.

Thus the region's most important resource is the land itself, and owing to a combination of factors the land is of diminishing value. Plowed up and mined for wheat during the years of the War wheat boom, the Plains states contain 165,000,000 acres of the most seriously eroded land in the U.S., and hardly a section in the area fails to show signs of damage by wind or water. By 1930 the region was growing half the U.S. wheat and had become the third-biggest corn producer, the largest sheep raiser, and ranked second in horses and cattle. But its cows give less milk than other cows, and its horses and chickens are valued lower at the market—in all, the realized agricultural income amounts to $530,000,000. Always arid, the Plains have been experiencing a chronic drought for nearly ten years, and farmers have stopped hoping for more than the present average annual rainfall of 18.7 inches. Wheat has sucked the subsurface moisture from the earth, the rain no longer flattens the dust, and a considerable fraction of the population can sit on their front porches and watch their livelihoods blowing away into the sky. As farmers go bankrupt, land reverts to the government by default of taxes, and much of it is returned to its original grass. Timothy and alfalfa replace wheat on thousands of acres, and the agronomists work ceaselessly to discover new crops suitable for the parched soil, new ways of utilizing the last drops of the scanty rain that falls.

It would be hard to say that these states conflict with other regions in view of the dominant conflict of the region versus nature. It resembles the South in that its main resource is apparently declining, yet it lacks the South's opportunities for expansion in other directions. Except for the $25,000,000 sugar beet crop, mining, oil, and range land, scenery and national parks are the chief assets of Utah, Colorado, Wyoming, and Montana, and tourists are their main source of cash.

THE SOUTHWEST

Historically the oldest, politically the youngest of the regions, the Southwest is a colonial economy exporting vast quantities of raw materials, importing most fabricated goods, and having more than a superficial resemblance to Brazil, Argentina, Venezuela, and Peru. It exports cotton for British, southern, and New England mills; cattle for the Chicago abattoirs; oil and minerals for the world. The region consists of Texas—where most of the developed resources are located and where the industrial dawn is breaking in the sparkling new cities of the eastern plains—Oklahoma, and empty New Mexico and Arizona.

The state of Texas—described in *Fortune* for December, 1939—is a thing apart; too big, too rich, too varied, too prophetic to be lumped in any general regional description, or synthesized in a paragraph or two. Bigger than any European nation except the U.S.S.R. and Germany, its widest points are more than 800 miles apart, and it has close to a tenth of the U.S. land area with a population of only 6,200,000—smaller than Greater New York. Texas grows more than a fourth of U.S. cotton and claims that it could supply the entire world. It furnishes close to 40 per cent of U.S. crude oil. On the coastal ranges it supports seven million head of cattle. Thanks to a $100,000,000 investment in irrigation ditches, the lower Rio Grande valley has already become a large producer of oranges, lemons, and grapefruit, and a distinct worry to the California citrus growers.

Nearly all of this fabulous wealth and growth are in East and Central Texas. West of Big Spring, Texas blends into the New Mexico-Arizona Southwest, with "centers" (*not* cities) separated by scores of miles of empty desert, incredible conformations of the land, always the hot sun, the high, dry air, the giant, theatrical, green cacti standing like sentries against the sky. New Mexico is Santa Fe, Roswell, and Albuquerque set down in 123,000 square miles with 422,000 inhabitants. Arizona is another 114,000 square miles, another 412,000 people, and Phoenix and Tucson, eternally bickering over each other's attractions. Phoenix is a spectacular working model of what other parts of the region may someday hope to be—a road or a fence separating cactus desert from lushly blooming irrigated fields of lettuce, orange groves, and every fruit and vegetable. Here is an American machine-conscious culture, rather than machine culture, built upon deep strata of ancient Indian and Mexican civilizations, and achieving a wholly pleasant compromise. In addition to the $77,500,000 annual copper output, tourists constitute a main source of income in Arizona and New Mexico, approximately $48,000,000 being spent by visitors. Arizona in particular visualizes itself as a tourist center and is often tempted to make a good thing better by legalizing gambling and relaxing the divorce laws to steal Nevada's lure.

THE FAR WEST

Nevada and California combine to form an almost indescribable region, with the infinite variety of California on one side of the mountains and the wild Nevada desert on the other. California is the second-biggest state in area and, with 6,154,000 people, is sixth in population;[1] Nevada has only 101,000 inhabitants and is forty-eighth in population, but sixth in area. Along with per capita income of $717, California has the fourth-highest total income in the U.S., whereas Nevada keeps herself going mainly by virtue of spinning roulette wheels, the eastern cartwheels dropping into slot machines, and the complacent magistrates handing down three thousand six-week divorces per year in Reno, "The Biggest Little City In The World." There is also a mining industry (chiefly copper) bringing in $14,000,000 annually; and there are minor livestock and farming activities in the infrequent irrigated portions of the state.

The great Golden State is a good deal like the amazing elephant encountered by the blind men. The coast line measures a thousand miles, runs from Oregon to Mexico. The northern quarter of California has some of the wildest forest and mountain terrain in North America; the southern quarter has an empty and dangerous desert—Death Valley. According to some experts, the finest ski country in the U.S. lies along the slopes of the Sierra Nevada; a few hours away the Pacific rolls onto golden beaches under palms and a semitropical sun. The contrast between the state's two great cities is as sharp as any—San Francisco a cosmopolitan, compactly built, sophisticated place, probably more completely unionized than any other U.S. city; gusty, vital Los Angeles, the booster and cheesecake capital of the world, attempting to become a city but still nothing but a garbled town sprawling across 450 square miles. "L.A." stands as immortal reproach to the subdividing realtors. It is bitterly anti-union, bitterly clear in its remembrance of the bombing of the *Times* by the McNamara brothers back in 1910.

Since Sutter's Mill in '48, California has produced something like $2,000,000,000 in gold, and its gold production is still worth more than $40,000,000 a year —including the driblets panned by thousands of prospectors working the streams and earning from a quarter to $5 a day. But more important than the gold is the agriculture, which accounts for a good 11 per cent of the state's income. California produces everything from avocados and citrus fruits in the South to the wine grapes of the San Joaquin. Virtually no crop refuses to grow in California, and practically no crops are overlooked, although citrus is the leading one. On the state borders fruit-inspection stations have been established for the ostensible purpose of preventing the importation of insects or fruit diseases, but in effect they form a barrier against fruit imports—diseased or otherwise.

A major part of California's industry consists of canning, packing, bottling, and other functions subsidiary to its agriculture. Although southern California is the chief center of the U.S. aircraft industry, and although more and more automobile-assembly plants have been erected by eastern companies, the state has comparatively few large factories. Its economy is in transition between the raw-material exporting economy of the Southwest and the agricultural-industrial economy of the Middle West.

THE PACIFIC NORTHWEST

Just as the Far West appears to be the least integrated of the regions, so the 250,000 square miles of Washington, Oregon, and Idaho are perhaps more closely unified than any other part of the U.S. Although the Pacific Northwest was explored by Lewis and Clark around 1805, its intensive settlement did not begin until the Northern Pacific linked Chicago with Seattle in 1883. Today it is closer to the frontier —topographically and economically—than the rest of the West, and, as of the census of 1930, less than half the population was native to the region.

The population today amounts to 3,200,000, or 2.5 per cent of the nation's total, whereas the Pacific Northwest has 8.3 per cent of the U.S. land, with a high ratio of resources to population. It has, for example, about 40 per cent of all U.S. potential waterpower, mostly accounted for by the Columbia River system. Yet this power is for the most part incidental to irrigation and water-conservation projects, because about 60 per cent of the region lies to the east of the Cascades, which block the rains from the Pacific. The mountains make for fogs and forests on the western slope, but semi-arid areas inland. Thus the whole economy of the Pacific Northwest revolves around the problem of bringing water to the land, and it is laced together by the branches of the Columbia, the main source of water. Today only a quarter of the 160,000,000 acres is in farms, and almost two-thirds of this land is suitable only for grazing. Here, and throughout the West generally, a good deal of the soil is potentially arable provided it can be watered, and the region looks forward to a conservative increase in productive farm acreage as the existing water supply is put to use. Grand Coulee alone will provide water for more than a million acres.

On the land that it currently farms the region grows over a fifth of the nation's apples, a quarter of the cherries, nearly a third of the pears, a tenth or more of the potatoes, onions, strawberries, green peas, and dry beans. It also accounts for close to an eighth of the wheat, over 10 per cent of the wool, and a slightly lower percentage of sheep and lambs. Mineral resources thus far have been scarcely touched, but even so the region mines large amounts of zinc, lead, and silver. However, its greatest source of wealth is the forest that covers the western slopes of the Cascades, representing about half the standing saw timber in the U.S. and producing roughly 40 per cent of the nation's

[1] With an estimated 13,300,000 in 1956, California is now also the second-biggest state in population.—EDITOR.

output of softwood lumber. Over 50 per cent of all wage earners in Pacific Northwest manufacturing are employed in lumber industries. Currently the annual cut of slightly under ten billion board feet runs ahead of the new growth by two or two and a half to one, and the region is becoming pocked with stranded communities decaying in the devastated cutover areas similar to those in northern Wisconsin, Minnesota, and Michigan. There is much talk of bringing the cut and the growth into balance, but so far few effective steps have been taken. Safe from destruction are 70,000-odd square miles of forest standing in three great national parks and on other U.S. Government land—land that amounts to a phenomenal 48 per cent of the region's total and an incredible 58 per cent of the area of Idaho.

The region is in competition with practically every part of the country. Its lumber competes with southeastern lumber; its wheat with the Middle West and Plains states; its orchards with those of the Northeast; its potatoes with Maine; its sheep and wool with the Southwest; and so on. Virtually its only noncompetitive export is the Columbia River salmon catch —and even that has Alaskan competition.

Meanwhile, with manufacturing accounting for only 16 per cent of its income, the Pacific Northwest must import nearly all finished goods, as well as oil, sugar, and other commodities. Ostensibly the heavy raw-material exports would balance the imports for an overall profit, but a catch exists in the form of freight rates. The region's markets are thousands of miles away—the fruit is shipped to New York, for example—and freight eats up from a quarter to a half of the farmer's wholesale price in the East, whereas the local growers have no such handicap. The result is that the Washington farmer, to compete with the Easterner, must be content to receive far less in net cash. When middle-western wheat growers were complaining about fifty-four-cent wheat, Pacific Northwest farmers growing the same wheat were realizing only thirty cents per bushel for their crop.

Conversely, the region is squeezed when it buys eastern manufactured goods. An Allis-Chalmers tractor delivered in Spokane would cost between 20 and 30 per cent more than the same tractor unloaded in Ohio. In effect the Pacific Northwest produces raw materials, pays a stiff price to get them out of the region, pays again to bring in its manufactured goods. Consequently, next to irrigation and power development, the freight-rate squeeze is the region's chief preoccupation, and few conversations go on very long without the subject's coming up and without the city of Chicago's being mentioned with infinite loathing.

However, these are familiar troubles in a pioneer economy, and the region will unquestionably outgrow them. For it has plenty of room, abundant resources, tremendous power, and perhaps more usable land. Cheap power is certain to lead to the creation of regional industries, and already Portland has begun an expansion that may make it the leading industrial city of the north coast. Seattle is a little San Francisco, economically and in spirit, with shipping and lumber to sustain it and Alaska acknowledging it as an "unofficial capital." Posters in the state of Washington announce that such-and-such is the "fastest-selling" article of its kind in "the Pacific Northwest and Alaska." The northern U.S. outpost, which seems so remote to the rest of the country, comes close to being a part of the Pacific Northwest region.

E PLURIBUS UNUM

From this hasty tour of 3,026,789 square and fabulous miles the secret of U.S. power emerges clearly. The U.S. is not great by nature or by accident. It is great by the act of man. The purpose of the political system invented by the founders of the republic was the political integration of sovereign states. But this political integration resulted in an economic integration far beyond anything man had ever attempted before. The economic interests of the states burst the boundaries of the states; they intertwined, merged, became compounded one with another. The result, as we have seen, has been the formation of shadow nations within a nation—seven of them by this count, fewer or more by others. The boundaries of these shadow nations are economic rather than geographical; they do not necessarily coincide with political sovereignties. The northern part of California seems to belong to the Pacific Northwest instead of to the Far West, and so does western Montana, though it is included in the Mountain States. The eastern half of the state of Texas goes with the old South, the western half with the Southwest. And so forth. The economic forces cut across political forces, check them, merge with political forces elsewhere, bind two into one. The action is like that within a huge retort in which dissimilar substances mix and compound, to create a new substance of a higher power. That new substance is what we know as the U.S.A.

This new entity is greater than the sum of its own parts. If the shadow nations were real nations, if the political boundaries coincided with the economic boundaries, then the area now known as the U.S. would be far less potent, far less rich than it is. Then New England would be struggling for food, and in the Northwest an automobile would be as rare as in other agricultural countries that have difficulty accumulating foreign exchange. It is when the Aluminum Co. of America contracts for waterpower in Oregon that the U.S. is created. It is when the rich coupon clippers on Manhattan are taxed to help build highways in empty Nevada that the U.S. lives. Every time a freight train crosses a state line, every time a purchasing department makes up its mind to buy an out-of-state commodity, every time an order clerk receives an out-of-state demand, the U.S. grows greater. For in these events, as in thousands of others, one is working for all, and all for one.

2. RESOURCES

THE CRISIS IN RAW MATERIALS*

It has taken a massive, five-volume report by a special commission to show that the United States has reached a major crossroads in resources. From here on out, the United States will be running into increasing deficits and rising costs in materials to sustain its growth—unless it takes thought and uses all the weapons of economics and technology in coordinated attack on the problem. The report in Fortune's words is "one of the greatest most readable government documents in the century." This condensation by Fortune from the opening to the summary of Volume I is an eloquent statement of the problem. Its eloquence derives in part from the sweep of data, in part from the caliber of the commission. Known informally as the Paley Commission, after its chairman, William S. Paley, chairman of Columbia Broadcasting System, Inc., its members were George R. Brown, chairman of Texas Eastern Transmission Corp.; Arthur H. Bunker, president of Climax Molybdenum Co.; Edward S. Mason, dean of the Graduate School of Public Administration, Harvard University; and Eric Hodgins, long associated with Fortune. The lucid Hodgins style is perceptible throughout this statement.

This is the crux of the problem: "The quantity of most metals and mineral fuels used in the United States since the first world war exceeds the total used throughout the entire world in all of history preceding 1914." What is more, even if none of the United States mineral deposits had been used and they were handed down intact to the next generation, a raw material crisis would arise in 1975. This crisis puts in a concrete setting the abstract notions of cost, scarcity, efficiency, and substitution of productive factors. It highlights the importance of imports from foreign countries for America's economic welfare.

The question, "Has the United States of America the material means to sustain its civilization?" would never have occurred to the men who brought this nation into greatness as the twentieth century dawned. But with the twentieth century now half gone by, the question presses and the honest answers are not glib.

The full report of the President's Materials Policy Commission, "Resources for Freedom," has as its central task an examination of the adequacy of materials to meet the needs of the free world in the years ahead. In area after area we encounter soaring demands, shrinking resources, the consequent pressure toward rising real costs, the risk of wartime shortages, the strong possibility of an arrest or decline in the standard of living we cherish and hope to share. As a nation, we are threatened, but not alert. The materials problem now demands that we give new and deep consideration to the fundamental upon which all employment, all daily activity, eventually rests: the contents of the earth and its physical environment.

None of us in the U.S., whether in civilian or military life, is easily accustomed to the idea that raw materials can be a problem. Indeed, America's problem today is precisely the reverse of the problem to which all our tradition has accustomed us. A hundred years ago resources seemed limitless and the struggle upward from meager conditions of life was the struggle to create the means and methods of getting these materials into use. In this struggle we have by now succeeded all too

well: so efficiently have we built our high-output factories and opened the lines of distribution to our remotest consumers that our sources are faltering under the constantly increasing strain of demand. We have always been more interested in sawmills than seedlings. We think about raw materials last, not first.

THE MATERIALS PROBLEM

Today, throughout the industrial world, but centering inevitably in the heavily industrialized U.S., the resulting materials problem bears down with considerable severity. The nature of the problem can perhaps be successfully oversimplified by saying that the consumption of almost all materials is expanding at compound rates and is thus pressing harder and harder against resources which, whatever else they may be doing, are not similarly expanding. This materials problem is thus not the sort of "shortage" problem, local and transient, that in the past has found its solution in price changes. The terms of the materials problem we face today are larger and more pervasive.

Powerful historical streams have converged to make the problem uniquely intense today. First, there has been a profound shift in the basic *materials position* of the U.S.—a worsening relationship between our requirements and our means of satisfying them. Second, other high-consuming nations, primarily in Western Europe, are in difficulties which stem from the serious depletion of their own domestic resources coupled with the weakening or severing of their former colonial ties. Third, many resource-rich but less-developed nations,

* From "The Crisis in Raw Materials," August, 1952.

especially of former colonial status, now focus on industrialization rather than materials export. Fourth, there lingers from the great depression a worldwide fear of the possible collapse of markets, which dampens the willingness of private investors and resource-rich countries to develop new free-world resources. Finally, a great schism divides the world between the totalitarian and democratic nations, disrupting normal trade patterns and making necessary costly measures of armed preparedness.

The nation's economic life calls for a vast and delicate balancing of multitudinous resources against continually changing needs and demands. The American pioneers had to destroy trees so that they could plant corn. In a more complex world, minerals, fuels, forest and agricultural products, the land on which these grow and the water that nourishes them must be variously dug, burned, felled, cropped, and constrained in interactions that reach further than we are aware of when we induce them. We grow and we destroy. We concentrate and we disperse. We nurture and we abandon. A chemist makes a crucial discovery, and the resource base for the production of women's stockings shifts from mulberry leaves in Japan to bituminous coal underlying West Virginia. A war occurs, and the material for tires and teething rings no longer comes from *Hevea brasiliensis* in Malaya but from Texas petroleum, natural gas, or ethyl alcohol made from molasses.

But these colossal interplays between resources more often take place in less dramatic ways; more often entirely within our own domestic economy and so slowly that we may be unaware of their significance for a decade. Energy for farming operations, once supplied almost entirely by draft animals, now comes chiefly from tractors, stationary gasoline engines, and electric motors. This considerable fact carries with it another, even wider ranging: in this process of change, the petroleum industry releases for other use no less than 60 million acres that would be necessary to feed draft horses. As prices rise and fall, the resultant of thousands of forces, steel replaces wood in housing construction, or vice versa, or concrete replaces both. Glass increases while brass diminishes; plastics from coke ovens supersede porcelain enamels; paint pigments begin to come from sands in Florida instead of from galena deposits in Missouri. The rise and fall of materials streams constitutes the great fugue of our industrial times.

To anticipate such moves in detail is beyond the capacity of even the most electronic intelligence; to attempt to plan them in detail would be like planning the fingerprints of one's great-grandchildren, and would fail for the same reason: too many accidents and unforeseeable forces. But because we cannot plan fingerprints we do not disregard the laws of genetics; and our inability to plan in detail does not mean that we can withdraw our intelligence from contemplating the future.

In contemplating the future, a prudent man can base his actions only on the best estimates he can make; commissions weighing policies can do no better. This report attempts no prophecies. But if our current generation is responsible for passing on to the next as best it can the prospects for continued well-being, then the first requisite is that we plan to meet successfully those requirements and challenges that now can be foreseen. Therefore, the commission has chosen, as the period to review, the quarter century stretching from the present to the year 1975—a date which seems sufficiently distant not to be strongly affected by our current (1952) defense-production problems, yet not so far as to be dominated by technological and other developments now wholly unforeseeable.

The eruption of war would alter the pattern of materials demand and the adequacy of supplies in swift and drastic ways. Yet if complete peace, confidence, and prosperity were to descend upon the world tomorrow, the materials problem would not vanish. Nor might it become less severe. If all the nations of the world should achieve the same standard of living as our own, the resulting world need for materials would increase to six times present consumption. Today's rearmament emergency may best serve us as a set of binoculars that brings apparently closer to us circumstances which would in any event confront us were we to take no action to avert them; in this sense it can be of great usefulness to us in emphasizing the problem we shall face and the actions we must pursue, *war or no war*.

THE FUNDAMENTAL CONCEPTS

This report can have significance only as the convictions held by members of the President's Materials Policy Commission are clearly stated:

First, we share the belief of the American people in the principle of growth. Granting that we cannot find any absolute reason for this belief, we admit that to our Western minds it seems preferable to any opposite, which to us implies stagnation and decay. Whether there may be any unbreakable upper limits to the continuing growth of our economy, we do not pretend to know, but it must be part of our task to examine such apparent limits.

Second, we believe in private enterprise as the most efficacious way of performing industrial tasks in the U.S. With this belief, a belief in the spur of the profit motive and what is called "the price system" obviously go hand in hand. This method, motive, and system have served uniquely well in America. We believe in a minimum of interference with these patterns of private enterprise. But to believe this is not to believe that this minimum must be set at zero. Private enterprise itself has from time to time asked for helps, or restraints, or counterpoises from government to keep the system working at its best. The commission sees no reason either to blink this fact or to decry it; as we see the future, the coexistence of great private and public strength is not only desirable but is essential to our preservation.

Third, we believe that the destinies of the U.S. and the rest of the free non-Communist world are inextricably bound together. This belief we hope will color everything we have to say about the materials problem. It implies, for example, that if the U.S. is to increase its imports of raw materials—as we believe it must—

it must return in other forms strength for strength to match what it receives. It is this commission's belief that if we fail to work for a rise in the standard of living of the rest of the free world, we thereby hamper and impede the further rise of our own, and equally lessen the chances of democracy to prosper and peace to reign the world over.

It is by these avenues of thought that the commission arrives at the formulation of the major premise upon which all the rest of its report is based: the overall objective of a Materials Policy for the U.S. should be to ensure an adequate and dependable flow of materials at the lowest cost consistent with national security and with the welfare of friendly nations.

THE BASIC APPETITE

The U.S. appetite for materials is gargantuan—and so far, insatiable. At mid-century, the nation uses up over 2.5 billion tons of materials each year to keep itself going and support its standard of living. With a population of 151 million, each person consumes, on an average, 18 tons a year. He uses about 14,000 pounds of fuel for heat and energy. He uses 10,000 pounds of building materials, 800 pounds of metals (winnowed from 5,000 pounds of ores). He eats nearly 1,600 pounds of food; this, together with cotton and other fibers for clothing, and with pulpwood for paper, and other miscellaneous products, mounts up to 5,700 pounds of agricultural materials. In addition he uses 800 pounds of non-metallics, such as lime, fertilizer, and chemical raw materials.

Such levels of consumption, climaxing fifty years of

phenomenal economic progress, levy a severe drain on every kind of resource we have: minerals, forests, soil, and water. In the first fifty years of the twentieth century, as population doubled and our total national output reached five times the 1900 level, the stream of raw materials increased in volume and value until, in 1950, it was worth two and one-half times as much (in constant dollars) as it was in 1900. In the mixture that made up this stream there were some significant differences, of which the most startling was that whereas our use of forest products actually declined 1 per cent in 1950 compared to 1900, our consumption of minerals, including fuels, was six times 1900 totals. In 1950 we were taking from the earth two and one-half times more bituminous coal, three times more copper, three and one-half times more iron ore, four times more zinc, twenty-six times more natural gas, thirty times more crude oil than in the year 1900. *The quantity of most metals and mineral fuels used in the U.S. since the first world war exceeds the total used throughout the entire world in all of history preceding 1914.*

This vast drain, greater today than yesterday, and inescapably greater tomorrow than today, upon resources that cannot be renewed has become the most challenging aspect of our present-day economy. A ton of ore removed from the earth is a ton gone forever; each barrel of oil used means one less remaining. Neither the next fifty years nor even the next twenty-five can see a growth in minerals consumption at the same increasing rate unless profound changes in trade and technology occur.

Even though they have been less urgently demanded,

U. S. Is Free World's Biggest Materials Consumer

With 9.5% of population and 8% of land area, the United States in 1950 consumed these materials.

With 90.5% of population and 92% of land area, other free countries in 1950 consumed these materials.

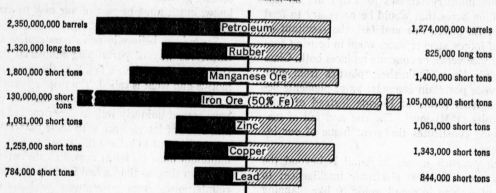

U.S.	Material	Other free countries
2,350,000,000 barrels	Petroleum	1,274,000,000 barrels
1,320,000 long tons	Rubber	825,000 long tons
1,800,000 short tons	Manganese Ore	1,400,000 short tons
130,000,000 short tons	Iron Ore (50% Fe)	105,000,000 short tons
1,081,000 short tons	Zinc	1,061,000 short tons
1,255,000 short tons	Copper	1,343,000 short tons
784,000 short tons	Lead	844,000 short tons

And U. S. Is Using Up Reserves Faster Than Other Countries
(1950 production as percentage of known reserves)

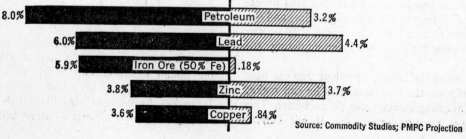

U.S.	Material	Other
8.0%	Petroleum	3.2%
6.0%	Lead	4.4%
5.9%	Iron Ore (50% Fe)	.18%
3.8%	Zinc	3.7%
3.6%	Copper	.84%

Source: Commodity Studies; PMPC Projection

"renewable" resources have also felt the strain. Ninety per cent of our virgin timber stand in the commercial forest area has been cut, and thus far we have done a poor job in growing replacement crops. At present we are using up our inventory of saw timber at a rate 40 per cent faster than its annual growth. Millions of acres are no longer in forest; other millions have gone to brush and inferior trees. Upon our agricultural land we have imposed a heavy burden of depletion; we have opened it, exploited it heavily, abandoned much of it after its fertility had been drained, and moved on to repeat the process elsewhere. Partly because of soil erosion, even water, once regarded as a "free commodity" of virtually unlimited supply, has become a problem.

The time has clearly passed when we can afford the luxury of viewing our resources as unlimited and hence taking them for granted. In the U.S. the supplies of the evident, the cheap, the accessible, are running out. The plain fact is that we have skimmed the cream of our resources *as we now understand them;* the pause must not be too long before our understanding catches up with our needs.

With less than 10 per cent of the free world's population and 8 per cent of its land area, the U.S. has come to consume almost half the free world's volume of materials. It is such growth of demand that is at the core of our materials problem; it is mainly our unwillingness to accept the status of a "mature economy" that challenges the adequacy of our resources to meet our needs. All the copper ever discovered in the U.S. would last only twenty-five years at the rate of consumption projected for 1975; all the lead would last only eighteen years, all the zinc only thirty years. In short, handing over the U.S. mineral deposits, intact and pristine as they were in Columbus' day, to our children in 1975 would scarcely help them solve their materials problem at all.

As a nation we have yet to face squarely such growing inconsistencies between our ambitions and the domestic bases upon which they rest. How did we get this way? And what are we going to do about it?

THE BASIC SHIFT IN POSITION

The U.S. has never been completely self-sufficient in raw materials: had we insisted on being so, our economic output and living standards today would be considerably lower than they are. We began as an "underdeveloped" nation, with rich resources but a shortage of manpower and capital, and little industry. Our own manufacturing grew: our foreign trade burgeoned and its composition underwent drastic change. U.S. exports of crude materials slowly fell in proportion as exports of manufactured products slowly rose. Opposite changes occurred in our pattern of imports. Finally, the decade of the 1940's marked a turning point in the long-range material position of the U.S.; historical trends long in the making came to a climax when the national economy moved just prior to the war from a long period of depression into a period, still continuing, of high employment and production. By the mid-point of the twentieth century we had fully entered an era of new relationships between our needs and resources; our national economy had at last not merely grown up to our resource base but in many respects had outgrown it. We had completed our slow transition from a raw-materials *surplus* nation to a raw-materials *deficit* nation.

The symptoms of this changed materials position are today numerous: We have become the world's largest importer of copper, lead, and zinc, whereas once we were huge exporters. We have begun to meet from foreign sources a sizable and growing portion of our needs for petroleum and iron ore, long the hallmarks of U.S. self-sufficiency. We have shifted from net exporter to net importer of lumber. There are today only two metals (magnesium and molybdenum) for which we are not wholly or partially dependent on foreign supplies. At the start of the century we produced some 15 per cent more raw materials than we consumed (excluding food); by mid-century we were consuming 10 per cent more materials than we produced.

THE PROJECTED DEMANDS

The size of future materials demands, and the adequacy of supplies, will depend upon the rate at which the U.S. economy and that of the whole free world expands. If we assume for the moment a favorable set of materials-supply conditions, the size of our national output by 1975 will depend mainly upon the size of total population and working force, the number of hours worked per week, the accumulation of capital that has occurred by then, and the rise of man-hour productivity.

Estimates of U.S. population for the future range between 180 million and 220 million; the commission has assumed, after consultation with the Bureau of the Census, a population of 193 million by 1975 and a working force of 82 million, in contrast with the 1950 figures of 151 million and 62 million. It has assumed a work week perhaps 15 per cent shorter than in 1950. It has further assumed an annual rise of about 2.5 per cent in production *per man-hour* against a somewhat smaller past rate of 2.1 per cent, because the commission thinks it reasonable to expect steadier levels of employment and economic activity in the future, in line with the avowed national objective of making major depressions a relic of the past. This does not preclude the possibility of milder fluctuations.

The fundamental assumption, drawn from this, may be wrong but seems unquestionably conservative: it is that the rate of growth of the economy in the next twenty-five years will be neither more nor less than what it has averaged over the last century, or about 3 per cent per year. Three per cent compounded results in a doubling every twenty-five years; thus by 1975 our total output of goods and services (the gross national product or G.N.P.) is assumed to be twice what it actually was in 1950. . . . Although it is assumed that our G.N.P. will double, past experience indicates that less than a doubling of total materials input can achieve this owing to the fact that G.N.P. will reflect more value added to materials by higher fabrication and a greater proportion of services. It thus seems that an increase in the total materials stream of between 50 and 60 per cent will suffice to achieve a doubling of the G.N.P. by the 1970's.

Based upon the foregoing, the commission has projected the general magnitude of demand in the decade 1970-80 for various major materials. These projections do *not* predict how much of each material will actually be available and consumed. Instead, they are estimates of what might be demanded *if relative prices of various materials remained the same as in early 1950,* which they are most unlikely to do. Moreover, the projections can make no allowance for unforeseeable new uses, sharp substitutions, or dramatic technological improvements.

In the difficult matter of projecting future demands, one point of overriding importance stands out: despite wide differences of judgment as to whether demand for some material will rise 50 per cent, or 100 per cent, or 200 per cent, the central point is that demand for everything *can be expected to rise substantially.* This may not be a popular dictum, particularly among some businessmen who may be more fearful of creating too much future capacity than of having too little. But the economic history of our times records more estimates of the future that were too small than those that erred on the other side. Many unexpected turns of fate will occur in the next quarter-century; one or more of them may have some deplorable effect upon business. But this commission sees no reason to assume that a world that has been growing economically by leaps and bounds for many generations will suddenly become static in this one.

THE ESSENCE IS COSTS

The threat of the materials problem is not that we will suddenly wake up to find the last barrel of oil exhausted or the last ton of lead gone, and that economic activity has collapsed. The real and deeply serious threat is that we shall have to devote constantly increasing efforts to acquiring each pound of materials from natural resources which are dwindling both in quality and quantity—thus finding ourselves running faster and faster in order to stay standing still.

In short, the essence of the materials problem is *costs.*

The real costs of materials are not measured primarily in money; they lie *in the hours of human work and the amounts of capital required to bring a pound of industrial material or a unit of energy into useful form.* These real costs have for some years been declining, and this decline has helped our living standard to rise. In this commission's view, there is a serious possibility that this downward trend in real costs may be stopped or reversed tomorrow—if, indeed, this has not already occurred.

There is no completely satisfactory way to measure the real costs of materials over the long sweep of our history. But clearly the man-hours required per unit of output declined heavily from 1900 to 1940, thanks especially to improvements in production technology and the heavier use of energy and capital equipment per worker. This long-term decline in real costs is reflected in the downward drift of prices of various groups of materials in relation to the general level of prices in the economy. Since 1940, however, this downward trend has in some cases been reversed. Whereas wholesale prices of commodities in general advanced an average of 105 per cent from 1940 to 1950, in that decade petroleum rose 149 per cent, zinc 119 per cent, farm products 152 per cent, lead 157 per cent, lumber 218 per cent. Others, including aluminum, iron ore, nickel, sulfur, and even copper, moved up less than the general level of wholesale prices, although some might have moved further in the absence of price ceilings.

This upward thrust of materials prices since 1940 is accounted for in part by failure of supply to adjust rapidly enough to sharp increases in demand. To this extent prices can be expected to settle back as supply catches up. But in many cases there is cause to suspect that present high prices show that pressure against limited resources is boosting real costs.

THE COSTS SOLUTION

If costs are the problem, what is the solution? The answer of this commission is that there is no *one* solution. There are, however, many flexibilities in our materials position, and we can succeed in averting the threat in the materials problem if we undertake a series of simultaneous actions which utilize these flexibilities to the full.

We can get more materials and more energy from domestic resources by pushing back the technological, physical, and economic boundaries that limit presently the *supply.*

We can alter our patterns of materials *use* by more efficient designs and processes—and by shifting the burden of use away from scarcer materials toward more abundant ones.

We can get more materials from abroad, on terms beneficial to ourselves and other free nations.

These opportunities are real and promising, but their full benefits will never be realized except by earnest and unremitting effort.

MORE FROM THE U.S.

The U.S. even today makes practical use of only a small fraction of its total resource base. Past depletions notwithstanding, we still possess a broader and stronger usable fraction of our resource base than ever before—mainly because, over the years, we have discovered resources and uses unsuspected by our ancestors. The bayberries of Cape Cod and the sperm whales off Nantucket were vital resources to the early inhabitants of Massachusetts; so was the buffalo to the plainsmen. It was irrelevant to them that nature had created huge pools of petroleum under the soil of Texas, great bodies of iron ore in Minnesota, waterfalls in Washington, and phosphates in Florida. It is equally irrelevant to us today that the candles, the whale, and the buffalo have all but vanished; it is of high importance that the resources of the West have been opened up, that the invention of the internal-combustion engine has made petroleum a valuable resource, that technology has taught us how to make aluminum from bauxite, and plastics from such abundant resources as coal, water, and air. By discovery, development, and technology, the materials stream which flows from our resources has been enlarged and its composition vastly altered.

To improve our balance, we need to work increasingly in six areas of supply and three of use.

SUPPLY

Exploration and discovery: Most major metal discoveries have been made by following surface ore exposures in mountain regions. By now few of these exposures remain undiscovered, but perhaps half the surface of the U.S. is covered by a mantle of "young" rocks, and geologists infer that ore deposits exist hidden below them as large and as rich as have ever been found in the exposed areas. We must improve geophysical and geochemical prospecting methods swiftly in the hope of discovering such ore bodies.

Fuller use of known resources: In coal mining we leave about 50 per cent of commercial grades of coal behind in the ground; we leave more than 50 per cent of petroleum in an average pool. Enough natural gas was wasted in 1950 to supply the gas needs of 11 million of the nation's homes. A considerable fraction of harvested resources also goes unused: only 65 per cent of the average tree that is cut ends up as useful material. These physical wastes are not necessarily economic wastes, but many extraction practices need intensive improvement.

Using lower-quality resources: The richest-grade resources are usually the cheapest; hence we skim the cream. Yet we have frequently found that today's use of the second best has advantages over yesterday's best. The newsprint industry, once confined to using northern spruce, can today use a faster growing southern pine, once useless to it. As the rich iron ores of the Mesabi approach exhaustion, we are learning to use lower-grade taconite ores.

Renewing renewables: The U.S. for generations has been mining out its renewable resources—forests, soil, and water. Restoration of severely depleted resources is slow and costly, if possible at all. We must learn more speedily that it pays to use such resources on a "sustained-yield" basis.

Finding work for presently unemployable resources: Perhaps the greatest increases in our usable-resource base could be achieved by learning to tap certain abundant components of our total resource base which hitherto we have not known how to use. The mix of materials we use today has little to do with the way in which these materials occur in nature. Among the ninety-odd known chemical elements only a third enter strongly into modern industry. Another third enter weakly if at all; the final third are just now beginning to step out of the textbook pages. There is much more aluminum in the earth's crust than there is iron—yet we use sixty times as much iron as aluminum. The most abundant metal in the earth, silicon, finds as a metal almost no use at all.

Synthesizing new materials: The most notable supplements to our materials stream in recent years have been the array of various highly versatile plastics, artificial fibers, synthetic rubbers, and the like. These synthetic materials may, in many cases, be superior to the article replaced, and cheaper as well. Science and technology, which have created many materials shortages by expanding demand, are challenged now to help solve the materials problem in a host of ways, not least of which is by synthesizing additional important materials from abundant or renewable resources.

USE

Shifting from scarce to abundant: The way we can shift our materials mix toward more abundant materials is seen in the case of copper and lead. As copper became scarcer relative to aluminum, aluminum moved in to perform certain of copper's functions. As lead became scarcer, plastics began to supplant it for such uses as cable covering. These examples make it clear that our attention should be focused just as much on expanding the output and use of *abundant* materials as upon enlarging the supply of *scarce* materials; for some purposes an extra pound of aluminum or plastics may ease the situation as much as another pound of copper or lead.

Making materials work harder and longer: The U.S. has been lavish in its use of materials, because of their comparative abundance in the past. Vast quantities of material have been wasted by overdesigning and overspecification. We have frequently designed products with little concern for getting maximum service from their materials and labor. We drive heavier automobiles than is necessary for mere transportation, and we adorn them with chromium because we like it that way. We blow thousands of tons of unrecoverable lead into the atmosphere each year from high-octane gasoline because we like a quick pickup. We must become more aware that many of our production and consumption habits are extremely expensive of scarce materials and that a trivial change of taste or slight reduction in personal satisfaction can often bring about tremendous savings. If we fail to act from such awareness, rising costs and shortages will eventually force us to it.

Giving materials a second life: The more materials we put into goods and structures, the larger becomes our stockpile of potential scrap. Frequently the man-hour cost of reclaiming this material is so great that recovery does not pay, but better techniques and better organization for handling scrap can add great tonnages to total supply.

Our strongest weapons for accomplishing improvements in supply and use, and fighting the threat of rising real costs wherever encountered, are in the application of larger quanties of energy to *work* and larger quantities of technology to *working methods*. How well supplied are we with energy and technology, *as resources*, to give us the flexibility we must have to support the burdens of the future? As of today the simple answer is: not well enough.

The previous contributions of technology to materials supply have been great, but the future contributions must be greater still. Most Americans have been nurtured on the romantic notion that technology will always come to the rescue with a new miracle whenever the need arises; after all, it gave us synthetic rubber and the atomic bomb in a hurry when the need was urgent. But isolated solutions of problems relating to individual materials are no substitute for the broad frontal attack technology needs to make on the problem as a whole. The criticism is not of our technologists but of our lack of national concern for the materials problem.

MORE FROM ABROAD

Even if no threat of war overhung today's world, the U.S. would still have to face the fact that our high-consumption economy no longer makes our domestic resource base adequate even to our civilian needs. The U.S. will find it increasingly worth while to turn abroad for more supplies of basic materials.

Some alterations in political thought may be necessary before such a policy becomes accepted as an everyday matter. Actually, there is little to be lost and enormous advantages to be gained by importing a much greater volume of raw materials in the future than we have in the past. We are in a good position to make bargains advantageous to buyer and seller alike.

The fact that nature distributed resources very unevenly over the face of the earth in relation to human population and consumption alone argues in favor of increasing integration of the various national economies of the free world. But the hard political facts of the mid-twentieth century add further great weight to the proposition that it will be to the mutual advantage of all freedom-loving peoples of the earth to achieve a greater measure of cooperation than ever before, founded on the principles of mutual help and respect. Such cooperation can succeed only if it is based on a clear understanding of the varying needs and resources of all the nations concerned, and the opportunities which lie in mobilizing the strength of all to meet the particular weaknesses of each.

AT THE LEAST COST

The task of overcoming the materials problem is far greater than one of merely locating enough physical resources. The task is to overcome the social, economic, and political obstacles in the way of foreign trade; to develop and apply more energy and technology to the materials field; to ensure a sufficient flow of capital into it; to guard our security, and concern ourselves at every point with insurance against rising cost. Such accomplishments can only be achieved by a consistent policy—that is, by intelligently directed action toward determined goals—as distinct from aimless drift and blind faith. A materials policy, broadly conceived, must provide a framework for public programs and for private actions such that all will move with reasonable harmony toward the same national objectives. It will not do to wait, and solve the problem "eventually"; while we are waiting we can encounter such a succession of shortages as to disrupt our cost pattern and defeat an "eventual" solution altogether.

The tests to be applied in government policy making are even more complex than those in private business. There is no magic formula to yield the right answers to the myriad questions that arise; each one must be judged on its merits and in its context. Yet there is one basic economic principle which, if applied to the limit of available facts and injected consciously into each judgment, can provide a basic thread of consistency throughout the whole field of materials policy. *With our economy facing stronger and stronger pressures toward rising real costs of materials, this commission believes that national materials policy should be squarely founded on the principle of buying at the least cost possible for equivalent values.*

This cardinal principle of least cost has application to all major sectors of materials policy: to development of resources, to energy and technology, to the difficult problem of weighing the claims of the present against those of the future, to imports of foreign materials, and to security. Its application is most often challenged, however, with respect to imports and security.

THE PROTECTION ARGUMENT

That our economy can best develop by obtaining its materials at the lowest possible cost is most often attacked by those whose costs are higher than those of foreign competitors. It is they who ask for restriction of imports on the grounds of "protecting the American standard of living from the competition of lower-paid foreign labor." This argument is often buttressed with the assertion that we should strive to be as self-sufficient as possible in view of the security risks we face.

The commission feels strongly that this line of argument is fallacious and dangerous. The idea that the American standard of living must be protected from low-cost foreign supplies based upon "cheap labor" is an idea based on unemployment psychology. In a full-employment situation the supply of any material from abroad at a price below that of our domestic costs (provided it does not represent a temporary dumping) does not lower the standard of living but actually helps push it higher. In the U.S. it enables us to use manpower and equipment to better advantage in making something worth more than the cheaper material obtained from abroad. Abroad, our purchases will contribute to a strengthening of economic life and improvement of working conditions in the nations from which we import.

It is true that where our industries face a considerable reduction in output, with employees and capital unable to transfer quickly to more remunerative activities, the government has the responsibility of easing the transition to the new situation. This, however, is hardly likely to be an important problem in the materials field, where even the declining industries are more likely to be faced with a shortage of manpower than with a surplus.

THE SECURITY PROBLEM

As, in one material after another, we reach the stage at which we must turn abroad for additional supplies, the point may be raised that we are endangering our security by dependence on foreign sources; on "fair-weather friends" whose supplies in time of war will not be available to us.

This point is substantial enough for serious consideration. The issue must be defined. *It is to gain the greatest security at the lowest cost.* Sometimes the least-cost route to security is to give special aid to domestic industry; sometimes it is not. When aid is indicated it is always best to tailor it to the specific situation. Self-sufficiency for many materials is impossible; for many others it is economic nonsense. It is certainly not true that for all materials an unqualified dependence on domestic supplies is the best in the end, even when physically possible. With some materials, peacetime dependence on domestic supplies may mean such depletion that, if war comes, a reserve which might otherwise have existed will have been destroyed. With some materials it is much more economical to depend upon expanded output in safe areas abroad and on stockpiles built in whole or in part on foreign supplies than to maintain a domestic industry behind elaborate and expensive protection. With some materials it may be advisable to maintain a domestic industry which normally supplies only part of our requirements but is capable of a rapid expansion.

The fallacy of self-sufficiency as a basic guide to a sound materials policy is that it costs too much. A 50-cent increase per barrel of petroleum or a 2-cent increase in the average price per pound of basic metals would add to our annual bill for these materials about $1 billion and $2.5 billion respectively. Yet it is not in dollars alone that the increased costs of self-sufficiency would be paid. Other countries in the free world find markets for their exports in the U.S., and we, to our profit, are a principal source of industrial products for them. Interferences with these normal channels of trade in the name of self-sufficiency would inevitably check economic growth both at home and abroad. The *political* consequences of self-sufficiency, with its accompanying damage to carefully established security arrangements, would prove even more serious.

In time of war the overriding problem of materials is to have enough safely available, and the question of costs becomes subordinate. In the period of preparation against the threat of war, however, costs remain a major concern.

Every war consumes more and more massive amounts of materials. The U.S. is becoming increasingly vulnerable through the growing military importance of metals and mineral fuels and our shrinking resources for supplying them. Of more than 100 mineral materials we use, about one-third—for example, sulfur, coal, phosphates, magnesium, molybdenum—are at present fully supplied from our domestic resources. Another third we get almost entirely from other lands; this fraction has assumed greater importance as advances in the technology of high-temperature alloys and electronics have brought into greater prominence such minerals as columbium, cobalt, high-grade quartz crystals, and others we do not possess. The final third we obtain partly from abroad and partly from domestic

output—materials like iron ore, petroleum, copper, and lead.

To meet or anticipate our needs from the supply side, we stockpile, and we seek reserve capacity in safe areas, domestic and foreign. On the supply side, civilian authority remains more or less in control. But on the demand side, the military, particularly in wartime, is in a commanding position. With each successive war, and now with preparation against the contingency of another, the military has become a greater and greater claimant against the materials of the whole economy. It would be impossible to fix a maximum percentage of military claims to the total economy and say "beyond this point you may not go." But even though the point cannot be fixed, it is known to exist. The military thus carries a heavy responsibility to hold its drain against the materials supply to the lowest levels consistent with adequate military strength; although progress has been made here, there is room and pressing need for much more.

TOWARD POLICY AND THE FUTURE

Closely linked with the least-cost principle is the notion of conservation of resources and materials. It is also linked with the question of this generation's responsibility to help provide for the next. Most thoughtful persons agree to some variation of this conservation idea, but there are wide differences as to how best—and how much—to protect the future claimants against the nation's resources.

The nation faces a very real and growing conservation problem, but many of our difficulties of agreement arise from a failure to recognize the economic dimensions of the problem and give proper weight to its dynamics. It is a popular fallacy to regard our resource base as a fixed inventory which, when used up, will leave society with no means of survival. A related fallacy is that physical waste equals economic waste; that it is improper to use materials in ways that make them disappear. This attitude can lead to devoting a dollar's worth of work to "saving" a few cents worth of waste paper and old string.

These fallacies together lead to a hair-shirt concept of conservation which makes it synonymous with hoarding. A sound concept of conservation, in the commission's view, is one which equates it with efficient use of resources, manpower, and materials: a positive concept compatible with growth and high consumption in place of abstinence and retrenchment. In developing America our forebears consumed resources extravagantly, but we are certainly better off in materials supply than they. It would be unreasonable for us to suggest that they should have consumed less so that we might consume more. If, then, through developing the opportunities inherent in the flexibility of our resource base, we can provide posterity with a better return of goods and services for its labor than we get for our own, we need not feel compelled to restrain specific consumptions of materials to make theirs even larger—any more than our New England forebears needed to conserve bayberries for candles to light a generation that lives by kilowatts.

Uncertainty over the future is the source of greatest difficulty in formulating national materials policy, yet it is basically because of this uncertainty that public policy has such an important role to play. In a sense, policy making and administration for materials is a huge national insurance business which seeks to protect the nation against tragic contingencies such as the collapse of living standards or defeat in war. More positively, it seeks to provide the best continuing chance for achieving the maximum growth and prosperity consistent with its means. Predictions have a useful role to play, but the nation cannot risk its future welfare by placing heavy bets on extremely optimistic assumptions. Neither can public policy be guided by the extreme of pessimism, lest we pay so much for insurance that we have little left for anything else.

An adequate materials policy for the U.S. must balance considerations of cost and security. It must take account not only of our own requirements and resources, but of those elsewhere in the free world. It must be concerned not only with our own economic growth but with the growth possibilities of the whole complex of nations of which we are inevitably the center.

The U.S., once criticized as the creator of a crassly materialistic order of things, is today throwing its might into the task of keeping alive the spirit of Man, and helping beat back from the frontiers of the free world everywhere the threats of force and of a new Dark Age which rise from the Communist nations. In defeating this barbarian violence, moral values will count most, but an ample materials base must support them. Indeed, the interdependence of moral and material values has never been so completely demonstrated as today, when all the world has seen the narrowness of its escape from the now dead Nazi tyranny, and has yet to know the breadth by which it will escape the live Communist one—both materialistic threats aimed to destroy moral and spiritual man. The use of materials to destroy *or to preserve* is the very choice over which the world struggle today rages.

3. POPULATION

SIXTY-SIX MILLION MORE AMERICANS*

As far as the national economy is concerned, babies are seemingly unimportant creatures, but if there are enough of them, they can have a tremendous impact on that economy. In fact, to the mercurial increase in the birth rate since 1940 goes a great deal of the credit for today's flourishing economy. This article analyzes why the birth rate has been booming the last fifteen years, what this will mean to the size and age composition of the nation, and how the American markets will be affected. There is also an important forecast: a moderate dip in sight to be followed by a second great baby boom.

Many Americans were fascinated to learn, last August 10, that the Census Bureau has a large, mechanical "speedometer," which records a net addition to the population every twelve seconds (it had been thirteen earlier in the year), and that the gadget showed there were then 160 million of us. *But just since that August day there has been a net gain of a million and a quarter.* Our growth in recent decades has looked like this:

1920 (*July 1*) .... 106 million
1930 .... 123 million
1940 .... 132 million
1945 .... 140 million
1950 .... 152 million
1954 (*January 1*) .... 161 million

Note that the U.S. population has grown as much in the past three and a half years as it did in the whole decade of the 1930's. In this brief period the American market has been enlarged by the size of a Texas and a Nebraska. Will the U.S. be able to keep it up?

Forecasting the future population of the U.S. is a parlous business at best—and no one knows that better than the demographers who have tried it in the past.

To begin with, one must make some broad political and economic assumptions. Let us suppose, first, that the U.S. remains at peace. Let us suppose, too, that the U.S. enjoys a reasonable prosperity. And let us suppose, finally, that Americans continue to show a preference for families somewhat larger than those of ten or fifteen years ago. Given these assumptions, we could venture the following population estimates with fair confidence:

1955 (*July 1*) .... 165 million
1960 .... 175 million
1965 .... 185 million
1970 .... 195 million
1975 .... 206 million

If the present population boom is dated from V-J day, 1945, and if 1975 is accepted as the most distant date for which sensible projections are possible, then the population boom may be summed up in these terms: the U.S. is not quite one-third of the way through a thirty-year period in which its population may well grow by 66 million.

The population boom is, of course, a reflection of the baby boom. In general, there are just four ways in which a country's population may be enhanced: immigration may be encouraged; emigration may be dis-

*From "Sixty-Six Million More Americans," January, 1954.

couraged; mortality may be slowed down; and fertility may be speeded up. The first two factors have not been very significant in recent years. Immigrants have been exceeding emigrants by less than 250,000 a year since World War II. In any case, the problems of migration can be pretty well guided by public policy, which, in recent years, has been fairly predictable. Mortality, though less susceptible to congressional direction, has also been predictable. A little less than 1 per cent of the U.S. population now dies every year.

The mercurial element in this picture is babies. Before the first world war the country's crude birth rate (i.e., births per 1,000 inhabitants) was around thirty. After the war it declined steadily, and at the bottom of the depression it was under nineteen. During the 1930's, it is true, the country's population increased by nine million. But it was apparent that this expansion could not have continued indefinitely without a rise in the birth rate. The frightening fact was that not enough girls were born during the decade to replace the women who would be growing out of the child-bearing ages. The 1930's, in fact, brought the smallest percentage increase in U.S. population in our whole history, and the lowest absolute increase since the decade of 1860-70.

Had the birth rate continued to decline, the demographers would have been right: the U.S. population would have stopped growing—at about 165 million—around the end of the twentieth century and would have begun declining soon afterward. Fortunately, the U.S. birth rate rose from the trough of the 1930's. By 1941 the rate was up to twenty, and during the early war years it hovered around twenty-two.* And in 1946, with the restraints of depression and war at last removed, the great baby boom began in earnest. Since the war the birth rate has never been lower than twenty-three and in one year (1947) it was up to twenty-seven. Total production for 1945-53: 33 million babies.

Historically, the mistakes of the demographers have proceeded mainly from a tendency to predict the future by simply extending the past. One of the more spectacular howlers was committed by a retired-merchant-turned-demographer named Francis Bonynge, who in 1852 enthusiastically forecast a cool 703 million for the U.S. by the year 2000. The modern demographers were led astray by the history of the birth rate. They noted that it had been declining for more than a hundred years. They noted further that the decline was general in Western industrial nations. On balance, there seemed to be no good reason for not extending the drooping birth-rate curve into the future. It would be easy to fall into the opposite error today, to assume that the recently rising birth rate must continue to rise. It probably won't. The intelligence now at hand suggests strongly that the number of annual births and the crude birth rate are due for a moderate dip in the next few years. No very bearish interpreta-

* The World War II rise in the birth rate is in curious contrast to the U.S. experience during World War I, when the rate fell. The difference is partially explained by the fact that the second war was preceded by a depression, which meant postponed births.

tion need be put on this prospect, however; the present birth rate is so high that a moderate decline will still leave the U.S. a dynamically expanding population. Beyond the "recession" in the birth rate, furthermore, lies the certainty of a second baby boom just as fabulous as the one of 1945-55, a certainty that must influence many marketing decisions that will be made even before the birth rate starts turning up again.

A LASTING BULGE

For many U.S. businessmen the forthcoming dip and subsequent boom in babies have implications too obvious to require much elucidation. Dr. Benjamin Spock, author of Baby and Child Care, is reasonably certain to benefit when births are on the rise. (Five million copies have been sold, in all editions, since the book was published in 1946.) Manufacturers of maternity clothes and baby food, operators of diaper services and nursery schools, will clearly be among the sufferers when births decline. And since, as Lord Keynes sagely observed, we are all dead in the long run, a decline in births would seem to mean even an eventual decline in the tombstone business.

But the point is that the 33 million babies born during the past nine years will affect more than a few specialized markets. They will constitute a kind of bulge in the U.S. population during their entire life cycle; their impact on both the size and age composition of the nation will not be transitory. Neither will their impact on the market.

As a case in point, consider the food market, explored at length in last October's Fortune. (See "The Fabulous Market for Food.") Though their requirements are special, and occasionally expensive, babies are not spectacular food consumers. A child of one needs less than 1,000 calories a day, a child of six less than 2,000. Since an extraordinary proportion of our population has been in the six-and-under group in recent years—it is now around 17 per cent—total U.S. calorie requirements have not kept pace with the rise in population. But the postwar babies will soon be growing into ravenous teen-agers. A seventeen-year-old boy ordinarily consumes more calories than a grown man; the figures are roughly 3,800 to 3,000 (for a moderately active man). From now until the 1960's, it seems probable, calorie consumption will rise about 3 per cent faster than the population totals. Applying the 3 per cent to a national food bill of $60 billion, it would seem that the food industry has some $2 billion worth of extra business implied in the changing size and age composition of the nation. The extent to which that potential can be realized depends, of course, on a great many things; no one knows just yet whether the teen-agers will be getting their calories from steaks or from bread and jam. But the potential is there.

The $15-billion automobile market (see "A New Kind of Car Market," Fortune, September, 1953) may derive some longer-range encouragement from recent fertility. The car-driving population, i.e., those fifteen to sixty-nine, will have increased by only 11 per cent from 1945 to 1955. The population as a whole will have increased by 18 per cent during those years. Here, again, the relationships are soon to be reversed.

From 1955 to 1960 the two rates of growth will be about equal; and after 1960 the potential drivers will be expanding even faster than the population. During the 1960's—whatever happens to the birth rate before then—the driving-age population will increase by more than 16 per cent, the population as a whole less than 13 per cent.

The prospects for automobiles are, indeed, not too dissimilar from those for many other durable-goods markets. From now until perhaps the late 1960's, perishables, soft goods, and services may be expected to enlarge their share of the market at the expense of the durables. As the postwar babies grow into adolescence, they will require more clothing, go to more movies, buy more phonograph records and athletic equipment. But they will not be ripe for the durables markets until much later—the late 1960's, say—when they marry and buy their own homes.

FOURTEEN MILLION WEDDING BELLS

Though the markets directly related to marriage are going to cool off a bit, they have, at least, had a remarkable growth in the past eight years. For this reason, it would be well to scrutinize the postwar marriage boom. Approximately 14 million marriages, involving almost twice that many Americans, have been performed in the postwar years. In consequence, the proportion of unmarried women in the marriageable ages has declined sharply. In 1920 almost one-third of the women in the fifteen to forty-nine age group were unmarried. The proportion remained about a third until World War II; but by 1945 it had dropped below 30 per cent, and in 1952 it was down to 22 per cent. Right now, it is not more than 21 per cent.

All age groups have participated in this surge to matrimony. In 1920 almost half the girls aged twenty to twenty-four were unwed; today the bracket is not much more than one-quarter single. The forty-five to forty-nine age group, which pretty much writes the final score, was 90 per cent married in 1920; it is now 92 per cent married. There are good reasons for believing that the figure will have climbed to about 94 per cent by 1965. This last statistic represents, roughly, the proportion of women who *ever* get married. Ninety-four per cent may probably be considered a sort of practical upper limit.

The marriage boom has meant not only that more women get married but that they do it earlier. For many years before 1945, the percentage of girls fifteen to nineteen who were married remained around 13. After the war the figure suddenly began rising; it is now about 17 per cent. Marriages in the twenty to twenty-four age group have expanded even more dramatically. About 56 per cent of all the women who marry do so in these five years. Back in 1920 about 12 per cent of all marriages were postponed until after the young lady was thirty; only about 5 per cent wait that long now.

Well, where do marriages, and the markets that directly depend on them, go from here? The fact seems to be that the marriage ratio (i.e., the number of women marrying in relation to the number reaching marriageable age) has already begun falling. It reached an all-time high in the years 1946-50, when it was a startling 124 per cent. During those years, in other words, the ratio was running about 24 per cent higher than would be required, in the long run, to marry off the entire feminine population. This extraordinary level plainly had to come down. In part it had been created by the shifting into the postwar years of delayed marriages. To a much larger extent, it reflected the increased proportion of women marrying in their teens and early twenties. The ratio was, in other words, a kind of borrowing from both the past and the future.

WHY A DECLINE?

The marriage ratio is down now to 97 per cent. Let us say that in the near future it will be around 95 per cent. That would still be much higher than the level of the 1930's (when it averaged about 89 per cent), but it would not be high enough to bring back the huge annual totals of the early postwar years. Remember, the generation now passing through the nubile years is the lean depression crop; the girls who are now

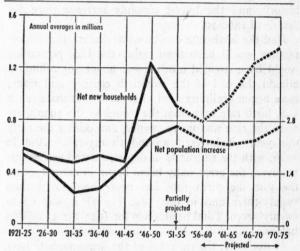

HOUSEHOLDS: THE DURABLE MARKET

The postwar boom in household formation has now slackened off, to the detriment of home building, cars, appliances, and the durables market generally; in 1956-60 the annual growth of new households will run about 100,000 less than in recent years. However, when the postwar babies begin to form their own households, the durables market will turn up again sharply. Furthermore, that market is helped by a long-run tendency for households to grow relatively faster than the population as a whole—i.e., for households to decline in size.

Data from the Census Bureau; projections by *Fortune*.

twenty to twenty-four were born in 1930-34, at the bottom of the depression—which means that relatively few of them were born. Right now there are about 5,300,000 of these girls around. When the war ended there were more than six million girls in this age bracket. But the dearth of girls at these ages is not the only reason for expecting marriages to remain lower. The girls are not only relatively scarce, but, since an extraordinarily high percentage of them are already wed, they are relatively ineligible. (These observations apply with less force to second and third marriages, which are not much affected by the shortage of younger girls. But *first* marriages are what primarily count for the American market.)

Recently, first marriages have been running at about 75 per cent of all marriages. The totals for the latter reached an all-time high of 2,300,000 in 1946. In the past five years they have been running at 1,600,000 annually. This rate is sure to come down as the number of first marriages drops—by perhaps 10 per cent—in the next few years.

This will doubtless be a matter of some dismay to the jewelers, caterers, and proprietors of honeymoon resorts, whose markets are directly affected by the marriage curve. But the market as a whole is affected less directly by the nuptial ceremonies; after all, it is not marriages that count so much as the subsequent formation of households and rearing of children.

WHY A BOOM?

For purposes of analysis, the 33 million babies born since 1945 may be divided into the three broad classes: births postponed from the Thirties; births that (because of a sudden fall in the age of marriage) came earlier than expected; and births normally expected. Needless to say, the parents of these teeming tots ordinarily made no such distinctions. The distinctions are necessary, however, to determine the future of the markets that have been swollen by the high birth rate.

How many births were postponed during the 1930's? To answer the question, one must first decide how many births might normally have been expected during the 1930's. The decision is not an easy one; unlike the steel industry, the mothers of the U.S. cannot be meaningfully rated as to total capacity. One can, however, gauge their past performance by number and timing of births at different ages.* Using the experience of the 1920's, it appears that over 33 million births might have been expected from 1930 to 1944. As it turned out, there were only about 30,900,000 births. By the end of 1944, in other words, there was a "deficit" of over two million births.

"Deficits" by Order of Births
(in thousands)

	1930-34	'35-'39	'40-'44	Total
First	421	336	−353	404
Second	276	532	71	879
Third	40	322	246	608
Fourth		109	156	265
Fifth		30	80	110
Sixth & higher			6	6
Total	737	1,329	206	2,272

In the early years of the depression the deficit was largely in first births, and was accounted for in large measure by the postponement of marriage. By 1933

* The estimates in this section on births postponed, made up, and advanced are for births to native-born white women only; detailed information is not available for other women.

there was a "backlog" of about 800,000 marriages. In the late 1930's the number of marriages slowly began to increase, and by 1940 the backlog was down to 600,000. These newlyweds of the late 1930's contributed heavily to making up the deficit in first births; note, in the table above, that first births in 1940-44 were 353,000 *more* than would have been expected for this period. But the deficits in second, third, and fourth births were not made up until much later. The above table makes it clear that by the time the great baby boom was beginning, the great deficit was concentrated in the second and third births.

Nearly all of these deficits, except for the small one in fifth, sixth, and higher births, have been made up in the past nine years. In other words, something on the order of 2,200,000 postponed births helped to make the boom. And these figures apply only to native white women; the figures for all U.S. women would come to about two and a half million births. Some 7 or 8 per cent of the 33-million baby boom is, in this respect, abnormal.

"ADVANCED" BABIES

But postponements from the past are not the only "extra." In addition to these, borrowings from the future have artificially souped up the birth rate of recent years. Just as women have been getting married earlier, so, quite logically, they have been having their first babies earlier. At first glance it does not seem entirely clear why a reduction in the age at which women have children should raise the annual birth rate. Why should it make any difference whether they have babies at twenty-three or at nineteen? The answer is that the age does not matter; the *change* in age does, however, because the number of potential mothers is being temporarily expanded. But an earlier age for first births does not necessarily mean *more* births in the long run, any more than an earlier draft age means more soldiers. There is only a temporary increase in the supply, followed by a drop to the old norm.

The age at which women become mothers has indeed fallen dramatically. The fact is that 14 per cent of native-born white women sixteen to twenty years old are now mothers, compared to 8.5 per cent in the 1920's. The percentage of mothers in the twenty-one to twenty-five group has gone up from 42 to 56 in the same years. In consequence, the entrepreneurs catering to young women have seen some interesting changes in their markets in recent years. A young mother does not ordinarily spend money—or have it spent on her—in quite the same way that an unattached young lady does. Soft goods (e.g., the young lady's wardrobe) and services (e.g., her recreational spending) are importantly affected. Instead of going out dancing, or to the movies, she is apt to stay home and watch television in the evenings. And since this young matron and her young husband have married with fewer resources than they would have had later, the TV set is more apt to be bought on credit.

Had the age of marriage and of first birth, and the spacing of subsequent births, continued in the pattern of the 1920's, then about 2,900,000 births to native-born white women in the past nine years would still be gleams in demographers' eyes. For *all* women, the effect of reducing the age at first birth has been to move some 3,400,000 births that would have come later into the 1945-53 period.

If we subtract the 2,500,000 "postponed" births and the 3,400,000 "advanced" births from the 33 million babies delivered during the past nine years, then the great boom is seen in a somewhat changed perspective. It remains a remarkable boom. Even when 18 per cent of the births are discounted, and when 27 million is seen as the "normal" birth total for the period, the total is impressive. But the portents are somewhat changed. With postponements and advancements of diminished importance, a decline in total births becomes virtually inevitable.

HOW BIG A FAMILY?

These somewhat bearish calculations need not have such gloomy implications for the future of the American market, however. To some extent, the decline in births will be offset by the growing proportion of births among higher-income families. Furthermore, there remains a great deal of uncertainty about the extent of this decline in births.

In many ways the most remarkable aspect of the recent baby boom has been not the staggering totals it produced but the way those totals break down. Specifically, Americans have not only been having more children, they have been having more second, third, and fourth children. Gallup polls, taken in 1941 and 1945, indicated then that the Americans' conception of the "ideal" family size was changing. The 1941 poll showed 40 per cent of the women twenty-one to thirty-four wanting only two children. By 1945 this had been reduced to 25 per cent. The big gainer was the group favoring four children; it moved from 21 to 31 per cent of the total.

Since about 1945, American women have been making this altered ideal something of a reality. The change, furthermore, has been felt all along the income scale. The middle classes, at least, are approaching a new norm; and it seems to center around families with three or four children.

THE FINAL SCORE

It will be more than a decade before the final score on the new family size is in. Completed families (i.e., those in which the mother is past forty-nine) have recently averaged 2.4 children in the population as a whole. This figure represents the end of a long decline; back in 1925 there were at least 3.5 children in the average completed family. It is unlikely that the national average will return to the 1925 level. Even the Gallup Poll ideal implies no more than about 2.8. The demographers are pretty much at a loss to explain the apparent trend. About all they have to offer is a general, and not very illuminating, statement that the "style" is changing.

The most dramatic change, in many ways, has occurred in the suburbs. It is clear that suburbanites have more children than urbanites (see "The Lush New Suburban Market," *Fortune*, November, 1953), but cause and effect remain somewhat tangled. It is certainly true that many people move to the suburbs precisely because they want to have children; and it is probably true, also, that once in the suburbs many parents find their notion of the "ideal" family size being enlarged. In the intimacy of many suburban communities, a family with only one child seems almost to call for some explanation to friends and neighbors.

The marketing implications of this tendency to larger households are rather complex. First babies revolutionize families' spending habits the most. By the time the later children come, many of the major adjustments have already been made. Furthermore, direct spending for the later babies is somewhat curtailed; the cribs, bottles, baby carriages, and playpens can all be used over again, and the market for this sort of product does not expand directly with the number of births.

But the problem is somewhat more complicated than that. For in middle-income families, at least, something changes at about the third birth; it is not just "more of the same." The most pressing change, of course, centers around living space. The first child, and probably the second one, can be put in the spare bedroom; but the third child calls, rather loudly, for a new home. Even the most intransigent apartment dwellers begin to feel, at about this point, that the heat is on them to buy a house—probably in the suburbs. Families who are already out in the suburbs when a third child arrives are there presumably because they anticipated the need; but even for them the added child may often mean a new home, or at least the construction of an extra room. Builders generally, with an eye on this increase in family size, have been putting up larger homes; the president of the National Association of Home Builders recently estimated that three-quarters of all the homes built in 1954 would have three or more bedrooms. In 1947-48 the proportion was one-third.

HOW MANY BABIES?

But despite the increases in family size, a moderate dip in the annual birth totals seems virtually inevitable. In the past five years births have fluctuated between 3,600,000 and four million a year. It is hard to see how the annual crop in the next five years can average more than 3,500,000; and this figure assumes that the "ideal" family size expressed in the 1945 Gallup Poll will be realized. If recent family size is continued, and not further enlarged, the crop could run as low as 3,100,000. The pleasures of populating the country will be increasingly those of the sparse depression generation. For this group to have as many babies as the U.S. has seen added in recent years would imply an almost unbelievable jump in ideal family size *beyond* the 1945 poll.

The fall will hardly be disastrous, however; indeed, a baby crop of over three million would have seemed unbelievably high to the demographers in the 1930's. And even the businessmen who are most directly affected by the curve of births may choose to consider the decline no more than a breathing spell. They, and a lot of other Americans (e.g., school-board members), may well want to catch their breaths. For in the middle and late 1960's, when the postwar babies begin to spawn, the annual totals will edge up rapidly. Five million babies seems possible for, say, 1975. And then, of course, when *those* babies are old enough to marry. . . .

Fortune *is indebted to Pascal K. Whelpton for general guidance on population trends and for data from his book,* Cohort Fertility: Native White Women in the United States, *to be published next month by Princeton University Press. Mr. Whelpton is Director of the Scripps Foundation for Research in Population Problems, at Miami University, Oxford, Ohio.*

4. PRODUCTIVITY

THE ENGINE: RISING PRODUCTIVITY*

By GILBERT BURCK

The fabulous American standard of living is primarily the result of the extraordinary productivity of U.S. industry. In the last twenty-five years our productivity has increased 2 per cent a year. Two vital questions are explored here: Why has U.S. production surpassed the rest of the world by so large a margin? Can American management keep productivity rising? The answer to these questions involves a basic survey of the whole American economy, the character of its people, the abundance of its resources, and the vitality of its institutions. Also discussed are the problems increased productivity solves as well as those it raises.

The supreme economic story of the past twenty-five years can be reduced to one simple, colossal fact: today the average American, though he works about 15 per cent fewer hours, has roughly 50 per cent more purchasing power than he had a quarter-century ago. This remarkable advance in material welfare is almost entirely a result of the fact that national productivity, which may be defined as average output per man-hour, has shown an average annual increase, since 1930, of more than 2 per cent a year.

The increase, despite the stresses of depression and war, has held remarkably steady over the whole twenty-five years. Forced to cut costs deeply, industry actually increased its man-hour productivity at somewhat more than the average rate during the depression (though total national output, owing to unemployment, dropped badly). Despite the inevitable inefficiencies of war production, despite the strikes and sloppiness of the reconversion period, American productivity did not fall off appreciably either during or immediately after the war. And since 1947 it has shown evidence of having risen by more than 3 per cent, and late last year by as much as 4 per cent. The payoff in U.S. living standards, as *Fortune's* series of articles on The Changing American Market (August, 1953, through August, 1954) has noted, was an increase in average per capita cash income, *even after very high taxes,* of some 13 per cent just between 1947 and 1953. The average U.S. family unit's cash income after taxes now stands at about $4,300. Thus it is, as a study by the Twentieth Century Fund (revised edition of *America's Needs and Resources*) puts it, that Americans who were in their thirties twenty-five years ago "have experienced a greater advance in our material

* From Gilbert Burck, "The Engine: Rising Productivity," January, 1955.

standard of living and a more pervasive change in our way of life than occurred in all the previous centuries of Western history."

The next twenty-five years, if anything, promise even more advances and changes. For American industry, as *Fortune's* series on The Dynamic Market for Capital Goods (September, 1954, through December, 1954) has reported, has invested $300 billion in laborsaving capital goods since 1945, and is expected to invest another $200 billion by 1959. Prodded by the current buyers' market, industry seems engaged in one of the most determined assaults on unit costs, and one of the fiercest strivings for volume, that the U.S. has ever experienced.

If last year's rate of improvement in productivity were sustained, the U.S. living standard would be doubled in about the next eighteen years. It may be that the 4 per cent rate of late 1954 represents an exceptional burst of productivity. But many conservative economists believe the U.S. economy in the past few years has broken through some barriers—that the rate of advance in American productivity, which has averaged roughly 2 per cent a year for the past hundred years, is moving toward a minimum of 2.5 per cent. One-half of 1 per cent compounded, applied to an economy as big as America's, is a potent fraction.

Can the U.S. *increase the rate of increase* in its productivity? How has American productivity advanced as far as it has, where does it go from here?

If U.S. productivity advances by 2.5 per cent a year for the next quarter-century, the annual cash income of the average American family unit in 1980, after taxes, will probably come close to $6,600, in 1953 dollars. What is more, this figure makes allowance for a decrease in working hours. Over the past hundred years, Americans have taken about half their potential income increase as leisure. If a similar ratio holds in the future, the average work week in the U.S. (including that of farmers, shopkeepers, professionals, etc.) will decline from forty-two hours today to about thirty-six in 1980.

All this will not merely expand U.S. industry, it will result in profound changes in U.S. industry. Some industries will not be able to, or just will not, improve their productivity as much as the national average improves. Since it is a fact that wage rates tend to rise with the national productivity, these industries will find themselves burdened with steadily higher costs, their products and services will become relatively more expensive, and their share of the expanding market will tend to decline.

If your wife is complaining about the servant problem, just wait until 1980. Servants will be nearly twice as expensive as they are now and will work 12.5 per cent fewer hours. A maid who now works forty-five hours a week for $45, in other words, would get $73 for some thirty-nine hours, or $1.85 an hour. Some people will still have maids. But it will cost 75 cents to have a maid wash and iron a shirt, whereas shirts will be little or no more expensive than now. Who will pay that much to have a $5 shirt washed and ironed at home? The implications: servants will probably become fewer and will be confined to fewer operations; efficient service organizations, including laundries of a kind not yet known, will take over everything else.

To assess the future of a business, look first at the way it uses manpower. Highly efficient industries like chemicals and petroleum refining, which have raised their productivity at better than the average rate, will probably maintain their extraordinary progress— though keeping it extraordinary may become harder. Industries like furniture and leather, which have a high ratio of labor "content" to unit of output, will be highly vulnerable to a rising wage level. To maintain even their "share" of the new market, they will have to find ways to manufacture with less labor. Garages and service stations will be forced to become far more efficient than they are now, as the cost of servicing and repairing cars rises still higher in relation to their first cost, and auto manufacturers will probably be forced to develop cars that need less servicing. The key to the economic future of America is that manpower, always expensive in the U.S., will become downright precious.

OUT OF THE "DARK SATANIC MILLS"

The progress of American productivity is by all odds the most important achievement in the history of man's struggle to wrest a living from his environment, and more than any other American achievement, it is what makes the U.S. uniquely powerful and hopeful. Our religions and our laws are inheritances from older cultures, but our economy is something new. And in our ability to increase production faster than population we have left the rest of the world far behind, and are leaving it further behind every day.

It can be argued that modern civilization begins not with the Greeks or the Renaissance or the Gutenberg press or the Declaration of Independence, but a hundred and eighty years ago, in the "dark Satanic mills" of England, whose managers first began to use machines to multiply the productive potentialities of the humble man-hour—that is, to increase output per unit of cost on a significant and rising scale. Until that time, all civilizations were alike in one basic respect: they had discovered no way of increasing their productivity greatly and continuously, and their total wealth, allowing for abundance or scarcity of usable natural resources, therefore bore an almost fixed ratio to the number of people producing it. People performed the same old jobs in the same old way; as Norbert Wiener has remarked, a Babylonian administrator would have needed no training to run an early Virginia plantation. It is true that some blessed principalities enjoyed comparative abundance without worrying about productivity, and it is also true that the Renaissance was accompanied by somewhat higher productivity. But these were temporary or relatively minor deviations from the rule that every nation, in terms of total wealth divided by population, was miserably poor. There was no genuine democracy because in the last analysis political democracy must be based on economic democracy, or the widespread distribution of wealth, and there simply was not enough wealth to distribute widely.

Management and machines changed all this. For the first time men were able to be optimistic about their future on earth without being foolish. For the first time a genuine, large-scale, working democracy became possible. For the first time mankind was able to multiply not only itself but its wealth per head.

Material progress, to be sure, is not wholly synonymous with everyone's definition of progress. Moreover, rising productivity makes possible undesirable consumption patterns like the juvenile consumption of TV thrillers. It usually results in "technological" if temporary unemployment, compels workers to move whether they want to or not, destroys ways of life and many non-material values that may have great merit. For rising productivity is both the result and cause of constant change, and constant change always is accompanied by some storm and stress.

But material progress is no longer a theory but a condition—and a condition that the whole world is now hot to enjoy. The time has long since come to make the least of its few disadvantages and the most of its advantages, which are palpable and legion. Rising productivity necessarily enthrones the consumer. Because machines not only displace but lighten labor, rising productivity makes labor continually easier even as it makes labor continually more precious. Because it tends to reward best those who contribute most to productivity, it endows money with the morality that it should have. Rising productivity raises plenty of new problems at the same time it is solving old ones. Even so, the central economic problem of the U.S.—and the world—is not so much what to do with productivity, but how to keep it rising.

THE BENCH MARKS

Just how much has America's productivity risen, and how does its growth compare with that of the rest of the world? At the outset let it be said that no one has yet measured with complete accuracy U.S. productivity or made wholly satisfactory international comparisons. Most productivity figures, for example, ignore basic values of raw materials and changes in quality of products. An apparent gain in dollar output per man-hour, if achieved mainly by wasteful use of natural resources, may end up as no long-term gain at all; on the other hand, the superiority of the 1955 Chevrolet over the 1930 Chevrolet, as a product, is not fully reflected in the gain in dollar value of output per G.M. man-hour.

What we do have, however, is a clear idea of many of the results of rising productivity, and from these we have a tolerably accurate idea of productivity's trend. First let us analyze the growth in America's production and wealth. Between 1850 and 1953:

The number of privately employed workers rose from seven million to 56 million, *or eight times*.

Total private man-hours worked annually, however, rose from about 26 billion to about 126 billion, *or only five times*. Reason: the average number of hours worked per week declined from about seventy to about forty-two, or by 40 per cent.

Yet national private (non-government) gross product—measured in constant 1953 dollars—rose from about $11 billion to $334 billion, *or about thirty times*, and private G.N.P. per worker rose from less than $1,500 to nearly $6,000, *or four times*.

Thus national productivity, expressed as private G.N.P. per man-hour (again in constant 1953 dollars) rose from about 40 cents to $2.64, *or more than six times*, averaging 2 per cent a year over the century.

Since a larger proportion of the population is working for money today than in 1850, our living standard, expressed as real per capita income, has increased *about five times*, or more than G.N.P. per worker.

WHAT IT TAKES

Most authorities agree that the U.S., Britain, and Western Europe were about equally efficient (or inefficient) about a hundred years ago; if the U.S. had an edge, it was over continental Europe, not over Britain, and at any rate the edge was nothing compared to the edge America has today. But then—mightily helped by European capital and immigrants—the U.S. began to forge ahead. Thousands of Americans left the farm for industry, fewer farmers produced enormously greater crops, and American industrial efficiency soared.

Today the U.S. manufacturing worker turns out from two to ten times as much per hour as his European counterpart, and U.S. farm and service workers doubtless boast a similar margin over their European counterparts. Thus, the U.S. *share* of the world product has risen steadily, even though Western Europe's share has recently increased sharply as Europe made good its World War II losses. And so it is that the 6 per cent of the world's population residing in the U.S. now

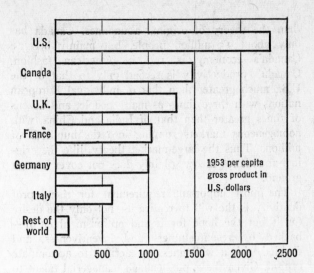

HOW LONG CAN IT KEEP UP?

These bars pose one of the most difficult economic and political problems facing the civilized world. Per capita gross product (and income) of the U.S. is now about twice that of such industrialized nations as the U.K. and Germany, and seventeen times that of the rest of the world. The "rest of the world" wants to catch up. But can it ever catch up with Western Europe, let alone the U.S.? And how much richer than the rest of the world can the U.S. afford—politically, militarily, morally—to be?

produces and consumes 40 per cent of the world's goods *and services*, and more than half of the free world's factory-made goods.

And why has U.S. production and consumption surpassed the rest of the world's by so wide a margin? The reason most commonly advanced by Europeans and many Americans is the abundance of natural resources in the U.S. But in the last analysis original abundance has not been a dominating factor in U.S. productivity. Like the red Indians before them, the early Americans were very poor. As Bill Nye once remarked of the Puritans, they had to dig clams all winter so they could have enough strength to plant corn, and they had to hoe corn all summer so they could have enough strength to dig clams. Even the homesteaders on the rich midwest prairies had to labor prodigiously for what today would be meager reward indeed. It was not until the Industrial Revolution was well under way that American productivity rose much above the level that had prevailed in Europe since the Middle Ages— and the relative abundance of natural resources was only one reason why it did. And today the U.S. is, if anything, penalized by its many natural resources. Thanks to price support and production-control schemes, Americans have to pay more than the world market prices (or what world prices would be if the market were free) for such things as grain, meat, metals, petroleum, fats and oils.

Another reason commonly advanced for American productivity is that the U.S. constitutes a huge homogeneous market. This reason has even less substance than the theory of original abundance. Canada has only about 15 million people, but mainly because Canada's economy is run in American fashion, Canada's productivity is second only to that of the U.S., much greater than that of individual European nations with three times as many people, and dozens of times greater than that of India and China, with homogeneous markets running into the hundreds of millions. Thus the large-market theory, like the original-abundance theory, plainly does not cover enough ground.

The most important requirement for rising productivity is the will to realize it—not only the desire for it but the hope for it and optimism about it—backed by resourcefulness and inventiveness, and coupled with a willingness to sacrifice to accumulate capital. Given these, plus enough managerial talent to organize work effectively, and the poorest nation can improve productivity a little. To improve productivity appreciably—that is, to introduce the division of labor on any scale—a nation needs a fair-sized internal market, and access to raw materials and plant and machinery. Later it needs access to a flourishing technology, whose inventions and innovations have been a major factor in the advance of productivity.

Yet that is not all. Even as life feeds on life, so productivity feeds on productivity. High real wages spur management to find ways of doing a job with fewer man-hours, and doing a job with fewer man-hours usually results in lower prices or still higher wages or both, and the cycle begins all over again. But the cycle plainly flourishes best when it suffers a minimum of artificial restrictions. Labor must be willing to be displaced, and willing to move when displaced. Management must be willing to operate in a tolerably free market, and to earn its reward by outdoing others. The ideal environment for productivity is an economy that is flexible, adaptable, competitive.

The only environment that has met all these condition, albeit imperfectly, is the American. Despite the heavy blows of depression and the scars of NRA, despite the vogue, for a decade or more, of the notion that the U.S. economy was at last "mature," despite all the rigidities and distortions imposed on the economy during World War II, despite the demands of Korea and the continuing demands of the cold war, it is fair to say that the U.S. economy today is more flexible, adaptable, and competitive than it was twenty-five years ago. The Europeans have had homogeneous markets, and abundant talent, and perhaps even more technical ingenuity than the Americans. What they have lacked are the American dynamism, optimism, versatility, and relative freedom from restraint and rigidity—all the traits that add up to what might be called a national *attitude* toward productivity. Thousands of European businessmen have recently testified to the existence of such an attitude.

THAT URGE TO GET AHEAD

To understand the American attitude toward productivity, we must begin with the American character. That character, of course, has been shaped by abun-

dance, even as a man used to money usually spends it more easily than one whose instincts have been chilled by want. Yet it was the American character that was also responsible for the American abundance. For although abundance begets productivity, only rising productivity can multiple abundance.

And what are the American traits that have been basically responsible for rising productivity? At bottom was the enormous energy of the American—restless, intense, unsatisfied, headlong. There was also a pervasive sense of equality, intolerant of pretense and disdaining class distinction; an almost contumacious individualism magnificently expressed in the old dictum that every 100 per cent American should live so that he could look any man in the face and tell him to go to hell; a pragmatic, intuitive, unintellectual approach to life's problems. And these traits, coupled with a lack of regard for custom and tradition, resulted in an unsurpassed ability to shift gears when it was time to shift them.

Add up these traits, and remember that all men of spirit and self-esteem harbor the germs of ambition, and you have another very important American trait: the urge to get ahead in the world, and the habit of judging a man's ability to get ahead by his success in laying hands on the almighty dollar. Taking everything together, this has been fortunate. The dollar can be a great corrupter of men, but it is also a great benefactor of mankind. The dollar has served humanity by functioning as Adam Smith said money should function—by harnessing man's dynamic, acquisitive instincts to raising productivity, by enabling the Invisible Hand of the market to function.

IS COMPETITION DEAD?

The yearning for the dollar was fortunately canalized and made socially useful, just as Adam Smith said it should be, by being subjected to the rigors of competition. Thanks in part to the national preoccupation with moral issues, the U.S. was the only nation to write the concept of competition into the law of the land. It has long been fashionable, to be sure, to argue that antitrust is beside the point and out of date, that competition in the old, classical sense of the word is dead. Of course it is dead. The old, classical competition is dead because it never existed save in the minds and textbooks of academicians. What did and still does exist is a kind of modified or workable competition that has stimulated productivity infinitely more than *no* competition would have. And that is the only reason for wanting competition.

Simply look around. The steel industry, any economics student can tell you, is not really competitive. Yet only recently, U.S. Steel built its $400-million Fairless Works to improve its competitive position. Fifteen years ago, any economics student could also have told you, the chemical industry was virtually a big price ring, hardly any better than a European chemical cartel. Yet today it has been invaded by many newcomers and encroached on by non-chemical companies, and the whole industry is acutely price and cost conscious.

Europeans who have taken the trouble to look closely at the American system have seen this clearly enough. Said the report of the British industrial-engineering team, published only four months ago: "It is our opinion that more than any other factor competition provides the [U.S.] drive to achieve the most economic usage of men, materials, machines, and money. . . . We are convinced that in the prevention of price rings and cartel agreements the effect of the [antitrust] legislation is to increase competition and efficiency."

DYNAMIC LABOR

It is precisely the combination of competitive spirit and yearning for the dollar—or, more exactly, for all that the dollar can buy—that accounts in the main for the important contribution of American labor to rising productivity. Labor's contribution? Aren't large, powerful labor unions fundamentally monopolies with much the same power to inhibit the growth of productivity as industrial monopolies and cartels? They are indeed. The point, however, is that American labor, unlike British and European labor, has not habitually exercised its monopoly power to inhibit change. British and European unions concern themselves primarily with making and maintaining as many jobs as they can, and secondarily with increasing wages. Thus German labor backs the legal revival of cartels because cartels will "stabilize" the market and employment; and German management, supplied plentifully with cheap labor, tends to use that labor inefficiently. Thus the British National Union of Railwaymen refuses to let management eliminate the state-owned railways' redundant workers, who may account for as much as 20 per cent of the staff, and thus all Britain pays more for transportation than it should.

American labor unions, of course, are in business to push their own interests, and some of them have been as guilty of featherbedding as any European union. The fact remains, however, that on the whole they differ radically from European unions in wanting higher wages above all else. At the rate American productivity is rising, about 1,500,000 fewer people will be needed next year to turn out this year's volume of goods and services. Labor doesn't exactly like this, but it has not made a policy of opposing it. In essence, labor wants the higher real wages that rising productivity makes possible, and expects business to invest capital to create new jobs to employ the workers displaced. All in all, U.S. labor well fulfills one of the basic functions of organized labor in a free, dynamic economy: that of prodding management into doing the job more cheaply.

The foreign observers, once again, saw all this clearly. They remarked on American labor's comparative willingness to change jobs and its acceptance of displacement, and they attributed these traits to better management, better human relations, the absence of deep-seated class warfare. "The trade unions," marveled Dr. Werner F. Gatz, scientific director of the Institut für Weltwirtschaft at the University of Kiel, "behave as if they were the entrepreneurs."

Above all, the foreign visitors noted, there is the American worker's desire for all the good things American money can buy. Better layout and longer runs do not cause the operative to work fast, a British boot-and-shoe industry observer noted, "but rather . . . those factors enable the operatives to earn as much as they can."

PROFESSIONAL ENTREPRENEURS

And so too with American management, whose enduring contribution to civilization is that it has made the American man-hour the most fruitful in history. What is the primary function of management in a dynamic society? It is, in the last analysis, to increase output per unit of input (or reduce input per unit of output), i.e., to increase profitability by increasing productivity. The manager who increases his company's productivity is discharging at once his major obligation to the owners and his major obligation to society. It could be argued, actually, that many of the "slave-driving" American managers who ruthlessly slashed costs in pre-union days contributed more to the long-term common good than many a latter-day "humanitarian."

Managers today, of course, know that they can achieve higher productivity by practicing a wise humanitarianism. They know the dollar value of public and human relations, and many practice them assiduously. They are, as the article on page 38 explains, becoming more professional and constantly enlarging their perspectives. Some are becoming "statesmen." A few, alas, are becoming stuffed shirts.

NO PLATEAU FOR PRODUCTIVITY

Well, can American management keep productivity rising? Isn't there a plateau beyond which output per man-hour cannot rise very much? The answer is that the opportunities for expanding productivity are so numerous that the nation's living standard *can* rise more in the next twenty-five years than in the past twenty-five, and more in the next hundred years than in the past hundred. Some of the reasons:

Rising productivity, as we have noted, begets rising productivity.

Technology is growing more productive. Industry is not only substituting machines for physical labor in specific jobs, and not only substituting machines for mental work, it is devising machines for work nobody has done before.

There will be plenty of capital.

Farm productivity can be improved immensely.

Distribution productivity, though rising has increased since 1900 much less than manufacturing productivity. Thus the pressure is mounting for reductions in distribution costs. The success of the mail-order and discount houses is doubtless just the beginning of a movement to eliminate a sizable portion of the man-hours now used to move goods from plant to consumer.

. . . BUT MANY OBSTACLES

There are, however, several factors that might prevent a steep rise in productivity. For one thing, as workers are displaced, or as better job opportunities develop elsewhere, workers must be willing and able to move. But they may not be so willing to move as they have been. More seniority privileges tie more workers to specific plants. So does the common habit of tendering workers *nonvested* pensions, that is, pensions that they cannot take with them when they leave the company. So would the guaranteed annual wage.

And more important than these are four basic forces, four great wielders of market power, organized not necessarily to increase the national product, but to get for themselves a larger share of the national product. Professor Clair Wilcox once described these forces as Big Business, Big Little Business, Big Agriculture, and Big Labor.

We have already noted big labor's power to restrain output and keep down productivity, and that U.S. labor has not generally abused that power.

Big business, thanks to antitrust, public opinion, and the sheer variety and creativity of the American economy, is probably the least fearsome of the four. But many industries are pretty much in the hands of two or three producers. And many companies, theoretically at any rate, can get so rich, dominate a market so completely, and gather so much momentum that they can relax and acquire the corporate equivalent of arteriosclerosis even while maintaining a façade of vitality.

TO PROTECT "COMPETITORS"

More ominous is little business' success in softening up the antitrust law with such amendments as the Miller-Tydings Act (legitimizing state fair-trade laws) and the recent McGuire Act (authorizing states to bind non-signers to fair-trade agreements), which in effect protect "competitors" against competition (though General Electric's recent decision to eliminate "suggested" list prices on major appliances will make these laws less enforceable than they are). There are also hundreds of local statutes, like those setting up milk cartels, all written to rigidify little corners of the market. Such are the obstacles in the way of improving productivity in distribution and services.

Organized agriculture has probably used its political power more purposefully than all the other three put together. The effect has been to hold back *both* agri-

cultural and industrial productivity. For high-level price supports have tended to maintain marginal farms and to hold a price umbrella over wealthy farms, to slow down mechanization, and thus keep on the land workers who could produce much more in industry.

To pretent that these anticompetitive forces do not exist in American life is the worst way of dealing with them. Anyone who looks can see them all at work in Europe, effectively keeping down productivity, crippling living standards, and throttling the hope and faith of the little man. Fortunately, there seem to be so many conflicting forces in the American economy, including Professor Wilcox's four Big's, that the anticompetitive forces do not have in practice the power they have in theory.

And what if U.S. competition does keep its vitality, and productivity rises at about 2.5 per cent a year? As we have noted, cash income (after taxes) of the average family unit by 1980 will rise to $6,600 (1953 dollars), the average work week will decline to thirty-six hours, and industries that use a lot of manpower per unit of output will be at a relative disadvantage.

Rising productivity is also sure to have a profound effect on American foreign-trade policy. By 1980, simply to keep our factories going, we shall probably have to import vastly greater quantities of raw materials than we do now. What is more, companies that now need protection to compete with foreign goods will, unless they increase their productivity sufficiently, need vastly more protection than they enjoy now. But the chances are at least even that they will not get it, save as it is unequivocally necessary for defense. For as our productivity rises, the ability of our most productive industries to invade foreign markets will increase. As we invade them, our ability to increase our own productivity will then depend increasingly on the expansion of those markets. But to expand those foreign markets we will have to let foreign industries into the American market. In short, rising productivity will render overwhelmingly obvious the economic advantages of an international division of labor, of concentrating on what we can do best and letting other nations concentrate on what they can do best. And, what is more, this is the only workable way of helping other nations raise *their* productivity—as they eventually must if the U.S. is to continue raising its own.

2. The Economy: Institutions

5. THE LABOR MOVEMENT

THE U.S. LABOR MOVEMENT*

Unlike its counterpart in Europe, the labor movement in the United States has not developed along proletarian or ideological lines. The American union is militant and successful; it is unique in the meaning it has for its member. It is his tool to acquire as an individual the status and security of a full citizen in a middle-class capitalistic society. The anti-proletarian and non-ideological orientation which characterized unionism in the United States is not only the key to its unique achievement and to its greatest danger, but also the key to the method by which it may extend the achievement and avoid the danger.

The stubborn refusal of the American labor movement to behave according to the so-called "laws of history" utterly baffles the European intellectual.

Organized labor is the strongest of our organized political pressure groups. Political action has always been important to American unionism. It has never been a pure "business unionism" concerned only with dollars and cents. But political action has been a tool for the achievement of union ends. The opposite approach—the use of unionism as a tool for the advancement of a political "ideology," as in Europe—has been considered here a "betrayal of unionism." That is why there is not a national American labor party.

Inside the American labor movement there is none of the ideological uniformity that characterizes European unions. A vast philosophical distance separates arch-Republican Bill Hutcheson of the carpenters from ex-Socialist Dave Dubinsky of the ladies' garment workers; yet they work together as vice presidents of the American Federation of Labor. And while the younger Congress of Industrial Organizations shows greater cohesion, the differences between Emil Rieve of the textile workers and Walter Reuther of the automobile workers might be enough to disrupt most European trade-union organizations. This diversity runs all the way to the individual local. Within the same union, within the same industry, within the same city, union practices, union policies, and even union oratory vary all over the lot.

American labor is not "working-class conscious"; it is not "proletarian" and does not believe in class war. Some parts of it are as uncompromisingly wedded to rugged individualism as the National Association of Manufacturers. Others want to "reform capitalism." If there were a standard or typical labor view on this subject, it would probably come close to that of George

W. Brooks of the strong and tough pulp, sulfite, and paper-mill workers (A.F. of L.), who says "labor's objective of 'making today better than yesterday' is predicated on its acceptance of capitalism."

Yet the American union is a militant union—more militant, perhaps, than its European counterparts. Not only can it point to steadier gains for its members in the form of wages and benefits than any other labor movement; it has also been demanding for itself more and more managerial power within the business enterprise. And it is capable of fighting for both its economic and its power demands with a ferocity and bitterness (to say nothing of a vocabulary) that could hardly be matched by any class-war union.

For however much similarity there may be between the objective conditions that gave rise to unionism throughout the industrialized world, the American union is unique in the meaning it has for its member, in the purpose and function it serves for him: *it is his tool for gaining and keeping as an individual the status and security of a full citizen in capitalist society.* That it has made the worker to an amazing degree a middle-class member of a middle-class society—in the plant, in the local community, in the economy—is the real measure of its success. The existence at the same time of real hostility to enterprise, management, and the economic system among the American workers is not only the measure of its failure; it is the greatest danger to the American labor movement—and perhaps also its greatest opportunity.

THE MORE IT CHANGES—

Twenty years ago it was easy to dismiss the peculiar characteristics of the American labor movement as signs of the "immaturity" of the American worker. The U.S. at that time, next to Japan, was the least unionized of the major industrial countries. Surely, so the argument ran, a bigger union movement in America

*From "The U.S. Labor Movement," February, 1951.

· 27 ·

would be as proletarian and as much dedicated to class war, as much anti-capitalist and socialist, as the union movements of Europe. The most confident expression of this view came from Harold Laski, the lord high keeper of leftist illusions. But the same view had been held inside the American labor movement itself all during the twenties—for instance, by the young men around the Brookwood Labor College, many of whom later on showed up among the moving spirits of the C.I.O.

Today the U.S. may well be the most unionized of the free countries. Certainly, as *Fortune* showed in its labor column last April, practically all production employees in "big" and "middle" industry are organized. Union contracts determine wage rates everywhere in this country, in unorganized as well as in organized businesses, for clerical as well as for production employees. This switch from an open-shop to an organized economy took only twelve years—from 1933 to 1945. They were years of depression and war, of tension and upheaval. Yet today's successful, strong, and militant labor movement is as little "proletarian" or "socialist" as the small and unsuccessful labor movement of twenty years ago.

Since 1941 there have been three major developments within American labor, all illustrating the same drift: the renascence of the A.F. of L.; the strong anti-ideological shift within the C.I.O.; and the eclipse of left-wing ideologies and philosophies within the labor movement itself.

All through the thirties and right up to World War II the A.F. of L. was the "sick man" of American labor, if not given up for dead. It was obsolete if not senile, hide-bound, unprincipled, inflexible, corrupt, and—worst swear-word of all—"petty bourgeois." Yet today the A.F. of L. has some eight and a half million members—twice as many as it had in 1941. In addition the bulk of the "independent" unions are A.F. of L. unions in their philosophy, their tactics, and their structure, though not in formal affiliation. Almost two out of every three American union members—10 million out of a total of 15 million—are thus organized on the A.F. of L. basis and in unions that derive in unbroken descent from Samuel Gompers.

Neither economic developments nor the small changes in tactics that have occurred within the A.F. of L. fully explain this renascence. Perhaps it is too much to claim, as some A.F. of L. men do, that it is precisely its anti-proletarian, pro-capitalist character that has been attracting the American worker. But one thing at least is sure: that the A.F. of L.'s middle-class character has proved no obstacle to its success, let alone, as was so confidently predicted only ten years ago, fatal to its very survival.

The C.I.O. at its start was hailed as the fulfillment of the intellectual's dream of a "class-conscious" and "proletarian" labor movement. What has actually been happening to the C.I.O. may be read in the career of the one bright young C.I.O. radical of fifteen years ago who actually made good, the automobile workers' Walter Reuther, by all odds the most dynamic personality in American labor today.

Where Walter Reuther stood politically was never exactly clear. He was certainly not just an "ordinary socialist." There was always a strong resemblance to the Henry Ford of thirty years ago—the Henry Ford who sent the "Peace Ship" to Europe to stop World War I, who had an opinion on anything and everything, and whom the Chicago *Tribune* once called an "anarchist." There was also a bit of the technocrat in Walter Reuther, this being the element of continuity in his many "Reuther Plans." But there was no doubt whatever that he also believed in the class struggle, in some form of socialism, and in a labor party to bring about the "necessary change in the system." These beliefs (rather than his ability and competence as a union leader) gained him the admiration of all the sentimental "friends of labor" among the intellectuals, from the *New Republic* to the amateur politicians of Americans for Democratic Action.

Yet the biggest labor event of 1950—if not of the entire post-World War II period—was a contract negotiated by Walter Reuther that goes further in its affirmation both of the free-enterprise system and of the worker's stake in it than any other major labor contract ever signed in this country. The General Motors contract is the first contract that unmistakably accepts the existing distribution of income between wages and profits as "normal," if not as "fair." This at least was the interpretation that was given within the U.A.W. itself to the acceptance of the existing wage structure as the basis for the next five years. It is the first major union contract that explicitly accepts objective economic facts—cost of living and productivity—as determining wages, thus throwing overboard all theories of wages as determined by political power, and of profit as "surplus value." Finally, it is one of the very few union contracts that expressly recognize both the importance of the management function and the fact that management operates directly in the interest of labor.

The G.M. contract probably reflects what Reuther himself has come to believe over the last few years—though he will surely continue to talk his old line and to ride it hard in his two union publications, the *United Automobile Workers* and *Ammunition* (two of the liveliest pieces of aggressive journalism in the country today). But his own beliefs or words are really none too relevant. The important thing is that this contract—whose significance everyone in the labor movement grasped immediately—has become the program on which Reuther hopes to unify American labor under his own leadership. This is strong evidence of the C.I.O.'s shift toward the George Brooks concept of unionism, "predicated on its acceptance of capitalism." And the force behind the shift is precisely the C.I.O.'s success in gaining for the unskilled and semiskilled worker in the mass-production industries what has been the goal of American labor in general: middle-class status and full citizenship.

THE BATTLE MARX LOST

Never have left-wing ideologies had so little influence on the American labor movement as they have today.

The Communists still control a small but strategic sector of American labor and have scattered but dangerous beachheads elsewhere, notably in the Ford local of the automobile workers. But in glaring contrast to twenty or even to ten years ago, the Communists stay in control only by claiming to be "bona fide unionists"; the mask is dropped only in the closed conventicles of the faithful. David Dubinsky pointed out last May that the old radical, socialist, and idealist movements which formerly were the source of union leaders have been drying up. There are no Wobblies today, no Jewish Bund, no Italian anarchists, no Debs, no Mother Jones. If there is any ideological influence in American labor today it is Catholic union theory —spread by a growing number of labor priests and Catholic labor schools and of considerable importance in several C.I.O. unions as well as in the building trades of the A.F. of L.

In historical perspective it appears that the flare-up of left-wing ideologies in the middle thirties was a freak, no more typical of the basic trends of American unionism since the 1890's than the economic stagnation of the period was typical of the basic trends of the American economy. In origins (Knights of Labor, etc.) the American labor movement was more socialist than the British, and in 1902 the A.F. of L. convention barely defeated a resolution endorsing socialism (4,897 to 4,171). This date corresponds to the date when British labor took the opposite turning—1899, when Keir Hardie committed the T.U.C. to the borning Labor party. Since then British labor has been increasingly dominated by the socialist intellectual. By contrast, the creed of the American labor movement, as summed up in that famous sentence of the Clayton Act of 1914, "The labor of a human being is not a commodity or article of commerce," traces back not to the *Communist Manifesto* but to that blackest of "black Republicans," Mark Hanna, whom Gompers joined in the leadership of the National Civic Federation.

CROSSING THE TRACKS

This anti-proletarian and non-ideological character of American unionism is the key to its unique achievement, to its greatest danger, and to the method by which it may extend the achievement and avoid the danger. Let us first consider the achievement, which is the democratic one of integrating unionism with American community life.

Any proletarian union movement, with its class-war creed, regards the existing community and its institutions as "instruments of oppression." All European union movements, including the British, have sought to build their own community organizations in competition with, if not in opposition to, those of "capitalist society." The American union movement, by contrast, accepts the community and its institutions.

In 1942 the C.I.O. was represented on ninety community-service programs; last year the number was 7,000. In Akron alone—the bloody labor-management battleground of the thirties—sixteen C.I.O. people serve on various boards of the Community Chest.

"We're in about everything in this town except the Portage Country Club," said one C.I.O. leader to John Dos Passos. There is still plenty of resistance by "polite society" against accepting the union leader. But the resistance is hardly more strenuous today than that always offered to the newcomer—for example, the resistance of the New York "society" of merchants and bankers in the 1870's and 1880's to the new industrial magnates.

In some places—one-industry towns with a strong union like Saginaw, Michigan, and the paper and pulp towns of Wisconsin—even this resistance is disappearing. There union men are accepted by the groups that run the communities and set the mores for them. Even the "service clubs" of the small businessman, such as Rotary or the Lions—once strongholds of anti-union sentiment—are beginning to bring union men in as members. There is also increasing acceptance of union men as normal and regular members in management workshops and panels. And there has been full union support for the Joint Council of Economic Education, an amazingly successful group of educators, businessmen, and unionists who are trying to educate Americans in the facts of the free-enterprise system through teaching high-school teachers.

THE DANGER: THROMBOSIS

There is a price for these achievements of democratic unionism. The less class war, the more group greed: a quiet division of loot or assumption of privilege at the expense of less organized members of society. Here is the peculiar danger posed by American labor to a free and mobile society: the danger of social thrombosis, of union feudalism.

Last November, Pan American Airways pilots threatened to strike. Their objective was not higher wages, shorter hours, or different working conditions. It was to deny jobs and benefits to a group of fellow pilots. Pan American had just acquired American Overseas Airlines. But the Pan Am pilots refused to let the American Overseas pilots come in except at the very bottom. Union leaders and government agencies both urged full acceptance of the seniority gained by the A.O.A. men during their years of service—in vain. The demand of the Pan Am Pilots was not motivated so much by fear of damage as by desire to gain a better position for themselves—at the expense of fellow pilots who had been unlucky enough to work for the less successful company.

The pressure for *exclusive* kinds of job security usually comes from the men and is often resisted by union leaders. It is in part an instinctive assertion of the property right—a property right in a certain job. The blame, if blame there be, lies not at the door of unionism but in the technical conflict between machine modes of production and American democratic ideals. It seems harder nowadays (though it may not be) to reach the top through individual effort in an industrialized economy. The workers respond to this supposed sacrifice of vertical mobility by claiming more security —and when this claim is asserted in a particular job, the result may be a real loss of horizontal mobility.

Union policy is not responsible for this danger, but the structure of U.S. unionism has paralleled and sharpened it. The value of the union card is highest in a small unit: there is one local per company, if not per plant or even per department. Seniority rights tend to be bounded by the local's membership. So are the "fringe benefits"—pension rights, severance pay, vacations, sick pay, profit shares, life insurance, etc.—benefits worth as much as 30 cents in some companies for every dollar paid in straight wages. The growing demand for these benefits is in itself a sign of the middle-class character of the American worker and of his union. They are among our major tools of integrating the worker into industrial capitalism as a full and responsible citizen. And they are necessarily grounded in his membership in one particular enterprise or in one particular industry. But these privileges and benefits are usually not transferable. They thus create the danger of tying the worker to his job. After a few years of service a man has amassed too big a stake to be willing to leave, even for a better job. They may also tend to convert the job into a property and the work group into a closed guild. In the typographical union a "priority system" protects a preferred job for a linotype operator even if the worker is forced out for years by illness, or, as in the last war, even leaves the industry for a defense job. Companies with generous pension or profit-sharing plans are under increasing pressure to restrict the hiring of new workers to sons or relatives of their present employees. The fear of just such "un-American" developments was partly responsible for the no-closed-shop provision of the Taft-Hartley Act.

But to halt or reverse this trend will require more than restrictive legislation. It will require considerable imagination in devising new techniques and procedures —above all, techniques to make job benefits transferable. It may aso require enabling legislation, the kind that encourages and rewards voluntary action. In attempting to solve this problem we will have to be careful not to weaken the desire of the American worker and of his union for a stake in the enterprise.

We also must not sap the strength of the local unit of unionism. Its vigor and autonomy, distinctive traits of American labor, are essential to it and serve a constructive function.

THE FEDERAL STRUCTURE

The American union—like so many other of our institutions—found it necessary to organize itself on the hallowed American principle of federalism. This followed from the physical nature of the country, from the spirit of its society, and from the union's approach to its task. The English, French, or German union can be satisfied with one national center of power and authority. The American union demands two centers of about equal strength and vigor, the local union and the national union.

A *national*, or industry-wide organization of real strength, is needed to prevent domination of the locals by management. It is needed to set policy, to develop standards for wages and contracts, to represent the union to public and government, and to accept responsibility for the economic and social effects of labor's actions. For every management that feels it would have no labor-relations problems if only it could work exclusively with the "local boys," there is another that has had to ask for the help and intervention of the national officers to settle a local situation that had got out of hand.

National policies and wage rates, however, are no more than the skeleton of American labor-management relations. The local is their flesh and blood. The local develops the spirit of the relationship as well as the rapidly growing "common law," the body of grievance settlements and arbitrator's decisions that define the rights and responsibilities of both parties. As with the federal structure of our system of government, so in the labor movement: local autonomy makes experimentation possible. While bad labor-management relations can be caused by national union officers alone, good union relations require good locals. Even in large companies (such as General Motors) in which mutual distrust is profound, and in which as a result all authority is apparently concentrated in the hands of top-management and top-union leadership, patterns of living and working together are quietly but steadily being worked out by local union leaders and by the local plant managements with whom they deal day by day.

Federalism is a difficult political system, and many or most American unions have not yet learned how to use it. The national leader is greatly tempted to centralize all power in his own hand, if only to remove threats to his tenure of office. In a few unions, notably John L. Lewis' coal miners, it has led to an all but complete destruction of local life and local autonomy; the locals are not much more than administrative units. Equally great is the temptation for the local leader to declare himself independent; in some of the railroad brotherhoods this has almost fragmented the union into a loose league of warlords whose perpetual feuding makes responsible unionism impossible. While unionism was struggling for recognition, these constitutional problems could be brushed aside. Now they are coming to the fore—so much so that more than one union has hired a professional management consultant to strengthen its internal structure.

When that structure is stronger, American labor will have the right machinery for consolidating and extending its traditional goal and for avoiding the danger of feudalism ahead of it. It can fulfill the worker's desire for full citizenship in a non-class society, and keep that society open and mobile. It can—if that is what the worker continues to want.

Many signs point to his still wanting these goals. All kinds of sociological studies reveal his desire to take pride in his job, in his product, and in the company he works for. As his income rises, he wants to buy stock in that company through some form of payroll deduction—a desire that has been voiced in companies large and small such as the Bell System, G.M., and Cleveland Graphite Bronze. One of the best popular guides to the reading of corporate balance sheets and corporate profit-and-loss statements was printed two years ago in the A.F. of L. house organ, *Labor's Monthly Survey,* and the Detroit *Labor News* recently ran an admirable treatise on investment and small-estate management. The visiting teams of businessmen and union leaders who have been studying American productivity under ECA auspices were all struck hard by the American worker's acceptance of increased productivity as in his own interest, by his pride in being a worker but also by his acceptance of the management function as necessary to his own effectiveness.

THE BASIC CONTRADICTION

All this is true—truer than ever. Yet it is not the entire truth. There is also another picture of the American worker—and it is the one major discord in the harmony of the American Proposition. We cannot assert that the big job of industrial society has been done, or that the industrial worker will surely remain "deproletarianized" in the U.S. For there undoubtedly runs a powerful undercurrent of hostility to management and to enterprise, to competitive economy, and to profits, throughout the American working class. There are only a handful of conscious collectivists in American labor. But throughout it there is a strong emotional reaction to anti-enterprise union oratory. And, much more threatening, there is steady support of collectivist and anti-business legislation. And an attitude that sees in enterprise and management THE ENEMY—rather than the opposing team in a rough and competitive game—is a proletarian attitude.

We cannot blame this attitude on the "foreign agitator corrupting the good American workingman" as management was wont to do only a few years ago. It is indigenous, and shared by the skilled "aristocrat of labor" as well as the unskilled man on the assembly line. We cannot explain it away as "economic illiteracy" that will yield to high-powered campaigns of "economic education." But we equally cannot explain it as expressing the "real" desires of the American worker as the left-wing intellectual is prone to do; the evidence is all the other way. The explanation does not even lie in past management sins. It lies in something much more difficult to change: lack of imagination on the part of managements and union leaders.

The American worker definitely wants to be a part of the business enterprise. He wants to consider it "his" business, its future "his" future, its prosperity "his" prosperity. But his everyday experience is one either of conflict or of lack of relationship between the interests, the prosperity, the profitability of the business and his own interests, his own prosperity, his own future.

The worker is told that his wage, his standard of living, and his job depend on the profitability, stability, and productivity of the enterprise. He knows that. But this relationship is not immediate, not visible, not part of the daily relationship between man and company. It has no impact on the worker's experience. What is real is all too often the opposite: conflict, or the total lack of mutuality of interest.

One illustration must suffice. It is possible to under-

The guaranteed annual wage, as the demand is generally known, or the guaranteed employment plan, as the U.A.W. more correctly terms it, is *not* simply a plan for supplementary unemployment compensation. If it were, then the auto workers as well as the auto companies would be better served simply by an improvement of the state unemployment-insurance system. Walter Reuther's aim is vastly different. What he proposes is a system of penalties to force the industry to abandon its seasonal pattern of production and marketing, to provide year-round work for workers with seniority. If he should win, then the next step—and this is the revolutionary aspect of his objective—would be to end the system of hiring a factory worker by the hour, and to pay him instead by the week or month.

Factory and construction workers have not always been paid by the piece or by the hour. In the guild and artisan system, apprentices and journeymen were paid nominal "salaries" by the masters, who kept them on in slow seasons. In paternalistic economies today, such as Japan's, or in countries like Italy and France, where Catholic social doctrine is dominant, workers are rarely fired even when unproductive costs become a crushing weight upon the enterprise. Paying a man by the hour or by the piece produced, and having him shift for himself if no work is at hand, was part of the economic calculus introduced in Protestant countries. A worker became a commodity, whose net yield could be reckoned to the penny. (Even today General Motors pays its workers by tenths of an hour worked.)

Toward "Middle-class" Labor

Trade-unionism, from its beginnings, has continually tried to break down this system. In craft markets, unions have sought to control the labor supply, define their own work rules, and create artificial scarcities. In mass-production work, where unions cannot control labor supply, they have sought through seniority systems and call-in pay (i.e., a guarantee of a minimum number of hours' pay for a worker called in at any time during a day) to minimize the use of labor time as a commodity. The most spectacular effort has been the enormous push for "fringe benefits" whereby a business is forced to assume the cost of a variety of welfare services for workers.

Reuther has now taken the final step in the attack on the "commodity" concept of labor. Since a large proportion of the corporate work force, principally white collar, today receives a full week's salary and a full year's income, regardless of daily or seasonal fluctuations,* he argues, the production worker is entitled to similar status. Reuther, the one-time Socialist, is seeking to make the American worker genuinely a middle-class individual. And that is the historic import of the negotiations this spring.

—Daniel Bell, "Beyond the 'Annual Wage,'" May, 1955.

* In the twelve largest corporations in the country, the salaried work force is one-fifth to two-thirds of the hourly paid production force.

stand why managements were caught so unprepared by the 1949-50 pension wave. But what is totally impossible to understand is why managements did not use the pension demands to make crystal-clear the connection between the company's prosperity and the employee's old-age security. There are proved ways in which this could have been done, simply and dramatically. Yet, as a result of management's handling of the issue, pensions to the worker have become another experience of conflict between his needs and the objectives of business, between "human values" and "greed."

It is the biggest challenge to American management today to design institutions that will tie the needs of business and of the capitalist system (profitability, independent management, investment of risk capital, productivity) directly and visibly to the major interests of the worker (income, job security, recognition and participation, promotional opportunities). Until this is done the American worker will not be able to be what he wants to be, a full citizen in a free-enterprise industrial society. Despite his beliefs he will be pushed by his daily experience into pressing for more and more anti-business laws, more anti-business taxes, and more government welfare. He may even, in an economic or political emergency, develop a susceptibility to that very collectivist infection to which he has hitherto shown such singular resistance.

But the development of new and positive policies that will institutionalize the worker's stake in the business enterprise and his responsible citizenship in capitalist society is equally a major challenge to union leadership. The anti-business undertow is a danger to American unionism as well as to business. It tends to push the union leader into opposition to the spirit of American society—a position in which he cannot function. But above all it is only in and through such policies that the American labor movement can develop what it so conspicuously lacks today: the appeal of ideals and of moral leadership. The very strength of the anti-business undertow is proof that it is not enough for a union movement to be free from a class-war and proletarian ideology. It has to have positive beliefs—or it will be in constant danger of infiltration by the very ideologies it rejects.

The left-wing critics of the American labor movement were wrong when they predicted its conversion into a European-type proletarian movement. But they were right in their assertion that it is not enough for labor to define its beliefs and aims in Sam Gompers'

famous answer to the question as to what labor wants: "More." Only a positive acceptance of the American Proposition, a positive creed, will strengthen both American society and the American labor movement. Only positive policies will make the union an instrument for the worker's responsible citizenship in capitalist society rather than just a device for getting more from it.

There are labor leaders who realize this and who work devotedly to develop such a policy. There is Clinton Golden—formerly of the steelworkers, now Labor Adviser to ECA—who has directed the research for *Causes of Industrial Peace*. There is Joseph Scanlon —also formerly of the steelworkers, now at M.I.T.— whose exciting work has been discussed in *Fortune*, January, 1950. There is the work done by the unions in the once strife-torn pulp and paper industry in the Pacific Northwest. But by and large today's union leadership cannot do the job. It has—almost without exception—come up in the bitter and violent fight for union recognition. Their very background makes it all but impossible for these men to take the lead in integrating the worker and the enterprise into one industrial society. As judicious and as conservative a man as Philip Murray, for instance, cannot help using the usual hate rhetoric of union negotiations, though it both embarrasses and frightens him.

But today's labor leaders are largely at the end of their career. Even in the young C.I.O., few unions have a young leadership. The majority will retire or die within the next ten years. Mostly their places will be taken by new men, unknown today. These leaders of tomorrow will be men of a very different background: men who have come up in the leadership of a local rather than in organizing a national union, who have learned their unionism after recognition rather than in battle, and who have served their apprenticeship in day-to-day living and working with management. It is to those men that we will have to look for the resolution of the major conflict within American society.

Looked at one way American labor has reached maturity. The last decade has proved the validity of its basic concept—the concept that was formulated fifty years ago when the young and small A.F. of L. turned its face against socialism. Looked at another way the history of American labor is just about to begin. For it is only now that it has achieved power and recognition that it faces its real challenge: to make fruitful its beliefs, its aims, and its power. The potential at least is there.

UNITED STEELWORKERS OF AMERICA*

The United Steelworkers of America (U.S.A.) is important because it is the nation's largest labor union and steel is the country's basic industry. Its history is filled with conflict and even bloodshed. This is a realistic account of the U.S.A. in action. The best way to understand any large union is to begin at the local and work upwards to the top "international" level. In this way one sees the routine workings of the union; the non-headline activities of the local officers, the grievance committee, the district directors, and the big-business top structure. The U.S.A. mirrors the personality of the late Phil Murray, one of the historic figures in the history of labor in America.

The United Steelworkers of America, C.I.O.—the U.S.A.—is the nation's largest labor union. From basic steel, where it represents over 90 per cent of 500,000 production workers, its sinews stretch out over the country into the iron-ore mines of the Mesabi, the aluminum rolling mills of Alcoa, Tennessee, the locomotive shops of Schenectady, the can factories of San Francisco, and myriad plants fabricating steel castings, railroad cars, steam shovels, stoves, bedsprings, and even mandolins. Around Pittsburgh there is a Steelworkers' local of dress-factory employees and one to which cabdrivers belong. The 803,746 members who paid dues to the union last August, together with their families, account for nineteen out of every 1,000 persons in the U.S.—enough people to more than populate the states of South Carolina, Wyoming, and Vermont. The Steelworkers is big unionism.

The U.S.A. is important not only because it is a big union but because steel is still the country's basic industry. The aphorism, "As steel goes, so goes industry," is just as applicable now that the union is on the offensive as when the Steel Corporation made the rules. So long as steel was unorganized the labor movement was limited. When Myron Taylor settled with John L. Lewis in 1937, it was the signal that U.S. industry in general was ready to capitulate. Last winter it was the steel strike that set the 18½-cent wage pattern that spread across the country. Before that there was the Little Steel formula.

What will an examination of the union and its relations with the steel industry yield today? What is the barometric reading of labor-management relations in Pittsburgh? The reading is, unfortunately, low. Mutual suspicion is the dominant fact—mutual suspicion and a conviction that toughness is a more tenable virtue than reason. The genesis of this suspicion is easy to trace. For forty-five years the steel companies crushed every attempt of the men to build a union. Most of the battles were bloody—from Homestead, where seven workers lost their lives in 1892 shooting it out with

two bargeloads of Pinkerton agents, to the Little Steel strike of 1937. With the aid of the Wagner Act, the workers won the war.

But armed truce, not peace, has followed victory. This half century of fear is too close to be forgotten. During these early struggles brute force elbowed its way into the moral code of the contestants, each of whom was convinced he was fighting the devil. Today, generally speaking—there are exceptions on both sides—neither management nor union believes the other recognizes its right to exist. Easy relationship is therefore difficult. The workers are convinced that the legally enforced recognition of their union may be taken from them if they don't keep their left up. This leads them to act at times as if they were still fighting a battle for survival, and were consequently blind to their own as well as the employers' stake in production and profits. Management deeply distrusts the wisdom of its employees' acting through unions and mortally fears that pressure from the rank and file, abetted by competition between individual labor leaders, will someday force union demands that will ruin the industry. As a result, industry in turn fights a wary, defensive war in dealings and negotiations, hoping it will thereby stave off some vague doom. This in turn merely confirms the union's suspicion that the employers would drink champagne at its funeral—which many of them undoubtedly would.

GANGLING GIGANTISM

Yet with all the slogans of class warfare that the U.S.A. so often uses—and that the conversation in the Duquesne Club so often justifies—the union is no mass crusade on its way to utopia. It is rather a big, slow-moving organization of essentially conservative members led by a pragmatic Christian, Philip Murray, and living, as he says, "by today's yardstick."[1] Its

---

[1] Phil Murray, an important figure in the history of labor, died on November 9, 1952, and was succeeded in the presidency of the U.S.A. by Dave McDonald, the secretary-treasurer of the article. —EDITOR

* From "United Steelworkers of America," November, 1946.

class-consciousness is as evanescent as that of the average American workingman. It is preoccupied with the grievances and pay envelopes of the men in the mills, whose needs are always immediate; it has little time and it is not pressed by the membership to fool with the problems of the day after tomorrow. Being reasonably clear of Communists, it doesn't dabble in foreign policy or international affairs.

For ten years Phil Murray has dinned the philosophy of responsibility into his officials, promoting those who could acquire it, trying to eliminate those, like the Communists, who seemed to be psychologically immune. There are signs that he has made progress. Most of the international's officials throughout the country have successfully made the switch from agitators to administrators, and the membership is expressing a notable preference for local officers who can carry on a successful negotiation better than they could lead a wildcat strike.

STEEL TOWN

U.S.A. is so big, so sprawling that you have to go to the local to see how it works, to a steel town dominated by one plant, one local union. Clairton, Pennsylvania, a not too ugly scar in the rolling green hills along the Monongahela, is one such community. The Clairton Works of Carnegie-Illinois stretches for more than three miles along the west bank of the river. Its twelve open hearths can turn out almost 1 per cent of the nation's steel potential. Its mills shape this steel into structural sections, such as beams, angles, and bars. But the key operation is the world's biggest coke works, which supplies the Carnegie-Illinois mills in the area with all their coke and coke-oven gas. The handful of workers who man the coke ovens can shut down most of the valley, as they have. Work on the ovens is dirty and unpleasant because of the fumes and heat; most of it is done by Negroes, some imported by the corporation for the purpose.

Most of the plant's estimated 4,600 production workers live in Clairton. The unpainted ramshackle houses down by the mill are reminders of the social price that has been paid to make western Pennsylvania the steel-producing center of the world. But near the top of the hill the atmosphere changes to middle-class American, with only the bulbous cupola of one of the Slavic churches to spoil the illusion of Main Street. Up beyond the center, away from the smoke of the blast furnace, stands Woodlawn Terrace, the brick-and-mortar evidence that the town is no longer a private-corporation preserve. This modern housing project was brought to the community by its labor mayor, Johnny Mullen, who helped organize the men in the mill and later used their support to change the political complexion of Clairton, as the union has changed it in scores of other steel communities.

Clairton's local union, No. 1557, U.S.A., now has 4,200 members. Its president, Simon H. Davies, who looks like an uncertain Clement Attlee, with his thinning brown hair and his well-clipped mustache, is a stillman in the byproducts department of the coke works and lives in Woodlawn Terrace. His living room is as neat as a furniture-store window, the kitchen behind is gleaming and modern, and, last autumn, on the side of the hill out back, his patch of corn stood higher than that of his neighbors. Every week he turns over his pay envelope of about $45 to his wife, keeping only the loose change.

Davies' close election victory last summer over Abe Kendall, the coke workers' most militant champion, is fairly indicative of the state of labor relations in Clairton. Kendall, an intense young man with a quick eye for injustice, played a leading role in several wildcat strikes during the war. Though Abe fulfills their requirement of toughness, most of the men seem to prefer Davies' steadier, earnest leadership, and would probably agree with him when he says, "We must use the proper channels. Wildcat strikes in the long run defeat your own purpose. The average workingman doesn't like to strike."

Two nights a month Davies goes down over the hill to preside over meetings of Local 1557, which are held in a converted store backed up against the mill fence. Smoke drifts through the windows and fills the room; conversation has to compete with the roar and clanking from the plant. On the drab walls are photographs of two men: Philip Murray and Franklin Roosevelt.

When Davies gavels the meeting to order, perhaps thirty-five men rise from their wooden seats to pledge allegiance to the flag. The fact that less than 1 per cent of the members bother to attend routine meetings is one of the officers' chief worries. Most members find it too much trouble to put their shoes on after dinner and go out and attend to the union's business. What holds Local 1557 together between contract negotiations is its handling of the members' day-to-day grievances about such matters as wage rates, seniority rights, and working conditions. "Outside the protection of the grievance procedure," Davies says, "the men hardly seem to care about the union."

In Clairton the workers often push complaints for internal political reasons or just to annoy the company. Management too often still stalls on grievances or passes the buck. The workers suspect that the plant superintendent feels that the union's main function is to protect loafers. On the other hand, the men are gradually becoming more familiar with the rights guaranteed them by their bible—the seventy-two-page agreement between U.S.A. and Carnegie-Illinois. They are no longer fighting so often for rights they don't have in a contract they don't understand. And management is beginning to interpret the contract more as a *modus vivendi* than as a restrictive legal document.

But anger often breaks through the reasonableness that nine years of contact have evolved. In the closing days of the war Abe Kendall asked that a summer relief crew be placed on the coke ovens when the official temperature reached 85° for three consecutive days. He felt that the 90° minimum in the existing agreement was intolerable. The union appealed this grievance from the foreman on through the department and plant superintendents up to the corporation executives in Pittsburgh—the final step in the grievance procedure prior to arbitration. There it rested while Abe and the other workers on the coke batteries, most of whom are Negroes, seethed.

The racial question has long bothered both Clairton and the union. The municipal swimming pool was closed for four years during a controversy over mixed bathing, at the height of which a fiery cross was burned on the hill-side. In the plant the Negroes have been more or less confined to dirty, low-paid jobs, and they feel that the union has not been aggressive enough in pushing their seniority rights to promotions. "Union means together, but this has been two unions," one Negro told a meeting of the local recently. "On our grievances, you've hardly fought for four or five cases, and wouldn't have done this, except that the coke batteries could close down the mill. I can act as good as anybody and I've gotten better treatment from guys who can buy and sell all of Clairton than from some of the $5-a-day men down here."

The Negroes may have felt that the stalling on relief crews for the coke ovens was just another case of discrimination. In any event, discontent, catalyzed by Abe Kendall, boiled over and the coke workers walked off the job. Most of the Carnegie plants in the valley shut down for lack of coke and gas, and the men did not go back until after one of Murray's ablest trouble shooters had spent several difficult hours arguing with a turbulent meeting of the local.

INCOME ACCOUNT

After this experience Kendall not only lost his campaign for the presidency of the local, he also failed to be elected a member of Clairton's seven-man grievance committee. Each committeeman handles the grievances of some 600 men and is recompensed by the union for time lost on this job. The local pays for his time on the basis of the man's usual wage, though an occasional grumbler in the crowd at the union meeting, where the expenditure must be approved, may complain that the bills are too high. In Clairton one man has asked over $100 for time lost in a two-week period.

Aside from the item, which is the largest in Local 1557's budget, chief expenses are for officers' salaries, the highest being Davies' $20 a month. The income of the local is derived entirely from its half of the $1.50 per capita monthly dues and a third of the $3 initiation fee. The other share is kept by the international. In its early days the union had considerable difficulty collecting dues; in one low month of 1938 it took in only $40. This problem was first solved by barricading the gates with dues picket lines. Since 1942, however, income has been stabilized by maintenance-of-membership and checkoff clauses in the contract. Until last June the dues were only $1 a month, of which 25 cents went to the local. Now the local is putting away 70 per cent of its increase in income to pay for the building it bought in September, which it hopes to make into a recreation center. It is making tentative plans to spend the rest for such come-ons as picnics and union bowling teams.

Last winter's four-week strike cost the union only one-tenth of its $8,000 savings. It learned that though the men may not attend meetings, when the strike was on the union was theirs to defend. It was the local's first official walkout in its nine years, but as drama it was a flop. The company made no effort to break it. One superintendent even provided the men at his gate with coal and a stove. But fear of company displeasure still touched some; even during the coldest weather, Davies found it easier to get men for night picket duty than day.

Some members feel that their actual gains from the strike are dubious; rising prices by late summer, they think, had almost wiped out their 18½-cent hourly raise. A few wonder whether the cost of living might have risen less if Murray had accepted the 15-cent increase offered by the steel corporations just before the strike. This dawning comprehension of the relation between wages and cost of living has turned the men's attention to demands for less elusive benefits—better pensions and more health, accident, and life insurance.

MAN IN THE MIDDLE

Up from the Clairton local the next level in the union organization chart is the district. The district director in turn represents the local in the international. The Clairton local is in District 15 under director James J. Thomas, a stocky blue-eyed Irishman, who worked for twenty-five years in the Hazelwood plant of Jones & Laughlin in Pittsburgh. The international pays him a salary of $6,000 a year plus a maximum of $10 a day for "legitimate expenses" and gives him five staff men and a stenographer.

In the U.S.A. the district director is the man in the middle. Below Thomas are the 30,000 men in the twenty-three locals in his district who now elect him every two years. They can throw him out of office if he doesn't settle their grievances, negotiate their contracts to their satisfaction, or get results from the international—or simply because some ambitious local rival gets too popular. Above Thomas is Philip Murray, who pays his salary, approves his expense accounts, appoints, pays, and controls his staff, and expects him to weed out Communists, transmit policy, maintain "unity," suppress unauthorized strikes, organize new workers, improve labor-management relations, comport himself like a responsible gentleman, and get re-elected.

In his role as servant of the men in his district, the most time-consuming function of the director and his staff is that of processing difficult grievances appealed from the plant to the corporation level, and, if necessary, on up through to arbitration. Most numerous and most complicated of the grievances concern the wage rates for new incentive plans. These rates are a fruitful source of mistrust, since neither worker nor foreman understands how most of them are computed.* They are set by industrial engineers, who, as the union so aptly puts it, "practice mathematical voodooism with a slide rule for the bosses." In self-defense, at least one smart district director has acquired a production engineer for countervoodooism.

District directors are currently struggling with another wage problem that has long afflicted the industry—pay inequities. The variance in hourly earnings for men doing equivalent jobs in different parts of a plant ranges as high as 50 cents an hour. To end the resultant feeling of injustice, the industry and the union are now undertaking the biggest joint wage-rate survey ever attempted in this country. In the process they are reducing the number of rates from hundreds to less than thirty, writing a job description for every position in the industry, and setting up a classification system to judge the worth of a man's hire far more precise than that of the U.S. Civil Service Commission. The fact that the parties can cooperate fully in this businesslike task shows that beneath the hostile surface there is at least evidence of normal relationships.

EMPLOYER RELATIONS

The assignment that calls for the greatest political courage on the part of the director is that of handling wildcat strikes in his locals. Men who get angry enough to walk off the job in violation of an agreement are not easily talked into going back to work, as one director discovered during the war when he was tossed bodily out of a local meeting three times in one night.

The director's most difficult job for the international is the political one of maintaining the "unity" of the organization, which Murray never ceases to stress. When a delegate to the union's biennial convention last May had the temerity to boo Murray from the floor, he received this lecture:

"People shouldn't boo in Steelworkers' conventions. That does not comport itself to the requirements of good conduct. I suppose a fellow who boos the chairman in this convention perhaps goes home at night after his day's work is over and boos his wife and the kids."

Murray expects the directors to maintain unity by using their prestige to smother potential disrupters before they reach the top in a local union. The methods used are not always conspicuous for their delicacy. On at least two occasions Murray has transferred directors to other jobs because their political tactics were too brazen.

The director's dearest task, of course, is to get himself re-elected. Sometimes this objective dovetails neatly with that of maintaining unity; if so, it may have the indirect effect of suppressing new ideas as well as new leaders. More often it is reached simply by

* The reason is obvious. This is the formula for calculating the earnings of a shear inspector in the U.S. Steel mill in Gary, Indiana:

$$\text{Total earnings} = (1.2 \times S \times R_b + \$.10 \times A + D \times Rg) \times (\text{Actual Ult. Yield/Std. Ult. Yield}).$$

doing a good job for the locals. The union has become a career for these men; they would take a considerable pay cut if they had to go back to the mill, and most of them would not be willing to jump the fence into management's lucrative preserve.

PITTSBURGH—PLUS

At the top of U.S.A.'s structure is the international, which occupies twenty-five rented rooms scattered over five floors of Pittsburgh's Commonwealth Building. With its staff of lawyers, accountants, publicity men, and production engineers, it is a businesslike operation engaged in servicing the members. It is also the leadership of an organization with a considerable potential for influencing the course of U.S. industrial, economic,

---

COMMUNISM IN THE C.I.O.?

The Timken Roller Bearing Co. of Canton, Ohio, recently divested itself of $25,000 by preparing a 3,100-page fourteen-volume "study of C.I.O. and Communist attitudes toward the American system of free enterprise. . . . On page after documented page," according to the publicity release that announced this curious project, "it reveals the astonishing coincidence of these attitudes as established by official publications and periodicals of both organizations, testimony before congressional and other hearings, general newspapers and magazines, books, speeches, and miscellaneous other sources."

The release then dwells, with curled lip and raised eyebrow, upon several aspects of past C.I.O. history—on the years when, as everybody knows, the organization was crawling with party-liners. It also takes note of some issues that found the C.I.O. critical of the workings of private enterprise, or asking for government intervention in the economy. None of this, of course, proves anything about whether the C.I.O. is Communist-influenced today. Grappling with this question, the release, unfortunately, becomes a bit vague; it says, "The chances are preponderant that as the known Communists were uncovered and expelled, new Communists, perhaps more clever at infiltration, were sent in to replace them."

Now there is no law that says Timken has to admire the economic thinking of the C.I.O.—whose Steelworkers, incidentally, have had the company sewed up tight for more than a decade. But the plain fact is that the C.I.O. *is not* Communist-influenced today, and fourteen volumes of "research" are not going to change the fact. On balance, Timken seems to have been stung: $25,000 out the door and a very little innuendo.

—"Editorial Notes," April, 1953.

---

and political history. Its president, two vice presidents, and secretary-treasurer direct a staff of six department heads and some eighty employees.

The secretary-treasurer, David J. McDonald, a

brightly groomed college graduate of forty-two, may appear to have chosen a union career by mistake, but he has done an outstanding job for the Steelworkers, whose financial affairs are firmly in his hands. In the twelve months ending last June he received $10,678,318 in dues and initiation fees. He sent back $4,336,639 to the locals, distributed $4,501,641 for administration of the districts, and spent $2,309,116 on the operations of the international. Last winter's nationwide strike, which cost the international more than $750,000, put McDonald in the red for that period, the first time this had happened since 1942, the year after the union paid off its loan to the United Mine Workers and started operating on its own. Last summer's balance sheet showed that McDonald had accumulated for the union a surplus of $4,600,000.

Through this centralized control of finance, Murray has been able to curb dishonesty, direct the organization with complete authority, and keep it financially healthy. Rackets have short lives in U.S.A. McDonald knows how every cent is spent. He approves all the expense vouchers of the directors and staff representatives, whose books and those of the international are audited semiannually and given widespread distribution and publicity. Even the books of the locals are combed over by a group of traveling auditors on McDonald's staff.

Two chiefs of departments are close advisers to Murray—Vincent Sweeney and Lee Pressman. Sweeney, who is one of the ablest labor publicists in the country, spent $101,000 during last winter's strike for nationwide broadcasts. Hitting for middle-class appeal, he featured speeches by friendly ministers and priests. Pressman, brilliant, articulate general counsel of both the U.S.A. and C.I.O., gets to Murray's left ear. His close friends are largely in the camp of the Communist party liners, and, for that reason, he has few supporters in the steelworkers' union. Despite Murray's deep conviction about Communists, which is that of the ardent Catholic and democrat, his sense of loyalty is unusually strong and he believes he can control this hard-working lawyer. There is also a potent emotional tie: the sentimental ex-miner cannot forget that during his struggle with John Lewis in 1941, Pressman switched fealty to Murray. Controlled or not, Pressman is one of the reasons why steel employers are suspicious of the union's ultimate goals.

UNION AIDS TO PRODUCTION

A function of one of the international's departments that shows promise of developing is that of production engineering, the province of research director Joseph Scanlon, former steel-company cost accountant and open-hearth helper. Scanlon has aided many small companies by using his knowledge of production and enlisting the aid of their workers. "If the fellow at the bottom of the heap can talk in safety," Scanlon says, "you find out plenty about what is wrong in a plant. And this is the kind of information management never gets."

Scanlon tells of the case of a manufacturer of stain-less steel, who in an overflow of patriotism after the war stocked up on returned veterans. Production fell off disastrously and the employer asked Scanlon to do something about it. Scanlon discovered that the boys spent half their time around the water cooler refighting campaigns. He then sent in a union time-study man, who persuaded the local union that unless it speeded up production and allowed a couple of the worst offenders to be fired, the plant would probably have to close down. "You can't run a good guy out of business," says Bill Jacko, the man on Scanlon's staff who made the study, "just because union members don't want to work."

About sixty companies have appealed to the union for help with production problems since 1942. The most generous response was to Cyrus Eaton's Portsmouth Steel, the small, high-cost plant supplying Henry Kaiser; Harold Ruttenberg, the union's former research director, became vice president in charge of practically everything. The oddest case was a little company in Ohio, the president of which became so irritated by general discontent, low production, and grievances in his plant that he gave control of the company to a committee, half of whose members are picked by the union. Everybody belongs to the union except the president. After a sum is set aside for depreciation and taxes, the profits are divided equally between the union members and the owner, who has been voted a salary of $12,000 by his employees. Production in the plant has risen 65 per cent; profits have more than doubled.

Scanlon wouldn't maintain that you necessarily give your company away to get production. But by taking workers into its confidence, he says, management can tap reserves of skill, ingenuity, and initiative that would push output far above previous levels. H. W. Seyler, general superintendent of the Clairton Works, thinks this is the bunk. He says that productivity will rise only when the labor market is less tight, and the men, who were coddled during the war, lose the feeling that they are irreplaceable.

MURRAY THE PATERNAL

Murray has carefully protected the organization from too much exercise of self-government. At the union's conventions, where once every two years the rank and file has its only real opportunity to formulate major policy, the 2,200 delegates find that all resolutions are carefully screened by appointed committees and cannot be amended from the floor. Those who want to speak against a resolution complain they have difficulty being recognized, that when they speak they are heckled by shouts of "question" from staff representatives scattered throughout the crowd, and that Murray uses both parliamentary and emotional devices to shut off debate on controversial issues. Murray points out that there are practical limitations to democracy; little business would be accomplished in a five-day convention without some direction from the chair.

Murray's paternalism is accepted, not because the men are too weak to rebel against it, but basically because they feel Murray would never seriously abuse it. He takes such pains to learn in advance what they want that they have little to grumble about when policy is pronounced. Murray organized steel, a feat that had never been performed. In the ten years since June, 1936, when the union was only twelve men around a table in Pittsburgh, average hourly wages of the mill-workers have risen from 66.5 cents to $1.35; they have acquired a yearly vacation and six holidays; they have a partly established property right to their jobs through the workings of the seniority system, and the man with a gripe against the boss now has the right to holler and be heard.

THE MUTUAL RIGHT TO STRIKE

Collective bargaining in steel is still in the hollering stage—and probably will stay there for some time to come. Why? In part because both labor and management cling to a residual desire to have it just that way. Both seem to suffer from an obsession that to lose your toughness is something akin to losing your honor. They talk about the dangers of mutual suspicion, but when it is replaced by real cooperation, they much prefer to keep the fact dark. Example: a friendship between a steel executive and a district director had opened inauspiciously in 1940 with a bitter thirteen-week strike. The district director was jailed regularly because he could not keep his fists down on the picket line. But after the battle, he and the chief company executive, like a couple of Irishmen, shook hands. This friendship proved real when the director nominated his former antagonist as impartial arbitrator of a stubborn dispute he was having with another company. The employer repaid the compliment last February during contract negotiations by guaranteeing his workers six days' work a week for six months—a long step toward the union's cherished annual wage.

It is characteristic of steel today that in telling this tale of peace both participants belligerently demand anonymity; publication, they say, would result in "irreparable damage" to their reputations. The reasons: some ambitious rival would see a chance to accuse the district director of being no longer a good union man because he had dropped his guard; the executive would be under fire from his fellow steelmen for softening up and "joining" the Steelworkers. This reaction is not unique. Another employer said he could not talk openly about the success of his union shop or of his monthly production meetings with the men because he liked to receive his supply of steel ingots regularly; a third, mentioning the above-average increase that he had granted his workers, added quickly, "Now don't get the idea we were generous."

It is true that, beneath the surface of hostility, both U.S.A. and the steel industry are building toward the day when suspicion has been minimized and they can become responsible partners in raising production and profits for the companies and living standards for the men. Their joint work on the wage-simplification study is a promising example. Another is the sensible manner in which they conducted the strike; the union made careful advance preparations to maintain plant property, and many employers privately assured the union they would do nothing to weaken it during the shut-down. Most important of all, probably, is the progress at the plant level, where out of the day-to-day handling of routine problems are painfully but surely growing mutual respect, a little more understanding, and some real confidence.

But before peace rules the steel country, the two tough giants, forced by circumstance to live in the same house, will undoubtedly throw a lot more furniture around.

7. THE CORPORATION

THE AGE OF THE MANAGERS*

By Herrymon Maurer

The corporation is the most common business form in the U.S. and the most influential. Two hundred of the largest corporations alone influence three-quarters of American business life. But the only way to understand what corporations are doing today is to study modern management since the corporation in itself is a lifeless legal fiction coming to life only through human decisions. The humans making the corporate decisions today are the managers, with their new instruments and calculations, preoccupied with the future. Moreover, the present trends in management practices are harbingers of the dangers and opportunities in the American economy of tomorrow.

For twenty-five years the managers of U.S. business have made it increasingly evident that this is indeed their age, not the age of enthroned wealth, entrenched tycoons, or enterprising manipulators of securities. Yet the role of managers—unlike that of the owners, magnates, and financiers of the past—remains incompletely

*From Herrymon Maurer, "The Age of the Managers," January, 1955.

assayed and popularly misunderstood. The older roles were settled and conspicuous. But modern management, self-conscious and even introspective, is engaged in constant study, experimentation, and change. The modern managerial breed is preoccupied, above all, with the future—not just the personal future, but the future of the corporation itself.

The rapid and accelerating changes of the past

quarter-century have produced a new sort of business leader, unwilling to be propelled aimlessly by the shifting winds and waves of immeasurable economic forces. A manager, indeed, might be defined as a man who wants to navigate his course of business as exactly and predictably as he can. While he makes various decisions by hunch, dead reckoning, or sudden reaction to current market conditions, he prefers to rationalize decisions, calculating the risks and analyzing the markets. He maneuvers not so much by feel as by instruments, which become more numerous—and more complex—year after year. The device of "linear programing" materialized only a few years ago, and the concept of "planning and control for profits" achieved wide acceptance only within the last five years. The various new tools, moreover, depend on other tools also relatively new: e.g., aptitude tests for future managers, precise cost-accounting systems, general economic forecasts, specific market projections.

All such tools and all the rational calculations of managers share one significant characteristic: they apply more to the economic hereafter than to the here-and-now of business life. Indeed, modern managers are distinguished by their concern with what profits, products, and markets will be in a tomorrow that may be several years to several decades distant. This preoccupation with futurity may prove to have good consequences—or bad. Will all the instruments and calculations of the modern manager rationalize away the responsibility, the intuitiveness, the personality, and even the dignity of the human beings who man large corporations? Or will they help the corporations to become still more capably managed, while remaining hospitable to the talents of individual men and women? The questions call for a new appraisal of the modern managers: where are they now, and where are they headed?

The pace setters of management are now, by definition, the top decision makers of the largest corporations. The influence of these executives is extensive largely because of the relationship between their corporations and the many smaller companies that big business tends to breed in increasing numbers. G.M., which employs over 475,000 people, is the direct source of employment for nearly 400,000 others in dealerships and distributorships, and indirectly for perhaps a million people in 21,000 supply companies. Sears has nearly 10,000 suppliers, which employ about 1,600,000 people. Swift's retail dealers number between 300,000 and 400,000. Westinghouse has between 100,000 and 125,000 distributors and draws on the labors of an incalculable number of supplier and subcontractor employees.

Since about one out of four business employees works for the 200 largest corporations, and since these corporations make employment for at least two additional persons besides every one they employ themselves, it is not too much to say that the management practices of the 200 largest corporations strongly influence three-quarters of U.S. business life.

1930 AND 1955

One clue to the vast economic and social consequences of management activity lies in the particular quality of competition that has become prevalent during the past twenty-five years. Large corporations are now increasing their size, activities, and earnings by creating new markets, increasing old ones, and developing new types of products. As regards new products alone, du Pont President Crawford H. Greenewalt has estimated that "half our present national working force is engaged in production and sales of things unheard of generally in 1902. A very large number are concerned with developments new since 1928. Should this trend continue, half our working population in the year 1978 may be making and selling things as yet unknown."

This type of new-product and new-market competition is not of itself a new thing; it was always a concomitant of our expanding market. But more and more managers have sharpened it into a conscious policy, by which they set out to stimulate future consumption by planning the lowest possible prices on the biggest possible output. Since managers seek in the long run to capture the highest possible sales and profits, it is significant that they emphasize decreasing price as a dynamic that makes for expanding production and, as a consequence, for lower unit costs and higher return on investment. Companies often respond to this dynamic by electing to take a temporary loss on certain products to increase their sales and consequently their production. Westinghouse, for instance, gave up the profit margin on its distribution transformers to build future acceptance for them. G.E. follows comparable practice, calls it "broadening the base."

Similarly, the dynamic concept of wages, which seemed so revolutionary when Henry Ford enunciated it in 1914, has been almost universally accepted by the managers. Partly in response to the pressures of organized labor, they treat high pay not only as an incentive to employee productivity but as a means for turning the workingman into a consumer, able in most cases to buy what he makes. An expanding market coupled with decreasing prices and increasing production is the basis for the widespread belief among managers in an expanding economy as a natural condition.

Consider now the social changes that have paralleled the growth of these concepts of management. Since 1930 not only have the poor become richer but the rich poorer. Child labor has disappeared. The gulf between classes has narrowed abruptly. Big houses are smaller, small houses bigger. Servants are disappearing from the homes of the well-to-do, and the street and sports clothes of the assembly-line worker are hard to distinguish from those of executives. Employees now take for granted goods, products, services, standards of living, levels of education, and even types of architecture that not long ago would have seemed beyond the reach of anyone but bosses. Meanwhile, paid vacations, medical benefits, insurance, and pensions have become prevalent among large corporations. Unionism, long fought violently, has within twenty-five years become a necessary part of large industrial establishments.

THE NEW TRANSACTION

More social change and marked alterations in management will probably follow the new preoccupation of business with the future. The lag in time between decisions and sales is increased, of course, by the technological complexity of new products and new plants. Nowadays, many managers find themselves committing funds for research, development, engineering design, and capital expansion that cannot produce income for five to ten or more years. They have to deliberate levels of price and pay, themselves complex considerations easily influenced by many still unknown factors, and they have to weigh as rationally as possible the effect of these levels upon distant levels of production and the even more distant shape of the market. Meanwhile, they have to respond as sensitively as possible to studies of what business conditions may conceivably be many months or many years hence.

Thus managers look ahead in a more sophisticated way than they formerly did. They make decisions that are considerably separated in time from the market transactions to which the decisions are supposed to lead. Du Pont spent twelve years' time and $27 million in research and development to get nylon into production. Before R.C.A. sold its first television set, it also put $50 million into research and development. Some years ago the Santa Fe purchased several hundred acres of land adjoining its properties in Los Angeles after a five-year study of what the land needs of the railroad might be fifty years thence. It takes Consolidated Edison two years to plan a modern complex generating station and from three to five years more to complete it. For some time Sears has been expanding its store selling area in the South (its square footage per capita of population is already greater there than in any other part of the country) out of a conviction that natural resources, population growth, and the stimulus of Sears' eleemosynary programs will make the South more prosperous fifty or so years hence. As early as 1929, Alcoa built a mill at Massena, New York, to roll large structural shapes for which there was not yet any market, and has recently built another at Davenport, Iowa, to roll unusually wide sheets although the market cannot begin to absorb the output for some years to come. In sum, big-company managers are engaged in a continuum of business decisions separated by a chasm of days, months, and years from a continuum of market transactions.

NEW FORESIGHT

Solicitude for what will be, and how it will affect the long-term production, prices, and profits of a corporation entails, first of all, a willingness to refrain from squeezing the last drop of profit out of current operation. Managers often fall heir to profits resulting from decisions made prior to their own appointment to decision-making jobs. This circumstance usually convinces them that foregoing of maximum profits and dividends today is often essential to provide a higher level of profits in another top-executive generation. In fact, almost any manager can point to particular uses to which today's profits can be put for tomorrow's profits: research, for example. Obviously, a decision to expand plant is an employment of money in hand to create money in some future bush. Sometimes profits are plowed back and dividends held down. Sometimes money is borrowed and current costs increased. And always there is the overhead of research, engineering, development, and design. Such decisions, of course, are encouraged by the federal tax structure with its provisions for capital gain and rapid depreciation.

The managers of large corporations, moreover, usually have concrete plans to ensure the flow of raw materials critical to the company's future earnings. Witness the exploration programs of the big oil companies. Witness also U.S. Steel's iron hunt. The corporation presumably could have found a more attractive return on its money than its high-cost tidewater Fairless Works, erected to process Venezuelan ore. But had the company not elected to build this plant, it would have lacked the means to compete with other manufacturers on the eastern seaboard. Comparable in urgency is American Can's intensive effort to find materials to take the place of tin, of which there is a free-world supply of twenty-three years if deposits adjacent to Communist areas are not lost, or enough tin for just five years if the deposits are lost. "So far as I am concerned," remarks President William C. Stolk, reviewing his company's efforts to anticipate the future, "this is the day after tomorrow."

Managers today do not merely look to the future, or guess at the future, or simply let the future come to pass. They consciously analyze, calculate, project, and predict. So rationalized are their decisions that they lead to conscious and continuous planning of the whole of a corporation's activities. This planning is flexible, to be sure; most programs provide for cutbacks at the drop of an index. But few programs can be cut out altogether. There are basic decisions, including commitments of money, that could be altered only by major economic reversals. When such basic decisions are being made from one to a dozen years ahead in a segment of U.S. enterprise potent not only in its immediate effect on the economy but also in its effect on an army of suppliers, subcontractors, dealers, and distributors, the economy no longer simply happens; it is to a very considerable extent planned. And the planning is done by the forward programs of managers themselves. The actual planning period is stretching constantly: many managers, indeed, project even the ordinary events of their businesses and draw up detailed profit-and-loss statements for a rolling five-year period.

NEW MARKETS

Novel as this conscious sort of planning is, it involves other novelties, one of which is anticipating and creating future markets. A calculated market, clearly, is something different from the market places of earlier times, or from the commodity and security exchanges of today. Most corporations today are concerned not with actual places of exchange but with market potentials for particular products in particular areas. Thus there is the Midwest rural market for cake mixes or the suburban market for air conditioners. In competing for shares in such markets, managers must draw on studies of economic trends, projections of population statistics, estimates of future income within the market, and other indications of distant sales potentials. The remarkable fact about this uncertain sort of market is that most managers are confident in their anticipation of it.

One reason for confidence is a belief by many managers that the planning process itself may contribute to the stability and growth of the economy and may help limit the swings of the business cycle. If G.M. has spent money during the past ten years that it must recover during the next ten; if du Pont is putting into production products that came out of a test tube eleven years ago; if U.S. Steel has committed itself not only to the costs of finding ore but also to the costs of transporting and processing it; if, in short, several hundred large companies, together with the small companies grouped around them, have gone to great expense in planning future products and plant and have taken great pains to calculate the chances of this expense producing future profits, then a significant stabilizing force has been brought to bear on the economy.

Since flexibility is a purposely built-in feature of most plans, managers can tailor part of their programs to the emerging shape of the economy. There remain, however, incalculable economic forces. It may be, for instance, that the heavy use of profits for capital expansion in recent years reflects stockholder interest in capital gains rather than in dividends; and it is conceivable that more expansion has occurred than the markets for goods justify. On the other hand, the caution with which managers tend to calculate future markets probably reduces the likelihood of such a dangerous imbalance.

Ask a manager how he actually makes plans and he will describe how his company is organized. While rational organization of the labor of many employees is a long-established fact of large enterprises, the organization of executives is recent. In most companies, indeed, the shift from one-man rule, or undefined rule, has occurred within the last twenty-five years. Authority and responsibility have been decentralized to the end that executives down the line may know what role they play in current activities and in future planning. At the same time, top managers are putting new emphasis on the function of central control, trying to find the correct balance between decentralization and integration of management.

THE NEW EXECUTIVE

Modern organization systems are seldom final. Just as managers are forever planning the future, so are they forever reorganizing themselves. But there is one crucial principle that does not change: on every execu-

tive level, many of the decisions are the result of the interaction of many men, even if the decisions are formalized by individual managers. Group management has become characteristic of the large corporation. The corporation's activities, particularly its future plans, are simply too vast for one man to keep in his head. Union Carbide, for instance, acts on the premise that major decisions for the future demand collective judgment. President Dial presides at committee meetings, but decisions result from an interaction of minds, with consequent compromises, and major commitments are always unanimous. "When you have more new things than you have money," he points out, "you don't do anything unless the reasons are overpowering and you all agree."

It follows that the job of such a manager as Morse Dial is to fuse the ideas of his fellow managers. In that role there is only limited scope for a man to practice some previous specialty. In decades to come, the U.S. is likely to see more and more managers who are not so much experts in law or finance or production or research, as in the art of management itself, and who still know how to get the highest volumes of sales and profits out of highly specialized undertakings. Of B. F. Goodrich's President William Richardson, a manager without formal training in chemistry, Sidney Weinberg has said, "I don't know any man who knows more about the chemical business." And du Pont's Greenewalt has noted that "specific skill in any given field becomes less and less important as the executive advances through successive levels of responsibility...."

THE NEW ATTACHMENT

Compared with businessmen twenty-five years ago, today's managers exercise less individual power, definitely take home less money, probably enjoy less popular recognition. Generally speaking, more money is to be had by entertainers, more power by men in government, more recognition by athletes. Under such circumstances, what motives make managers work—work harder, longer, and with greater dedication than the men of twenty-five years ago? The motives are unquestionably mixed, ranging from money and success to satisfaction in making mammoth organizations tick. But many top managers profess an additional motive growing out of the group deliberation that so often decides future business plans. For good or ill, the corporation is frequently the executive's club, and to some extent (or so his family complains) his home. Leroy Wilson, late president of A. T. & T., liked to stress the satisfactions of working with like-minded people. Union Carbide executives actually refer to their company as "the community." James T. Leftwich, president of F. W. Woolworth, says simply, "We live Woolworth."

This bond to the company is reinforced by a significant trend toward setting recompense for managers essentially by policy. There is a declining turnover of top executives in most industries (notable exceptions: aircraft, textile, amusements), and recompense can seldom be set in terms of competitive bidding for talent. It is set most often in terms of "what the job is worth." This development reflects the increasing confinement of executives to the preserves of their own companies. And the confined executive may well be the sort of man who centers his entire life around his company, from which alone he is certain of employment, and to which alone he is able to look for old-age income. The policy-set salary thus becomes a symbol of a community closed to outsiders.

In many ways the development of a community of executives can be salutary. The corporation ceases to be a mental abstraction or—what it is legally supposed to be—a fictional person, devoid of spirit and life. It becomes a group that gives a man the sense of being an integral and valuable part of a common effort. The group, moreover, meets his money needs, offers legal advice, medical service, loans when needed, advanced education, even travel. It takes note of the birth of children, regularly attends funerals.

Group management, however, has pitfalls. Big companies already have unique traits and habits, so that it is possible to speak of a G.E. man or a G.M. man or a Bell System man (once labeled *homo telephonicus*). Cohesiveness is one of the certainties of life at B. F. Goodrich, top money-maker among rubber companies per dollar of sales. "We all work so closely," says one Goodrich man, "that we know what each other is thinking." If such closeness of purpose should lead to dull uniformity of mind, there would be danger: obvious danger to the profits and productivity of American industry because of closed-mind business thinking wherein each executive would repeat a line of ideas common to the group, and wherein no executive would offer fresh slants or new flashes of insight. A more insidious danger would be the violation of the democratic belief that the individual human being is unique, unrepeatable, and no man's copy.

These dangers, to be sure, do not show up conspicuously among contemporary managers, most of whom have experienced the rough-and-tumble of individualistic enterprises in times past. Young executives, however, obviously lack this experience. There are signs, moreover, that some companies select and advance young executives partly on their ability (and even that of their wives) to conform to a company pattern. There are also signs that an increasing proportion of younger managers, unlike their elders, are sons of men who were themselves executives. Thus there

arises the unhealthy possibility of a self-perpetuating managerial elite.

NEW OPPORTUNITIES

Group enterprise, indeed, offers alternatives both hopeful and horrible. It is conceivable that such enterprise will be the prototype of social slavery, that it will be the agent of a soul-rotting decay that shreds the last remnants of man's dignity. But it is also conceivable that the large corporation will emerge as a new social force whose basic drive is the creativity of individual human beings. The American people will, of course, make the choice between these alternatives, but the actual shaping of the alternatives will in large part be the work of tomorrow's managers.

Some of the managerial decisions will have to do with the forms of group enterprise itself. Others will center on more diverse social responsibilities. Already the new management provides or extends employee benefits, supports charitable and educational activities, works at cut-rate profits for the government—a dollar a year in the case of du Pont's and G.E.'s atomic projects. There have been experiments with guaranteed annual pay, with wage increases based on productivitity. There are an increasing number of programs to bring employees as well as executives into the corporate community. Such a program at Jersey Standard has helped maintain peaceable labor relations for more than thirty years.

NEW RELATIONSHIPS

The question for the future is how well the new management, and the American people, understand the relationship between these social responsibilities and the economic functions of the modern corporation. And here the beginning of wisdom lies in two propositions:

All the "strictly economic" functions of management have weighty social consequences.

The ability of modern management to carry out its "social" responsibilities rests on economic performance —i.e., profitability.

It is futile for a big corporation to talk of being "a good citizen" if it is not meeting the first test of corporate citizenship: production and distribution at such prices and in such volume as to elevate the U.S. standard of living—on profit margins that assure its ability to attract capital, raise productivity, and yet again enhance the standard of living. It is equally unrealistic for a big corporation to pretend that the market is the only payoff on its activities; a corporate decision to have *no* social policies is actually an economic decision with adverse effects on profits.

Much of U.S. management would subscribe to the foregoing, but few managers are entirely free of embarrassment in explaining to employees or the public the "social" value of profits or in explaining to fellow managers the "economic" value of decency. This slowness in recognizing the essential unity of a company's multitudinous affairs suggests that managers themselves are not yet fully aware of the logic of the large corporation with its emphasis on doing now whatever will contribute most to the health (i.e., profits) of the corporate community in the future.

This difficulty is important because a substantial part of the American people adhere to stereotypes about managerial enterprise, even though the stereotypes are only rough caricatures of business activity twenty-five or more years ago. Many people still suppose that managers are the rapacious spokesmen of "vested interests" threatening the economic stability of the country.

NEW EXPLANATIONS

Obviously, the persistence of such misunderstanding means that large corporations, only recently rehabilitated in public esteem, are still potentially subject to attack in the future, conceivably to increased government control. Today's managers cannot be held wholly responsible for the misunderstanding. Managerial enterprise is too new to be understood quickly and fully, let alone explained. The responsibility therefore falls upon tomorrow's managers. Certainly it should not take many more years' experience in the logic of the large corporation to find ways to explain the dynamism and stability that managerial planning brings to the economy, or to make clear that the strenuous competition vital to productive efficiency is not of a dog-eat-dog character.

Nor should it be difficult to demonstrate that large corporations are subject not only to law but also to effective economic controls: first, competition itself, which ensures high production at low prices and also measures efficiency and foresight; second, the economic vote of customers, to which managers must respond sensitively if they want to stay in business; third, the major test of competence, profits on investment; fourth, public opinion.

Nor should tomorrow's managers find it hard to demonstrate the concern of big companies for social values. The large corporation today is not out of harmony with a papal encyclical (considered radical when issued in 1891) which declared that a market wage was not necessarily a just wage, voiced approval of unions, and emphasized that people other than property owners had needs. Nor is the corporation out of harmony with comparable but unofficial statements published in the late Forties by the Federal Council of Churches. Managers would agree that man is not a mere economic creature, that labor is not a mere commodity, that the fullest possible employment is a social good, that prices should stimulate consumption, and that workers should get more than subsistence pay.

NEW MEN

How well tomorrow's managers will do their social and economic jobs depends on the sort of men—alert, creative individuals or conforming robots—that managers now in office are choosing to succeed them. And making the right choice is clearly complicated by the existence of group-minded executive communities, many of which—fortunately not all—are in effect closed to outsiders.

Here is an immediate opportunity that can have far-reaching benefits. Today's managers can reverse the long trend toward advancement strictly from the inside, outlaw the executive closed shop, and re-establish an executive market in which their various companies can actually bid for talent. Today, when the art of management is more important than special skills, executives ought to be free to circulate more easily than in the past. And such circulation as does occur indicates that neither the group deliberation nor the *esprit* typical of the new management would suffer from occasional infusions of fresh talent. Indeed, the first job of the present generation of managers may well be to keep the future managers out of institutional ruts.

THE URGE TO MERGE*

By WILLIAM B. HARRIS

Everyone—economists, politicians, and the public—is concerned about the concentration of business. In other words, there is concern about the present "urge to merge," for the most common source of concentration is through consolidation. The postwar movement of industrial consolidation is contrasted in this article with the two earlier great merger movements in American history. The four reasons underlying the combination of companies today at such an astonishing rate are analyzed in detail. Examples of horizontal, vertical, and conglomerate mergers are presented.

Mergers of important U.S. industrial corporations are taking place at the astonishing rate of about forty-five a month. This is a count only of those mergers big enough to receive national press notice; probably a score of lesser companies "disappear" daily through the same process. In the past eighteen months many well-known companies have come into the merger news. Names like Packard, Studebaker, Nash, Hudson, Burlington Mills, Olin Mathieson, and Bethlehem are but a few of the more familiar. The frequency with which companies like these are being linked together to form larger combinations has recently provoked cries of monopoly and demands for antitrust action. Attorney General Brownell, recognizing a growing political problem in the merger trend, a few weeks ago put the managers of Bethlehem Steel and Youngstown Sheet & Tube on notice of immediate antitrust action if they should consummate their proposed merger. However, Mr. Brownell's attitude is not likely to stop this merger movement, now nine years old. Even the amendment to the Clayton Act in 1950, passed to stop mergers before they were made, proved futile.

Since 1946, interest in mergers has been so broad that practically every corporation in the U.S. with a net worth of $1 million has been approached with a merger proposition, or has itself approached another company with a deal. If a company is largely owned by its management and has been doing well in a growth industry such as chemicals or electronics, merger propositions may well have been so numerous and so attractive as to interfere with the efficiency (and the peace of mind) of the management. Ordinary companies have also been flooded with merger offers; and even some ill-favored corporations, losing money and presumably unloved and unwanted, seem to be involved in merger negotiations about as much as more fortunate firms. The fact is that in this movement of industrial consolidation, the third great consolidation in U.S. industrial history, anything goes. Contrary to historical precedent, giants have not merged with giants, but it would be difficult to find a giant that has not acquired a small company or two just to "round out the picture."

The first great merger movement, dating from 1890

to 1904, was relatively simple in motivation. It consisted of building vertical, fully integrated, monster corporations for the purpose of monopolizing markets, or at least dominating them. These trusts were put together by bankers, and the securities they offered were so thoroughly watered that it took a generation of industrial growth and the inflation of a world war to dry them out. No merger of today has been negotiated to monopolize a market, although the prospect of lessened competition is always present in some degree. Also, none of the mergers today are of mastodon size; the largest of them, Olin Mathieson, involved total equities of $236,100,000. And unlike what happened in the first round, securities resulting from mergers today are bone dry when offered.

The second great merger movement, starting just after the end of World War I, was checked temporarily by the sharp depression of 1921, and then skyrocketed through all the rest of the 1920's. Like the first movement, it was a banker's field day. Corporations were merged to provide glamorous new securities for a speculation-mad public. Stocks of merged companies sold quickly at huge premiums, and the unions became so frequent and dizzy that even Wall Street was amused. "Now we'll put Worthington Pump and International Nickel together and get Pumpernickel," the bankers cackled. When the crash came it was discovered that much of this merging was evil, particularly the sale of public-utility holding-company debentures and preferred stocks. The Insulls and the Hopsons of the period, and the bankers who worked with them, put Wall Street under a cloud from which it has never fully emerged.

THE NEW MATCHMAKERS

Most of today's mergers are initiated by the operating executives of industry itself, not by "financiers." The bankers who get involved in the negotiations—and of course many do—work either for a fixed fee or a thin percentage. This is true of the "finders," too. Finders today generally are quite respectable, although there is a scattering of seamy characters who peddle their ideas with no authority from the principles they talk about so intimately.

Although solid figures are scarce, it appears that since 1945 there have been some 7,500 mergers impor-

* From William B. Harris, "The Urge to Merge," November, 1954.

tant enough to be noted by financial journals or services. Value of the companies merged probably approaches $15 billion to $20 billion. That is roughly 10 per cent of the $185.5-billion value currently placed on net current assets of all industrial corporations. Corporate formation appears to go on vigorously (there were 740,000 industrials last year, compared to 450,000 in 1945), but it is certain that the merger movement has resulted in whittling down the population of independent corporations in the $1-million net-worth league and increasing the size of larger companies.

There is political dynamite in this trend, for much of the American public believes that bigness is bad per se, that it keeps the little man down. Much of the public also believes that government has a responsibility to maintain prosperity. Here is a fine contradiction. For most of the government's moves to support the economy have a somewhat inflationary character, and every inflationary move hits the small businessman first—because of his higher degree of risk—pushing him into consolidation for the protection inherent in larger accumulations of capital. Added to the pressures of inflation are corporate income tax rates, which make capital formation so laborious that the small corporation itself is driven to seek merger in order to grow enough to stay alive.

But neither politics nor government regulation seems likely to deter the present merger movement. There are four underlying reasons for the movement, and unless there are basic changes in the economy, the trend will go on at about its present rate.

REASON NO. 1: MERGING FOR GROWTH

Few American executives any longer consider it safe to cut out a nice little share of a market and sit with it. A minimum objective is to keep pace with the normal growth of the general economy, and merger is the quickest and cheapest method. Merger can be horizontal (broadening a company's base in similar markets), vertical (moving forward to the consumer level or back to raw materials in an industry), or conglomerate (banding together companies in dissimilar industries). Industrial imperialists, out to build bigger and bigger companies for power, must merge if their objectives are to be met in a lifetime. Growth and merger are so closely related that it is impossible to name a prominent corporation that hasn't a whole series of mergers in its history.

The more successful a company is in a single field, the quicker it reaches its limit of growth. Even if it is in a dominant market position, a company can become static unless it broadens its base. Consequently, many corporations move horizontally by merger into similar markets. This is what is happening at Continental Can. General Lucius Clay, its chairman, has emphasized Continental's transformation into a "packaging company," not just a can manufacturer. He has bought or merged with numerous strategically located paper-container manufacturers, and last year, through a series of acquisitions, expanded further into flexible packaging and plastics.

A merger campaign can result in opening up completely new markets to the absorbing company, and forcing other mergers. A conspicuous case is that of Food Machinery, a native of San Jose, California, now a $223-million corporation. This company originally supplied machinery to food packers, and to farmers growing high-value crops—a sprawling market, but all related to food. In 1943 Food Machinery bought Niagara Sprayer & Chemical Co., a bulk supplier of insecticides to farmers. Its management discovered that profits from insecticides were safe only when the supply of basic raw materials was captive. A few years later Food Machinery moved boldly back into raw materials in a vertical merger with Westvaco Corp., then the largest independent supplier of chlorine, an insecticide basic. Since then, a succession of mergers in the chemical field has made it a machinery-chemical company with 41 per cent of its sales in chemicals, the industry that paces the general economy in growth.

Vertical mergers, the classical form of monopoly, have been as prevalent as horizontals in this movement, but it would be hard to call any of the recent ones monopolistic. They are mostly growth mergers or consolidation moves like those made by Continental Can and Food Machinery. Smaller producing companies, based on processes or on patents that are likely to become obsolete before they expire, are merged with companies having better facilities and credit so that the product can be exploited quickly.

GROWTH ACROSS THE BOARD

The conglomerate merger, made by joining companies engaged in dissimilar businesses into a combination operating-holding company, and maintaining them as separate divisions, is a new merger force. No conglomerate giants have been built yet, but some husky middleweights have appeared. Colonel Willard F. Rockwell's interests in less than ten years have built assets from $22 million to $189 million (*Fortune*, "Cool Col. Rockwell, and the Companies He Keeps," March, 1954). Louis Wolfson, the young Florida financier who has challenged Sewell Avery for control of Montgomery Ward, is busy building Merritt-Chapman & Scott and New York Shipbuilding, two companies he controls, into conglomerates. There are scores of other smaller conglomerates, and many of them were started for the degree of protection found in being just a little bigger.

Smaller companies banded together feel safer, in terms of credit and supply, than when they stand alone. Thomas Evans, president and assembler of the nine disparate companies that make up H. K. Porter Co., Inc., of Pittsburgh, calls this "the protection of little bigness." Running one small business, Evans argues, is just too dangerous an occupation. If it is growing, a small business is invariably undercapitalized and therefore vulnerable, and if it isn't growing it isn't worth having.

Bigness, although popularly disapproved, has virtues: the larger the corporation, the greater the risk it can take in the development of a product. A case in point is a sonic oil-well drilling device offered some years ago to scores of medium-sized corporations. Several million dollars were needed to bring it to market, and none of these companies could take the chance. It went to $260-million Borg-Warner, which is now studying the tool's exploitation after having spent nearly $5 million proving it. Another advantage of size, in these days of high-priced tools, lies in the large sums of cash made available from depreciation charge-offs in big operations. Large depreciation charges enabled Ford, a big company in a tight squeeze, to get through difficult times without going to the money markets for capital. Even moribund giants command respect: consider American Woolen and its much-fought-over $27 million in cash.

GROWTH: THE CAPITAL-GAINS ROUTE

Great capitalists like Mellon, Rockefeller, and Whitney, who reached out from their original industrial bases and put together huge combinations in other fields, do not operate today, but much lesser capitalists, banded together and following a leader, are running in packs to control a wide variety of enterprises. These capitalists, whose money has come from capital gains, are reaching out for more capital gains, and the leverage factors in a company built by a number of successful mergers can be highly attractive to them.

Louis Wolfson asserts that besides his own family he has about a hundred or so men of means who are following him. These people are said to be his protagonists in the Montgomery Ward fight. They followed him to Merritt-Chapman & Scott Corp., into his Washington, D.C., Capital Transit deal, and later into New York Shipbuilding Corp. New York Ship now has assets of $48 million, against assets of $27 million when he took it over; Merritt-Chapman & Scott's assets have grown in a series of mergers from $16,200,000 to $63,800,000 since 1949.

One characteristic of this kind of risk capital is that its managers seek mergers with companies whose stocks are doing badly, or whose futures have been dimmed by changing markets or poor managements. Such companies usually can be picked up at about their net quick value. If they cannot be rehabilitated, the fixed assets are put on the block. Sale of fixed assets can be a windfall profit, which, added to net quick, provides additional capital to the mother company for a similar deal.

REASON NO. 2: MARKET MERGERS

The changing American market exerts continuous pressure on corporations to merge. Market factors have to do with the development or obsolescence of product, shifts from buyers' to sellers' markets (and back), regional market developments, shifts in supply, substitutes in raw materials—a maze that can make a normally stable corporation dizzy. This was particularly apparent after the war.

At that time industry encountered heavy demand and acute shortages of materials. Companies of moderate size, which never before had had a supply problem, found themselves unable to fill orders. They were faced with the choice of merging their suppliers or being merged. There are literally hundreds of such cases. Some were marriages for the moment; Studebaker, for example, bought Empire Steel in 1947, and sloughed it off two years later when steel supplies loosened up.

As markets grew, many companies found that certain of their original distribution patterns had fallen out of balance. This was particularly true of the burgeoning markets of the Southeast and Southwest and the Pacific Coast. To catch up regionally, companies with trademarked products merged with existing distributing agencies or with companies possessing manufacturing plants. Even capital-goods companies used the merger to solve their regional distribution problems. U.S. Steel, for example, which bought the war-built Geneva steel plant, absorbed Consolidated Steel to get quick access to Pacific Coast markets (and got itself into an antitrust action, which it eventually won). W. R. Grace, in a little deal, bought Thurston Chemical in Joplin, Missouri, for fertilizer sales and plant capacity in three midwestern states in which the fertilizer market was booming. In this deal Grace paid a small premium to induce William Thurston, founder of the Joplin company, to head its entire fertilizer operation. The practice of merging to get management (and incidentally a company) is practiced by many corporations, particularly by those moving into new regions or new markets.*

Scores of mergers are brought about either by changing tastes in products or by new technologies opening new markets within a corporation's distribution system. For example, the automatic washing machine enjoyed a tremendous postwar demand. Avco Corp., large manufacturer of radios, television, refrigerators, and ranges, found merger with Bendix Home Appliances a rapid, if expensive, way to fill this hole in its product line.

REASON NO. 3: TAXES GENERATE MERGERS

The attractions of income from tax-free securities, when compared to the problems of retaining earnings subject to corporate and personal income taxes, are great enough to precipitate mergers today. In the case of a man with a million dollars employed in a business, the arithmetic of tax-free vs. taxable earnings remains constantly before him. He must inevitably question the advisability of continuing to risk this money in business. If his company is earning 20 to 30 per cent after taxes and is enjoying solid growth, the decision to go ahead with the risk is fairly easy. But if his per cent of earnings on capital drops after taxes even to 15 per cent (national average earnings on capital employed in all corporations in 1953 was 10.4 per cent) he has a major decision on his hands. Fact is, even a drop to 15 per cent may force him to sell at under book value.

Let us assume, however, that he can sell his business for the $1-million book value. After paying capital-gains taxes he will have 75 per cent of his fortune

* Grace's bet on Thurston did not pay off; he resigned two years later after Grace merged with Davison Chemical.

left. Depending upon his tax bracket, this reduced sum, put into tax-free governments, can give him net income equal to 12 per cent earnings on the whole sum employed in his corporation, without either short or long risk. In this instance it takes a hard-shelled entrepreneur, or a bachelor with no dependents, to turn down a reasonable offer to merge.

Having an estate liquid enough to pay inheritance taxes is an urgent tax problem that can be solved easily by merger. It is particularly urgent for the owner of a business whose securities are selling far above book value. An almost perfect example is the merger of Benson & Hedges, manufacturer of the first popular filter cigarette, Parliament, with Philip Morris. Benson & Hedges, run by seventy-two-year-old Joseph Cullman, patriarch of the powerful New York Cullman tobacco interests, grew surprisingly from sales of $2 million in 1941 to $27 million in 1953. The Cullman family's control of Benson & Hedges stock, which rose prodigiously, could have caused inheritance-tax problems that would have embarrassed even the Cullmans. That Joseph Cullman was shrewd enough to make his deal with Philip Morris just before the tobacco stocks went into a quick decline is beside the point; the time had come for him to get the liquidity that inheritance taxes demand in a large estate, and the only way Cullman could get it quickly was in the Philip Morris trade.

LOSSES ARE ASSETS SOMETIMES

Accumulated loss provokes mergers of corporations facing dreary futures; it also makes a corporate shell (a company stripped of all physical assets) attractive. The value of this red ink is due to the loss carry-back and carry-forward provision of the income-tax laws. Using this provision, a corporation can carry back part of the losses to offset previous profits on which it has paid taxes, and gets a check from the Treasury Department for the difference. Thus a corporation pays taxes on its average earnings over a period of years instead of having to pay huge sums one year and none the next.

Merging losses for tax avoidance is frowned on by the Treasury, which has attempted over the years to write provisions into the Revenue Act to make the practice difficult. Until the new sections are tested in court, however, merging to avoid taxes is likely to go on unabated.

REASON NO. 4: MERGER FOR SURVIVAL

Mergers between companies in sick industries, and between companies plagued by high unit costs and declining volume, became more and more common during the past few years of hot market competition. Too much capacity has depressed railroad-equipment manufacturers, textiles, and alloy steels. High costs in face of declining volume have affected the industrial-machinery, automobile, and coal industries. Mergers for survival during the past year have been so frequent that the corporate pattern of at least two industries, textiles and motorcars, has been transformed, and many companies are so changed their names are no longer descriptive of their businesses. Pressed Steel Car, which once made nothing but freight cars, has merged itself out of the car business.

The industry that has undergone the biggest change is textiles, now in the fourth year of the deepest depression ever—a depression of its own making, for practically every corporation in it not only overbuilt new low-cost capacity after the war, but retained all of its old high-cost capacity. Today there are still millions of dollars' worth of capacity that can be bought up for from 20 to 30 per cent of replacement cost, which in some instances is less than half of net book value. Owners are clamoring to sell or merge at these discounts just to stop losses. Fortunately for them, there are still some optimists left in textiles.

THE VANISHING INDEPENDENTS

The situation in automobiles has worsened only for the high-cost manufacturer. Last year there were six independent companies, now there are three. In the automobile business, volume under 150,000 to 200,000 annual units is produced only at high cost. This explains the strikingly bad showings of Hudson, Nash, and Studebaker over the past year. Individually these companies could not command sufficient volume to install the expensive machinery necessary for low-cost production. The Nash-Hudson merger resulting in American Motors Inc. and the Studebaker-Packard marriage indicate—on paper, at least—that new firms can reach volumes that will permit low-cost production and profit. Together, the firms also have better credit.

High cost has forced the mergers of several of the larger coal companies. Here size provides the resources to buy the automatic machinery necessary to achieve low-cost production. One merger (Pittsburgh Consolidation Coal Co.), after the usual slow start, is now

"This company, Mr. Spencer, has one of the finest tax losses that can be bought anywhere at any price."

producing earnings considered sensational in this long-depressed industry. The trend is toward bigger producing units, and is smiled upon by the union.

NEW ANTITRUST OUTLOOK

The whole process of antitrust enforcement has undergone a great change since the cellophane case was decided against the government in 1953. The Department of Justice went into that case confident of winning it. On a per se basis du Pont was a vulnerable giant since it controlled 75 per cent of cellulose wrapper in the industry market. Du Pont countered with a skillfully prepared market analysis of all wrapping materials, which disclosed that there was more to cellophane than making it. Cellophane had to be sold against some ten other major kinds of flexible packaging materials, and was just one product in a huge industry. This study showed that cellophane accounted for only 17.9 per cent of all flexible wrapping materials. It competed badly in several markets, and only in one —cigarette outerwraps—was it a dominant material. Unless the decision is reversed by the Supreme Court, the case appears to have shifted antitrust-enforcement philosophy back to the "rule of reason" of the 1920's.

Essentially, this means that management, using its own data, can itself decide how much of a market it can exploit safely through a merger without inviting an antitrust action. Economists and statisticians, in other words, take the place of lawyers in helping management reach decisions of this kind. How good this is for the economy and how much it will lessen competition, only the future will tell. Rule-of-reason enforcement has undoubtedly slowed down enforcement of antitrust; neither the Department of Justice nor the Federal Trade Commission has the budget or trained personnel to watch the markets constantly and move against a company or a group of them trying to rig one. The threat of antitrust action probably will stop flagrant attempts to minimize competition, but it need not stop a merger if management's conception of the market position after merger is sound in antitrust terms. If Eugene Grace, for example, believes that the proposed merger of Bethlehem and Youngstown will strengthen competition in the steel industry (and many outsiders believe it will), chances are the merger will go through.

There is a saying on Wall Street that a major merger or consolidation movement marks the beginning of the end of a boom. Future historians may call this one "The Consolidations of the Managers in 1940-50's." There is also a good chance they will report that this one did not portend the end of a boom.

9. TAXATION

TAX REFORM: IT CAN HAPPEN*

Taxes, one of the vital parts of fiscal policy, affect business decisions and the economy as a whole. The emphasis in this article is on reform of the nation's makeshift tax structure. The promising new idea—a "down-payment" program of tax reform—is introduced. Important questions discussed are: What is the critical point in the level of taxes? Who ought to get relief first? What reforms are politically and economically feasible? Should tax cuts be used primarily to stimulate consumption or investment? Reference is made to the opinions of Colin Clark, Dan Throop Smith, Robert Nathan, Leon Keyserling, the Committee of Economic Development, the U.S. Chamber of Commerce, and the National Association of Manufacturers.

When a query about the Treasury's forthcoming tax program was put to them recently, the top officials of the department, sitting in a druidic circle, merely peered at one another secretively and answered with separate, sphinxlike smiles. Mr. Humphrey was sympathetic with the public's curiosity about what the Treasury intends to do. But otherwise he was as uncommunicative as the portrait above him of ex-Secretary John Snyder in bright fresh oils.

The Treasury had several good reasons for keeping mum. Any predictions might mislead businessmen and consumers into making decisions now they would be sorry for later on. The program in the end will be what Congress decides, which may not be what the Treasury is going to recommend. Moreover, it would be impolitic of Mr. Humphrey to annoy Chairman Dan Reed of the House Ways and Means Committee by making the Treasury's ideas public before both sides have had

* From "Tax Reform: It Can Happen," December, 1953.

time to reach some working compromises.

And finally the Treasury is in the midst of reorienting its entire fiscal thinking. The dominant idea earlier was to balance the budget. But it is now becoming increasingly evident that the budget is not likely to be balanced in fiscal 1954 or even 1955, and the Treasury is no longer even promising that it will be balanced in fiscal 1956 or 1957. Consequently the Treasury is shifting the emphasis of its policy to the more appealing idea of tax reform. And such embarrassing shifts are not made right out in public.

There was logic, of course, behind the change. When Mr. Humphrey talked so sternly last spring about balancing the budget, the principal threat appeared to be inflation, on which continued high taxes and "a sound fiscal policy" would have had some cooling effect. Now that the economy is showing a mild but pronounced deflationary bent, a rigorous fiscal policy might well have too cooling an effect. And although political expediency in an election year may not cut much ice with Mr. Humphrey, it will cut a lot of ice with some of Mr. Humphrey's fellow Republicans. People around the White House are now beginning to refer to "the fetish of the balanced budget."

And so the Treasury has developed a theme to fit the new situation, "expanding productivity." This may sound a little vague but should be taken to mean that nothing (such as overwhelming taxes) shall be allowed to inhibit the growth of the U.S. economy. From now on the Treasury is apparently going to give priority consideration to some much-needed reform of the Internal Revenue Code.

THIS TIME MAY BE DIFFERENT

U.S. taxpayers have been hearing about tax reform for years on end; almost every Congress opens with a sonorous exchange of bipartisan promises to do something about the tax structure. But the last recodification of the sprawling system occurred in 1939 when the total tax take was only $5.5 billion, as against $69.7 billion today, and the revenue sources were vastly different.* During the Eightieth Congress the House managed to pass a fairly comprehensive reform bill but it got lost to sight in the closing days of the Senate. Something else always comes up.

Tax reform has two parts, only one of which is to reduce the country's aggregate tax burden. The other phase is the problem of untangling an obsolescent and inequitable system. There are those who hold that since most inequities stem from high rates, the obvious cure is to cut the rates and let's have no nonsense about it. This cure has an inner logic but is simply impractical so long as defense requirements remain as large as they are now. It is still possible, however, without the Administration's committing itself to extensive tax relief, for it to bring about some extensive structural revisions.

This, at any rate, would appear to be the Treasury's reasoning, and the reasoning of a number of members of the Joint Committee on Internal Revenue Taxation. Out of such thinking may emerge a piece of tax legislation unique in U.S. history.

The effort would be to write a program that would set up the framework of reform while limiting actual reductions to a token amount. The new code, for example, would recognize the principle that double taxation of dividends should be avoided, but limit immediate relief to, say, a 5 or 10 per cent cut in the dividend levy. In addition, there would be undertaken certain overdue technical reforms that would not involve any large amount of revenue loss. In this "downpayment" reform bill the new tax structure would be complete; all that would remain for future Congresses would be to increase the reductions as the fiscal situation permitted. The very existence of such a structure would exert considerable pressure for continued relief.

As things look now, this is precisely what will be

*In 1939, corporate and personal income taxes provided 55 per cent of federal revenues, excise taxes 34 per cent; in 1953, income taxes provided 84 per cent, excise taxes only 13 per cent. The personal income-tax base has been broadened from 7 million taxable returns in 1939 to 44 million in 1953.

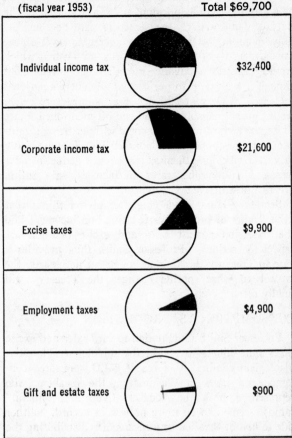

WHERE THE GOVERNMENT GETS ITS MONEY

(fiscal year 1953)   Total $69,700

Individual income tax $32,400

Corporate income tax $21,600

Excise taxes $9,900

Employment taxes $4,900

Gift and estate taxes $900

In millions

proposed and what Congress and the U.S. taxpayers, along about next spring, will be heatedly discussing.

WHERE DO WE START?

The proposal will sharpen all the arguments on priorities of reform, and in some respects make the problem of writing a fiscal 1955 tax program even more difficult. Discussion will rage over favored treatment and discrimination. Who ought to get relief first? What reforms are most needed? What reforms are politically and economically feasible?

Hardly two economists agree either on basic questions or basic premises. Who, for example, gets finally socked with a tax that may be passed along dizzily through the labyrinthine price structure? What is taxable capacity? When and in what segments of the economy do taxes become so oppressive that they destroy incentive and thus discourage economic growth? Colin Clark, the Australian economist, has set the critical point at 25 per cent of national income, yet federal, state, and local taxes in the U.S. now eat up 30 per cent of the national income. The greatest industrial growth in the U.S. has been in the period since 1941 when taxes have been the heaviest in history. New industries have been created, old industries expanded, and the phenomenon of middle-class buying power, described in *Fortune's* articles on "The Changing American Market," has invigorated the entire economy as never before.

Harvard Professor Dan Throop Smith, who is now the Treasury's top tax adviser, not long ago declared at a Tax Institute Symposium at Princeton, that: "The nature of a country's tax structure may be considerably more important than the aggregate level of the tax burden. . . . We could devise a tax system which would throttle economic growth and development though it took only 10 per cent of a country's national income. . . . Or we could devise a tax structure which would go appreciably beyond the oft-mentioned figure of 25 per cent of national income without being significantly repressive or inflationary." Inordinately heavy taxes on risk investments, inadequate deductions for losses, high marginal rates on incomes, said Smith, create a destructive tax system.

Secretary Humphrey's chief tax adviser thinks that "the dogma of progressive taxation [on incomes] and the obsession against sales and excise taxation are especially serious." Professor Smith thus provides a clue to Treasury thinking, although not necessarily the answer to what specific changes the Treasury will finally recommend.

CONSUMPTION VS. PRODUCTION

Professor Smith's inclination toward sales and excise taxes puts him squarely in the middle of a familiar ideological conflict. At a recent C.I.O.-sponsored conference on taxes in Washington, the speakers, who represented both the "conservative" and "liberal" camps, seemed to be more or less in accord. Neither side talked of taxation as a means of redistributing the wealth, making the interests cough up their ill-gotten gains, or the like. There was even, astonishingly, substantial agreement that top surtax rates should be reduced. Where the economists divided was over this question: in so far as tax cuts are feasible, should they be used primarily to stimulate consumption or investment?

The "conservative" position as expressed by George Cline Smith, of the U.S. Chamber of Commerce, and Herbert Stein, of the C.E.D., paralleled Professor Smith's: the first step toward expanding the economy is to create a salubrious climate for private enterprise and investment. The *primary* objective of tax reform should be to encourage production, which will lower prices and increase employment, thus increasing consumption.

New Dealers like Robert Nathan and Leon Keyserling, on the other hand, held that the tax structure should be weighted in favor of wage earners to stimulate consumption and hence full production. They favored priority tax relief for the group with incomes of less than $7,500 (who receive 60 per cent of after-tax consumer cash income). On the same ground, the "liberals" stood obdurately against imposing either a general sales or manufacturers' excise tax.

Now it is painfully apparent that the tax system has been redistributing U.S. wealth for twenty years and it cannot be denied that taxes have helped create the country's remarkable mass-class market. But there is considerable opinion that the U.S. has gone about as far as it safely can in redistribution of income through taxation. Any further substantial gains for the lower and middle income groups must come from expanding productivity. That means revising the tax system so as to provide more stimulation to enterprise and investment—but without bearing down *more* heavily on consumption (i.e., through a general sales tax or manufacturers' excise tax).

If that policy is to be carried out, what reforms in the structure are indicated?

THE 52 PER CENT LOAD

The immediate question on corporate income taxes is whether they should be cut from 52 to 47 per cent next April 1, as scheduled. It is no question at all with the rough-and-ready school, which holds that the way to reform taxes is just to cut. And the producer-first argument would also seem to point to the 52 per cent corporate tax rate as a good place to start.

Yet there is considerable doubt, even among business groups, that this is a high-priority sector. The Chamber of Commerce favors the scheduled reduction. The National Association of Manufacturers and the Committee for Economic Development, at this writing, are engaged in some soul-searching to decide just what they think.

Secretary Humphrey, however, has committed himself to the fight to maintain the 52 per cent rate, and in the present circumstances he would seem to be right. There is no sign that the corporations are doing too badly under the burden. Although it is no defense of the tax, the fact is that much of it is passed along to consumers. Corporate taxes certainly need ultimate reduction but they are a low-priority item now.

FASTER WRITE-OFFS?

If there is some soul-searching among businessmen over corporate income tax rates, there isn't any over the question of depreciation allowances. Here businessmen are in resounding accord: the problem should be put at the top of the reform list. This is partly a political strategy. Business can appear in a much more appealing role protesting a "grave inequity" than coming out for straight cuts in the rates, and the effect of reforms in the depreciation allowance would be some immediate tax relief. But more than just strategy is involved; the question of depreciation allowances is fundamental in an economy devoted to expanding productivity.

The nub of the trouble is that businessmen are not presently allowed to write off capital investments as fast as they think advisable—or as fast as economists believe is desirable to stimulate capital outlays. Until recently, business was under Treasury orders to make estimates of the reasonable life of equipment and write it off over that period and nothing less. On the taxpayer, moreover, was put the burden of proving that his estimates were not foreshortened, and over him, like Big Brother, hovered the Treasury with its own studies of how long machinery *should* last. Challenging a Treasury agent's estimate meant hiring engineers to make studies and lawyers to defend the case, so that more frequently than not companies simply swallowed the Treasury's estimates and surrendered the tax allowance to which they might in fact have been entitled.

Last May the Treasury decided that the depreciation rates, once determined, should be left alone, which has been some relief. But there still remains a set of estimates of useful life that almost every businessman naturally considers too low, as well as accounting procedures that recover too little of the investment in the early years and take inadequate account of losses when equipment is scrapped prematurely. The effects of the present measure have been highly deleterious. Many companies have been discouraged from discarding obsolescent machinery until it has been written off. (Machinery salesmen say they get turned off with that plaint more often than with any other.) The present law has discouraged modernization and capital outlays.

The dramatic post-Korea investment boom demonstrated what can be accomplished through accelerated amortization to spark both big and little business expansion. Pointing out that investment risk is reduced by quicker tax-free recovery of capital outlays, Under Secretary of the Treasury Folsom recently said, "The credit position of the small businessman would be improved. . . . [There would be provided] better access to bank funds for hard-pressed businesses which have no recourse to the ordinary sources of equity capital."

THE DOUBLE BITE

Since dividends are a share in what is left after one tax has been taken out, it is widely argued that it is unfair to tax them again. The hotly pursued stockholder gets bitten on both cheeks. Advocates of soak-the-rich naturally do not find this distressing, since more than half of all corporate dividends go to individuals with incomes of $25,000 or more. But to the people who put up the bulk of the risk capital for U.S. enterprise, the provision seems both harsh and unethical. And there is a further injustice (and loss of revenue) in the fact that millions of dollars of individually small dividends go unreported.

Double taxation also produces a serious economic distortion. Since common and preferred stocks are the only investments subject to such a tax, high-bracket funds have tended to flow away from stocks and into investments with lighter tax penalties or none at all; e.g., municipal bonds, real estate, and oil wells.

However, abolishing the tax entirely would be too big a blow to the Treasury. A rough estimate of the annual loss in revenue would be $3.5 billion. But token relief from this double penalty—say a tax credit equal to 10 per cent of the income from dividends—would cost an estimated $750 million in revenue. Further, a system of corporate withholding of the basic income tax on dividends to prevent evasion would place an unwelcome bookkeeping burden on corporations but would also offset an estimated $300 million of the loss.

HOW MUCH IS UNREASONABLE?

Another high-priority reform, particularly pertinent to small business, is the overhauling of Section 102 of the Internal Revenue Code. Section 102 is not properly a tax at all but a penalty on "the unreasonable accumulations of corporate surplus." Its direct take is minuscule but its punitive effect is large. Under 102, accumulations of surplus beyond what the bureau decides are the "reasonable needs" of the business constitute prima-facie evidence of intent to evade personal income taxes on dividends. A penalty of 27½ per cent on top of all other corporate taxes is thereupon applied to all surplus up to $100,000; 38½ per cent on all surplus over $100,000.

The law, however, does not define "unreasonable," as indeed it cannot. Most small companies must finance expansion out of retained earnings, and funds must be accumulated for several years in anticipation of capital outlays. So-called standard practices in an industry may be completely irrelevant to a company's future plans. The company may have no access to information about its competitors' accumulations and so may not know what the standard practices are. And yet the burden of proving that its accumulations are not unreasonable is on the company, while the bureau can hold up "standard" practices as a criterion. With the odds against it, a company is thus vulnerable to bureau threats of assessments under 102. Under that threat it has often hastened to make settlements in the bureau's favor on other issues.

The other flagrant feature of 102 is that a corporation has to pay the penalty tax on the entire accumulation, not just that part of it the bureau deems unreasonable.

So long as dividends are taxed twice, some such provision must be retained to prevent taxpayers from hoarding their earnings. But the burden of proving the accumulation "unreasonable" should certainly be shifted to the bureau, and the penalty applied only to that portion of the accumulation the bureau can show is unreasonable. The penalty taxes, on the other hand, should be made even heavier in order to make unjustifiable hoarding unattractive; even now some owners of closed corporations prefer paying the penalty to paying themselves dividends subject to 92 per cent personal tax rates.

TAXABLE VS. REAL INCOME

Because it cuts the widest swath through the economy, the personal income tax is the one most widely discussed, and with the least objectivity. Almost everyone has a gripe, the main one being that rates are too high.

As high as surtax rates are, however, quite a bit more income remains after taxes than is generally supposed. It has been argued, for example, that confiscation of all incomes over $10,000 would produce only $3 billion to $4 billion more revenue. The statement is true—but only so far as "taxable income" is concerned. Actual "cash income" is considerably larger than "taxable income"; thus the over-$10,000 group retains $41.2 billion of cash income after paying $17.4 billion in taxes, according to *Fortune* estimates. In any event, with present revenue needs what they are, the personal-income-tax take cannot be reduced materially, nor can much of it be shifted to lower income groups without cutting consumption unduly.*

The personal-income-tax *structure*, however, can be made more equitable. Many of the inequities in the present setup arise from the fact that tax rates do not

---

* Indeed, the Administration has indicated its opposition to the scheduled half per cent increase in the social-security tax, which for low income groups would more than counterbalance the relief from the January 1 cut in income-tax rates.

press down on comparable income groups with equal severity. Professor Walter W. Heller of the University of Minnesota, using Bureau of Internal Revenue audits and Department of Commerce studies, estimates that the individual income tax is "50 per cent effective for farmers, 60 per cent effective for rent recipients, 70 per cent for small businessmen, 80 per cent for dividend recipients, and 90 per cent or more for wage and salary earners."

Businessmen and the self-employed can exploit deductions that are on the borderline of personal consumption (e.g., transportation, meals, "entertainment"). But a working mother cannot claim as a business expense what it costs her to have her children cared for. (There has been such a to-do kicked up over this one that it is almost certain to be fixed.) Moreover, such evasions as underreporting, open to the farmer and the small businessman, are pretty much closed to the salary earner whose taxes are withheld.*

SHELTER FOR TAXPAYERS

Over the years an intricate pattern of "loopholes" has been punched in the law, and these have afforded comfort for some taxpayers. (Accidental loopholes, i.e., tax-avoidance possibilities unforeseen by Congress, are not so common as deliberately created loopholes.) The great haven of "tax-sheltered investments," for example, the use of nontaxable trusts, and the techniques of converting ordinary income into capital gain through corporate dexterity are all well known. What has made it possible for some taxpayers to live with the surtax rates at all is the variety of ways in which income can be removed from their reach. But this, of course, is no defense of the present structure, which creates injustices between one taxpayer and another; most taxpayers are not in a position to switch income from one category to another.

But businessmen and the self-employed have legitimate gripes too. Capital gains are taxed at only 26 cents on the dollar, to be sure, but the present law allows only the most niggardly kind of deduction on net capital losses: a maximum of $1,000 a year for six years.

Such injustices should be corrected. For example, the law should be more rigorous in its specifications of what capital assets are subject to the preferential capital-gains rate, and, on the other hand, should give taxpayers a better break when they suffer capital losses. Depletion allowances on oil wells and other natural resources should probably be reconsidered and perhaps reduced to levels more closely related to actual attrition, unless it can be plainly demonstrated that the national interest requires such subsidies—which, in effect, discriminate against all forms of investment not benefited by high depreciation allowances. (Even then, there is a question whether tax benefits are an appropriate subsidy device.)

In the past, the chief method used to correct inequities has been to rescue taxpayers who thought they were being discriminated against by opening up new

* It has been estimated that more rigorous enforcement of the present taxes would yield at least $500 million more revenue —perhaps as much as $1 billion.

holes through which they too could wiggle. This method, however, tends to compound the evils. Arrant inequities, such as the top surtax rates, should be corrected, but, at the same time, a determined effort should be made to write a tax program that makes taxation much more nearly equal in its effects on similar amounts of income from dissimilar sources.

PURITANICAL TAXES

It is this area that is attracting the greatest attention from prospectors for new revenues, and it is as confused and filled with injustices as any of the others. On April 1 [1954], when the 1951 laws that increased certain excises expire, the rates on a number of items (e.g., liquor, automobiles, cigarettes, gasoline) are due to drop with an attendant loss of about $1 billion in annual revenue. There is some sentiment, however, for keeping the rates where they are.

By and large, selective excise taxes spring from a moralistic attitude. The schedule of rates is a dictum on what are "luxuries"—in other words, on what citizens should or should not spend their money for. But even the moralistic attitude is inconsistent. The woman who buys a fur coat pays 20 per cent; the woman who buys a cloth coat pays nothing—although the fur may be rabbit and the cloth cashmere.

A number of other excise taxes are hangovers from World War II, when the government deliberately discouraged the consumption of critical materials and the use of overburdened services—e.g., by placing a 20 per cent tax on leather goods, a 15 to 25 per cent tax on telephone messages. Obviously these taxes can no longer be justified on the original grounds.

There are only two ways to approach excise-tax reform without sacrificing federal income. One is to widen the schedule to include sufficient new items to make up what would be lost by reducing the presently unreasonable high rates on a few items. The other is to expand the system into a general sales tax that would increase total revenues.

A general tax at the manufacturers' level is, in fact, being seriously considered, for the persuasive reasons that such a tax is easy to administer and would be more or less concealed from the consumer. Because of the markup system, however, such a tax would raise retail prices considerably more than the actual amount of the tax. The jobber would add his *percentage* to the manufacturer's price, the wholesaler would add his percentage to the jobber's price, and so on. It is estimated that with this pyramiding the consumer could end up paying from $1.70 to $1.80 in order to provide the government with $1 of additional revenue.

POLITICAL DEATH AND TAXES

The full proceeds of a retail sales tax, by contrast, would go directly to the government. A sales tax would be more difficult to administer, however, and thirty-two states are already mining this seam (at an average 2 per cent) and would loudly protest the federal government's horning in. Advocacy of a sales tax, moreover, involves a kind of martyrdom involved here that the Republican Party is probably not willing to undertake.

The compelling argument against either tax at the

moment is not that the sales tax is regressive, i.e., more of a burden, relatively, for the low income groups than the high, but that excise taxes have a more depressing effect on consumption than do income taxes, since they lower the value of savings as well as of current income.

What may very well be done is to rewrite the excise schedule with an eye to more evenhanded justice. Some items now exempt might be subjected to excises —though not enough to justify the label of a "general" sales tax. In other words, the cashmere coat might be taxed as well as the rabbit skin, but both at more moderate rates. At minimum, the aim should be to keep the total excise take somewhere near the current $10-billion level.

HOW TO WIN FRIENDS?

In the main, this kind of argument can be applied to the whole tax picture. Where reforms can be made with little sacrifice of revenue, they should be carried out. All the reforms here suggested could mean a loss of as much as $10 billion in annual revenue—in addition to the $5 billion of scheduled cuts. This is palpably more than the nation can afford in fiscal 1955. The down-payment principle of tax reform, therefore, has considerable economic logic. By laying out a broad pattern for future tax relief, moreover, such a program would also have political appeal and would be a monumental step forward, after some fourteen years of improvisations.

10. MONEY

GOLD: DOWN BUT NOT OUT*

By RICHARD AUSTIN SMITH

Gold does not circulate freely today, but the yellow metal is still the principal support of the world's currency. What happens to gold can seriously influence the foreign trade and the domestic welfare of the world's nations. Analyzed are the economic meaning of the developments in the gold market, the dwindling of the U.S. hoard, the decline of the gold smuggler, and the Soviet foreign sales. Discussed are the proposed increase in the price of gold and the return-to-gold-coinage movement.

It is somewhat ironic that the American public, proprietor of the greatest gold pile the world has ever seen, was generally bored by the subject of gold— until the Russians began their spectacular sales of late last year. Gold to an American was something he could take or leave alone, attractive enough in jewelry, but certainly not worth hoarding when that meant a brush with the law. He preferred to put his spare cash in something that would earn money, like stocks and bonds or real estate, and had more than a little difficulty understanding why foreigners liked to sink theirs in gold, which merely stored it without earning anything. He dozed through the greatest period of gold smuggling the world has ever seen, unmindful of its results except as the ingenuity or daring of some particular smuggler was celebrated in the press. But the Russians were something different. If the Soviet Union was unloading quantities of gold, then it was likely to have some malevolent effect on the U.S. and its citizens.

It was high time that Americans did wake up and begin asking questions, for a lot of important things have been happening in gold. Whether Americans knew it or not, the permanence of the French gold hoard, the gold output of the Russian slave, a joint South African-British move to raise the price of gold, and a congressional move to put gold coins back in the pockets of U.S. citizens—all these could have a serious effect on their jobs, their purchasing power, even their military security.

Over the past eighteen months two momentous things have happened to gold. First, the premium market, that once fruitful playground of the smuggler

*From Richard Austin Smith, "Gold: Down But Not Out," March, 1954.

and speculator, has collapsed; second, the U.S. gold stock has undergone a depletion of 6 per cent. From an international point of view, the depletion—really sales to foreign countries—is all to the good, for it is a demonstration that the rest of the world is on the way to selling more to the U.S. than it buys, and with the proceeds salted down in gold will be better able to withstand any adverse fluctuations in future trade balances. To be sure, these foreign gold reserves are in part a consequence of the $6.7 billion spent last year in offshore procurement and other forms of foreign aid; growth of the foreign reserves has also been assisted by restrictions against U.S. imports. Even so, possession of gold has such a cheering effect on the finance ministries of the world that barriers to U.S. trade, particularly in the sterling area, have now a better chance of being reduced. Domestically, the effect of our gold sales has been more tangible. There's nothing to be alarmed about in so far as the *rate* of "loss" is concerned, for the $1.4 billion leaving the U.S. in 1952-53 could be repeated for seven years before bringing our $22.1-billion holding—60 per cent of the world's monetary gold—down to the amount legally required to back our currency (at present levels of currency and bank deposits: $11.9 billion). But a foreign country, when it buys gold here, gets it from the Treasury and pays for it with a check on a U.S. commercial bank. The banks, their reserves being depleted by this amount, can lose part of their lending power, which results in tighter credit for American business.

The other milestone, the collapse of the premium market in gold, is just as important, for it signifies a turning point in the economies of several nations and presages the return of millions of dollars to normal channels of trade and investment. Premium gold (gold that in terms of local currency brought more than $35 an ounce, the U.S. Treasury price) owed its existence to the deep distrust many nationals had for their governments after the end of World War II. To such nationals, gold coin and bullion were the only safe storehouse of value; they were proof against the sort of inflation that even in America made promissory paper, like government bonds, an unappetizing investment. In China during 1946-48, $100 million worth of gold went into private hoards every year. In France, where fiscal aberrations are endemic, the hoard of privately held gold last year reached an estimated total of $6 billion —a far greater dollar value than that of all securities listed on the Paris Bourse.

OUT OF HIDING

The economic consequences of the premium market in gold were a general weakening of those countries where substantial hoarding was going on and a disruption of normal trade. Money was going into a sterile, nonproductive commodity instead of being used domestically or internationally for reconstruction and expansion. Such a dissipation of resources had a painful interest for the U.S.; our foreign aid was not intended to make matters easier for hoarders but rather to make up the difference between the earnings of national resources, used at maximum effectiveness, and the cost of essential imports. The premium market reached its apogee in 1949 when gold prices stood at the astonishing figure of $68 an ounce in Hong Kong, almost double the official U.S. price. Korea gave gold trading a boost in volume, if not in price. But by the autumn of 1953 premiums had all but vanished. Gold was selling at $35.25 in Zurich, $34.90 in Paris, right around the U.S. bench mark. The importance of the event needs no underscoring. During 1953 roughly a third of the world's gold production exclusive of the U.S.S.R.—24,800,000 ounces—went into official monetary reserves; in 1951 it had been only a sixth.

Partly responsible for the disintegration of the premium market were such factors as a lessening of international tension, a slump in Middle and Far Eastern commodity prices after the Korean war, and the obliteration of the Chinese market by Communist edict. But the biggest reason and the most significant one was the renewed confidence of the citizens of a number of foreign countries in their respective currencies and their governments' ability to deal with inflation. In France, the most sophisticated of Continental markets, gold was actually being, in the unlovely word of the economists, dishoarded, and the money put to work. As for the U.S. dollar, what had happened to gold made it look solider than ever—so solid, in fact that some foreign governments decided our federal securities at their higher interest rates were more attractive than speculations in gold.

Just how long this pleasant state of affairs may continue is at best conjectural. There should be no metal shortage to drive the price up again, for the South Africans, the world's No. 1 producers with almost half of the total output in 1953, expect a steady increase over the next decade. The new Orange Free State and West Rand gold fields, for example, will boost South African output 50 per cent. On the other hand, the new gold reserves, accumulated in an era of trade barriers and currency restriction, have yet to stand the ordeal of convertibility, and the premium market itself might be quickly reawakened by a war scare, an American recession, or the simple depletion of these same reserves by adverse trade balances. There are, however, some very solid reasons for hoping the change is a relatively permanent one. As M. A. Kriz, New York Federal Reserve's foreign-research chief, emphasized in the *Engineering and Mining Journal* (February, 1954), the recent increase in reserves was not the result, as in 1950, of a depletion in raw-material stocks or of a rise in the prices of primary commodities from the sterling area. It came rather as a consequence of record agricultural and industrial production in Western Europe and an increased reliance on monetary and fiscal policies to ensure that that production earned a maximum of dollars.

Unfortunately for the prospects of a healthier world economy, the disintegration of the premium market does not signify an end to the hoarding of gold. To be sure, speculative demand—the bone and muscle of the premium price—has subsided, but the savings demand is still very much in evidence even if it is not robust enough to push the going rate substantially above $35 an ounce. National attitudes toward gold hoarding, generations in the making, cannot be changed overnight.

THE GALLIC VIEW OF GOLD

In France the speculative hoarder comes and goes with the prospects of arbitrage or the waxing and waning of that hope of all gold traders, a boost in the U.S. buying price. But apart from the speculators' activities, there is a large and permanent group of Frenchmen who regularly embalm their savings in gold. Some simply have large profits to hide from the tax collector or the police, others act defensively out of fear of a government that has at one time or another instituted devaluations, nationalization of industry, a "solidarity" (net worth) tax, the calling-in of bank notes for exchange (followed by the temporary blocking of the 5,000-franc note), and a surprise stamping (registration) of Treasury bonds. Many businesses go so far as to keep a third to a half of their reserves, in gold—an unwholesome policy that starves banks of reserves, fosters long-term interest rates of 9 to 11 per cent, and makes industrial expansion difficult and costly. Even the otherwise successful Pinay ("good as gold") loan of 1952—which guaranteed principal repayments in francs pegged to the price of gold at a future date—scarcely loosed the Frenchman's grip on his napoleons. The Pinay bond offering pulled in only $42 million in gold.

Such unwavering devotion to gold quite naturally created a vigorous postwar market for it in Paris and other French cities. Typically, South African gold came into the country for refining at Cie des Métaux Précieux or Comptoir Lyon-Alemand, two big plants in Paris. The bullion was then loaded on planes (since France's membership in the International Monetary Fund prohibited gold imports or exports other than those in transit or for refining) and flown to Switzerland, where a free market was re-established in December, 1951. From Switzerland it was either smuggled directly back to Paris or across the Italian-Swiss border to Milan. A profitable coin factory in Milan then minted the bullion into gold napoleons, at a profit of 30 per cent per coin, and supplied them to the smuggling trade for the return journey to France.

BRACELETS VS. BANKS

In another of the world's great "sinks" for gold, India, hoarding is if anything more a part of the national life than in France. Banks are located only in the larger cities; investment opportunities in sound stocks or bonds are not generally available to attract the savings of the middle and upper classes. Even real estate is a difficult venture because of antiquated land-tenure laws and the vast number of handkerchief-size holdings. Every village, however, has its goldsmith. Here farmers exchange their rupees for bullion after the January harvest and then at a charge of about 10 per cent often have the gold fashioned into jewelry for their wives to wear, temporarily. Here, too, come fathers to buy gold dowries for their daughters, in anticipation of the marriage season, which immediately follows the harvest, for under some local Indian laws women cannot own property; their sole security lies in jewelry—streedhan, or "woman's wealth."

The price of gold naturally rises during this period of heavy demand, even though smuggling has a seasonal increase too, thousands of ounces coming in under the fish in dhows, in false-bottomed bird cages, automobile doors, shoe soles, and now and then the human colon. By September some of the farmers find themselves wanting cash to buy seed for the spring planting and jewelry is automatically bought back by the goldsmith at the going gold-billion rate. The hoarder has lost at least 10 per cent on the transaction and maybe more, depending on how seriously the gold owners have taken the traders' cunning rumors about dumping by the Reserve Bank of India or, more recently, massive sales by the Russians.

ENTER THE COMMISSARS

When the last of these rumors materialized in October of 1953, the impact was felt not only in India but, characteristically, in gold markets all over the world. There had always been a great deal of nervous speculation about what Russia was doing or might do with its gold. Lenin had once declared: "We will use our gold for no other purpose but the building of comfort stations on the streets of our cities. . . . That is all gold is good for." The fact, as is not unusual with Soviet pronouncements, was something else again.

Gold mining in Communist Russia had continued under high priority at a volume estimated to be between $70 million and $330 million a year, and the Soviet gold hoard is put down at anywhere from $2.5 billion to $10 billion. A standing labor force of roughly 200,000 political prisoners had been mining the metal in the bleak Siberian wilderness around Kolyma; lately, however, gold production has reportedly slumped to $70 million as miners were diverted to uranium and the 200,000 to 300,000 Chinese replacements, obligingly supplied by Mao from his pool of 30 million political prisoners, dug disappointing amounts of metal before half of them died of cold and starvation.

Actual sales from the U.S.S.R. in 1953 totaled $106 million, $78,700,000 going to Great Britain alone. The first wild interpretations of the Russian sales were pretty much of a piece with those that usually came into vogue at each dip in the postwar market. The Russians were waging economic warfare; they knew large-scale dumping would wreck the market; the falling value of gold reserves in capitalist countries would force banks to retire proportionate amounts of currency; the tightening up of the money supply would cause a slump, unemployment, social upheavals, ad infinitum.

So picturesque an explanation might have had some credibility were the price of gold at its 1949 peak, but the premium market was then on its last legs. Moreover, Russia probably still possessed the world's second-biggest gold hoard, and would certainly be unwise to do anything that might seriously depreciate one of its greatest assets; the direct employment of gold as bribes for espionage and political favors, particularly in the Orient, would likely be far more effective, ounce for ounce, than any quixotic fiscal use the metal might be put to.

A more sophisticated explanation is built around Russia's use of gold as a lever to pry loose some of our less resolute partners in NATO and the European Defense Community. Up until now East-West trade has either been proscribed or, by virtue of the ruble's shady reputation as an international currency, severely limited. Aside from hides, coarse grains, timber, and oil, Russia has very little to offer in exchange for Western goods; Soviet manufactured articles certainly are too high-priced and too shoddy to compete successfully in the export markets of the world. Last year the Soviet Union suffered a trade deficit with the U.K. of some $25 million and, pinched for sterling, had to limit its buying of rubber in the Far East. But suppose East-West trade were expanded on a hard-money basis and payments in Soviet gold conditioned on a friendlier attitude toward Soviet objectives—what then?

SOFT GOODS AND SLAVES

Certainly it would be sound business from the Russia viewpoint to buy Western goods with the half ounce of gold mined each day by the average Kolyma slave; even at current prices, Kolyma miners are producing $17.50 worth of gold, for a labor cost of not much more than their twice-daily ration of thin cabbage-and-carrot soup; a day's wage for European labor, which will produce some of the goods bought with Kolyma gold, averages $4.50.

Competitive advantages of this magnitude are quite an improvement on Marx's original proposition that gold being a product of labor is no more than equivalent to any goods of equal labor content. But while it is certain that the Communists will try for political concessions as part of the selling price of any metal they market, the possibility of influential quantities of gold being used in East-West trade has been much overplayed. The Russians can be expected to use their gold sparingly in the knowledge that should war come, gold rather than their paper currency will have to assume the complete burden of buying them essential materials. Thus while the U.S.S.R. will use its gold for the settlement of trade imbalances and to buy consumer goods for the restive Russian people, it can be expected to do so only in moderate amounts. How long the sales will continue is anybody's guess: Malenkov's emergency three-year program to raise Soviet food and consumer-goods output might be successful enough to take the pressure off gold; on the other hand, a widening of the incipient "sterling gap" could keep the Russians selling gold to buy pounds. In either event there is little about the Russian gold sales that should disquiet the West—provided the foreign exchange is used for consumer goods and not strategic materials.

On the contrary, the sales are something to cheer about. They underline the weakness of the Soviet in the international market place and its internal ferment. A further reason for satisfaction lies in the fact that gold-bought consumer goods will increase the monetary reserves of Western Europe, an essential step toward convertibility, and may even have a direct effect on the U.S. economy. Some of the Russian gold sold to the British last year has already been used to make up a part of the U.K.'s annual $142-million debt payment to the U.S. As Europe's own reserves grow, Europeans may be far more willing to buy from our mountainous stockpiles some of the cotton, corn, and wheat they need.

THE POLITICS OF PRICE

The real danger to Americans is not in some Russian legerdemain with gold but rather in changes we ourselves are being urged to make in U.S. gold policy. The U.S. gold price, a cardinal feature of that policy, has long been under attack by groups and individuals who want to have it increased. When the U.S.—and the world—was going through the recession of 1937-38, they argued that a boost in the price of gold, by writing up the value of existing monetary reserves, would create additional money and promote economic recovery both at home and abroad. Now that the trend has been toward inflation, an increase in the price of gold, it seems, is also justified, for the metal, as a commodity, should keep pace with the rise of other commodities.

The gold-mining companies, naturally, have played so flexible a viewpoint for all it is worth. Their understandable concern is over profits, squeezed between rising costs and a selling price that hasn't been changed in twenty years. But gold, as most producers will admit privately, *is* a monetary metal, not a commodity. Its value in the last analysis is determined by what the U.S. Treasury will pay for it. Sometimes, as in the Thirties and at present, the "free" market price of gold would be substantially below $35 an ounce were it not for the support of the stable Treasury price. Producers cannot reasonably expect a fixed price on the down side and an elastic one on the up.

A far more difficult group to answer are the economists and government officials, principally from the sterling area, who talk of there not being "enough gold to go around." Their proposition runs along these lines: at the present rate of production the volume of gold is insufficient to keep up with the terrific increase in in-

comes and bank credit (hence with prices); if this brake on the money supply is not to cause a serious deflation, the price of gold must be increased. Such a markup would loosen credit and promote "international liquidity," since the value of gold now in central banks would be raised, permitting the issuance of additional currency; it would also bring about an expansion of gold mining with a salutary effect on the world's monetary reserves.

How seriously the British take this proposition can be seen in the fact that the Chancellor of the Exchequer, R. A. Butler, urged it upon the U.S. Government in the official economic talks of June, 1953, and South African Premier Daniel F. Malan had an understanding with Churchill that the latter would pursue it with Eisenhower last December at Bermuda. Distinguished British economists have argued for it at length, Roy Harrod going so far as to suggest that the U.S. price be doubled. But for all of that, the benefits of the move are dubious while the dangers are plain.

THE UNINVITED

If the price were raised, not 100 per cent as Mr. Harrod would prefer, but say 50 per cent—a daring enough figure—the markup from $35 an ounce to $50 would result in the upward revaluation of monetary stocks outside the U.S. by $5.9 billion. But who would benefit by the windfall?—not primarily the nations whose lack of "international liquidity" was the ostensible excuse for the revaluation.

Canada, the "hard currency" countries of Western Europe (Switzerland, Netherlands, Belgium, Portugal), and the dollar-area nations of Latin American—none of which have a balance-of-payments problem—would profit most since they hold close to 40 per cent of the gold outside our borders. Russia, with perhaps the world's second-biggest holding, would also be a substantial if unwelcome guest at the banquet. The sterling area, on the other hand, while it would get an increase in the value of future gold production, could only count on an immediate appreciation in its reserves of $1 billion, France of $247 million, Italy of $148 million. And once the price were in effect, new difficulties would be certain to arise.

An increase in the value of gold automatically throws commercial advantages to producing countries, while more goods (as expressed in devalued currencies) are demanded from non-producers for a given quantity of metal. South Africa, as a producer, would have a 50 per cent greater claim on the goods and services of Great Britain for the same amount of gold.

Would the U.K. be able to meet this *additional* burden on her productive capacity? She has not been able to satisfy the import requirements of the sterling area since the war; indeed it was her failure to do so plus the ability of the U.S. to meet the quantity, quality, and time requirements of world trade which created that famous dollar gap. Would simple liquidity bring about a long-needed change in the pattern of British production—a shift, for example, away from textiles and toward the heavy equipment now in such demand? Would it correct poor merchandising, market analysis, salesmanship?

GOLD, THE PALLIATIVE

This gets down to the fatal weakness of the price proposal: no superficial remedy like an appreciation in gold will cure the trade imbalances of today. Gold can overcome temporary dislocations; deep-seated dislocations demand a structural readjustment, complicated and painful, in international trade.

The material advantages of our increasing the U.S. price come down, principally, to one offered by Roy Harrod. As gold flowed to this country, our reserve would be built up to the size that might be demanded of it if there is to be a World War III, in which we would likely be involved from the outset. "At $22 billion the U.S. external reserve must be regarded as miserably inadequate," he says. "Britain . . . overspent externally some $50 billion [$72 billion in 1954 dollars] in the second world war." This advantage is at least partially nullified by the circumstances under which it would be possible for us to accumulate the gold: the economic weakness of our friends and allies. But it is far outweighed by the dangers a price rise in gold would bring to the American citizen. The devaluation of the dollar attending a markup of gold could very well start a new round of inflation with an immediate slump in sales of U.S. savings bonds, a rise in redemptions, and a hedging of capital. Federal difficulties with refunding might then force the government into greater reliance on the banking system with a consequent expansion of bank credit and the money supply.

While a rise in the price of gold is patently unwise at this time, it would be just as unwise for the U.S. to put the idea permanently out of mind. Thirty-five dollars an ounce is not a sacred price tag. U.S. population and production growth may someday require the kind of enlargement of the domestic money supply that is best accomplished by higher gold prices. But that day, barring unforeseen circumstances, is still five to ten years over the horizon.

THE CASE FOR COINAGE

A second serious assault on U.S. gold policy has been engineered by a small but dedicated group demanding a return to gold coinage. Senator Styles Bridges has already introduced their bill—the Gold Redemption Act of 1954—and hearings are scheduled for the present session of Congress. Fundamentally these partisans—a mélange of sincere sound-money men, hungry gold miners, and incipient hoarders—believe that if everyone could turn in his dollars and get gold coin for them, fiscal sanity would automatically return to the U.S. Whenever a citizen was distressed by the outlook for stability of the dollar, he would express his concern by simply presenting various amounts of currency for redemption in gold coins. An automatic shrinkage of money and credit, moderating the inflation, would then result as the Federal Reserve banks called in *four* times the amount in bills that they had lost in gold. During deflations, so the theory runs, the hard-pressed public would turn in its gold (for bank notes) and the newly created gold reserves would expand the money supply enough to get things rolling again.

Unhappily the practice of gold-coin redemption, far from performing an automatic function in monetary management, has been a nightmare in times of crisis. It enabled monetary control to be wrested from the hands of those charged with administering it and given over to an impulsive public. In 1928, when the Federal Reserve was struggling with inflation, there was no coin redemption by a sapient public, exercising an automatic brake on the boom. That didn't come until 1933, when the country had gone from the inflation into a deep depression. The result has been succinctly described by Dr. E. M. Bernstein, research director of the International Monetary Fund, and a lifelong student of gold: "The public depleted our gold reserves, endangered the banking system, and almost destroyed the economy."

Two independent instruments of monetary control like gold-coin redemption and our Federal Reserve System obviously should not exist side by side. The Federal Reserve, which was created in part to compensate for the inflexibility of the money supply under gold coinage, completely superseded coinage in 1934, when it became so painfully clear that gold redemption was not a stabilizing influence on the economy. The defects of redemption are just as real today as they were in the early Thirties; indeed, the problems of finance involved in our budgetary deficits, refunding of the national debt, and cold-war expenditures would, if anything, make redemption's operation much more capricious.

Gold-coin redemption should be rejected. As Allan Sproul, president of the New York Federal Reserve Bank, said sometime ago, "The integrity of our money does not depend on domestic gold convertibility. It depends on the great productive power of the American economy and the competence with which we manage our fiscal and monetary affairs."

THE NET OF GOLD

It is disquieting to think how much depends on the steadiness of our hand in gold matters. Holding the bulk of the world's $36.7 billion monetary gold supply, we possess through gold the means of increasing or decreasing the value of money all over the globe and through money influencing the patterns of life. A whisper from us on price would reverberate like a thunderclap in the world's treasuries. The smuggler, now grumbling idly over his wine in some border café, would be in business again, more slaves might be put to work in Kolyma, less jewelry sold in Bombay. But we ourselves are caught in the same net of gold and must bear the consequences of any faulty decisions. Today, rather than tinkering with the price of gold, we can do much more to promote international liquidity through a continuation of limited foreign aid, a liberalization of our own trade policies, and an active backing of any sound moves toward currency convertibility. Such a policy entails neither a perilous devaluation of the dollar nor unselective assistance; using it, we can strengthen friends, nudge laggards, and leave our enemies none the richer. We would do no service to our friends or ourselves if we aroused new doubts about the stability of the dollar, simply to accommodate nations who have better, albeit more painful, means of setting their houses in order.

MANAGERS OF THE DOLLAR*

This story of the historical struggle between the Treasury and the Federal Reserve exhibits the importance of monetary policy and summarizes its recent history in the United States. Also it is an instructive case study of the Federal Reserve's "open-market" operations and the Treasury's financing techniques. References are found to the important Douglas report on monetary credit and fiscal policies and to the studies of George L. Bach and E. A. Goldenweiser on the proper role of the Federal Reserve.

The late Lord Keynes once remarked that people would be following his teachings a generation after they were obsolete. It is a hundred to one that if Keynes were head of the Council of Economic Advisers he would not be a quasi-Keynesian, like Leon Keyserling, but would be appalled at the government's dogmatic reliance on fiscal policy and its contempt for monetary policy.

One of the tragedies of our times is that few people—not merely laymen but Congressmen and even some bankers—can give a rational account of these vital instruments. Aside from price and other direct controls, which in the last analysis only repress but do not eliminate inflation, fiscal and monetary policies are the two major means of achieving relative economic stability, *and they should be used together*. The essence of fiscal policy is a countercyclical budget and tax policy: you run a Treasury surplus to damp down inflation, and you run a Treasury deficit to buoy up a slumping economy. The essence of monetary policy is that you control the money supply mainly by contracting or expanding credit.

To understand why these policies should be used together, think of the economy (greatly simplified) as a pair of scales with all the goods and services piled on one side and all the money (mostly bank credit) on the other. When money heavily outweighs goods and services, the government extracts part of it in the form of a Treasury surplus. But it doesn't take out enough to strike a balance. That is the job of Federal Reserve, to which Congress delegated the power to "regulate the supply, availability, and cost of money."

Fiscal policy can be counted on to make only the roughest adjustment in the money supply; monetary policy must do the rest. In the words of the highly regarded Douglas report, "Monetary policy is strong precisely where fiscal policy is weakest; it is capable of being highly flexible. It can be altered with changes in economic conditions on a monthly, daily, or even hourly basis."

WAR BY DEFICIT

Monetary policy was discredited in the 1930's because oceans of cheap money were unable to stimulate investment much. The problem, indeed, was not to regulate the flow of money but to get somebody to use

* From "Managers of the Dollar," February, 1952.

it. Federal Reserve helped by exerting "a steadying influence on the capital market," i.e., by occasionally buying and selling government securities solely to maintain an orderly market for them.

The arrangement was made to order for the deficit financing of the war. Without much urging, the Reserve "patriotically" agreed to sustain the market for the duration by purchasing any government securities left in the market at the low interest levels then prevailing: ⅞ of 1 per cent for one-year certificates, ⅜ of 1 per cent for ninety-day bills, and 2½ per cent for long-term bonds. By the end of the war the Reserve held $25 billion worth, mostly of short-term, low-yield securities, and member banks held $80 billion.

Long before the war ended, these securities began to bother the Reserve Board. The demand for credit, it knew, was sure to boom after controls were lifted. The banks would create reserves for profitable loans by selling their low-interest governments to the Reserve. So long as the Reserve bought governments at par or better, the banks would have no incentive to refrain from selling them. They would, in short, be able to monetize a great part of the national debt. And since the process of extending bank credit involves a potential expansion of the money supply by more than five times, they could monetize the debt not dollar for dollar, but by more than five dollars to one.

Now Federal Reserve was created by Congress as a strictly independent agency to regulate money and credit in the interests of economic stability. Like the Bank of England, it was also expected to maintain working relations with the Treasury. But here it was working with the Treasury to the extent that it was about to default on its prime mandate. In Marriner Eccles' own words, the Reserve was about to become an engine of inflation.

CHEAP MONEY AND POLITICS

Although Mr. Eccles brought the situation to the Treasury's attention in 1945, the Treasury was not impressed. It insisted that the Reserve support the price of government securities to keep the interest rate down. The Treasury by this time had a vested interest in cheap money. Its original job, of course, was to collect and disburse federal revenues, and in the course of a hundred and sixty-two years of superintending the nation's finances it assumed a number of distantly related activities. But thanks to the increase in federal debt the Treasury's big job in these latter years lies in what is known as debt management—taking account of the debt, judging the money market, and issuing and refunding securities.

The end of the war saw many of Federal Reserve's fears come true. Because the government had raised about $150 billion by taxation, the national debt had risen by $230 billion, to $278 billion. But the government's failure to pay for more of the war in cash need not have doomed the U.S. to postwar inflation. The trouble was that only about half the $230 billion the Treasury had borrowed had been in the form of relatively non-inflationary loans, such as savings bonds sold to citizens. More than $100 billion was held in central and commercial banks, and was thus directly inflationary.

Both the Treasury and the banks tried to get much of this inflationary potential into the hands of individuals and savings banks. But there was not time. As soon as price and wage controls were lifted, commercial banks, savings banks, and even insurance companies wanted cash for loans. To get it they sold part of their government-bond holdings to the Reserve Banks, which duly bought them at or above par. Between 1946 and 1950 commercial bank loans increased from $25.7 billion to $51.7 billion.

Note that the boom in bank loans was not as great as

Where Money Is Really Made

Down near the Potomac River, where the railroad bridge crosses from Washington to Virginia, stand two nondescript structures that look less like government buildings than like factories. They house the Treasury's Bureau of Engraving and Printing which is unique among government bureaus in that it neither collects anything from the taxpayer nor costs him anything. Engraving and Printing is in the business of making new currency, stamps, bonds, and 1,500 other such items for 100 different government divisions. In so doing it makes enough money for itself—about $30 million a year—to break even after depreciation and amortization. It does not, however, make its money by holding out some of the stamps or currency. It bills its customers just as any other printer does, and since its customer is the government, it never has trouble collecting.

The bureau's biggest customers are the Treasury and Federal Reserve. Every day it turns out for them about $37 million worth of new currency, which is counted by hand no fewer than thirteen times, and every day a similar amount of old and battered currency is incinerated at the bureau in the presence of a so-called Committee on Collections. The bureau's other customers include Internal Revenue, for which it makes the spirits and tobacco stamps; and the Post Office Department, for which it turns out no fewer than 22 billion postage stamps a year, requiring 2,500,000 pounds of paper for the stamps and 750,000 pounds of dextrin for gumming them.

---

it might have been. A good part of the pressure on prices, at least up till 1950, was accounted for by expanded consumer credit and backlogs of consumer and business savings. It was also the result of the low-cost housing program, which allowed the Veterans Administration and FNMA ("Fanny May") in effect to extend credit at the rate of $5 billion a year. Nevertheless, it seems true that if the Reserve had refused to support the price of governments immediately after the war and let them find their own level in the market, much of the inflation after 1945 could have been avoided. Even Marriner Eccles, to his later regret, shared the general feeling that any drastic tightening up of credit might result in a disastrously heavy cashing of bonds.

But the Reserve's independence and its very reason for existence were at stake. And there was also the large consideration that the very size of the government debt, which now constituted a full half of all public and private debt, actually gave it more power to influence the money supply than it had ever possessed. The Reserve therefore began to assert itself. Early in 1946, against the protests of Secretary Vinson, it eliminated the preferential discount rate of ½ per cent at which it made loans to member banks on short-term securities during the war. In the summer of 1947 it finally got the reluctant consent of Secretary Snyder to end the pegging of short-term Treasury bills, which were then advanced from ⅜ of 1 per cent to 1 per cent. But during the next two years it made no move to unpeg long-term bonds.

SUPPORT FROM OUTSIDE

Then, in 1949, the Joint Committee on the Economic Report, founded in 1947 to educate Congress on the annual report drawn up by the Council of Economic Advisers, established a subcommittee on monetary, credit, and fiscal policies, under Senator Douglas. The subcommittee produced, early in 1950, what is generally regarded as the ablest inquiry into the subject since the National Monetary Commission of 1908-11, which prepared the way for Federal Reserve. The report came out strongly both for the independence of Federal Reserve and the use of monetary policy to check inflation, regardless of its effect on federal debt service charges. "Our monetary history gives little indication," it said, "as to how effectively we can expect appropriate and vigorous monetary policies to promote stability, for we have never really tried them. . . ."

The report was not adopted by the Joint Committee, however. The President's Council of Economic Advisers, by then under the chairmanship of Leon Keyserling, prepared a rebuttal that deprecated monetary policy and advanced the Keynesian argument that "Low interest rates are always desirable. We should retain the advantages of cheap money and adopt other measures [direct controls] to curb inflationary forces." But as the subcommittee made clear and Senator Douglas himself later pointed out in a Senate speech, the issue was not the interest rate at all; the issue was the expansion of money stemming from Federal Reserve's practice of unlimited bond purchases.

The issue was brought to a head by the roaring "post-Korea" boom.

The inflation of 1950-51 was partly the result of the Treasury's insisting on keeping down debt service charges. Yet the resulting price advances increased the budget by at least $6 billion, or more than the whole annual charge on the national debt. By the summer of 1950 Federal Reserve was being widely criticized for following the Treasury. So in July, after buying government securities heavily, the Reserve decided not to continue to buy short-term securities at the same low rate. When Treasury paid no attention but announced a refunding operation at a low rate, the Reserve bought the new Treasury issues but sold enough of its other government securities at high rates to offset a large part of its purchases. It was this bold if belated action that first exposed the serious cleavage between the Reserve and Treasury.

"HISTORIC . . . IMPERTINENCE"

The showdown came, of course, early in 1951, when the Treasury attempted to browbeat Federal Reserve into supporting the 2½ per cent rate on its long-term bonds. In a speech before the New York Board of Trade, Mr. Snyder implied that Federal Reserve had agreed to support the Treasury. Neither the board nor the Federal Open Market Committee had agreed to any such thing. The press was indignant. "For the moment at least," commented Edward H. Collins, financial editor of the New York *Times*, "the fact that the policy enunciated by Mr. Snyder was, as usual, thoroughly unsound and inflationary, was overshadowed by the historic dimensions of this impertinence."

Then Mr. Snyder got Mr. Truman to help him. Mr. Truman called the Reserve's entire Open Market Committee to the White House and gave them an almost insultingly presumptuous lecture on the patriotic importance of supporting government credit. It was the first time in history that a President had tried to influence the committee so openly. The President exacted no promises. He simply followed the meeting up with a letter, publicly released, thanking FRB Chairman McCabe for his commitment to support "government credit . . . at present levels."

COMES STABILITY

The Reserve acted quickly to repudiate this clumsy attempt to impose Treasury's will on it. Marriner Eccles, who had been demoted from the chairmanship by Truman in 1948, released the official minutes of the "confidential" White House meeting, which flatly contradicted the idea that Federal Reserve had committed itself to anything. Federal Reserve then suggested official negotiations. Whereupon the President, at the suggestion of Leon Keyserling, appointed a "compromise" committee consisting of Federal Reserve Chairman McCabe, Secretary Snyder, Director of Defense Mobilization Charles E. Wilson, and Keyserling himself.

The committee eventually drew up an eleven-point anti-inflation program, but it came too late. For William McChesney Martin, then Assistant Secretary of the Treasury but a friend of Federal Reserve's point of view, had been applying his high persuasive talents to bringing Secretary Snyder around to some kind of compromise. Partly because of Mr. Martin's good work, partly because neither Treasury nor the Reserve wanted Keyserling and Wilson in on the deal, an "accord" was arrived at on March 3, five days after the committee was appointed.

The Treasury, it was announced, would offer new *non-marketable* 2.75 per cent long-term bonds, for which it would exchange its 2.5 per cent bonds of 1972. The next week the Reserve pulled the peg by withdrawing its standing offer to purchase government long-term bonds at 11/16 of a point above par. Within a few weeks the market price of the old 2.5 per cent bonds fell three points or more below par. Significantly, however, they fell no lower. Just as the advocates of unpegging had predicted, buyers came in heavily, relatively few holders wanted to sell, and Federal Reserve intervention was not needed to check the fall in prices.

MONETARY POLICY IN EFFECT

It was not a complete victory for the Reserve, but it was a great victory for monetary policy. The Reserve was still committed to maintain an "orderly" market for government bonds. But its refusal to peg them tightly soon had a deflationary effect that flabbergasted the detractors of monetary policy and astonished its advocates. Yields on riskier investments became less attractive. Institutional holders of government bonds thought twice before they sold them at, say, 96 to create reserves for more lending.

Almost at once banks and insurance companies, already heavily committed to buy mortgages but no longer able to sell government securities at a price high enough to make buying mortgages worth while, suddenly stopped making commitments for this building paper. By mid-April last year residential mortgage money had almost vanished in large areas.

And despite the inflationary omens of the times, business began to make an effort to scale down its huge inventories. The public, always panting to buy if shortages seem imminent but hanging back when things seem plentiful, refrained from buying until prices fell. The current buying strike of the public, of course, cannot be wholly accounted for in such easy terms; plainly the people's unwillingness to buy as fast as inventories piled up also has a lot to do with the current stability. But Federal Reserve's action surely contributed to the astounding and agreeable fact that the price level remained almost stationary in 1951.

INDEPENDENT RESERVE

Never have the functions of Federal Reserve been subject to more examination and discussion. Most of it, fortunately, seems to redound to the Reserve's credit. The current Patman subcommittee of the Joint Committee on the Economic Report originated in the fact that Representative Wright Patman, who was a member of the Douglas subcommittee, disagreed with the findings of his colleagues. All his life Mr. Patman has been an easy-money man and suspicious of dam-bankers; he believes that Federal Reserve should be owned by the government. But the answers in the subcommittee's investigation, beginning this month, may not give him great comfort.

Other recent studies are certainly partial to the Reserve. Professor George L. Bach, once a Reserve economist and author of the Hoover task-force report on the Reserve, would bring it closer into government councils and give it more say. E. A. Goldenweiser, formerly director of Federal Reserve's division of Research and Statistics, in his book *American Monetary Policy,* suggests making the chairman of the board of governors a Cabinet officer.

The only trouble with these schemes is that they do not guarantee that the President, Chairman of CEA, or Secretary of the Treasury will turn out to be a man of surpassing knowledge and wisdom. And giving Federal Reserve more weight in Administration circles in return for its independence is hardly possible without subordinating it to older members of the executive family.

The facts, in short, add up to leaving Federal Reserve substantially as it is now—politically independent, not supported by government funds, free to make its strategy, trying hard to settle its differences with Treasury privately, as the Bank of England and the Exchequer always settle theirs, but never afraid to carry its case to the press and public should the occasion demand it. It is precisely because Federal Reserve has been independent that it has been able to vindicate monetary control as an instrument of economic stability.

TOO MUCH MONEY

The vindication of monetary policy, to be sure, does not mean that doubts about and arguments against it are no longer valid. Many economists have doubts and fears. Alvin Hansen argues that the relative price stability of the years 1948-50 cannot be explained only in monetary terms, and no monetary policy except a destructively deflationary one could have prevented *some* price increase after Korea. Abba Lerner argues that a monetary policy strong enough to prevent labor from enhancing inflation would have to be deflationary enough to prevent the "extra 10 per cent or so of output that we need right now."

And monetary policy cannot do everything. It did not work in the depths of depression. It cannot easily make consumers buy when they do not feel like buying (as recently), or refrain from spending their savings when they should refrain (as in 1946-47). It cannot prevent labor from asking for more than its productivity justifies, as it always seems to do. And the demands of labor are potentially highly inflationary. A 10 per cent increase in the nation's wage-and-salary bill adds $18 billion to personal income.

Yet the fact remains that stability comes first, that in a fairly stable economy labor is easier to deal with, and the market disposes of the nation's resources remarkably well. The so-called wage-price spiral is often, if not usually a *result* rather than a cause of inflation. The real cause of all inflation, at all times and everywhere, is too much money.

Certainly nothing that has happened in the past few years suggests that the conclusions of the Douglas subcommittee are any less valid than they were in 1950. Congress, said the subcommittee, should instruct the Treasury and Federal Reserve that primary power to regulate the supply, availability, and cost of credit belongs to the Federal Reserve System. "Treasury action," it said, must "be made consistent with the policies of the Federal Reserve."

3. National Income

12. INCOME FLOWS

THE HYDROSTATICS OF THE DOLLAR*

This discussion of the value of the dollar in terms of a water system manifests the interdependence between the flow of spending and the role of the banking system. National income, prices, production, the flow of spending, and the quantity of money are not isolated economic realities; they influence and condition each other. Attention is called to the importance of the different income flows and their capacity for change.

Could one energetic man foretell the course of prices in detail, he could use his knowledge to destroy capitalism. Every other participant in business would be up against a competitor who could ruin him. An odd feature of the price system is that, while it is assumed to require a good deal of insight and intelligence on the part of those who function in it, it survives because of universal ignorance of the future.

One can, however, identify the forces that determine prices and therewith the value of the dollar. Few economists have ever been able to do so without resorting to analogy, and if it is recalled that things can be expounded but never proved by analogy this is a useful device. Of all the things the price system may be said to resemble, it is probably most like a water system. The flow of water through reservoirs and conduits may be likened to the flow of incomes and expenditures in the economy—and by a simple exercise in imagination, the expenditures can be considered as offset by a pumping system representing production. But there is also the problem of how the water supply enters the system—what replenishes it and how it is controlled. In short, what is the source of the money and what limits its supply? This article deals with these two issues—first, how money is spent in the U.S. economy and, second, where the money comes from.

The flow of spending in relation to production is shown on the pages following in the form of an imaginative isotope of a metropolitan water system. (The reader should note carefully the specifications of this wholly distinctive waterworks.) The most important source of spending is by consumers for consumer goods, which, it might be added, is one of the hallmarks of an individualist society. It is an implicit assumption of that society that the sole and sufficient purpose of economic activity is to provide the individual with what he eats, wears, and enjoys.

The reservoir of consumer spending draws on a number of sources of which by far the most important is wages and salaries. It follows that whatever happens to wages and salaries is profoundly important in the total flow of spending. A 1 per cent increase in this

item, for example, is equivalent in effect to a. 10 per cent increase in consumer credit, or a 16 per cent increase in expenditure for new manufacturing plant.

Wages and salaries are important for another reason. Given the proper circumstances, which include an adequate supply of money, they have an autonomous tendency to rise. In an industrial economy wages will go up whenever it is evident to union leadership that employers can afford to pay more, or when increases in the cost of living dictate an effort to get more pay.

PRODUCTION, INVESTMENT, AND TAXES

Important though wages and salaries are as a source of spending in the U.S. economy, they provide only slightly more than half the total flow. Moreover, spending has two dimensions: its absolute magnitude and its capacity for change. To get the substance of this abstraction, the reader should refer again to page 70, where the recent changes are shown by the differences between 1945 and present water levels. The movement in wages and salaries has been relatively small compared with that in farm, business, and professional incomes. It has been radically smaller than the change along the investment watercourse. The increase in expenditure for capital goods and equipment has contributed substantially to the *total* increase in spending since the end of the war.

In an ideal world, size and capacity for change would be uniquely combined in the pump, on the right, representing physical production. In a world where production adjusted itself automatically to what was spent, there could be no inflation. For a good many months, unhappily, there has been little spare plant and less spare manpower in the U.S. economy—the pump has been operating at capacity. Apart from secular advances in labor productivity, an uncontrollably gradual process, the principal chance for higher production has been from new additions to existing plant. But this, as a moment's study of the chart will suggest, could be accomplished only by a corresponding increase in investment spending along the watercourse on the left. The immediate result for the consumer would be increased competition in the markets for goods.

During the last year or two there has been a surprising unanimity in error between conservatives and

* From "How Sound is the Dollar?" April, 1948.

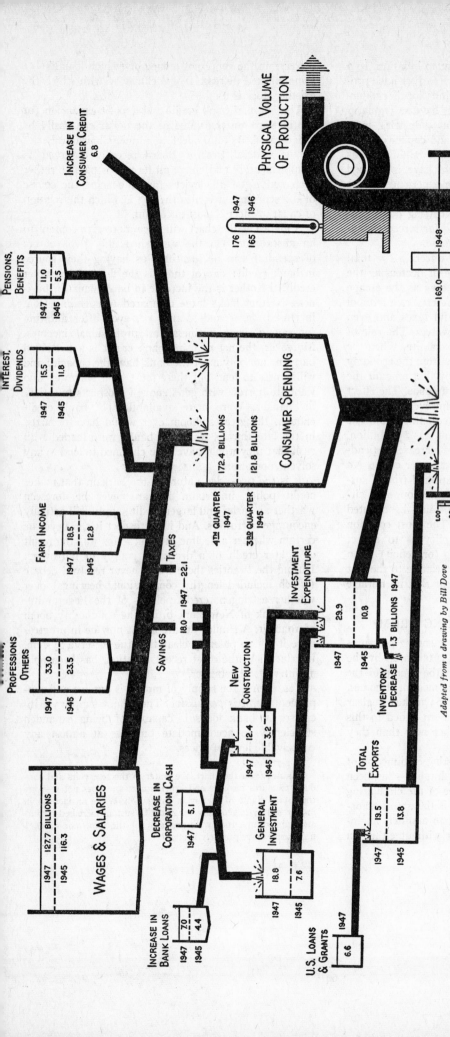

Adapted from a drawing by Bill Dove

This water system resembles that of no city on earth but it does depict the forces that determine the value of the U.S. dollar circa 1947-48. From the top comes the flow of purchasing power that citizens, corporations, and foreigners pour into the market on the right. Out of that market the pump at the bottom, now operating well above its rated capacity, absorbs purchasing power, which is what production does. So long as purchasing power exceeds production (plus what is drained off by government surplus), the market, shown by the consumer price index, will rise to the discomfiture of some, the pleasure of others. The dollar, shown against a gauge calibrated to its pre-war purchasing power (1935-39 = 100), will fall. As and when spending falls below production it can as safely be assumed that prices will fall. The total volume of water flowing through this system—and being pumped to start another round—shows the actual flow of incomes and expenditures in the economy. The increase in flow since 1945 suggests, though it does not measure, the increase in the money supply necessary to sustain the higher income, expenditure, and prices of 1947. Figures are for fourth quarter of 1947 or third quarter of 1945 at annual rates except increases in bank loans (1945 and 1947), government cash (not budget) surplus, and government loans and grants, which are annual figures. The figure for corporation cash includes government securities and shows decrease in the twelve months preceding July 1, 1947. These latter figures, though not strictly comparable, show orders of magnitude. The production index is based on 1935-39 = 100.

liberals on the relation of investment to inflation. In a thousand after-dinner speeches conservatives have proclaimed that "The only answer to inflation is production and MORE production." Liberals have as regularly denounced the unwillingness of some industries, most notably the steel producers, to expand capacity. Both have been arguing for a policy that, at a minimum, was unreal and that, at its worst, could have intensified inflation. There was nothing in the experience of the thirties to suggest the wisdom of trying to maintain the purchasing power of the dollar by cutting down production. Much of the recent demand for forced expansion of production makes no more sense.

A much more forthright way of affecting the total volume of spending is by increasing or decreasing the government surplus—shown on page 63 as the escape valve at the bottom of the main reservoir, a symbol that does small justice to the painful taxes and even more painful politics that its use involves. The role of the government surplus is perfectly definite. When the government is collecting more money from the economy than it is spending, it is lessening by that amount the pressure of demand on the supply of goods. The effect of a deficit is exactly the reverse. However, the reader should make careful note of the size of this item. The cash surplus of the Treasury last year was $5.6 billion, which was substantially less than the increase in spending resulting from the increase in consumer credit. No vast deflationary effect should be expected from a surplus of this size just as, under other and opposite circumstances, no magical expansion should be counted upon from a deficit of equal size. The most common error in connection with fiscal policy is to expect miracles from a government surplus (or deficit) when a moment's examination of its size, relative to the rest of the economy, should make it clear that no miracle is to be expected.

WHERE IS THE MONEY COMING FROM?

Production not only absorbs the spending pressures in the economy (barring only what is taken up by the government surplus), but it is also the source of the incomes from which the spending or most of it comes. But a glance at the chart on page 63 makes it clear that, since the war, something has been added to this flow. All of the reservoirs are higher now than they were two years ago.

What has occurred—in an interesting conjunction of the language of economics and hydraulics—has been a substantial increase in the volume of the circulating medium. Since the act of spending is the act of transferring money from one individual to another, an increase in spending could not occur without either an increase in the supply of money or (which is unlikely) some marked increase in the efficiency with which the existing stock is used.*

The effect of bank credit and deposit expansion (or contraction) on the value of the dollar can easily be exaggerated. Its total effect, as former Chairman Eccles of the Federal Reserve Board recently observed, is "supplemental" and above all its role is passive rather than active. Of all devices for influencing the course of the economy, it is also the one in which the relation of cause to effect is most uncertain.

A glance at the chart will once more give content to an abstraction. On the watershed only two sources of spending can be identified as having their source in bank credit: one of these is the flow of consumer credit, the other is the increase in bank loans for business. Neither looks large compared to spending from increased wages and salaries or, even after allowing for saving, from business and professional incomes. Moreover, the act of using bank credit is a two-sided bargain: not only must the bank have the capacity and willingness to lend but there must be a borrower who wants to borrow with good enough prospects to satisfy his banker. Were mere availability of bank credit enough, the greatest boom ever would have occurred in the late thirties when the banks were loaded with cash that they would have been charmed to lend to any solvent borrowers.

It is the two-sided nature of the bargain that makes credit policy uncertain. It can never be foreseen whether an easier and larger credit supply will actually encourage borrowers. And in retrospect it can never be certain whether a decline in bank loans was the result of tighter credit or a decreased supply of borrowers. During the twenties there was a never resolved debate (which included lengthy congressional hearings) over whether astringent credit policies of the Federal Reserve Bank of New York broke the commodity boom of 1920-21. A similar debate might now be in progress were it not so patently clear that the Reserve System, in relation to the most recent inflation, has been only an interested bystander.

Yet, even if the supply of money is passive and supplementary, it *is permissive*. The money supply via increases in bank loans is capable of being expanded sufficiently to accommodate business at almost any conceivable level of prices.

* As noted on the chart, the water in the reservoirs and conduits measures incomes and expenditures and does not measure the total volume of money in circulation. While an increase in money supply is generally necessary to sustain increased income and expenditure, the two items are not the same nor do they necessarily move precisely in step.

WHY DO PEOPLE BUY?*

Classical economists considered the consumer a purely passive agent. It was Lord Keynes who assigned the consumer an important role in the economy when he built his doctrine around the theory of how the consumer behaves and stressed savings' vital influence on the level of national income. Here Keynes' fundamental psychological law is tested by an examination of the facts, especially those gathered by the Survey Research Center of the University of Michigan under Professor George Katona, author of Psychological Analysis of Economic Behavior *(New York, 1951). The important economic function of selling usually ignored in consumer theory is held to be capable of becoming a vital force for the welfare of the economy.*

The most illustrious economist of our times, the late Lord Keynes, made his reputation largely on the proposition that people do not automatically buy enough to maintain prosperity. He wrenched the thinking of the capitalist world away from production and toward consumption; his theories were built around the behavior of the consumer. Yet Lord Keynes never seriously considered the possibility that "selling"—the persuasive element in distribution—might have a measurable effect on how much people buy.

And Keynes is not the only one who neglected salesmanship. Few economists before or since have paid much attention to it, to say nothing of taking it seriously. Selling and advertising, writes Harvard's J. K. Galbraith in his new book, *American Capitalism,* "may be waste but they are waste that exists because the community is too well off to care." Most economists, indeed, tend to regard selling as an excess of capitalism, a kind of bug in the distribution process. They make no functional distinction between distribution and selling. If the distribution process were ordered rationally, they imply, it would consist almost entirely of packaging, shipping, warehousing, and sending goods to market. They do not grant that selling or the art of persuading people to buy can affect appreciably the over-all volume of consumption. To them the consumer buys for a variety of causes, but rarely if ever because he is sold.

In eighteenth- and nineteenth-century Europe, where most economic ideas originated, distribution without persuasion was natural. The problem there was (and often still is) to produce enough to maintain a substandard living. The U.S. today is uniquely different. The standard of living is so far above subsistence that it is fair to say that production is no longer a problem —in the sense that it is *the* problem in all the rest of the world. Distribution, in the mechanical sense of moving the right goods to the right market, is not a problem. In the years ahead, barring the deluge of war, the problem of American capitalism is clear: will people spend enough to buy back what they produce *at a high and rising level of production?*

The economists' answer: not necessarily. And the

economists should not be airily dismissed; they may be right. But have the economists overlooked something, the new something called selling? Is the consumer really predictable? Does he act with the rational self-interest of "economic man"? And finally are economists correct in assuming that the whole apparatus of American selling is powerless to move the index of consumption by the relatively few points that spell the difference between prosperity and depression?

These are some of the questions that need to be asked about American selling. There are no pat answers; perhaps the questions can't be answered satisfactorily until much more is known about the consumer. But there is in very recent history a storehouse of experience: the "savings spree" of 1951. It is a good place to start asking the questions. This phenomenon, the most stunning economic surprise since 1929, provides a vivid demonstration of the unpredictability of the unsold consumer, the narrow margin between boom and recession, and the role that salesmanship *can* play.

The "saving spree," significantly, was preceded by the spending spree that began immediately after the Korean war broke out in June, 1950. Never, probably, has the outbreak of war been so violently inflationary. Everybody remembered all too clearly what happened "last time"—the shortages, the rationing, the black markets. Everybody acted as if he had to stock up for a war of indefinite duration. One hotel proudly announced that it had laid in a ten-year supply of liquor. One government agency bought a 247-year supply of loose-leaf binders.

But an urge to save lurked underneath all the furor, and amazingly strong it seems to have been. The very excesses of the boom naturally strengthened that urge. In any event, inventories began to increase faster than sales even in the latter part of 1950. With General MacArthur's advance to the Yalu River in October, savings increased and buying dropped sharply. Although China's entry into the war sparked a new buying wave, this wave began to peter out by early 1951. It was in March, 1951, that the consumer clutched his pocketbook to his breast, spat in the face of world economic forces, and began to save a higher proportion of his disposable income than he ever had in peacetime. By

* From "Why Do People Buy?" April, 1952.

April his reaction was in full swing, and in the second quarter he was piling up net savings at the phenomenal rate of nearly $20 billion a year, a tenth of disposable income. He did even better in the third and fourth quarters. To put it another way, the increase in his savings alone nearly canceled out the increase in defense spending during 1951. Prices remained steady.

THE BAD GOOD TIMES

Rarely has an economic phenomenon been so pulled apart, dissected, analyzed, and mulled over. There is even a school of thought that pooh-poohs it. The year 1951, this school says, was after all the second best (after 1950) in peacetime history; the noise was made by retailers, who always judge this year's sales not by, say, a ten-year average, but by last year's. One expert has essayed to show that in reality 1951's department-store sales were normal, and that stores should not be surprised if the current ratio of sales to disposable income continues indefinitely.

Other analysts, particularly those in department-store organizations, sharply question the accepted figures on savings, openly arguing that the only remedy for the sales lag is less government spending and reduced taxes. That the savings figures are not wholly satisfactory there is no doubt. "Savings" figures generally include insurance, payments on homes, and social-security contributions, most of which could not have been arbitrarily spent on goods. But the facts belie most such arguments. Had people bought in 1951 as they did in 1950, there would be nothing to argue about. And the fact also remains that in 1951 the con-

sumer's savings in cash, securities, and net debt liquidation (but not life-insurance premiums) came to $6.5 billion more than the same categories of savings amounted to in 1950. The consumer, in other words, would have spent $6.5 billion more in 1951 had he saved as he did in 1950.

This may no longer seem like big money to a people accustomed to talk in an offhand way about hundreds of billions. But it has a tremendous leverage. Between October, 1950, and May, 1951, retail inventories rose by $3.2 billion. If the consumer had spent $6.5 billion more in 1951, business probably would have "boomed." Prices would have stayed firm or advanced—in short, much of the inflation that everyone predicted with such cocksure sagacity probably would have materialized.

One of the things that most people have yet to appreciate adequately is the incredibly small difference between "over-supply" and "scarcity." In 1951 the auto industry made 5,300,000 cars, or just enough to keep a "scarcity" from developing. Another 500,000 automobiles, everything else being equal, would have meant "oversupply." In 1950 refrigerators were "scarce"—yet manufacturers sold 6,200,000 of them. "Scarcity" quickly becomes "oversupply" when the consumer is possessed by the urge to save and is permitted to indulge it, and "oversupply" quickly becomes "scarcity" when he is possessed by the urge to buy and is permitted to indulge it.

But why didn't the consumer buy as much as he could have in 1951? Practically every expert, recognized and self-appointed, has a reason. One such

---

THE OLD SAVING HABIT

Among family units above the $7,500 level, spending habits change markedly: they begin to save a much greater proportion of their income. To measure this saving tendency, *Fortune* made an analysis of 1953 incomes, based on a Federal Reserve Survey of Consumer Finances and a BLS Survey of Consumer Expenditures in 1950, the latter released for the first time.

The analysis shows that, on the average, families with $4,000 to $5,000 cash income saved 10 per cent of the "top" or "extra" $1,000 of their incomes,* families with $5,000 to $7,500 saved virtually the same proportion—11 per cent—of their "extra" income. But families with $7,500 to $10,000 saved nearly 20 per cent of the "extra" income. And families with still higher incomes saved at a much higher rate—nearly 40 per cent of their "extra" income.

It is almost precisely at the $7,500 line, in other words, that savings begin to rise steeply (and spending, as a *percentage* of income, begins to fall). And why do savings rise so steeply? First, people with high incomes save a much greater percentage of their "extra" income than people with low incomes, just as they always save a higher percentage of their total income. Second, *all*

*The statistical concept: "extra" income is the difference between the average income of one group and the average income of the next-lower group; "extra" saving is thus the difference between the average savings of one group and those of the next-lower income group.

consumers whose income is rising from year to year tend—at least for a while—to save an extraordinarily large percentage of their additional or incremental income. It was on this often observed phenomenon that the late Lord Keynes based a large part of his economic philosophy. It is a fundamental psychological law, he said, "that men are disposed, as a rule and on the average, to increase their consumption as their income increases, but not by as much as the increase in their income. . . . For a man's habitual standard of life usually has the first claim on his income, and he is apt to save the difference . . . between his actual income and the expense of his habitual standard. . . ."

But what does this kind of saving portend for future years? If consumers' income rises as our projections have suggested, and if consumers keep on saving the same percentage of their incremental income that they did in 1953, the over-all U.S. savings rate would rise from nearly 7 per cent (1953) to about 10 per cent. Actually, of course, consumers' cash income would not keep on rising under such conditions because so high a savings rate would probably result in a shrunken economy. A nation that wants to have money to spend must spend money.

Well, then, how much "should" consumers save? Over the past half century, American consumers have spent, on the average, 93 per cent of their income and put the other 7 per cent into savings—which include

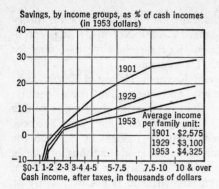

Savings, by income groups, as % of cash incomes (in 1953 dollars)

1901
1929
1953

Average income
per family unit:
1901 - $2,575
1929 - $3,100
1953 - $4,325

Cash income, after taxes, in thousands of dollars
$0-1 1-2 2-3 3-4 4-5 5-7.5 7.5-10 10 & over

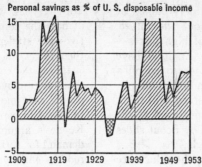

Personal savings as % of U. S. disposable income

1909 1919 1929 1939 1949 1953

CONSUMER SAVING HABITS:
A HAPPY PARADOX

cash, bank deposits, accumulations of cash value on insurance policies, and equity payments on houses. Now, there is nothing sacred about this savings percentage, for it is merely an average encompassing very wide fluctuations indeed; as a matter of fact, consumers never have saved precisely 7 per cent of a given year's total income. It is possible that business or government will spend unusual amounts in 1959, and that the U.S. could be prosperous with consumers saving as much as 10 per cent of their income—which they last did in 1941, when the U.S. began to arm. It is also possible that consumers could save only 3 per cent with no damage to the economy—which happened in 1947, when people were catching up on World War II shortages. But these were exceptional years. Savings much above 10 per cent might have serious consequences for the market. Experience suggests that the economy of 1959 would balance properly if savings amount to something around 7 per cent of consumers' projected $278-billion cash income.

"God's Dice Are Loaded"

And the fact is that consumers with rising income, at some point or other, *do* shift their saving habits and begin to spend more. This shift is the subject of the highly encouraging chart at the top of the page. *It shows that, on the average, people on every income level, for a half century or more, have been saving an ever smaller percentage and spending an ever larger percentage of their incomes.*

The progression has not been steady. Obviously millions of consumers do not step up their spending at any uniform rate; one man who has been raised from $7,500 to $8,500 may go on saving at a high rate for years; another may save at a high rate for only one year. But over the long run the decline in the rate of savings displays a steadiness amounting almost to inevitability. *Consumers in the $3,000-to-$4,000 income group, for example, saved 9 per cent of their income in 1901, only about 5 per cent in 1929, and only 4 per cent in 1953; consumers in the $7,500-to-$10,000 group saved a fourth of their income in 1901, 15 per cent in 1929, and 10 per cent in 1953.* (All figures are in 1953 dollars.)

At first blush, this may seem impossible. Haven't total consumer savings, over the years, worked out to 7 per cent of cash income? How, then, can people be saving a steadily smaller percentage of their incomes *at every income level?* The answer is simply that the *number* of people in the high-saving upper brackets has increased almost exactly enough to compensate for the reduced percentage of saving by all groups.

Without this compensation the dynamism of the American economy could not exist. To repeat, if people whose real income is rising did not increase their spending sufficiently, the percentage of national income saved would rise to the point where trade would be stifled and real income would be reduced.

Emerson would have been delighted with this automatic compensation. "The dice of God are always loaded," he wrote. "The world looks like a multiplication table, or a mathematical equation, which, turn it how you will, balances itself."

The Economic Bellwethers

But why do individual Americans, most of them happily ignorant of any law of universal compensation, spend a progressively larger percentage of their income over the years? A good many theories have been advanced to explain the tendency, but at bottom is the simple fact that there are more and more things to spend money on today. It was partly because a $5,000 family in 1900 could buy nothing like the number of things that are considered necessities for a $5,000 family today that it saved about 16 per cent of its $5,000 (1953 dollars) against about 6 per cent for today's $5,000 family. Rising productivity and rising real income, in other words, beget the standard of living that nourishes them.

This rise in the nation's living standard is paced by consumption bellwethers who are sold on a new product, adopt that product, are emulated by others whose acceptance gives it the mass support that converts it from a luxury into a necessity. The masses have been very well served, economically speaking, by the well-to-do who act as economic guinea pigs.

But these well-to-do, let it be noted, are no longer the very rich. In the homogenous community that is America today, the bellwethers are the $7,500-and-over families. Unable to outdo other families by any extraordinary margin, usually disinclined to be dramatically different, they keep a jump or two ahead of the rest, who hustle to follow as soon as they can. And it is this continuous emulation of the continually advancing—and steadily more numerous—bellwethers that keeps the long-term, over-all savings rate manageably low.

—Gilbert Burck and Sanford Parker, "The Consumer Markets: 1954-59," August, 1954.

reason is the "fact" that many consumers balked at buying because they felt insecure about the future. Another is that they balked because of high prices— just as high prices of soft goods in England have caused even the austerity-ridden Britons to go on a kind of buyers' strike. A related reason is that people, though their wages have more than doubled, still think in terms of 1940 prices: the traveler, outraged at the 25-cent redcap fee, the housewife by Boy Scout shoes at $9 a pair and beef at $1.25 a pound.

Still another related reason given for the reluctance to buy is the perverse but psychologically sound one that people buy when goods seem to be growing scare. Finally, there is the notion that the average consumer today can buy so many things with his money that he has become, in the words of Arno Johnson of J. Walter Thompson, a man with great discretionary spending power. Beardsley Ruml likes to talk about consumer *un*necessities. "Today as never before," he says, "the ordinary individual can get along without purchasing for his day-to-day requirements. . . . The consumer is free—free to postpone, free to reduce, free to anticipate, free to switch from one *un*necessity to another."

But these reasons by themselves afford only partial clues to the consumer's behavior. Who is this consumer, and why *does* he behave as he does? On this question, alas, it is possible to throw only a meager and fitful light. We know there are roughly 52 million "spending units" in the country—a "spending unit" being defined as all related persons living at the same place who pool their incomes for major expenses. We know how these "spending units" break down by income, how much each income group saved or spent in any year, and, as the result of special surveys, what each of these groups did or intended to do under certain circumstances. But we still lack many elementary statistics such as who owns what brand of autos, stoves, etc., and when they were purchased. And as yet we have few valid generalizations on consumer behavior under common circumstances—for instance, which individuals increase their savings and for what reason.

THAT MAN KEYNES AGAIN

The most important or at any rate the most consistent work in "psychological-economic" fact gathering is being done by the Survey Research Center of the University of Michigan, under Professor George Katona, author of *Psychological Analysis of Economic Behavior*. The center not only does considerable investigation in its own right, it makes the field surveys for the Federal Reserve Board's highly regarded annual "Survey of Consumer Finances." Well aware that consumer behavior has been generally regarded as a bunch of immeasurables, Professor Katona nevertheless thinks consumer behavior can be investigated empirically, and that someday the Research Center may be able to suggest under what circumstances a certain pattern of consumer behavior is likely to appear. But not enough of this investigation has been done to formulate sound generalities. Anyone wanting to account for the consumer and his proclivities in a large way must perforce turn (as indeed Katona himself has turned) to the late

Lord Keynes, who built his doctrines around a theory of how the consumer behaves. Not many sales executives are students of Keynes; the time has come for them to get out the books again.

It was the core of Keynes's Theory of Employment that unemployment and depression come because people save more than business at the time is willing to invest in capital goods. When a man saves $10,000, Keynes's argument went, he reduces by $10,000 the demand for certain consumer goods and thus, of course, reduces employment in the industries that make them. The trouble is that the $10,000 is not necessarily or immediately put to work creating new jobs in heavy goods. Then there are fewer jobs and fewer purchases, and the downward drift toward depression commences. Savings without works, Keynes kept emphasizing, are distinctly bad; and the ultimate remedy for too much saving is government spending.

To account for the propensity to save, Keynes decided that a "fundamental psychological law" governs human spending and saving. He stated the law thus: "Men are disposed, as a rule and on the average, to increase their consumption as their income increases, but not by as much as the increase in their income. . . . For a man's habitual standard of life usually has the first claim on his income, and he is apt to save the difference which discovers itself between his actual income and the expense of his habitual standard; or, if he does adjust his expenditures to changes in his income, he will over short periods do so imperfectly. Thus a rising income will often be accompanied by increased saving, and a falling income by decreased saving, on a greater scale at first than subsequently."

And how has this "law," which has been accepted by most economists if only because nothing else is more acceptable, worked out in actual practice? Is there any correlation between it and sales effort? The figures before the 1930's do not lend themselves to a reliable interpretation one way or the other. But during the 1930's the trend seemed generally to uphold Keynes. From 1932 to 1935, consumer expenditures followed Keynes and exceeded disposable income, as well they might have, since people were using up savings to live. Between 1935 and 1940 consumer savings increased faster than income. And during the war Keynes's law fulfilled itself with a vengeance. Incomes rose swiftly, but savings rose still more swiftly. The consumer saved what till then had been unheard-of sums, at unheard-of rates. In 1942 he saved $25 billion, or 22 per cent of the national disposable income; in 1943 and 1944 he saved more than $30 billion, or nearly 24 per cent. But the wartime increase, of course, proves little one way or the other, for the consumer was under unusual and heavy pressures to save. (Survey indicated that the "shortages," contrary to general opinion, did not play a large role in his decision to save.)

It is hardly to be expected that a close analysis of consumer spending *after* the war would verify Keynes's thesis. No matter how much the consumer's income was increasing, he would not be likely to continue to save after having saved so much and bought so little during the war. And so it was. An analysis of "dissaving" (spending in excess of income) in 1946 and 1947 by Professor Katona shows that although disposable income increased by 6.6 per cent, over-all savings did not increase, as Keynes's law says they should, but actually declined (from 18.5 per cent of disposable income in 1945 to 2.3 per cent in 1947). What is more, there was a vast increase in "dissaving." And it all happened without much sales effort on the part of American business, which as a whole almost forgot how to sell between 1941 and 1949. But the survey noted that this abnormal spending would probably be followed by saving. In another analysis Professor Katona examined the effect of income changes on the rate of postwar savings. This was inconclusive, contradicting Keynes at points and verifying him at others. The most significant conclusion emerging from such studies was that people's buying seems governed by expectations: when they expect good times, they buy more than when they are dubious or pessimistic.

Taking everything together, Keynes's law seems hard to verify by experience. But in so far as it suggests an underlying desire to save on the part of consumers, it can claim a certain validity. Surveys made by the Michigan center as early as 1946 indicated that people might start to save again once they had filled their wants. From 1947 there seems to have been a definite swing toward savings. In 1948, net consumer savings, thanks to a second- and third-quarter spurt, advanced to $10.5 billion, or 5.6 per cent of disposable income. In 1949, owing to the resumption of buying after the "inventory recession," net savings declined to $6.3 billion, or 3.4 per cent of disposable income. But despite the wild spending and dissaving after the Korean war, savings were $10.7 billion in 1950. And the "Survey of Consumer Finances" made by the center in January and February, 1951, printed in the *Federal Reserve Bulletin* of April, 1951, gave clear indications that people were planning to buy less, not more, durable goods. In retrospect it seems that anyone who had noted these signs with Keynes's law in mind might have guessed what was coming. And it is perhaps arguable that what happened in 1951 might be interpreted as a kind of delayed fulfillment of that law.

THE REAL REASON

Actually no economic theory anticipates what was possibly the most important and relevant explanation for 1951. And in the sense that all the other reasons commonly given for 1951's savings are only excuses, they do not anticipate the important explanation either. The explanation: people buy for a number of reasons, a major one being that they are sold; and business wasn't selling as it should have been. It hadn't been, indeed, since prewar days. Just as salesmanship was caught napping in the short "inventory" slump of 1949, it was caught wanting in 1950 and 1951. True, many companies had organized for the selling that they knew lay ahead. But even the most determined of them found their resolution softening in the heat of the sellers' picnic "after Korea."

The difference between boom and stability in 1951,

as we have noted, was a matter of some $6.5 billion. If salesmanship were as highly organized and proficient as it has been and should be, might it not have persuaded people to spend $6.5 billion more than they did? Unless the American selling apparatus is nothing but a luxury that only an inordinately wealthy and somewhat insane nation would tolerate, the answer is obvious. Selling could have. The government's fiscal policies being what they were, the U.S. can thank its luck that under the circumstances it did not.

AND IN 195X . . .

And how successfully will it tackle 195X, that much-discussed year when the military boom wears off, and production in a vastly expanded economy must again go into the civilian stream?

Many experts, particularly department-store owners and durable-goods makers, take a dogmatically optimistic view of the long-term prospects. The events of the past years, they say, are abnormal; the long-range trend is not toward saving but just the opposite. With all people sharing more equally in the national income, the argument goes, there will be less to save on the part of the upper income groups because there will be fewer large incomes. Pension programs, old-age insurance, unemployment insurance, and so on have fostered and will continue to foster a feeling of security that will result in a continuous and high level of spending.

It is nevertheless possible to make an excellent case for just the opposite, that people will feel the urge to save more and more. True, incomes have tended to become equalized. But it is also true that no less than 44 per cent of the personal income is still earned by those making more than $5,000 a year, and that as a group they have more to save than ever. And many people who never could save can now do so, for the equalization of U.S. incomes is being achieved while the real per capita income is steadily advancing.

CONSUMERS' DISCRETION

Thus it may be that the absolute savings potential is greater now than it ever has been. As Mr. Ruml and others keep insisting, the area of optional or discretionary buying is growing immensely rather than contracting. Just what percentage of the nation's income is spent optionally is almost anybody's guess. Arno Johnson of J. Walter Thompson defines it as what is left after the bare necessities of food, clothing, and shelter are paid for. He estimates it today at around $105 billion, or 45 per cent of 1951's disposable income, or two and a half times as great as in 1940. Other estimates are considerably smaller, for they place a more liberal interpretation on the cost of food and clothing and include some transportation.

But in the sense that discretionary purchasing power represents goods whose purchase can be *postponed* it does not have to be large to be important. When people delay purchasing goods, they do not necessarily accelerate their buying later on to compensate for what they didn't buy earlier. As Keynes observed, "An act of individual savings means—so to speak—a decision not to have dinner today. But it does not necessitate a decision to have dinner or buy a pair of boots a week hence or a year hence or to consume any specified thing at any specified date." Such is the kind of saving that can throw a monkey wrench in the economic machine. It is the margin between "oversupply" and "scarcity," and it is no more certain than the unsold consumer's whim.

Thus on the one hand we have the Keynesian uncompensated saving, whose ultimate solution may be capital formation by government works. On the other, we have the forces of salesmanship striving to prevent accelerated saving, indeed to keep savings down to the minimum needed for capital formation.

DOES SELLING RAISE DEMAND?

The alternative, of course, may not be quite that sharp. It is just possible that the system can jog along without real selling and without running into a depression. All Keynes tried to prove with his Theory of Employment was that the system might stabilize itself at less than full employment. And it is not straining probability to imagine a prosperous, stabilized economy in which people regularly save 10 per cent or more of their disposable income—i.e., an economy with a high rate of capital formation or "donation diplomacy."

On the other hand, nobody has proved that Keynes's basic analysis is wrong. It is a commonplace that businessmen do not like to expand when consumption is declining. Even the progressive motor industry does not plan vast expansion of production facilities when the outlook for sales is bad, and even the boldest and most resourceful dress manufacturer prefers to spend a year at Miami Beach when business in general is bad. There is no reason to suppose industry will change

its habits in the near future. It was this entrepreneurial reluctance to buy capital goods, indeed, that drove Keynes into his partiality for more or less permanently low interest rates. High interest rates may encourage savings, he argued, but they do not encourage capital formation when capital formation should be encouraged most.*

Why didn't Keynes pay more attention to the role of selling? Because selling had not rescued the U.S. from the depression, he may have concluded (as some of his followers have concluded) that selling is so much wind and noise generated by what Americans stubbornly insist on calling competition. Most economic thought, as a matter of fact, has tended to regard selling primarily as a device for increasing one company's sales over another and has tended to doubt that it has any important effect on the *aggregate* consumption.

Not even the most enthusiastic exponent of the art would claim that selling can turn depression to boom. But doesn't it really play a preventive role? Isn't it or couldn't it be a means of sustaining aggregate national demand?

To answer these questions in the affirmative, the businessman obviously must behave as if a major aim in life were to demonstrate that Keynes and the other economists were wrong. Defining salesmanship, as *Fortune* has defined it, as everything that contributes to the salability of a product from the time it is conceived until it is finally used up or worn out, the businessman must practice salesmanship as he never has practiced it before.

* He perhaps should have gone into this more deeply. The crypto-Keynesians in Washington have taken him so seriously that they apparently prefer inflation, via the monetization of the public debt, to the smallest alteration in the interest rate.

14. DISSAVING

THE COMING TURN IN CONSUMER CREDIT**

By GILBERT BURCK AND SANFORD PARKER

This article reviews the much debated rise in consumer credit which plays so portentous a role in accelerating consumption. It analyzes how much consumers have borrowed and why they have gone into debt. It examines the crucial question whether consumer debt can keep rising and what will happen to the economy if it does not.

Consumer short-term debt, perhaps the most controversial force in the booming U.S. economy, is approaching a historical turning point. Having risen at an abnormally fast rate for ten years, it must soon adjust itself to the nation's capacity for going in hock, which is not limitless. Whether the rate of growth in consumer debt will slow down is no longer the question; as this article will demonstrate, it *must* slow down. The question is when it will slow down, and how. There are, to oversimplify only a little, three ways that the decline can occur:

1. Debt growth (not debt itself) may coast downward so smoothly and gradually that the whole turn

** From Gilbert Burck and Sanford Parker, "The Coming Turn in Consumer Credit," March, 1956.

will be virtually painless.

2. Debt growth may slow down erratically, with painful effects for those industries—notably automobiles, appliances, TV, and all their suppliers—that have received the biggest stimulus from the abnormal rise in debt. For the economy as a whole, however, these consequences might be offset by growth and expansion in other industries, and the transition to a lower rate of debt growth could pass off without serious damage.

3. Finally, however, there is the possibility that debt may continue for a time to mount furiously, until it has reached a level where it has heavily overloaded consumers with fixed debt payments and overexpanded the industries depending on these consumers. Then it could go into an abrupt decline, and if this happened

at a juncture when other critical components of the economy were turning *downward*, the turn in consumer credit would powerfully accelerate a general recession.

THE HEADLONG SPENDERS

Consumer debt, clearly enough, creates worrisome economic problems, and to some theorists it still presents a considerable moral problem. Roger Babson once wrote a book called *The Folly of Installment Buying*, which covered most of the angles, moral and economic. Yet even Mr. Babson admitted that consumer short-term debt is not a theory but a reality, and a durably and quintessentially American reality to boot. As foreign observers from Tocqueville on have noticed, Americans, unlike Europeans, care not so much for money as money as for what money will buy them; and unlike Europeans they exhibit, in the words of Emerson, an "uncalculated, headlong expenditure." This has made them the world's greatest consumers; it has helped make the American market the most expansive and dynamic the world has even seen.

The American genius for consumption has also made Americans the world's most ardent debtors. But consumer debt in the U.S. is not confined to people who have spent their whole income in agreeable consumption and then find themselves strapped for cash in a sudden emergency. Indeed, the distinguishing mark of American consumer debt is that it carries no broad connotations of emergency or of irresponsibility: it is a respectable arrangement by which many millions of people live, for considerable periods of time, "beyond their means." Because automobiles and the other consumer durables that serve and embellish the U.S. living standard are expensive, and call for what might be called a capital outlay, a large majority of Americans have let others finance these goods for them.

It is sometimes argued, indeed, that since World War II, installment debt, incurred as it has been in large measure by young couples with children, has offset the savings of the older and more affluent, and so helped prevent a recession. Whether it did or not, there are certainly sound reasons why consumer debt can rise at a somewhat faster rate than the nation's real income without seriously imbalancing the economy. Durables like automatic laundries, and appliances have almost eliminated part-time help, autos have cut down carfare; time payments on these durables thus replace some of the operating expenses of former days. What is more important, the low-income groups are constantly graduating into the middle-income groups, whose consumption of expensive durables is high. This movement in itself would justify a considerable part of the postwar growth in consumer debt.

However beneficent some of the past effects of consumer debt, and however plausible the justifications for some of the recent increase, the fact remains that the recent rate of increase is too high to be sustained indefinitely. Inevitably there will come a time when the economy must be deprived of the extraordinary stimulus it got from the soaring growth of debt in the past.

WHEN REPAYMENTS CATCH UP

An excellent short-term example of what happens when consumer debt expands too fast is afforded by what is happening in the U.S. right now. Last year American consumers, mainly because they bought (mostly on easy credit) two million more cars than they bought in 1954, increased their debt outstanding by $6 billion—from $30 billion to $36 billion—and thus added $6 billion to the economy's buying power.

But debt, alas, must be repaid, and short-term debt soon. Repayments are rising and will continue to rise. In part because of the unprecedented credit expansion last year, auto sales are declining this year by one million or more units, and debt incurred is, of course, declining with them. At the same time, repayments are advancing sharply and catching up with new debt, and savings—since short-term debt repayments *are* a form of savings—are rising too. Thus consumer debt outstanding will increase little, if at all, in 1956, and this will deprive the economy of a whopping $6 billion worth of buying power it had in 1955. As *Fortune's* Roundup has shown, this reduction will be a major factor in bringing about a slight contraction in total business activity this year. Were this reduction not offset by expanding factors like the boom in capital goods, it would exert a much more serious and depressing effect.

What concerns us here, however, is not merely the current fluctuation in debt but its long-term trend, which has been steadily and sharply upward. As the chart on page 72 shows, consumer short-term debt has been increasing somewhat faster than the nation's disposable income over the whole period since 1923, when detailed figures were first available. But during the past ten years, while disposable income rose at an average of 6 per cent a year, consumer debt rose at an average of *20* per cent a year. That is why President Eisenhower's recent Economic Report expressed anxiety about consumer debt, and suggested a congressional study of consumer credit controls. That is why all sophisticated economists, and many responsible bankers and businessmen, particularly those with accurate knowledge of the 1920's, are disturbed. The tendency to abuse consumer credit in boom times, as Allan Sproul, president of the Federal Reserve Bank of New York, recently warned, "is a process that cannot go on indefinitely. There will come a time when repayment of old debt will catch up with new extensions of credit."

When credit goes on a real binge, too many millions of dollars worth of assets are put into production, too many thousands of people are employed, and too many billions of dollars worth of sales are generated, so to speak, ahead of time. Every extreme acceleration breeds an opposite if not equal deceleration. When the binge tapers off, as taper off it must, so do sales, employment, and asset use, with their deceleration intensified by debt repayment. A mere decline in the rate of debt *increase* can, as a matter of fact, result in an actual *decline* in production.

CREDIT CRAZY

The bald, unadorned figures of consumer-credit expansion smell of a credit binge. The number of U.S. spending units—families and individuals living alone—

has increased from 51,200,000 in 1948* to nearly 55 million today, or by 7 per cent. But the total number of debtors has risen 65 per cent, increasing from 22 million in 1948 to more than 36 million. More than two-thirds of all spending units are now burdened with short-term debt. Their total debt has much more than doubled, increasing from $14.4 billion in 1948 to $36 billion, with $6 billion of the increase occurring in 1955 alone. All Americans today may be divided into two parts—a declining minority that owes no installment debt and whose liquid assets are rising steeply, and a large and growing majority whose debt is increasing and whose liquid assets are, on the average, actually declining.

And the human trends behind the figures suggest even more strongly a credit binge. During World War II, rationing and high incomes not only generated extraordinarily high savings but caused consumer short-term debt to drop from 11.5 per cent of disposable money income (in 1940, the high till then) to 3.7 per cent in 1944, the lowest level since records were kept. Despite the vast accumulation of savings, however, debt, as a percentage of disposable income, began to rise at a precipitous rate almost as soon as the war ended. Then as now, the evidence shows, the rise was led by young, middle-income couples with children— the returned G.I.'s and other families in the vanguard of the great migration to the suburbs.

They and many others like them fell into installment debt in a natural, almost a routine, fashion. Dept no longer bore the cachet of irresponsibility and poverty. Great sales organizations and consumer-finance companies, ensconced in buildings as reassuring as the Federal Reserve and directed by men resembling loan sharks no more than bishops resemble loan sharks, were underwriting or directly extending credit to consumers. The most stately banks, having wised up to the profits in consumer credit, were condescending to fill the fiscal wants of the common man.

As the prosperous years rolled on, there seemed little necessity to get out of debt. Pension plans, social security, health insurance, and the spreading belief that the government could be depended on never to let another depression occur—all these seemed to eliminate the need for much net balance. So more and more consumers, possessed by a kind of mass compulsion to lose not a month in living up to a community standard, found it easy to regard short-term debt as corporate managers regard it—as a way of acquiring capital goods whose immediate use is worth more to them than the carrying charges.

The fact is that the $28 billion in installment debt this year will cost consumers more than $4 billion in carrying and interest charges, or about 16 per cent on the balance over the year. This is a big price for lower and middle-income groups to pay for the luxury of postponing the reckoning a little.

* The year 1948 is a good point of departure because the postwar increases in consumer debt prior to 1948 might be considered merely a recovery from the freakishly low level of debt that prevailed at the end of the war.

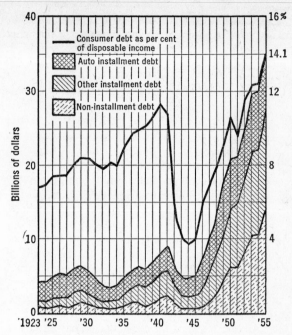

TOTAL CONSUMER DEBT OUTSTANDING

For ten years, while the nation's disposable income has been rising at an average rate of 6 per cent a year, consumer short-term debt has been rising at an average of 20 per cent a year. From a wartime low of 3.7 per cent of disposable income, it increased to 14.1 per cent, against a prewar high of 11.5 per cent.

MORTGAGE ON WHEELS

Now let us examine in more detail the kind of debt U.S. consumers have taken on, and see how loaded up they are. Only 23 per cent of the $36 billion outstanding is non-installment debt, such as charge accounts, doctor and hospital bills, and single-payment loans. Non-installment debt has been growing only moderately fast, rising from $3.2 billion at the end of 1945 to $5.4 billion at the end of 1948 and to $8.3 billion at the end of 1955.

The bulk of the increase in consumer debt is accounted for by installment debt, which has risen from an abnormally low figure of $2.5 billion at the end of 1945 to $9 billion at the end of 1948, and to no less than $28 billion at the end of 1955. The major factor in the rise, accounting for over half the debt outstanding and nearly half the debtors today, is the automobile.

BORROWING FROM THE FUTURE

Automobile paper outstanding has risen from $455 million at the end of 1945 to $3.1 billion at the end of 1948 and to no less than $14.3 billion at the end of 1955 (or 360 per cent since 1948). The proportion of cars bought on time has risen from 40 to more than 70 per cent. Cars alone accounted for nearly $4 billion of 1955's $6-billion rise in consumer credit.

Automobile debt is not the only installment debt rising much faster than disposable income. Others have risen from $5.9 billion in 1948 to $13.6 billion, or by 130 per cent. These forms are (1) housing repair and modernization loans, (2) "other consumer paper," and (3) personal loans.

New house *construction* has been and probably will continue to be a mainstay of U.S. prosperity; yet perhaps the most dangerous trend in the New Economy today is an excessive and in many ways alarming rise in residential *mortgage debt*. Measured against all relevant yardsticks of healthy economic growth—the rise in disposable income, in the value of houses, in new construction—mortgage debt is rising too fast. In the eight years between the end of 1945 and the end of 1953, the net rise in mortgage debt—new mortgage debt minus debt repaid—averaged $5.9 billion a year. In 1954 the net rise was *$9.7 billion,* and in 1955 it was no less than *$13 billion,* bringing total nonfarm mortgage debt to $89 billion.

Fortune has previousy demonstrated that consumer short-term debt cannot go on rising at the rate it has been rising recently, and that the inevitable slow-down in its growth could be painful to the economy. The same general observations apply to mortgage debt—but with double force. For its annual net rise in dollars, and hence its impact on the economy, is more than twice as great.*

And this is not the whole story. The paid-up equity in houses, now slightly under $200 billion, should logically be rising, for consumers' incomes have been rising. Actually, however, paid-up equity in U.S. houses has declined by about $5 billion in the past three years. In 1952, average equity per owner reached a high of $8,700; by the end of 1955 it had fallen to $7,800.

Taking everything together, consumers last year obligated themselves to $17.5 billion of new mortgage debt—$8.8 billion on new houses and $8.7 billion on "used" houses. Since, in the aggregate, house owners paid back $4.5 billion on old debt, the net rise in mortgage debt was $13 billion. Not all of this borrowed money went into houses. Owing to the growing practice of borrowing on old houses, five billion dollars or more of "mortgage money" went out elbowing its way into all corners of the economy, demanding everything that money is entitled to—automobiles, appliances, soft goods, entertainment, even stocks on Wall Street. This money helped accelerate prematurely, so to speak, the fortunes of the businesses that sell these goods and services.

In 1928 and 1929 total residential mortgage debt outstanding amounted to 24 per cent of disposable income; in 1945 to 13 per cent; in 1955 to 35 per cent. Housing payments, it is true, provide a more accurate measure of the abnormal growth of mortgage debt because they include rent payments and real-estate taxes, and thus compensate for the fact that mortgage debt, owing to the rising proportion of house owners, tends naturally to grow faster than disposable income. In 1945 annual housing payments amounted to 6 per cent of disposable income; in 1955 they had increased to 9 per cent or by half.

* This article is concerned solely with mortgages on one-to-four-family nonfarm houses.

How Far and How Long?

Borrowing from the future, even at the current rate, can probably keep up for some time—but not indefinitely. In 1955 the net increase in mortgage debt came to 3.4 per cent of the gross national product. Just consider what would happen, by way of extreme example, if that increase were to continue indefinitely to amount to 3.4 per cent of G.N.P.

Since the economy will nearly double by 1975, the net annual rise in mortgage debt, being a constant 3.4 per cent of G.N.P., would nearly double too. (In fact, since mortgage-debt repayments would be increasing rapidly, the total of house mortgages incurred would probably have to triple.) The resultant net new construction would raise the total value of houses from $286 billion today to about $750 billion by 1975. Mortgage debt outstanding—now $89 billion—would rise to $250 billion by 1965 and $500 billion by 1975 —or from 31 per cent of the value of all houses today to 55 per cent in 1965 and to about 66 per cent in 1975. Mortgaged houses, which now account for $180 billion of all housing value, would account for $380 billion in 1965, and about $750 billion in 1975—i.e., all houses would be mortgaged.

This *reductio ad absurdum* demonstrates clearly enough that mortgage debt cannot rise indefinitely as it has been rising. It almost certainly can never rise to 66 per cent of the value of all houses.

—Gilbert Burck and Sanford Parker, "The Danger in Mortgage Debt," April, 1956.

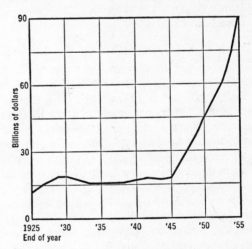

TOTAL NON-FARM MORTGAGE DEBT OUTSTANDING
(1 TO 4 FAMILY HOUSES)

The wicked 1920's showed nothing like this. In the five years 1925-29, mortgage debt outstanding increased from $13 billion to $19 billion, or 46 per cent. But in the five years between the end of 1950 and 1955 it increased from $45 billion to $89 billion, or by nearly 100 per cent, with the actual dollar rise accelerating year by year.

Repair and modernization loans have nearly doubled rising from $843 million at the end of 1948 to more than $1.6 billion.

More important is "other consumer paper," which is offered by retail outlets and which has more than doubled, rising from a little less than $2.8 billion at the end of 1948 to about $6.4 billion. Among the most significant developments in this category is the growth of retail interest-bearing credit in department stores. Almost the whole department-store industry is now actively pushing interest-bearing debt, and is soft-pedaling charge-account debt.

Other retail outlets are in the act. In 1928 less than 5 per cent of Sears, Roebuck's retail sales volume was made on time; in 1941 the percentage was 28; today it is 41—on $3.5 billion of sales. How much net is derived from installment-interest charges Sears does not say.

One of the hottest "innovations" (though apparently it dates back to 1935) is the interest-bearing charge account known as the revolving credit account. The store extends, say, a $240 line of credit to a customer, who obligates himself to pay $20 a month on the outstanding balance, plus a "service charge" of 1 to 1.5 per cent a month. Canny operators describe the plan as chiefly a device to increase sales, but candid ones admit that the interest charge is a juicy source of profit. The scheme has put soft goods on the installment plan in a big way.

Finally, among the major forms of installment debt, there are personal cash loans, which have increased from $2.2 billion at the end of 1948 to $5.5 billion, or by 150 per cent. About 40 per cent of the loans are made by small-loan or "consumer-finance" companies, more than a third by banks, and the rest by credit unions and others. In the thirty-eight states where small-loan companies are supervised, they have some ten million borrowers.

"THE VALLEY OF DEBT"

Whether or not many consumers are, technically speaking, "pyramiding," the evidence mounts that they have begun to pile debt on debt to a significant degree. Many, having got extended terms from auto dealers, are taking advantage of the lower monthly payments to go in hock for appliances or furniture, or to buy soft goods on revolving credit. As a matter of fact, some seem to be borrowing cash to make down or time payments on expensive durables like autos.

That more and more people are having trouble with repayments is argued by the spectacular rise of some 300-odd credit-counseling companies, which help debtors get themselves straightened out, for a good fee. Some counselors are shady operators, under the interdiction of Chambers of Commerce and Better Business Bureaus, but some appear to be honest and functional; and good or not so good, so many could not exist if a growing body of debtors were not in trouble.

The largest debt-consulting company, before it got into trouble, was New York's two-year-old Silver Shield, which, for a fee of 15 per cent of a "hopelessly" indebted man's outstanding debt, helped him to escape from his "Valley of Debt." Silver Shield's average client owed money to no fewer than ten creditors, and some owed to as many as forty-five. This astounding

circumstance is explained by the fact that banks and loan companies do not exchange information because they don't want to reveal the names of their customers to competitors, and by the fact that most application forms have little space under the item "other creditors." "And what's a guy going to do when he sees that?" asks one heavily hocked debtor. "Ask for another form?"

NOT ENOUGH NON-DEBTORS

Such are the dimensions and the most significant characteristics of the huge increase in short-term consumer debt in the past seven years. Why, to come to the most critical question of all, can't it go on increasing this way?

Installment debt has, as we have seen, risen from $9 billion in 1948 to nearly $28 billion. Auto paper has risen much more sharply than other installment debt, from $3.1 billion to $14.3 billion. Thus installment debt outstanding has grown from 5 per cent of consumers' disposable money income in 1948 to 10.9 per cent in 1955. If this rate of increase were to continue another seven years, installment debt outstanding would have to rise to about 17 per cent of disposable income in 1962. How it can is hard to see.

For the rise in total installment debt was a compound of two factors: (1) the number of installment debtors increased from 19 million in 1948 to 35 million in 1955, or by 85 per cent; and (2) average debt per debtor rose from $475 to $800.

First of all, the *number* of debtors cannot rise over the next seven years as it has over the past seven. The proportion of debtors is already extremely high precisely at the income levels that would have to account for any future increase: 78 per cent at the $3,500 level, 81 per cent at the $4,500 level, 76 per cent at the $6,000 level—an average of close to 80 per cent, compared to about 48 per cent in 1948.

For all practical purposes, these percentages are pushing their limits. There are, and always will be, some people even at these income levels who don't have to incur installment debt and don't want to. And there is little chance that the non-debtors in either the lowest or top income groups will join the army of debtors in sufficient numbers to swell the ranks very much. The former can't afford to, and in the upper-income group, which accounts for most of the non-debtors, people are growing steadily more liquid.

But let us extravagantly assume that the proportion of debtors in the middle-income groups can rise from 80 to 90 per cent, and so generate four million more debtors by 1962. There will also be four million more spending units seven years from now than there are today, and perhaps 2,500,000 of them can be expected to go in debt. And because more families will be moving up from the low-debt-low-income brackets, perhaps 1,500,000 additional debtors will come into being. This adds up to eight million more debtors—a rise in the next seven years of at most 23 per cent, against an 85 per cent rise in the past seven.

A NATION OF FIFTY-PERCENTERS?

Which leaves only one way the past rate of debt growth could be sustained: installment debt *per debtor* must increase much faster than it has increased in the past seven years. This would put an intolerable burden on consumers. Let us look, for example, at what would have to happen to the spending units in the $3,000 to $7,500 groups, which would have to account for most of the rise. The average debt outstanding in these groups is nearly 15 per cent of the debtor's disposable money income. If the national consumer debt is to go on rising as it has been, his indebtedness would have to increase to more than 20 per cent of his disposable income. Can he elevate his debt this much?

The only way to tell is to look at the average consumer's obligations. The nation now funnels 30 per cent of its disposable money income into fixed payments—13 per cent on installment payments and the other 17 per cent on other fixed housing payments. The debtors in the $3,000 to $7,500 groups, however, spend on the average 40 per cent of their disposable income on fixed payments—17 per cent on installment payments and 23 per cent on other fixed payments. And no fewer than 25 per cent of these middle-income debtors spend more than 50 per cent of their disposable income on fixed payments—more than 20 per cent on installment payments and the rest on other fixed payments. Since these spend another 25 per cent of their budget on food, they obviously are carrying all the fixed payments they can.

If, then, the debtors in these middle groups were to increase their installment debt outstanding to more than 20 per cent of their disposable income, they would have to funnel fully 23 per cent of their disposable income into installment payments. That is, nearly all debtors in these middle groups would be funneling 50 per cent of their disposable income into fixed payments.

For all practical purposes, debt probably will have reached its peak long before fixed payments rise this high. Debt growth, in short, will almost certainly turn down before seven years are up.

DETERIORATED ASSETS

The distortion of consumer budgets by debt pretty well disposes of the frequently advanced argument that debt can be expanded because debtors' short-term asset position has improved greatly—that the $30-odd billion worth of cars and other durables they own has offset their debt rise.

Actually, the short-term asset position of debtors (liquid plus durable assets minus debt) has not kept pace with their incomes, which have risen 31 per cent since 1948. It has not only failed to keep pace, it has apparently declined a little. For in their optimism, debtors have let their liquid-asset position deteriorate markedly. The average debtor's per capita liquid assets have declined from $1,800 in 1948 to about $1,600 in 1955, even while his debt per capita was rising from $475 to nearly $800. These figures, moreover, tend to overstate debtors' liquidity because their asset figure is swollen by the circumstance that some people with high liquid assets do occasionally buy something on time.

What will happen to the economy in dollars of purchasing power can be estimated roughly. If installment debt were to rise at the rate it has been rising over the past seven years, it would, as we have seen, increase from its present 10.9 per cent of disposable income, or

$28 billion, to nearly 17 per cent of an enlarged disposable income, or about $56 billion. But this, as we have also seen, is a virtual impossibility. A reasonable figure, *Fortune* estimates (from the long-term growth in debt-income ratio), is about $42 billion. In the next seven years, in other words, installment debt should rise no more than an average of $2 billion a year, or $2 billion a year less than if it continued to rise at its recent rate. And the economy will get a proportionately smaller stimulus from the rise than it got in the past seven years.

This letdown obviously presents no great problem if the debt growth tapers off gradually. And even if it slows down erratically, to repeat, the pain may well be confined to a few industries like automobiles and appliances. The rest of the economy, if other industries are expanding, may hardly notice it.

BINGE'S END

But the habit of taking on more debt is one of the economic forces that do not readily slow down of their own accord, and it would be naive to underestimate the possibility that debt could continue to mount precipitously in 1957 and 1958. Relaxation of terms has not yet reached its theoretical outer limits. More and more consumers, prodded by their endless wants as well as by easier terms, could postpone maturities further and further, push the average indebtedness closer to the maximum, and finally hock themselves to capacity to consolidate their debts. All of a sudden, so to speak, the day would come when a significant body of debtors would find themselves boxed in by their own fixed payments, unable to respond to the lure of relaxed terms—indeed to any lures. The credit binge would end, and industries depending on it would be hard hit.

What would happen then, once again, would depend on the rest of the economy. If house construction, the capital-goods industry, commercial construction, and others were starting or already in the throes of a readjustment of their own, a general recession would be hard to avoid. If, on the other hand, other industries were rising, the drop would be well cushioned.

As for government's role, the rate of debt increase is now beginning to slow down, and there is no case for any immediate action; tightening credit terms right now, indeed, would be just what the economy doesn't need. If, on the other hand, debt should pick up and take off again in 1957, some kind of braking action might be necessary. Meantime, as the President's Economic Report has recommended, both Congress and the Council of Economic Advisers would do well to keep watch on the nation's phenomenal urge to borrow.

Data for this article were prepared under FORTUNE's *direction by Alan Greenspan of Townsend-Greenspan & Co. Basic aggregate credit data before 1929 came from a variety of sources, since 1929 from Federal Reserve Board. Postwar distribution of aggregates from data collected by University of Michigan's Survey Research Center; prewar distribution from data by BLS and Department of Agriculture. Fixed payments aggregates from data of Federal Reserve, Department of Commerce, Institute of Life Insurance, etc.; distribution of fixed payments from data of the Survey Research Center.*

THE DYNAMIC MARKET FOR CAPITAL GOODS*

By GILBERT BURCK AND SANFORD PARKER

Investment in capital goods is the key to the nation's economic destiny. Capital goods play an economic role completely out of proportion to their dollar volume—although that is not small, totaling about $37 billion a year. The wide fluctuation in the sales of capital goods inspired J. M. Clark's "acceleration principle," which has a prominent place in most business-cycle theories. This article examines the critical issue: Can and will sales of capital goods expand at the rate they must expand if the economy itself is to expand? The answer introduces the question of the proper balancing of saving and investment. Finally, the prospects of stabilizing investment are explored.

The best economic news in years is that the often-predicted and much-feared post-Korean slump in capital goods has failed to materialize, and that the capital-goods market appears to be expanding once more. This good omen, which has gone practically unnoticed in all the jubilation about the current improvement in general business conditions, contains the real key to the national economic destiny. Let only this trend strengthen, and the nation's growth and prosperity automatically and quickly gain strength. But let the trend begin to disintegrate, and the nation's economic health begins to disintegrate.

The trend is turning up despite the fact that American business has spent no less than $300 billion on capital goods in the nine years since World War II, and despite the fact that a lot of worriers, professional and amateur, have shaken their heads and argued that each billion already spent is one more reason why capital-goods purchases must soon decline. The probability is, however, that capital-goods spending over the next five years will at worst average no less than the near-record $36 billion of 1954, and it may rise as much as a third higher. Between now and 1959, the U.S. will probably spend around $200 billion on capital goods. This is a truly stupendous prospect.

There are three reasons why the behavior of the capital-goods market is of surpassing importance:

1. Capital goods are the "procreative property" of industrial society—the manufactured goods whose sole function is to produce and distribute other goods and services—and as such they are basically responsible for rising productivity and national wealth. The chief economic difference between primitive and civilized man lies in civilized man's facility in creating and using capital goods. A nation must learn to create and increase a stock of those goods if it wants to progress; a nation that fails to replace or increase its stock begins automatically to retrogress.

2. Capital goods in themselves constitute a sizable and important part of the U.S. economy; last year their sales came to $37 billion—more than the factory value of all new cars, new homes, and other durable goods for consumers taken together.** They include the innumerable machines, buildings, and equipment that make, process, transport, and display the nation's goods and services; and the five million people who make them are scattered over nearly every industrial area of consequence.

Tick off a few of the important capital goods and you are soon calling the roll of America's oldest and newest factory towns—the locomotives, forgings, and transformers of the great Delaware Valley industrial complex; the machine tools of Bridgeport, Connecticut, and Cincinnati; the turbines and generators of Schenectady, New York, and Lynn, Massachusetts; the pumps and irrigation machines of Alhambra, California; the hoists and cranes of Portland, Oregon; the locomotives of La Grange, Illinois; the air-conditioning machinery of Decatur, Alabama; the office machinery of Endicott, New York, and Oakland, California; the trucks and buses of Flint; the mill equipment of Birmingham; the earth-moving machinery of Milwaukee, Cleveland, and Peoria.

3. This is indeed a lot, but this is not all. What is vastly more important, capital goods play an economic role all out of proportion to their dollar volume. For they not only *exaggerate* but *accelerate* and sometimes lead the pace of the economy as a whole. When business in general falls off, the capital-goods business tends to decline much more and thus to intensify the general decline; when business in general advances, the capital-goods business tends to race ahead of it and thus to intensify the general rise.

Economists of such widely varying stripe as Karl Marx, Wesley Mitchell, and John Maynard Keynes have agreed that this eccentricity of the capital-goods market is a critical factor in business cycles, and their theories about it in the main differ only as to why and how the tendency occurs. Some economists have built whole theories of the business cycle on the concept of the "acceleration principle," originated by Columbia's J. M. Clark. This principle says capital-goods buying is affected merely by the *rate* of change in national output—i.e., even if national output is growing, a decline in the rate of its growth will result in a decline in the volume of capital spending.

Fully formulated in all their intricate and prolix splendor, the theories based on the "acceleration prin-

---

*From Gilbert Burck and Sanford Parker, "The Dynamic Market for Capital Goods," September, 1954.

** Capital goods as defined in this article include only business expenditures on plant and equipment—no government armaments, roads, or other public works; no personal-consumption spending even on autos or other durables.

ciple" probably try to cover too much ground, but there is no doubt about the two assumptions on which they rest: not only does capital-goods volume accelerate the swings of the economy as a whole by fluctuating more than the economy as a whole, but the total stock of capital goods cannot increase faster than consumption very long before a general decline sets in. History, indeed, has put its cachet on these two assumptions. Capital-goods buying fell much more than general business in the panic of 1907, the recession of 1921, and in the great depression of the 1930's. In doing so, it intensified all those declines.

It is no wonder that the state of the capital-goods market became a prime subject for the "postwar planning" movement that gathered way a dozen years ago, even when World War II was at its very height; no wonder that the age-old notion of "stabilizing" business investment has caught the imaginations of businessmen as well as economists since the war. The subject has been explored by, among others, the Committee for Economic Development, the National Association of Manufacturers, and the U.S. Chamber of Commerce. And in 1951 even the academic, conservative National Bureau of Economic Research organized a conference on how to even out business investment, and it has bound the essays and papers delivered at the conference into an imposing volume entitled *The Regularization of Business Investment.*

Business certainly has worried and is worrying about the capital-goods "situation." Only recently the rail-equipment industry, alarmed by the decline in railroad spending, which had anticipated and reflected the decline in railroad net income, organized a committee to do something about the inability or unwillingness of the railroads to maintain their capital-equipment purchases.

THE NECESSARY 93 PER CENT

So let us consider the outlook for sales of capital goods during the next five years. Can and will they expand at the rate they must expand if the economy itself is to expand? Arthur F. Burns, Chairman of President Eisenhower's Council of Economic Advisers, has remarked that the U.S. can and should advance its gross national product from the current level of about $360 billion to $440 billion in 1959. Last month, in the concluding article of its year-long series on the changing consumer-goods market, *Fortune* estimated that a $440-billion G.N.P. would yield a consumer cash income, after taxes, of nearly $280 billion—which, however, would depend on consumers' spending of about $265 billion, or about 93 per cent of their cash income. If capital goods claimed exactly the same share of the G.N.P. in 1959 as in 1953, they would amount to nearly $45 billion, or 25 per cent more than the $36 billion of 1954.

Whether capital-goods spending will increase that much depends, at bottom, on whether consumption keeps reasonably close to its potential growth. At this point the argument may sound like double talk. If consumer buying depends on capital-goods buying, and

capital-goods buying depends on consumer buying, which depends on which the more? This gets us into the classic hen-egg argument about business cycles. Let us therefore refine the proposition: the capital-goods business, in the long run, cannot prosper without a consumer market strong enough to keep the nation's capacity busy. High consumption, in turn, depends on a high level of consumer income and a low level of consumer saving. Thus "oversaving" could have a very depressing effect on capital-goods spending and consumption in the next few years—as it probably did in the 1920's.

ORDERS ARE UP

Well, are people likely to "oversave" in the next few years? As *Fortune* pointed out last month, people whose income is rising tend to save a very large part of the increment over the short term; but this tendency is offset, at one point or another, by a long-range tendency to spend a larger *percentage* of their income. And the prospects for specific markets, added up last month, make the chances reasonably good that the long-term trend will assert itself sufficiently to keep spending comfortably close to 93 per cent of consumer cash income, as it should if the economy is to be balanced at a high level of activity. This conclusion, of course, assumes that labor will continue to demand and get its share of rising income. It also assumes that business will take a more dynamic view of its prospects than it did in the 1920's, when it all too often preferred the "certainties" of fixed prices and a more or less stationary market to the "hazards" of an expanding market. Nothing can be more hazardous, in a nation whose productivity is rising as fast as America's is rising, than for business to set a stable, "fixed" market as its goal.

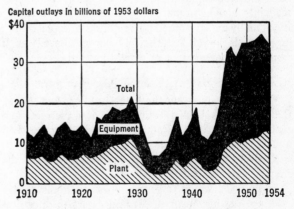

Capital outlays in billions of 1953 dollars

OUTLAYS ARE RISING OVER THE LONG RUN

Save in depression and war years, capital outlays (expressed in constant 1953 dollars) have shown a steady growth; shortly after World War II they again achieved the growth trend they achieved before 1930. Note the rising preponderance of equipment: this occurs partly because plant lasts longer than equipment, partly because technological progress renders equipment obsolete faster than plant, partly because highly productive modern machinery may take less space.

The signs for capital-goods buying, so far, are good. Capital-goods spending in 1954 will very nearly match that of 1953. Orders are up, and producers say they will start to increase output late this year or early next.

It may be that too much of this new capital investment is accounted for by a relatively small number of big companies whose needs will soon be satisfied, and that capital investment therefore will soon reach a peak and then turn down abruptly, instead of continuing on to new highs. Or, what is more hopeful, it may be that many companies, goaded by rising labor costs and new technology, are increasing their investment primarily to become more efficient. Or it may just be that business as a whole is confident the consumer market will expand, and is getting ready to serve that market, both by expanding and by improving plant and equipment. All these make sense today. Future articles in this series will explore their relative importance in examining the markets, industry by industry.

But here let us size up the weaknesses and strengths of the market *as a whole*—assuming that U.S. consumption will expand as it must expand to realize a $440-billion gross national product in 1959.

Fair warning: long-range data on the stock of capital goods have been accumulated only recently; the data are crude, and the techniques for analyzing them relatively undeveloped. Moreover, aggregate figures may conceal significant developments in certain sectors of the economy. The projections, therefore, should be regarded largely as guides to thinking about the market as a whole.

Now, capital goods are usually divided into two main classes: those purchased as replacement of existing stock, and those purchased to expand capacity. The line between the two is vague and wavering; nearly every replacement, in this day of rapid technical progress, involves some addition to capacity; and many machines bought primarily for an expansion of capacity actually replace others. The notion of replacement, however, is a valid statistical concept, based, as it were, on the death rate of capital goods.

REPLACEMENTS ARE RISING

The most significant and encouraging fact about the projections is that retirements and therefore the replacement need of capital goods are rising and will almost inevitably continue to rise:

Replacements are necessarily growing because the stock of capital goods is constantly growing.

Equipment, which is shorter lived than plant, has been accounting for a steadily larger portion of capital outlays.

Specifically, much of our postwar capital goods— largely equipment—is now already growing old or obsolete. By 1959, 28 per cent of equipment produced between 1946 and 1950 and 9 per cent of that produced between 1951 and 1953 will have worn out.

It is true that the existing stock of capital goods may be larger than indicated; the survival curves are based on U.S. Treasury estimates of useful life, and much equipment lasts longer than the Treasury as-

sumes. All in all, however, replacements can be expected to amount to $23 billion in 1959—up from $18.2 billion in 1954, $17.4 billion in 1953, and $15 billion in 1950.

What will happen to the sales of capital goods bought for expansion is a harder question to answer. National economic growth obviously must be accompanied by a growth in capital stock. But how much growth?

The record since 1929 is puzzling. The U.S. did not add much to its capital stock in the 1930's, and added little more than needed for munitions in the 1940's. Yet wartime production increased enormously, and the ratio of capital stock to output—the "capital-output" ratio—consequently declined greatly. Business apparently had on hand much equipment and plant that did not show up in the statistics because it had passed the retirement age. Plant and equipment, of course, were utilized beyond normal capacity. The expansion of the stock of capital goods since World War II has occurred at a rate 50 per cent faster than the historical rate.

A dollar's worth of new equipment, moreover, can sometimes (though not always) be so much more productive than a dollar's worth of old equipment that it now takes less money to buy a unit of new capacity than it did several years ago. And there is a tendency to install new equipment without building new plant, thus reducing the capital-output ratio.

Yet again, there is evidence that capital investment in manufacturing has outstripped output. According to a series of calculations by Charles F. Roos of the Econometric Institute (and used with permission of the institute), the margin of unused capacity over output in mining and manufacturing, which was about 15 per cent in the late 1920's and only half that much after the war, rose to 15 per cent again a year ago and is now fully 25 per cent.

BUT EXPANSION MAY NOT BE

What does all this mean for 1959? If the capital-output ratio should resume the downtrend that occurred after 1929, the 1959 outlay for expansion would at worst be $13 billion, against $19.5 billion in 1953 and $17 billion this year. This is unlikely because much of the "excess" factory capacity is old and many non-manufacturing businesses in the U.S. still seem "undercapitalized." If, on the other hand, capital stock maintains its unusually rapid postwar growth rate, capital outlays for expansion would come to all of $25 billion in 1959—which also is unlikely. The middle or probable projection is that business in 1959 will buy $19 billion worth of capital goods for expansion. This would correspond to the over-all historic rate in the growth of U.S. capital stock, and it would probably also allow for less strain on capacity in 1959 than in 1953.

Add to each of these projections the $23-billion replacement figure, and the total capital-goods projections for 1959 are as follows:

Low projection: $36 billion
High projection: $48 billion
Middle or probable projection: $42 billion

So rising purchases of replacements coupled with a leveling in purchases for expansion should result in a steadily rising volume of capital expenditures. This conclusion, however, is subject to two major qualifications, one bearish and one bullish. The bearish qualification has already been mentioned: specific capital-goods markets may vary widely, and must be examined individually for weaknesses not readily apparent now.

The bullish qualification is that the projections are largely based on measurements of past trends, and thus cannot make allowance for the unmeasurable propensity to change that is the distinguishing characteristic of American markets. And never has the capital-goods market been subject to more change—to technical changes producing more efficient and useful capital tools, to operating changes making for more efficient use of those tools, and to changes in corporate buying habits and financial policies making for more efficient replacement and expansion policies. All these can make the middle projection seem conservative.

THE DYNAMICS OF RESEARCH

Probably the most important factor making for change is the growth of American research. In 1941 government and business spent less than $1 billion on research and employed 87,000 research engineers and scientists; last year they spent about $4 billion ($2.8 billion of it accounted for by work performed by industry), and employed 192,000 research engineers and scientists. Thus research expenditures, expressed as a percentage of gross national product, have been growing faster than G.N.P., and now claim 1.1 per cent of it. By 1959 research expenditures, with a $440-billion G.N.P., may come to 1.24 per cent or some $5.5 billion. Big corporations are steadily increasing their expenditures on research. Westinghouse, for example, now spends 5.8 per cent of its sales dollar on it; American Cyanamid 5.3 per cent. Company after company, replying to *Fortune's* survey of capital outlays, reports rising research expenditures.

Some of the impact of research on capital expenditures is obvious enough. Research in productive processes that is well planned and executed creates a need for capital goods over and above the goods that are needed to take care of normal growth and physical obsolescence or replacement. Not so obvious is the fact that research, invention, and innovation have a "multiplier" effect on capital goods use—their very application often calls for large expenditures on "conventional" plant and machinery. The development of instruments for blind flying, for example, stimulated spending on airplanes because it made commercial air travel practical; the atomic-energy installations at Paducah, Kentucky, demanded a tremendous expenditure on ordinary power equipment.

INNOVATORS AND IMITATORS

Moreover, the bulk of American research is devoted to the application of basic inventions to immediate use. As the economist Joseph Schumpeter made so clear, sheer invention plays a minor role in capital investment. What counts is the innovators—the men who adapt the inventions and make the "new combinations" —and their imitators. Without pure or basic research, of course, no economy can advance. But an economy can also do a lot of brilliant and original basic research without getting very far. It is in innovating and adapting that American superiority is so pronounced. And the time required to make a wide-spread application of an innovation is steadily declining.

Andrew Jackson Higgins, the late New Orleans boat builder, used to build speedy river craft that he sold both to revenue agents and to moonshiners. When he turned out a new model, he sold it to, say, the revenuers, and as soon as he sold that model he developed a still better and faster model and sold it to the moonshiners, and so on. His changes came rapidly, and he sold his boats rapidly. "What I practiced," he said, "was progressive obsolescence." The dynamics of research today are such that a research-minded capital-goods manufacturer finds himself automatically practicing progressive obsolescence.

Finally, the immediate outlook is reinforced by what Dr. Irving H. Siegel of the Twentieth Century Fund calls "repressed acceleration of technological change." That is to say, the recent business readjustment or recession has made most companies anxious to increase efficiency. They cannot expect large reductions in basic wage rates, so they want to add to their capacity without adding proportionately to their labor force.

MORE MACHINES, FEWER MEN

And rising labor costs may also make for more capital expenditures than the projections indicate. One of the most significant and least appreciated facts about the American economy as it is now expanding is that, barring the dissolution of labor unions, *the national wage level is bound to keep on rising so long as the nation's productivity rises*. This puts every company on the spot. With basic wage rates essentially beyond its control, a company can keep its labor costs in line and maintain its competitive position only by improving productivity. And that means it must not only use more machines but create new machines, or new combinations of old machines, to do jobs formerly done by men.

The argument is sometimes advanced that rising labor costs also push up the cost of machines, and for a company that is using capital goods to full advantage, seriously reduce the advantage of new machines. But capital-goods prices are notoriously sticky; they fluctuate less than direct labor costs. And they are still relatively low. Labor costs rose twice as fast as capital-goods costs between 1941 and 1947, and although capital-goods costs have been rising faster since 1947, they are still "cheaper," relatively speaking, than labor— up 85 per cent from prewar, against the 130 per cent increase in manufacturing labor costs. At all events, the majority of corporations replying to *Fortune's* survey report that they find more opportunities to save labor costs now than in 1939-41, or even in 1947-48.

DEPRECIATION FINANCING

The financing of capital goods, assuming no recession or war, should become progressively easier. The main reason it should become easier is that depreciation charges have been increasing swiftly and greatly —owing not only to accelerated depreciation but to the growing stock of capital goods plus the growing part of that stock accounted for by high-priced equipment. In 1947 and 1948 corporate depreciation charges came to about $6 billion, or about one-third of corporate capital outlays, with retained profits accounting for about 50 per cent and new issues about 20 per cent. Today corporate depreciation charges are $15 billion, or about half of all corporate outlays, and retained earnings account for about 30 per cent. By 1959 corporate depreciation charges should amount to nearly $20 billion, or considerably more than half of all corporate outlays (which represent some 80 per cent of all business' capital outlays).

Now some experts hold that neither depreciation money nor the ability to raise outside money is a major factor in determining the level of capital outlay; profitability, they say, comes first. But the fact is that most small companies regard and always have regarded financing as a limitation on investment because they don't want to commit themselves to "outside" debt. And large companies are becoming less concerned with financing problems precisely because depreciation charges are growing so large.

What is more, the new tax law liberalizes depreciation practices for new investment somewhat. It gives a company the choice of four methods, including a broadened version of the declining-balance method, which, unlike the straight-line method, applies the depreciation rate not to the full original cost but to the unamortized balance, and allows a company to write off two-thirds of the cost of an asset in the first half of its life.

THE KEY IS RISK

The relatively small decline in capital expenditures this year—only 4 per cent against an 8 per cent decline in industrial production—suggests that capital-outlays are becoming less volatile, at least over the short run. One reason may be that large corporations are taking a strategic, long-term view of their capital needs—or at any rate, a longer view than they did before the war.

Corporate methods of deciding on capital expenditures vary greatly from industry to industry and company to company. But in general they are still described by economists and management consultants as vague, irrational, inconsistent, and unscientific, with too much emphasis on short "payoff" periods. Even companies that confess to a methodology often end up by making highly *ad hoc* judgments. Machinery salesmen, for example, report that some customers, despite clearly demonstrable saving with a new machine, refuse to scrap an old one because "it has not yet been written off." Others refuse to replace a machine because it has been written off and "isn't costing us anything." The conclusion seems obvious: let companies adopt better methods of deciding on capital outlays, let them try to "regularize" those outlays, and both they and the economy as a whole will benefit.

But it isn't so easy as all that. That the buying habits of great, well-heeled companies seem more fickle and irregular than the spending habits of the most untutored consumer is not a hard paradox to resolve. The key to the paradox is risk. Plant and equipment outlays are definitely if not infinitely postponable. Just as a consumer postpones the purchase of a new car if his prospects are bad, so a company postpones the purchase of capital equipment if its prospects are bad. Even if the company has the money it cannot be sure the investment will pay off. The equipment may be obsolete by the time it can be employed profitably, or the market may have changed. Even if the equipment is bought at a bargain price, therefore, it may turn out to be a poor bargain.

And so with spending in boom times. No company is going to postpone spending if postponing it means a loss of competitive position. "The causes of cyclical fluctuations in investment are deep-rooted and inescapable," says management consultant Joel Dean, who specializes in capital expenditures. "The shifts in the firm's schedule of demand for and supply of funds dictate a pattern of investment. Departures from this pattern for the purpose of stabilizing capital expenditures will result in gains that are relatively small and dubious as compared with the ensuing large and certain cost and risks."

But many other economists, while agreeing that completely uniform capital spending is inconsistent with a dynamic economy whose course is determined by a multitude of independent decisions, believe that a significant number of companies can adopt a long-range approach without taking undue risks.

Melvin G. de Chazeau, of the Cornell University School of Business and Public Administration, consultant to the committee for Economic Development, is a prominent advocate of *noncyclical* planning— "with primary consideration for market conditions and trends rather than for the timing of cycles" because "it becomes increasingly probable that the government would exert the full power of its economic strength to prevent major fluctuations, and there is growing confidence that it would succeed in this objective—thus making major fluctuations that much more avoidable through non-governmental action." Much of business, in other words, can and should behave as if the long term trend of the U.S. economy, which is steadily upward, were the only trend that matters much.

THE "SCIENTIFIC" VIEW

Business as a whole may not yet be ready to adopt noncyclical planning, but the fact remains that it has in one way or another come far toward doing so. Partly because it is sharply aware that it will be blamed for any depression induced by a capital-goods slump, partly because American management is steadily improving all its techniques, many big companies are taking more "scientific" views of capital-goods expenditures.

Nearly half the companies responding to *Fortune's* capital-goods survey, indeed, report that they plan outlays over a longer period now than they did immediately before the war, and about a third plan longer now than they did just six or seven years ago. Long-term planning pays off, they say, because it enables them to budget in advance. It also enables them to have new capacity ready to exploit upsurges in demand.

"No area of management," says George Terborgh, research director of the Machinery and Allied Products Institute, "has advanced so rapidly as the determination of capital expenditures." Terborgh himself has played a large role in that advance by his work on "dynamic equipment policy." Though few corporations have adopted the replacement formula Terborgh developed (many find it too complicated), his views, according to Professor Ross Walker of the Harvard Business School, have had an "explosive impact" on corporate buying practices.

There remains an important consideration: how can regularization and the long-term view be sold to companies that suffer from a violently fluctuating demand for their goods? Take machine-tool manufacturers, who both sell and buy capital goods. They usually have the money to buy only when their own sales are high; and when their sales are high, alas, an inordinately large part of their profit goes for taxes and not for capital expenditures. They find themselves suffering the same injustice as self-employed people like artists, writers, doctors, and other professions. Because their income is concentrated in a few years, they may pay twice the income tax, over say a period of ten years, paid by people whose aggregate incomes are just as great.

The solution, some visionaries believe, is cyclical bookkeeping—that is, the practice of averaging profit-and-loss figures over a period of years rather than striking them annually, somewhat as losses are even now carried over. This would not only encourage feast-or-famine companies to spend more on capital goods, it would give them every incentive to spread their purchases more evenly. However, a long time will surely elapse before such schemes achieve acceptance, and meantime business will have to get along with its present bookkeeping.

But only recently a new spirit of enterprise has arisen among capital-goods manufacturers. Until recently the art and science of selling capital goods, for a large part of the industry, differed little from the art and science of selling those goods fifty years ago. The selling technique of many capital-goods companies, from locomotive to lathe manufacturers, could be summed up in a sentence or two: "We'll sell you anything you want to buy. Have a cigar (or a drink)!"

This attitude seems to be changing. The machine-

tool industry has refurbished old tool-leasing schemes whose purpose is not only to get more new tools into the hands of customers but to sell customers on the advantages of buying the tools. The schemes have been in effect only a few months, but they seem eminently successful and may help reduce the high percentage of old and obsolete machine tools.

The venerable Jones & Lamson Co. of Springfield, Vermont, is not stopping at tool leasing. Its new president is H. L. Andrews, formerly a General Electric executive vice president, and Mr. Andrews is bringing consumer-goods selling tactics and strategy to machine tools. Convinced that most owners of old and obsolete tools don't understand how much they're losing with their old tools, he has set up a marketing department, hired an operations-research man, increased his sales force, and embarked on a campaign to sell the benefits of increased productivity by person-to-person demonstrations and chalk talks.

$200 BILLION IN FIVE YEARS

The outlook, to be sure, is not one of unrelieved optimism. It is possible, to repeat, that an imbalance is building up, and that it may induce a decline in total outlays; the possibility will be taken up in detail in future issues, when specific markets are examined.

On the other hand, there are many unmeasurable forces that can increase the demand for capital goods by 1959 by much more than the "probable" projection suggests. The "multiplier" effect of an expanding technology and of rising labor costs, the easing of financing problems, a new sales-mindedness among capital-goods makers, and above all the gradual adoption of a long-term point of view by business itself—all these amount to a kind of revolution in business' approach to capital goods; and it will be discussed in detail next month. Taking everything together, the outlook for $200 billion worth of new capital goods in the next five years, even after the $300-billion capital outlay of the last nine years, is astonishingly good.

Data for this article is based on the work of George Terborgh, research director of the Machinery and Allied Products Institute. Fortune has modified Mr. Terborgh's data on capital outlays and replacement to include construction of farm buildings other than dwellings, oil drilling, and capital charged to current account. Capital-output and capital-worker ratios for manufacturing are based on data from Daniel Creamer of the National Bureau of Economic Research. Projections and updated estimates for recent years are by Fortune.

WHAT CAUSED THE GREAT DEPRESSION*

By GILBERT BURCK AND CHARLES E. SILBERMAN

The great depression was one of the most important events in all U.S. history. It profoundly changed the nation economically, politically, and socially. Everyone who experienced the depression wonders whether it can happen again—without being too clear on what happened the last time. However, a great deal more is known about what caused the depression than is commonly believed. This article presents the best over-all analyses of that disastrous event. It synthesizes the important theories and facts about the causes of the depression, including new data prepared for Fortune *by Dr. Paul Boschan, expert on national income, as well as material from an unfinished treatise by Professor Robert A. Gordon.*

When General Motors, on January 3, 1955, jumped nine points in a single hour, one small stockholder spoke the minds of many people, shareholders and non-shareholders alike. "In just an hour," he said, "the value of twenty shares went up by $180. Wonderful! But is *it* going to happen again?" By "it," of course, he meant the disaster of 1929, the Eniwetok of all busts, the crash that rocked the very foundations of the Western world. And his question, which Americans had been asking for ten years with slowly declining concern, was now being asked with renewed anxiety.

Yet even the most anxious often have only the sketchiest idea as to what really went wrong in the 1920's. And many have forgotten exactly what a cataclysm 1929 turned out to be. It precipitated America from the greatest decade of material well-being any nation had until then enjoyed into a decade of despond and doubt and frustration such as few nations have ever endured. The great depression, much more severe in the U.S. than in other Western countries, has been described as second only to the Civil War in its effects on the country, but in most ways it was much worse. It split the nation not geographically but mentally. It robbed otherwise rational men of their ability to be rational about economics. It degraded and stultified American capitalism, and turned some of the country's most creative—and also some of its most practical—minds to the facile promises of fascism, technocracy, social credit, socialism, and Communism. It brought despair and even hunger to millions of ordinary people, and planted blind resentment in their hearts. It wasted a total of nearly 200 *billion* man-hours. It did something that no foreign enemy, national disaster, or old-fashioned "panic" had ever done: it paralyzed, for years, American growth.

And just what *did* cause the depression? Was it simply unrestrained stock-market speculation? Or was it some basic, obscure defect in the economy? It is amazing how many well-informed people, well aware of the overwhelming pertinence of the subject today, have only the vaguest and most confused notion of

what actually happened in the Twenties. Their confusion, it is true, is easily pardoned. Nearly all the critical examination of the Twenties was done in the Thirties, when the basic problem was still how to get out of the depression, or in the war years, when the big problem seemed to be to avoid a postwar depression. Although dozens of eminent economists have expounded the reasons for the great depression and although they agree on most basic facts, they disagree considerably on which facts are the most important.

Alvin Hansen, leading American disciple of Lord Keynes, believes that the 1929 debacle was the result of the fact that several major investment booms came to an end at the same time that the economy's "maturity" was resulting in too much saving and in a general decline in investment opportunities. Lionel Robbins of the London School of Economics, however, argues that there was too little "real" saving, and that investment expanded unduly and then collapsed because it was financed by a volatile supply of bank credit rather than by stable saving habits. But Sumner Slichter of Harvard, heading a committee to study the depression, found no shortage of real saving in the 1920's, and argued that the rabid speculation of the day made businessmen fear a stock-market collapse and business recession, and so led them to cut back inventory and capital outlays. And the late Joseph Schumpeter of Vienna and Harvard believed that the transportation and agricultural revolutions fomented by the Fords and McCormicks, like all such waves of innovations, could not sustain themselves indefinitely and were bound to end in depression regardless of the stockmarket boom.

This article tries to synthesize the important theories and facts about the causes of the depression, including new data prepared for *Fortune* by Dr. Paul Boschan, expert on national income, as well as material from a still unfinished treatise on the interwar period by Professor Robert A. Gordon of the University of California. As the second in *Fortune's* Twenty-fifth Anniversary series on the development and direction of the "New Economy," this article also examines the 1920's as the portentous decade whose evolving mass markets prepared the way for today's Great Breakthrough into the new mass markets of the 1950's.

* From Gilbert Burck and Charles E. Silberman, "What Caused the Great Depression," February, 1955.

THE FERMENTING TWENTIES

And what was the matter with the economy of the 1920's? Looked at as a collection of aggregate figures, that economy seemed and still seems a model of stability, a fitting opening for the New Era of perennial, prosperous "normalcy" that Waddill Catchings and other prophets of the Roaring Twenties plausibly thought was just beginning. Early in 1929 the President's Committee on Recent Economic Changes, headed by Herbert Hoover while Commerce Secretary, published in two large volumes what is still the most thorough analysis of the 1920's. Its eminent contributors, not having the advantage of hindsight, could find no grievous defects in the economy.

On the contrary, they were full of enthusiasm for the nation's rising income, growing mass markets, rising productivity, high employment, economic balance, managerial prudence—for many of the very virtues, let us note well, that seem to endow today's economy with so much power and stability. Even that great student of the business cycle, Wesley Mitchell, in a wary, yes-but summary of the committee's analysis, agreed that the stability of employment in a period of great technological advance (and hence technological displacement) was, in the last half of the decade, something to rejoice about. Alas, even the decade's most eminent and careful analysts overestimated the stability of this expanding economy.

Let us define a stable, expanding economy as one whose major components, such as production, consumption, employment, and investment, are advancing in a kind of dynamic harmony. When one of the components advances too fast or fails to advance fast enough, dislocations may occur. The trouble with the 1920's, as things turned out, was that, in the last half of the decade, over-all stability concealed the fact that rising components were offset by declining ones. The balance was precarious because the rising components, being in the last analysis dependent upon the others, could not rise indefinitely.

This cyclical trend downward, which will be discussed in detail later, was neither so great nor so growing that it might not have been reversed as all business cycles hitherto had been reversed—at worst by a classic depression (but certainly not one as bad as that of the 1930's), or at best by a short, mild adjustment. What finally occurred was the most severe depression in history; and it occurred, in the main, because the nation's rational enthusiasm for sharing in the splendid future of American business degenerated into the exuberant excesses of unrestrained stock-market and real-estate inflation, manipulated on a scale never before practiced, and spiraled faster and faster in by people who had let their avarice get the better of their common sense. For the stock-market inflation put a false front of prosperity on the economy, postponed the inevitable reckoning, and converted what might have been a routine recession into a cataclysm.

Some of the dislocations of the 1920's were the result of new products and new processes. Oil began to replace coal, rayon began to compete with cotton. Some of the dislocations were inherited from World War I.

When American agriculture was called on to feed Europe, for example, farm prices doubled and farmland values and mortgage debt shot up. Then in the deflation of 1921 these prices and values fell almost as far as they had advanced, while farm debt increased. Agricultural prices recovered somewhat, but what with excess farm capacity and a declining world market, they turned down again after 1925.

And some of the dislocations of the 1920's were hidden, so to speak, in the very temper of the people. Americans, then as now (and now as a hundred years ago), were dynamic and restless, bursting with ambition and self-assertiveness, casting old habits to the winds, bristling with new ideas and new developments. The U.S. in the 1920's was, indeed, in a state of unusually violent ferment, politically, socially, morally, intellectually, *and* economically. One extreme generated another. No sooner had the country washed its hands of the idealism of World War I and declared allegiance to the ideal of "normalcy" than its new normalcy became a state of continuous abnormalcy. No sooner had it given itself over to the high-minded hypocrisy of prohibition than it proceeded to disregard not only prohibition but a whole inheritance of customs and morals. Its variety and energy enabled it to try everything with unflagging enthusiasm.

Above all, there was the old frontier delight in gambling for big stakes. Partly because people wanted to get rich quick, partly because they were congenitally optimistic, they debauched themselves not only in the Florida land boom but in a dozen other minor booms whose busts did no harm on a national scale. And who would have guessed that the stock-market boom would be different?

SITUATIONS OF STRENGTH

All this zymotic energy was, up to a point, a wonderful thing. Because American productivity or output per man-hour grew at a near-record pace, production expanded much faster than population. Henry Ford, who had raised his production from 19,000 cars in 1909 to 785,000 in 1916, had in his intuitive but immensely impressive way shown how rising productivity means lower prices and higher wages. Thanks to a shortage of workers in World War I, labor had demanded and got a large share of rising productivity, and its real wages had risen 30 per cent between 1914 and 1923. Thus labor both created the beginnings of a mass market and prodded management into higher efficiency. So mass production was the talisman of the day. Machinery output increased 50 per cent between 1923 and 1929—while industrial production itself was rising 25 per cent.

As industries "rationalized" and consolidated, modern salesmanship and advertising bloomed in all their early glory. Mass production was followed by mass distribution—though, as we shall see later, perhaps not soon enough. Chain stores began to spring up, Sears, Roebuck began to build stores in the suburbs.

And so, between 1920 and 1929, industrial production rose 45 per cent, and gross national product 43 per cent, while employment rose only 17 per cent. Unemployment, large by today's standards, showed no increase when expressed as a percentage of the labor force. So the aggregates looked just fine.

To see how the economy really shaped up, let us look closely at the major trends—first at the components that rose steadily throughout the decade and gave it so much stability. For one thing, there were government expenditures (15 per cent on roads), which even in those "unregimented" days were considerable, rising from $6.2 billion in 1920 to $8.2 billion in 1929 (in 1929 dollars). More important were the consumer non-durables and services. Their sales, taken together, rose steadily from $46.5 billion in 1920 to $70.1 billion in 1929, or 50 per cent.

Sales of non-durables alone, in the same period, rose from $25 billion to $37.8 billion or 51 per cent, but consumption of food, which accounts for a major part of non-durable consumption, rose only 27 per cent. Remember that food, in those days, was merchandised as food, more often than not in bulk, and in much plainer and simpler forms than are common today. Out-of-season fruits, precooked and exotic comestibles that are part of every plumber's diet today were then either nonexistent or rarities consumed only by the well-to-do.

The consumption of other non-durables, however, nearly doubled, rising from $9.7 billion in 1920 to $18.3 billion in 1929. Not only did mass markets develop for cigarettes, gasoline, and other "luxuries," the American standard of clothing was rising. As American Woolen Co. was already learning, even workmen wanted something other than blue serge for their Sunday suits. Silk stockings, usually made of fibers from Japan, were astonishingly expensive by today's standard—the cheaper ones cost about $1.50 a pair—but even the poorest high-school girls found it *de rigueur* to clothe their limbs in silk.

Consumer services, which include rent, recreation, utilities, cleaning, public transportation, financial and legal expenses, and so on, did very well, too. Their sales rose from $21.5 billion in 1920 to $32.3 billion in 1929 (in 1929 dollars), or 50 per cent. Here, too, was the beginning of a great new mass market. Consumption of gas and electricity doubled between 1919 and 1929. The number of wired homes increased from 8,700,000 in 1920 to more than 20 million in 1929, while expenditures on telephones more than doubled. And expenditures on personal care nearly doubled between 1920 and 1929, reflecting no doubt the rise of the now ubiquitous beauty shoppe.

Much of the increase in services, of course, was accounted for by the top income group, which received twice as large a percentage of the national income as it does today. Expenditures on domestic service increased by more than 50 per cent between 1919 and 1929, and brokerage charges and interest, generated by the stock-market boom, increased nearly ten times in the same years. But taking everything together, the growth of non-durables and services was impressively broad. As Hoover's *Recent Economic Changes* rejoiced, it was the timely development of the mass services, which in effect absorbed the population increase, that saved the

nation from a critical unemployment problem in the late 1920's.

THE WEAK TRENDS

The record of consumer durables and residential construction, however, was not so consistently good. These two had been the economy's major source of strength in the early years of the decade, stimulating immensely, in turn, consumption of non-durables and the establishment of new services like gas stations and garages. Durables rose 38 per cent between 1920 and 1923, and home construction a phenomenal 165 per cent. But both were also responsible for the economy's later weakness. They not only stopped growing, they declined between 1926 and 1929—consumer durables by 5 per cent, house construction by no less than 37 per cent.

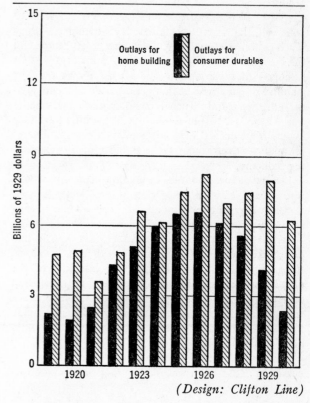

Outlays for home building   Outlays for consumer durables

(Design: Clifton Line)

THE ECONOMY HAD MANY WEAK SPOTS

The weakest spots in the late Twenties were consumer durables and residential housing, both of which turned down after 1926—by 5 and 37 per cent respectively.

Sales of most durables, including radios and washing machines, rose sharply, then dropped. Sales of mechanical refrigerators, by contrast, were a minor source of strength, increasing from fewer than 5,000 in 1920 to 778,000 in 1929. But the great source of strength in consumer durables, not only accounting for most of the rise in the early years of the decade but moderating the decline later on, was the passenger automobile, that quintessentially American device for augmenting the ego of the individual and freeing it from many of the restrictions of time and distance. Sales of cars rose from 1,900,000 units worth $1.8 billion in 1920 to 3,900,000 units (a 100 per cent rise) worth $2.7 billion in 1926 to 4,800,000 units worth $3 billion in 1929 (all prices wholesale).

Note, however, that the *growth* in auto sales, especially in dollars, *did* taper off. Why? For one thing, dollar value per unit dropped as the industry saturated the class market and shifted to a mass market. For another, it is obviously impossible for any new product to maintain its early growth *rate*—a fundamental fact on which Joseph Schumpeter erected much of his wave theory of depressions.

Again, the mass-production industries did not have the mass markets they have today. Finally, auto manufacturers, for all their high-pressure salesmanship, did not measure their markets as accurately or tap them as effectively as they do today. Henry Ford was a good if somewhat extreme example. Because he believed in giving the people any model they wanted so long as it was the Model T and any color they wanted so long as it was black, he put out his Model A two or three years later than he should have, and so restricted the market.

TOO MANY "HOMES"

What accounted for the spectacular decline of residential construction in the late 1920's was that both house and apartment construction had outpaced their market. Partly because mass immigration had ended, the U.S. population growth rate turned down sharply. Population had increased 14 million between 1910 and 1920, another 9,400,000 between 1920 and 1925—but only 7,200,000 in the next five years. Yet the building industry, rushing in to make up for the deficits of World War I, which concentrated so many people in the cities, erected 937,000 housing units in 1925 (only 22 per cent less than in 1954 when the urban population was some 40 per cent greater). And the overbuilding was usually accompanied by a bank-loan-fed inflation in real-estate prices, which like stock-market prices often outran real values and discounted future values egregiously.

A LOPSIDED MARKET

A part of the faltering in both the housing and durable markets is explained by the fact that the middle-class market was much smaller than it is today, both because average income per capita was lower and because the national income was not so evenly distributed as it is today. As *Fortune* showed in "The Changing American Market" (August, 1953), 15,600,000 or 43 per cent of all family units in 1929 received less than $2,000 cash (1953 dollars) whereas 11,700,000 or 23 per cent of all family units do so today. The 43 per cent obviously was not in the market for much except bare necessities.

The concentration of income in the upper groups actually increased, especially in the latter half of the Twenties:

The share of the disposable national income claimed by the top 1 per cent of incomes, between 1920 and 1929, increased by half, from 12 per cent to 18 per cent. And the share claimed by the top 5 per cent increased from 24 per cent to 33.5 per cent.

Between 1920 and 1929 profits, interest, and rent, which went largely to upper-income groups, increased 45 per cent, whereas total wages and salaries, which comprised the bulk of the income of the lower and middle-income groups, rose only 13 per cent. At the same time consumer prices, after rising between 1922 and 1926, declined only 3 per cent between 1926 and 1929.

Between 1920 and 1929, while factory productivity or output per man-hour was increasing 55 per cent, hourly wage rates in manufacturing rose only 2 per cent. One reason for labor's surprising inability to get more benefit from its rising productivity was that the labor movement, after the bitter strikes of 1919, was persuaded into uncritical "cooperation" with management. This was the great era of company unions, open shops, and shrewd paternalism. It was also an era of weak labor leadership. "If he [Judge Gary] sent less than ten hay wagons of roses to [Gompers'] funeral [in 1924]," wrote H. L. Mencken, "then he is a niggard indeed. For Sam got upon the back of the American labor movement when it was beginning to be dangerous, and rode it so magnificently that at the end of his life it was tame as a tabby cat."

There was also a growing imbalance in the distribution of corporate profits. Corporations with profits of more than $1 million accounted for 65 per cent of all corporate profits in 1925, 71 per cent in 1927, and 80 per cent in 1929. Economists argued that monopoly pricing and excessive market power accounted for a great part of the trend toward profit concentration. Actually, big companies tended to dominate profit figures partly because they had the resources to become more efficient. Their ability to "administer" prices cannot be overlooked, however, in accounting for the fact that consumer prices did not fall as rapidly as productive efficiency rose.

THE HEADY PHILTER

Let us recapitulate. Undeveloped marketing methods, declining population growth, declining foreign investment, low farm prices, sticky consumer prices, the real-estate inflation, and the substantial and growing concentration of profits in large corporations and of individual incomes in the upper-income groups even as the luxury markets were becoming saturated—all these caused the growth of consumer durables practically to stop in the mid-Twenties, and caused residential construction to turn down sharply. Thus it was inevitable that business' capital outlays would stop growing, and might even decline. The combination clearly made for a cyclical adjustment.

But before a genuine adjustment to correct the imbalances could occur, the stock-market boom began. This boom, by mounting and accelerating a false recovery early in 1928, postponed a real adjustment, and put the economy on an increasingly precarious footing.

It enabled hundreds of thousands of speculators to spend more on luxuries than they otherwise would have spent, and thus superimposed a consumption boomlet on the stock-market inflation. Above all, the stock-market inflation helped maintain business' capital outlays at a level unjustified by business conditions.

Those outlays rose from $6.8 billion in 1920 to $9.3 billion in 1926. Instead of falling when consumer durables and residential construction turned down in the mid-Twenties, capital outlays continued around the $9.4-billion level until 1929, when they actually jumped by $1.3 billion. The stock-market boom, by driving down yields, made new-issue flotation cheap and easy, and encouraged business to buy more capital goods than it needed.

The stock boom stimulated overbuilding of commercial and office structures; physical volume of commercial building in 1929 was larger than it ever has been since. And the boom also resulted in speculative excesses, such as mortgage bonds issued for amounts greater than costs. Some $8 billion worth of mortgage bonds were sold between 1920 and 1929.

The stock-market boom, in other words, not merely concealed the defects of the economy, it seemed to cure those defects. The patient's blood count was dropping, but the heady philter of speculation deluded him into believing he never felt better.

BOOM UNRESTRICTED

And what started the stock-market boom? For one thing, dividends began to catch up with profits in the middle Twenties, and the advantages of investing in stocks consequently became evident to more and more people who had more and more money to invest—a condition not too different from the mid-Fifties. The concentration of profits in the blue chips also made them inordinately preferable to other stocks.

There were no restrictions on margin such as there are today. The amount of cash a man needed to buy a share was decided by brokers and their banking connections, and in the mid-Twenties, 10 per cent was usually sufficient. And there were virtually none of today's restrictions on pool operators, who could drive up the price of stocks by selling them to one another.

In this unhealthy state of affairs, the Federal Reserve, in August, 1927, actually made speculative credit still more plentiful—by reducing the rediscount rate from 4 to 3.5 per cent and by purchasing government securities in the open market. The Fed did this partly to encourage business at home, which was then slipping a bit (the "adjustment" of 1927), but principally to help Britain stay on, and France get on, the gold standard. The widespread agreement that the Fed's action bears considerable responsibility for the stock-market inflation is more than shared by Herbert Hoover. "But the policies assumed by that System," he writes, "must assume the greater responsibility. . . . There are crimes far worse than murder for which men should be reviled and punished."

Before passing on, let us note the dilemma that faced the Federal Reserve. If it was expected to use monetary policy to avoid deflation and depression, how could it stop the stock-market inflation? The Fed was a relatively new institution that had been denounced for causing the 1920-21 crash by its stringent credit policies. And the Fed lacked the power it now has to set margins, and the backing of an SEC with the power to police the issuing and buying and selling of securities.

"WICKED MANIPULATIONS"

Starting about 1928, the market ceased to be a reasonably sober reflection of economic conditions and became a morbid demonstration of mass avarice. Before mid-1928, broadly speaking, a man paid a certain price for a share of stock because he was pretty sure it would return him more, over the long run, than a bond or other investment, and he was inclined to bid up the price only when he felt his judgment of the company's earning power was correct. After mid-1928 people bought stocks on about the same basis they had bought Florida real estate only a few years before.

It has been estimated that enough Florida lots were sold to provide one for every family in the U.S.; and in his book *The Legendary Mizners,* the late Alva Johnston wrote that some Miami lots could justify their 1925 price only if 200-story skyscrapers were erected on them. Many of the shares in the 1929 stock market could have justified their prices only by the year 2000.

But the "market" in those days represented not merely the spontaneous reactions of hundreds of thousands of speculators. It also represented the contrived pressure of operators who sold dubious foreign bonds, who promoted domestic issues many corporate layers removed from any productive property, who peddled the ubiquitous tips, and who worked the many variations of the pool racket.

The boom "set the stage for wicked manipulations and promotions," Herbert Hoover remarks accurately. "It also furnished ammunition to radicals for their attacks on the whole American system. The exhibition of waste, fraud, and greed . . . appears in their literature as a typical phenomenon of our free civilization, whereas it was the exception."

When two or three million little speculators entered the market, the pickings were all the better. It is true that the common people were given plenty of warning; Roger Babson was only one of many doom criers. But as every decline promptly turned into recovery and a still greater ascension, people who had nervously considered selling when they had a 30 per cent profit grew ever bolder; if their shares had now doubled in value there was no reason why they shouldn't triple. Many outward signs, moreover, were good, at least until early 1929.

THE GREAT CREDIT INFLATION

What gave the boom such uncontrollable momentum was that a great part of the stock buying was done on credit—how much nobody knows, but certainly much more than was done recently, when more than 40 per cent of all *individual*—i.e., non-professional and non-institutional—transactions were made on margin.

Brokers' loans, which had amounted to $1.5 billion in 1923, increased from $4.5 billion early in 1928 to more than $7 billion by June, 1929, and to $8.5 billion by fall. By then the average yield was less than a third of the interest that speculators had to pay to carry the shares.

About three-quarters of the money came not from the banks, but from individuals and corporations that saw a chance to make 10 per cent or more, with no risk to speak of, on their spare cash, and let the banks handle it. Many companies, indeed, floated new issues not for capital investment but for the sole purpose of investing the cash in the call-money market. And it was this tremendous rise in speculative credit that tightened credit for ordinary business operation—which was one reason why the Federal Reserve was reluctant to restrict credit still more.

So Anaconda rose from 54½ early in 1928 to 162 in September, 1929; G.E. from 128¾ to 396; Montgomery Ward from 132¾ to 466½; Radio from 94½ to 505 (without paying a dividend); Westinghouse E. & M. from 92 to 313. And thus it was that the total value of stocks on the New York Stock Exchange rose from $49 billion in December, 1927, to $87 billion on October 1, 1929.

"SO FOUL A SKY . . . ."

Such "appreciation," occurring when margin requirements were only 10 per cent (though they rose to as much as 50 per cent in the summer of 1929), meant that a man with $10,000 in cash in January, 1928, could have put it in blue chips and theoretically run it up to more than $1,500,000 by August, 1929. For $10,000 would have given him about $100,000 worth of "buying power," and within two or three months a 10 per cent rise in stock values would have given him another $100,000 or so in buying power, and he could, in this fashion, have doubled his "equity" every three months or less.

By early 1929 hundreds of knowledgeable people, among them the governors of the Federal Reserve, were wringing their hands, and dozens of magazines and papers, including the New York *Times* and the *Commercial and Financial Chronicle,* were calling the folly what it was. But almost nothing could be done.

The Federal Reserve issued its famous warning of February 2, 1929 stating that a member bank "is not within its reasonable claims for rediscount facilities when it borrows either for the purpose of making speculative loans or for the purpose of maintaining speculative loans. . . ." Although call-money rates went up to 20 per cent in February, and for a while it seemed as if a monumental "correction" would occur, the market receded only temporarily. Whether Charles Mitchell's audacious follow-up statement that his National City Bank, to avoid a panic, was prepared to lend $25 million in call money at rates beginning at 15 per cent started the market upward again is debatable. But upward the market went. The Federal Reserve's last attempt to stay the tide by raising the rediscount rate to 6 per cent in August, 1929, however, may have had some effect on the market. The Dow-Jones index had risen from 315 in June to 380 in August, and rose only one point higher in September.

As the madness of 1929 approached its climax, the stock market not only failed to anticipate the general state of the economy—which it usually does by six months or so—but it lagged behind by several months. The market rose despite the fact that inventories had begun to mount in midsummer, that wholesale prices had turned down in July, that industrial production had declined in August, and that capital-goods orders had tapered off as early as March.

In a more narrow or "technical" sense, the crash had actually been signaled by a turndown in low-priced securities late in 1928, and by sporadic temporary declines in the summer and early autumn of 1929. (The market, then as now, was selective.) Some of the bears were obviously selling short. The warning signs grew with successive waves of selling in September and early October, 1929, which reduced prices 15 per cent below their peak. And the grand October liquidation culminated not merely in the famous Black Thursday of October 24, when nearly 13 million shares changed hands and thousands of margins were exhausted, but also in a still blacker Monday and Tuesday the next week. By the end of October the Dow-Jones index had fallen to 230—from a high of 381 in September.

THE MARKET'S REVENGE

Of all the man-made forces behind the break and the ensuing panic, few were more powerful than the short interests, which began to mount in midsummer. "The short interests," says Sidney Weinberg, "were substantially responsible for the severity of the stock-market crash." Today a short sale cannot be made except at a price higher than the last reported sale. In those days short sales could be made at prices below the market level, and thus could be used to drive down and demoralize the market. One of the most spectacular short-sellers was Albert H. Wiggin, chairman of the Chase Bank, who made $4 million selling short between October and December 11, 1929. What gave Mr. Wiggin's achievement a great deal of adverse publicity later on was the disclosure that he not only sold short before and during the crash, even while he was a leading member of the famous bankers' consortium to stabilize the market, and that he had not only made the $4 million selling his own bank stock short, but that he had sold some of the stock to his own bank, and borrowed from his bank to buy the stock to cover his short sales.

An even more important factor in the panic than short selling, perhaps, was the fact that marginal speculators, when forced to cover their debts, had to sell the stock or turn it over to the brokers. The more stock they put up for sale or turned in, the more prices fell—and of course the more stock that had to be sold. Worse, panicky outside lenders called in their loans, which forced the sale of stock to repay the loans. The volume of brokers' loans declined $2.5 billion in three weeks. To avoid losing their shirts, brokers tried to sell in an orderly fashion the stocks they took over. But every time the market rallied, the new rush to sell precipitated a new decline. Neither speculators nor brokers were any longer free agents, expressing their faith in the future of the nation's business (which has turned out to be a pretty well-founded faith), or betting that a given stock was worth so much. They were flotsam in the torrent, and the fact that they were sensitive and even intelligent flotsam that did not believe in being rushed away by torrents did not help them at all.

This peculiar ability of a chaotically falling market to take its revenge not only on speculators but on the whole economy that lets it occur cannot be overemphasized. It was overlooked for a good time after the crash. Some called the crash a Prosperity Panic, in which, as Professor Irving Fisher put it, the lunatic fringe was being shaken out. "The depression in Wall Street," said the New York *Sun,* "will affect general prosperity only to the extent that the individual buying power of some stock speculators is impaired. No Iowa farmer will tear up his mail-order blank because Sears, Roebuck stock slumped."

THE GRAND LIQUIDATION

Alas, the forces the crash set in motion penetrated to every corner of the economy, where powerful deflationary influences—declining construction, declining consumer durables, declining farm prices—were already at work. The crash further deflated all values and almost destroyed the U.S. banking system.

When the 1920's ended, shattering as the end was, few Americans as yet understood what they were in for. One of the few who did was the hitherto dogmatically optimistic Andrew Mellon. Mr. Mellon now had only one "hope" for the nation: "Liquidate labor, liquidate stocks, liquidate the farmers, liquidate real estate." If Mr. Mellon's formula had included business, it would have come close to being a good description of what eventually happened.

17. DEPRESSION

WHY THE DEPRESSION LASTED SO LONG*

By GILBERT BURCK AND CHARLES E. SILBERMAN

The great depression was not only severe but it dug in deeply and lingered on for almost ten years, coming to a close with the 1937-1938 recession. The present history of those poignant years attempts to tell why the depression had such a prolonged existence. It also shows how the great blunders of the thirties, no less than the great reforms, have contributed to the strength of the New Economy of the fifties. The importance of a wise fiscal policy emerges as one of the most profitable lessons from the depression.

Ninety-six million Americans are, in one sense or another, "too young to remember the depression." Only 45 million living Americans were twenty or older when the great depression began (see chart on page 89). But for all 164 million Americans, the depression is an extraordinary legacy. It was, and remains, one of the most profoundly influential events of our domestic history; some have put it second only to the Civil War. For the great depression not only paralyzed the nation's growth for the better part of a decade, distorting and frustrating the lives of millions, it left in American life an undertone of uncertainty and fear that has survived the ten most prosperous years in history. At the same time, it lodged in American law many reforms that are among the buttresses of the New Economy of the mid-Fifties. Above all, it left the U.S. a body of economic experience that has imparted to the New Economy a remarkable balance and power.

The present article, which examines the 1930's in the light of the best economic opinion of 1955, attempts to tell (1) why the depression dug in so deeply and lasted so long, and (2) how the experience of the depression decade affects today's economy.

The basic reason the depression lasted so long was, of course, the economic ignorance of the times. Economics is one of the most elusive subjects that has ever engaged the intelligence of man, and economics has never been more baffling or elusive than it was in the 1930's. Venerable economic principles, the principles on which industrial civilization was erected, were suddenly

* From Gilbert Burck and Charles E. Silberman, "Why The Depression Lasted So Long," March, 1955.

powerless to account and prescribe for what was happening. All that most experts understood was that something new was happening, and it was years before they knew just what to make of it.

Neither Herbert Hoover nor Franklin Roosevelt, alas, knew what to make of it. Herbert Hoover, the very symbol of laissez faire, switched from laissez faire to a modified interventionism. But he would not desert his convictions on the inviolability of the gold standard and the balanced budget, and he ended up by prolonging the deflation without mitigating it very much. Roosevelt, on the other hand, unhesitatingly and even gaily threw over laissez faire and embraced a managed economy. But he, too, was haunted by the ideal of a balanced budget, and his deficits were too small to counteract the decline in private spending. And in 1936 he lost his nerve and practically balanced the 1937 budget—with disastrous results.

THE SPIRAL BEGINS

The depression had begun, as *Fortune* related last month, because of several basic weaknesses in the outwardly strong "New Era" economy of the 1920's. Among them were an increasingly lopsided distribution of the benefits of rising productivity, declining population growth, and relatively ineffective marketing techniques; because of these weaknesses, expenditures on consumer durables began to slide off in the mid-Twenties, and expenditures on home building fell sharply. Farm prices and income also fell. These declines made a correction practically inevitable.

But the correction, which might have been moderate

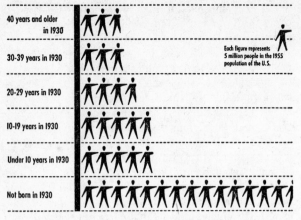

40 years and older in 1930	☥☥☥
30-39 years in 1930	☥☥☥
20-29 years in 1930	☥☥☥☥
10-19 years in 1930	☥☥☥☥☥
Under 10 years in 1930	☥☥☥☥☥
Not born in 1930	☥☥☥☥☥☥☥☥☥☥☥☥☥☥

Each figure represents 5 million people in the 1955 population of the U.S.

WHO REMEMBERS THE DEPRESSION?

Only a little more than a fourth of the present population of the U.S. was more than twenty years old in 1930. These are the Americans with firsthand, adult recollection of the whole of the hard times of 1930-40. And only 27 million living Americans, fewer than 17 per cent of the total, were more than thirty in 1930, i.e., old enough to be pretty well established in a job or business or standard of living.

---

had it occurred in 1928, was temporarily forfended by the stock-market boom, which erected false props of prosperity under the economy. It artificially stimulated certain forms of consumption as well as capital spending. Stocks kept soaring up even after business had turned down. Thus the boom in stocks, by postponing the correction and creating overcapacity, made a moderate correction impossible. The patient was in a bad way, but the heady philter of speculation deluded him into thinking he had never felt better. His first reaction, after his fortune changed for the worse, was that he would get better soon. But it was not long before his basic weaknesses exacerbated his illness and all but ruined him.

At first, many observers argued that the stock-market crash would affect only those who had lost money in it. Even these were a considerable deflationary force. Millions of people, rich and poor, even those who did not have to pay off margin accounts out of income, were forced to economize. The luxury market began to soften rapidly. And the great soft spots in the economy—consumer durables, housebuilding, and farm prices—grew softer still.

What is more important, the whole nation was heavily and precariously in hock to itself, and falling prices and the liquidation of security and real-estate values made the burden intolerable. In 1929 the interest on corporate debt took 40 per cent of all corporate profit before taxes, against about 10 per cent today. Nonfarm mortgage debt—most of it callable in five years—was equal to 50 per cent of disposable income, against only 36 per cent now, and interest rates in 1929 were 50 to 100 per cent higher than they are now. Farm mortgage debt came to more than 150 per cent of farm income, compared to 63 per cent now.

The banking system, despite the creation of the Federal Reserve in 1913, was not half so strong as most

people thought it was. It was still a frontier system, hospitable to boom and vulnerable to bust. It contained too many small and weak banks, and only a third of all banks were members of the Federal Reserve. There was no deposit insurance. Too many bankers had acquired the habit of manipulating and promoting "securities." Even in the prosperous 1920's about one out of every five commercial banks failed. Now the banking system was up against challenges that would have strained the strongest one.

When the stock and real-estate markets cracked, the banks already had nearly 25 per cent of their assets in security loans and 10 per cent in real-estate loans. The colossal decline in value of securities—$45 *billion,* or more than 50 per cent, by 1931, for those on the New York Stock Exchange alone—weakened the banks immeasurably. So did the real-estate decline. Farm prices and incomes collapsed, and the defaults on farm mortgages brought down many farm banks with them. Inflated urban real-estate values, on which mortgage debt was based, also collapsed. As Secretary of the Treasury Andrew Mellon told Herbert Hoover in the early stages of the depression, "There is a mighty lot of real estate lying around the United States which does not know who owns it."

In the meantime, every intelligent businessman, watching inventory accumulate and sales and profits drop sharply, knew he had to retrench. So business cut back purchases of inventory and capital goods, and industrial production declined 20 per cent within a year after the crash. Although business responded to President Hoover's pleas and for a while maintained wage rates, it laid off workers across the board. Not only did all these cutbacks contract the consumer market, the consumers who still had high incomes worried increasingly about their jobs, and began to cut their own spending. Few seemed willing to mortgage an uncertain future to buy durables like cars and appliances. And so business was forced to retrench still more.

FLIGHT OF GOLD

Thus, for a full year and a half, the whole economy slid downward. But in the spring of 1931 there seemed to be signs that the worst was over. Industrial production and gross national product, which had declined 30 per cent and 15 per cent respectively, actually turned up slightly. Stock prices rose, and President Hoover was quoted as saying that prosperity was just around the corner.

Even as he spoke, however, ominous tidings were coming from overseas. Europe's economies, which had been buoyed up during much of the 1920's by U.S. loans and large U.S. imports, were confronted with a virtual cessation of both. The big problem of these economies, too, was debt—not only to one another, but to the U.S. Their ability to pay those debts was not helped by the passage of the ill-famed Hawley-Smoot Tariff of 1930, which, signed reluctantly by Hoover, gave the rest of the world notice that it would have a difficult time earning the dollars to pay the U.S. As the situation worsened, gold and foreign exchange—"hot money"—moved frantically from country to country, looking for a refuge and wrecking credit systems in the process. The Kredit Anstalt, the largest bank in Austria, suddenly closed its doors in May, 1931, and every bank in Europe trembled. Business declined sharply, and even the cartel-dictated price structures began to crack.

Although Hoover met this challenge with imagination and resolution—he personally drafted and sold to key members of Congress an international moratorium on debts, described by the London *Economist* as the gesture of a great man—the gesture availed little. By September, 1931, Britain was forced off the gold standard. Fears that the U.S. would follow, plus the fact that U.S. production had turned down again, led to panic flights of foreign capital from the U.S., and of U.S. gold into foreign coffers and hoards at home. In slightly more than a month, beginning in mid-September, the U.S. lost $725 million worth of gold.

The Federal Reserve, which had previously adopted an easy-money policy to stimulate business, found its gold reserves threatened, and elected to protect the gold stadard in the traditional way. On October 9, 1931, as though fighting inflation, it raised its rediscount rate from 1.5 to 2.5 per cent, and a week later to no less than 3.5 per cent. This served to check gold movements, but at the sacrifice of any chance of domestic recovery. Interest rates rose, stock prices dropped abruptly, production declined, and banks tightened credit—and the credit-tightening process started liquidation all over again. And, of course, the banks' attempts to "get liquid" made it steadily harder for everybody to "get liquid."

Bank failures, which had numbered 158 in August, rose to 522 in October—the largest number in any month before or since. It was at this point that fear, Roosevelt's "nameless, terrifying fear," gripped the country. Hoarding rose $500 million in two months. Unemployment rose still higher while industrial production fell still lower—12 per cent in three months. What had capped the crisis, what had turned it into the most serious financial panic in U.S. history, seemed to be Herbert Hoover's determination to remain on the gold standard in the face of the world financial crisis.

IN THE DEPTHS

This is not to say that Hoover's policy, as so many believe, was one of doing nothing. Contrary, too, to popular myth, Hoover's economics were not incorrigibly laissez faire. Many of his associates, particularly Andrew Mellon, urged him to let things alone, arguing that the liquidation would end quickly, as previous liquidations had ended, if only left alone. But Hoover pointed out that the vast majority of Americans no longer lived and worked on the land, and no longer could sit out a depression on the farm; the depression meant heavy unemployment in the cities, and untold and unprecedented suffering. So he had announced late in 1929 that recovery was the government's responsibility. In 1930-32 he actually introduced many of the important measures that later became the bases of Roosevelt's recovery program. Through RFC he supplemented private credit for business with government credit. He created a little employment through public works. He plugged for high wage rates. He tried to cope with farm surpluses by withholding them from the market. And he tried to expand credit.

Having done all this, however, Hoover stuck doggedly not only to the gold standard but also to the balanced budget, which remained for him the categorical imperatives of the free-enterprise system. Their abandonment under any circumstances was something that could be seriously considered only by knaves, collectivists, or crackpots. It was primarily to save the gold standard that he pushed through the Glass-Steagall Act of February 1932, which allowed the Federal Reserve to use government bonds to back the currency, and so released $1 billion in gold for possible export. Although Hoover ran deficits in 1931 and 1932, these were largely involuntary. And it was to balance the budget that he persuaded the American Legion to forgo demanding a bonus, vetoed a direct relief bill, and took a resolute stand against "squandering the nation into prosperity."

To be sure, practically everybody in 1931 and 1932 thought as Hoover did—including Franklin Roosevelt. Practically nobody understood what today is commonly understood—that a deficit, if it occurs when a nation's resources and labor force are only partly utilized, need not be inflationary. Although John Maynard Keynes was already arguing in the press that deficit financing could cure the depression, it was not till 1936 that he launched the "Keynesian Revolution" with his *General Theory of Employment, Interest, and Money*, which, among other things, popularized the notion that a government's finances should be managed primarily in terms of their effect on the economy's stability.

Another and less academic partisan of deficit spending was a then obscure Utah banker named Marriner Eccles, who had never read Keynes. What the government should do, he told his scandalized banker friends, was not merely to loosen credit, not merely to devalue, but to spend more than it took in, in order to increase the nation's buying power.* The government of 1930-32, he argued, was like the stewards on the doomed *Titanic*, who locked all the staterooms so that nothing could be stolen as the ship sank.

CROSS OF GOLD

Taking everything together, history may well agree with the verdicts of Walter Lippmann and the late A. D. Gayer, the Columbia University monetary economist. Professor Gayer argued that Hoover's inconsistency was disastrous, that either he should have followed Andrew Mellon's formula and let deflation take its natural, brutal course, which might well have been a swifter course, or he should have supported employment and personal income directly besides shoring up banks, insurance companies, and railroads. He succeeded only in prolonging the decline without mitigating it very much. As for Lippmann, he argued in the 1930's that the one real difference between the Hoover and Roosevelt administrations was the former's

* Later on, as Federal Reserve governor, Eccles also argued consistently enough that in inflationary times the government should reduce the nation's buying power by running a surplus.

refusal to abandon the gold standard, and that the Hoover Administration crucified itself on a cross of gold.

By the close of 1932 the whole nation had been pretty well crucified on the same cross. Industrial production stood at only 50 per cent of its mid-1929 level, and gross national product had fallen 40 per cent, to $67 billion (1929 dollars). Nearly 13 million men—some estimates ran to 15 million or 16 million—were out of work, not counting several million more on short weeks. Wages and salaries had fallen 40 per cent.

Since people always stop buying postponable things first, the worst decline was suffered by the durable-goods business, which had boomed early in the 1920's. Unlike the volume of non-durables and services, which in real terms declined no more than 15 per cent, that of durable consumer goods dropped 50 per cent. Auto production fell from 4,600,000 in 1929 to 1,100,000 in 1932. Residential construction withered away to less than 25 per cent of its 1929 volume; only 134,000 new nonfarm units were started in 1932, compared to 509,000 in 1929, and 937,000 in 1925, at the peak of the residential boom. Because corporations (taken together) lost $2 billion in 1932 and again in 1933, and because excess capacity was depressing prices in almost every industry, business cut its purchases of capital equipment (producer durables) by 50 per cent, and cut industrial and commercial construction 70 per cent.

Meantime, the financial crisis grew more acute. The Dow-Jones average dropped to 40, mortgage foreclosures rose sharply, and bank failures mounted. In the first two months of 1933 hoarding increased by $900 million, and the merest rumor was enough to start a run on a bank. Farm-mortgage riots spread all over the Midwest as farmers took over foreclosure sales and forced the resale of foreclosed properties to mortgagees for a few dollars.

The great mass of people, including most businessmen, were not only bewildered and panicky, but angry and frustrated, ready to try almost anything that plausibly offered relief. Some of them fell for demagogues like Huey Long, with his "Share Our Wealth" platform, and Dr. Townsend and his old-age pensions, and Father Coughlin and his "Social Justice" campaign. Some of the more intellectual were much affected by books like Stuart Chase's *A New Deal,* a large part of which was devoted to expounding the "loathsomeness" of laissez faire—not the laissez faire of Adam Smith, who elevated the consumers' interests above all others, but a horrendous straw man embodying the worst traits of Jesse James, Daniel Drew, and Charles Ponzi. The book's title, significantly, was later appropriated by Franklin Roosevelt's Brain Trust to describe the Administration's aims.

A few of the nation's leading intellectuals went Communist or near-Communist. But actually the heyday of party-lining came later, and was more a response to Hitlerism and the Spanish Civil War than to events in the U.S. Such "leftism" as manifested itself at the depths of the depression was mainly in the pragmatic, idealistic American tradition of acting violently against injustice and oppression. And the wonder is not that so many Americans went left but that so

few did. In November, 1932, the Communist party pooled only 103,000 votes, and the Socialist party 885,000, vs. 15,800,000 for the Republicans and 22,800,000 for the Democrats.

ENTER F.D.R.

The election of Franklin Roosevelt, and his refusal to join Hoover in committing himself to a "sound dollar" before his inauguration, may have accelerated the flight of gold and cash from the banks. Hoover still insists that the bank crisis could have been averted if only Roosevelt had committed himself to maintain the gold standard. But the second flight of gold had occurred in the spring of 1932, before the election, and the financial crisis that followed probably rendered inevitable the bank holiday of 1933.

By inauguration day, at any rate the holiday *was* inevitable—most states had already closed their banks. Roosevelt acted promptly, proclaimed a bank holiday on March 6, and on March 9 he jammed through Congress the Emergency Banking Act, which validated the holiday, furnished capital to distressed banks, and provided a plan for reopening all banks save the hopeless ones. Within three days 75 per cent of the Federal Reserve member banks were reopened and currency was flowing back to them.

THE ROVING QUARTERBACK

When Roosevelt took office his advisers were full of ideas, many conflicting, about what had gone wrong—the nation's capital stock had been overexpanded, prices had been "managed," labor hadn't got a fair share of income, public utilities had been antisocial, and so on. But at first Roosevelt and his Administration had one important broad, fixed objective: to raise production by stimulating purchasing power, and to achieve this objective they were willing to try anything plausible. In a press conference Roosevelt compared himself to a football quarterback who can call only one play at a time, and must decide each play on the basis of how the previous one worked.

This pragmatic, experimental approach was perhaps the only intelligent one in those early days of the New Deal, and for a time it worked very well. Roosevelt's cheerful ignorance of economics, far from being a handicap, was if anything an advantage, for it made him receptive to the new and unorthodox. The trouble came later on, when it became necessary to stop improvising and choose a sound approach to the nation's problems and stick to it.

But the earliest measures of the new Administration, in March, 1933, were consistent enough. In his 1932 campaign Roosevelt had, much to his later embarrassment, argued eloquently against an unbalanced budget. "Stop the deficits," he had implored. "I accuse the Administration of being the biggest spending Administration in peacetimes in all our history." And the first thing the New Deal had to do, after reopening the solvent banks, was to "restore confidence" by demonstrating that it could cut expenditures and balance the budget. An economy act was passed, and federal salaries and other costs were cut. What would have happened if this deflationary course had been followed to the bitter end is hard to say, but even most business-men by this time were afraid to let it happen.

THE MULTIPLE ATTACK

At all events, the Administration reversed itself and moved rapidly toward credit expansion, monetary inflation, price and wage rises, relief payments, and public works. The most important decision was to go off gold, and the decision was in effect forced on Roosevelt by an inflation-minded Congress. On April 20, 1933, Roosevelt placed an embargo on gold, and thus in effect took the country off the gold standard.

There followed, between 1933 and 1937, a continuous avalanche of congressional acts and executive orders dealing with recovery. There were steps primarily designed to raise prices and boost purchasing power—though some of them involved various reforms. There was, of course, pump priming by means of a bewildering succession of public works and relief measures. There was the Federal Emergency Relief Administration, the Civilian Conservation Corps, the Civil Works Administration, and PWA, which under "Honest" Harold Ickes spent so little money that WPA had to be formed under Harry Hopkins. Partly as a result of these measures, federal expenditures rose from $3.7 billion in 1932 to $8.2 billion in 1936 (in 1929 dollars).

There was TVA, which got the government into the power business in a colossal way. There were aids to agriculture like "parity" prices and the AAA, which raised prices by paying farmers to restrict production. There were several labor measures, discussed later, which raised union membership from about two million in 1932 to over 11 million in 1941. There were a variety of measures easing home and farm mortgages. And there was the social-security system, founded in 1936.

Among the solidest early achievements of the New Deal were the laws reforming and strengthening the banking system, such as the Banking Act of 1933, which provided for deposit insurance and for the divorce of investment and commercial banking; the Banking Act of 1935, which centralized Federal Reserve power, particularly over open-market operations; and the Securities and Exchange Acts of 1934-35, which reformed the issuing and buying and selling of securities. Sidney Weinberg, who fought hard against the Securities and Exchange Acts, now says he would go on a crusade against any move to repeal them. And Professor Milton Friedman of the University of Chicago, one of the leading orthodox economists, argues that the Federal Deposit Insurance Corporation is by all odds the most important of the changes affecting the cyclical characteristics of the American economy, perhaps even more important than the establishment of the Federal Reserve.

THE BRIGHT BLUE EAGLE

The most inconsistent New Deal creation, the one that remains the supreme example of the Administration's let's-give-it-a-try, all-things-to-all-men approach, was NRA, or the National Recovery Administration, created in 1933. NRA was a kind of state-run super-cartel, with a genially ferocious dictator in the person of General Hugh ("Ironpants") Johnson in charge and a new national flag in the form of the "bright badge" of the Blue Eagle. Had NRA survived and succeeded, it would have accomplished publicly all that any group of European cartelists, meeting behind closed doors and puffing big cigars, has ever been able to accomplish. It would have wiped out the antitrust acts and committed the whole nation to planned restrictionism, with government, capital, management, and labor restricting together.

NRA's immediate genesis seems to have been a 1933 memo by Gerard Swope, president of General Electric, who advanced industry's plausible argument that cutthroat competition in a depression would make things worse rather than better. NRA put a floor under wages and hours, and through Section 7a guaranteed labor the right to organize and bargain collectively. Since productivity had been rising, this was long overdue. But NRA also allowed business to get together and adopt codes that incorporated price-fixing and production-restriction agreements, which might well have hamstrung the increase of American productivity. Hundreds of businessmen took their codes before the redfaced, wisecracking Johnson, who assured them he would crack down unmercifully on the chiselers. Fortunately for the U.S., there were too many chiselers in business even for General Johnson. Long before May, 1935, when the Supreme Court declared the NRA unconstitutional, the codes were being violated all across the nation.

The labor provisions of the act started a wave of unionization, and they, too, encountered employer resistance. Section 7a of the dead NRA, however, was quickly replaced by the National Labor Relations Act (the Wagner Act), which specifically authorized collective bargaining, defined unfair employer practices, and set up the National Labor Relations Board to help enforce the act.

THE CONTROVERSIAL LAG

For all their inconsistencies, the New Deal's early measures did achieve their major aim: they raised farm and industrial prices and wages, and so stimulated consumption and industrial production. Gross national product, rose just about as fast as it had declined, and by the third quarter of 1937 stood 5 per cent above its mid-1929 level. Industrial production had also passed the 1929 peak, and volume of consumer non-durables was 10 per cent above 1929. This, however, was not full recovery. Because the national working force had increased 10 per cent and its productivity 15 per cent, true recovery, that is, fairly full employment, would have meant a G.N.P. at least 25 per cent higher than in 1929. As it was, there were still more than seven million unemployed early in 1937.

What blocked full recovery, and so perpetuated mass unemployment, was the fact that the durables sector of the economy hardly recovered at all. By 1937 the volume of residential construction was still 40 per cent below its 1929 level, industrial and commercial construction was 50 per cent below 1929, and producer and consumer durables were 5 and 6 per cent below 1929, respectively. Why did they lag?

The story of residential construction may be told simply. There had been considerable overbuilding in the 1920's, and the low incomes and low household formation of the Thirties created little additional demand. The birth rate fell 19 per cent, and people doubled up. And so long as lenders feared that new houses would have to compete with houses on which they had foreclosed, or held shaky mortgages, they were reluctant to give mortgages for new construction. Then, too, building costs did not fall so much as costs in general.

The stagnation in capital spending—on industrial and commercial construction and producers' goods—is not so simple a story. The volume of commercial construction was so great in 1929 that it was not equaled again until 1954; thus the overbuilding and speculative real-estate inflation of the 1920's were among the main reasons why 1937's volume remained only half of 1929's volume. Then, too, commercial construction is closely related to the rate of home building, which was low.

Even the fact that the 1937 volume of producers' goods was only 5 per cent below its 1929 volume was disappointing. For there was (and is) occurring a long-term shift in capital spending from plant to equipment, and thus the volume of producers' equipment relative to the trend was actually low. And why did not this capital spending on equipment and plant recover?

TOO MANY ADJUSTMENTS

One answer popular in the late 1930's was Alvin Hansen's theory of secular stagnation, which blamed oversaving at a time when investment opportunities were declining, thanks to the economy's "maturity." What seems today a more plausible reason is that business probably was not able to adjust to all the changes that confronted it in a few short years:

The reform of the credit system, as well as SEC regulations, were badly needed, but probably discouraged new-issue flotation.

Legalized unionization elevated wage rates 41 per cent in 1933-37. Even harder to accept, for many businessmen, was that unions had to be recognized and bargained with.

Increasingly higher taxes altered the calculations on which investments had been based. In his attempts to balance the budget, Hoover had raised tax *rates* drastically in 1932. The New Deal raised them further, and added new taxes—e.g., excess-profits taxes, social-security taxes, and the undistributed-profits tax. It had also closed many loopholes, such as personal holding companies. As business and income picked up, therefore, tax payments rose even more. Federal receipts more than tripled between 1932 and 1937, rising (in 1929 dollars) from $2 billion to $6.8 billion, or nearly double the 1929 figure of $3.8 billion.

Banking regulations, unionization, and higher taxes, of course, are commonplace enough today. But the speed with which business had to adjust to them had a lot to do with its reluctance to make capital investment. Its adjustment problems were not eased by the increasingly uncompromising attitude of President Roosevelt. He had provocation, it is true. Some businessmen were venting a virtually psychopathic hatred of "that man." Roosevelt went on to assume that all businessmen, save a few New Deal "captives," were enemies of the people. His 1936 message to Congress was studded with such fighting phrases as "entrenched greed" and "resplendent economic autocracy," and his campaign speeches were even less conciliatory. "They are unanimous in their hate of me," he boasted with a certain accuracy of those who opposed him. But then he added childishly: "I welcome their hate."

NOT ENOUGH SPENDING?

Yet there remains one other important circumstance that probably contributed greatly to the lag in capital goods. What really shapes business decisions to buy capital goods is not a vague sense of confidence or doubt, not necessarily even an inflationary or deflationary government policy, but the outlook for sales and profits. Partly because of rising wages, partly because of rising taxes (and partly because 1929 profits were unusually high), profits in the 1930's did not recover so fast as wages and production. Corporate profits in 1937, after taxes, were 43 per cent below their 1929 level, and the sales outlook for the durable industries was still bad. But could anything have been done about *that?* The government could have kept taxes down by running somewhat bigger deficits. And why didn't this high-spending government run bigger deficits? Simply because Roosevelt was constantly plagued by the ideal of a balanced budget and by congressional advocates of sound money, and never seemed to understand quite how an unbalanced budget need not be inflationary (though he actually needed some inflation). Thus is irony defined.

HERE WE GO AGAIN, BOYS

And it was the lack of a consistent New Deal fiscal policy that was partly if not largely responsible for the disheartening recession of 1937-38, the steepest economic descent on record. In a few months the nation lost half the ground it had gained since 1932; industrial production fell 30 per cent, unemployment passed ten million. Stocks plummeted; e.g., New York Central declined from 41½ to 10 in about six months.

The reasons for the recession seem clear enough today. The 1936-37 boom, fed by the 1936 soldier's bonus, pushed up industrial production, commercial loans, and stock prices. Settlement of the automobile sitdown and other strikes led to a rash of wage increases. Businessmen, fearing that rising wages would mean higher prices, and expecting the government to continue to run a deficit, put their money into goods, speculatively placing orders for both current and future needs, and touching off an inventory boom. Yet rising wages did not increase consumption enough to stabilize the economy, and they did not because the government's irresolute fiscal policy in 1937 reduced its contribution to the nation's buying power by $3.2 billion, or more than the inventory accumulation and more than the aggregate wage increase.

How did this happen? It happened because in 1936 Roosevelt had begun to worry about inflation and the mounting pressures of business and the press, and had tried to balance the budget. He had even vetoed the 1936 soldier's bonus. But Congress had passed a $1.7-billion bonus over his veto, so in 1936 the government ran a deficit of $3.4 billion (1929 dollars).

In 1937, however, the government had no bonus to

pay, and so spent $1.2 billion less than it did in 1936. At the same time, moreover, it collected $1.5 billion in new social-security taxes, practically none of which it disbursed. So for all practical purposes Roosevelt and Secretary of the Treasury Morgenthau balanced the budget. And thus it was that they reduced the government's contribution to the nation's buying power by more than $3 billion. Businessmen, seeing their inventories mount while sales (especially of durables) fell, curtailed orders. By the late summer of 1937, the landslide began to gather way.

Franklin Roosevelt, who had been so hospitable to the new economics (up to a point), now found himself in the same frustrating, discouraging position that Herbert Hoover had been in five and six years before. For the first time in his associates' memory, Roosevelt was unable to make up his mind quickly on an important issue. Even while Secretary Morgenthau was promising another balanced budget, Roosevelt was conferring and discussing and mulling over the problem. Finally, on April 14, 1938, a full seven months after the recession began, he countermanded Morgenthau and asked Congress to appropriate $3 billion for relief, public works, housing, and flood control. The economy revived quickly as inventories were rebuilt, and by late 1939 most of the lost ground was recovered. But full employment was not restored until 1942, when World War II was in full swing.

THE HERITAGE OF REFORM

For all its fumbling and faulty signal calling, the New Deal passed on to the postwar generation a heritage of reforms and practices without which today's economy would not be nearly so strong and well balanced as it is. Aside from social security and financial reforms, the most important features of the heritage are the practices that enable our economy to remain a market economy despite big business, big unions, and big government, which have no place in a classic market economy of many small suppliers, each without significant control over the market.

Labor's right to organize its own unions and bargain collectively, for example, may give labor what sometimes amounts to monopoly power, but a vigorous labor movement helps solve the major problem of an economy whose output is increasing much faster than its population: how to distribute the benefits of rising productivity as fast as they are created.

Another important legacy of the great depression is an expanded understanding of how delicately a big economy is balanced, and the extent to which the government can or cannot effectively check imbalances before they grow serious. What with the growth in the government's fact-finding activities, the imbalances of the kind that eventually ruined the economy of the 1920's could not today go unnoticed, and it is unlikely that they could go uncorrected.

Today, at all events, we have the spectacle of a Republican Administration talking in a way that not merely would have astonished Calvin Coolidge, but in its calm assertion of responsibility in a relatively minor swing of the business cycle might have given pause even to Franklin Roosevelt. "Definite and deliberate steps were taken to promote a stable prosperity,"

Dwight Eisenhower told Congress last January, in discussing the 1953-54 recession (in his annual Economic Report). The steps included a reversal of the Administration's hard-money policy and an unhesitating if temporary abandonment of its attempts to balance the budget. Together with "automatic" stabilizers like unemployment insurance and reduced tax payments, these steps more than offset a $4.4-billion decline in income derived from manufacturing, and gave people $1 billion more to spend than the year before. Says the report: "This remarkable result—namely, a rise in disposable personal income accompanying a 10 per cent decline in industrial production—has no parallel in our recorded economic history."

THE PRICE

But all the depression-generated reforms and practices were not realized without a price. They encouraged a general idea that if a little government is a good thing, a lot of government is that much better. Specifically, they encouraged a belief that only continually *expanding* government expenditures and deficits can sustain prosperity. They encouraged those thinkers who solemnly proposed to cure the abuses of private monopolies by replacing them with government monopolies. They were, of course, a godsend to many politicians and bureaucrats. And the trend toward bigger government was strengthened by World War II, when the government had to control prices, allocate materials, and ration goods and manpower.

The inevitable reaction, both at home and abroad, set in shortly after World War II, when the much-heralded postwar crash never came, when in fact inflation turned out to be the great problem. There was a general realization that a market that is imperfect by strict classical standards is vastly better than none at all, that competition does work, that inflation in prosperous times is an evil less reprehensible only than dogmatic liquidation when millions are unemployed, that business and the businessman are worth a new vote of confidence.

This reaction, however, is not merely a pendulum's swing back to the 1920's and the decadent laissez faire Stuart Chase described so indignantly. The reaction may be best described in terms of Hegel's opposing thesis and antithesis, out of which a new synthesis is born. In his last Economic Report, President Eisenhower tried to indicate its direction. Discussing the doctrinaire manifestations of the old and the new positions, he described one as insensitive to the misfortunes of depression, the other to the inequities of inflation. "Each carries the danger of undermining, sooner or later, our system of free competitive enterprise. . . . The need of our times is for economic policies that recognize the proven success of sustained economic growth and betterment . . . and respect the need of people for a sense of security as well as opportunity." Such is the tendency of the New Economy, which if wisely guided can accelerate the astonishing progress that has enabled the material well-being of Americans to advance more in the past fifty years than the material well-being of the human race has advanced in all the previous centuries of Western history.

4. The Market

THE NEW BUYING "HABITS"*

This selection from Fortune's famous article, "The Changing American Market," analyzes consumer expenditure patterns and investigates the reasons why people buy what they buy. The recent rapid increase in "discretionary" income emerges as a volatile influence on consumer buying "habits." This influence is revealed by an instructive chart which compares the percentage increase of expenditures on individual items with the percentage increase of all consumption expenditures. Reference is made to Arthur F. Burns's summary of the present status of consumption theory.

Economists and even merchandisers often describe the consumers' buying "habits" as if they were a "function" of income. They relate those "habits" to income, project that income, and then complete the syllogism by predicting buying changes. This is becoming increasingly unreliable. Precisely because the new mass-class market has so much "discretionary" income, it can buy so much more in the way of frills, novelties, and variations. And so it grows more vulnerable to competitive selling, and even pure whim, and does not buy according to fixed pattern.

Now, consumer spending is usually sorted out into spending on (1) nondurables—food, clothing, tobacco, gas, and oil, etc.—which account for more than half of all outlays; (2) services—housing and household operation, recreation, personal services, etc.—which take about a third; and (3) durable goods, autos, furniture, etc. which take the rest.

Recently these three major categories of consumer expenditures have varied significantly. The most important variations are that nondurables now account for 54 per cent of all consumer outlays, against 48 per cent in 1929, and that services account for only 33 per cent, against 40 per cent in 1929.

The reasons *appear* to be easy to fathom. The decline in service expenditures has been to a large extent the result of prewar and wartime decline in housing costs. This, in turn, was the result of rent control and low interest rates, which automatically reduced the proportion of money people have found necessary to spend on housing. The trend is now reversing. Housing costs as a percentage of total consumer expenditures have risen from 8.8 in 1947 to about 10.8 today. They seem almost certain to rise further as interest rates and rents go up, and as housebuilders, taking advantage of the migration to the suburbs, push their attractive products hard.

Much harder to account for are the consumer's increased food expenditures (his largest single outlay)—from 24 per cent of disposable income in 1940 to about 29 per cent today. Food expenditures, expressed as a percentage of national income, have tended to decline

over the long range. But here they are, going against all the projections. A larger per cent of the national income is going to the lower groups, who normally spend more of their income on food than the upper groups. Can it also be that the middle groups are becoming more food-conscious, and beginning to consider good food as the expensive but necessary luxury that even moderately well-off Frenchmen regard it? Or is the increase the result of competitive innovations within the food industry, with its new frozen and packaged varieties? Such are the questions that future market studies will answer.

CLOTHES AND SHOES

Now look at consumers' outlays on clothing and shoes, which are next in size to food and housing. Except in World War II, when durable goods were practically nonexistent, outlays for clothes and shoes, expressed as a percentage of total outlay, have declined slightly for twenty-five years—from 12 to 9.5 per cent. Why? The phenomenon has several explanations—the automobile, which has reduced wear on shoes and informalized clothes design; the trend to lighter and cheaper clothes, and to vacation and sport clothes; and last but certainly not least, Adam Smith style competition.

Competition among clothes manufacturers has been a large factor in producing reasonably priced, good-looking mass-produced garments that in many ways are superior to expensive custom clothes of years ago. Certainly a man or woman can dress more elegantly and more variously on a smaller expenditure (in real dollars) than he or she could thirty years ago. Or, for that matter, than he or she can in any other nation today. The fact that no European nation has developed a ready-made clothing industry that can hold a candle to America's tells a lot about both European and American business and markets.

The consumer's outlay on autos and parts has tended in the past to remain fairly constant in good years—about 4 per cent of his total expenses. Owing to war-created backlog, however, it rose above 5 per cent in 1949, and 6 per cent in the Korean war buying boom of 1950.

*From "The Changing American Market," August, 1953.

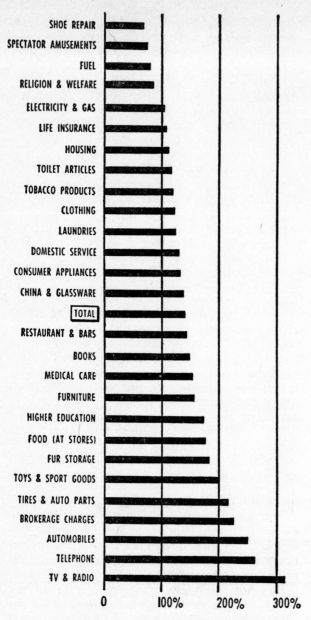

SHOE REPAIR
SPECTATOR AMUSEMENTS
FUEL
RELIGION & WELFARE
ELECTRICITY & GAS
LIFE INSURANCE
HOUSING
TOILET ARTICLES
TOBACCO PRODUCTS
CLOTHING
LAUNDRIES
DOMESTIC SERVICE
CONSUMER APPLIANCES
CHINA & GLASSWARE
TOTAL
RESTAURANT & BARS
BOOKS
MEDICAL CARE
FURNITURE
HIGHER EDUCATION
FOOD (AT STORES)
FUR STORAGE
TOYS & SPORT GOODS
TIRES & AUTO PARTS
BROKERAGE CHARGES
AUTOMOBILES
TELEPHONE
TV & RADIO

0   100%   200%   300%

(Chart: Clifton Line)

PER CENT INCREASE IN CONSUMPTION EXPENDITURES
FROM 1941 TO 1950-51 AVERAGE

Why the spread? A host of important variations in
consumer expenditures do not show up in broad groups
because they tend to cancel one another out. This
chart, therefore, gets down to some of the specific items
that make up the broad group.

Data: Percentages by *Fortune*, from Department of Commerce and BLS figures.

And it may well come close to 6 per cent this year.
Even making allowance for the fact that recent high
sales are still the result of the wartime lack of cars, the
industry is doing well. Its unit volume is declining
relatively to population, but its dollar volume is rising.
What it has done, is to sell *more* car with each unit—
more improvements and gadgets like power steering
and power brakes. It has, in short, successfully elaborated on what are essentially a few basic cars.

The market for household appliances, which take
about 1.5 per cent of the consumer's dollar, is really a
group of discordant markets whose significant variations are not necessarily reflected in the over-all figures.
This generalization, however, can be made: most appliances in use are relatively new. The prosperity of
the appliance business will therefore depend to a large
degree on the development and sales of new products
like air conditioners, freezers, and garbage-disposal
units. The mass-class market is there—if the new
appliances are forthcoming. A good example is the remarkable rise of TV.

Now look at a few expenditures in the smaller categories. Between 1941 and 1947, making no allowance
for the changing value of the dollar, personal-consumption expenditures just about doubled; between 1947
and 1950-51 they increased by another 20 per cent for
a total rise of 145 per cent.

Purchases in restaurants and bars hit 138 per cent
by 1947. But then, perhaps reflecting the trend to the
suburbs and the availability of durables, it slowed up
a bit and just reached 149 by 1950-51. Telephones,
which are certainly a good measure of the general
increase in living standards, hit 122 by 1947 and went
on to score a resounding 261 by 1951. Thanks to the
American's restlessness, moving and warehousing expenses were well above the average in 1947, and hit no
less than 199 by 1951.

So far as they can, the figures indicate that tastes
and preferences of people have broadened and risen.
Fenton Turck, consulting engineer, calls this elevation
the "American Explosion," and compares it to the beginning of the Periclean Age of Greece. He is jubilant
about the increasing expenditures for books, photo developing and printing, higher education, flowers and
seeds, phonographs and records, attendance at operas,
the growing number of symphony orchestras and local
opera companies. He also notes that design of draperies
and furnishings is far better than before the war. He
is, of course, right. But what is this great explosion? At
bottom, it is the rise of the great new homogeneous
middle market, big and resourceful enough to support
innumerable smaller markets and variations.

"A SCIENCE OF CONSUMPTION"

By now, it should be clear, nothing is more important
than the inclinations of the consumer. He has money,
he has a big choice, he can buy as he desires, and he
can stop buying many things for quite a while. What
is he likely to do? How would he spend the money if
the government reduced his taxes by 10 per cent? Can
he be persuaded to buy contraseasonally? Except in
small samples, nobody knows.

His "habits" have accordingly become a major preoccupation of American economists. Last year's annual
report of the National Bureau of Economic Research,
entitled "The Instability of Consumer Spending," outlined the new approach. It was written by none other
than Dr. Arthur Burns, now Eisenhower's chief economic adviser, who in the lead essay reviewed the growing concern with consumer attitudes. Dr. Burns began
by giving the consumer credit (as *Fortune* had done

shortly before) for checking inflation in 1951 by perversely going on a saving spree.

"The subject of primary interest concerning consumer demand has become the consumer himself—that is, his actual behavior and the kind and degree of regularity that characterize it," Dr. Burns said. "How, in what directions, and in what degree is the current spending of individual families influenced by the size of the family, the age of its members, their occupation . . . their income . . . the amount of their liquid assets, their highest past spending, their expectations concerning future incomes and prices . . . and by still other factors? How, in what directions, and in what degree is

the consumer spending of a nation influenced . . . by advertising expenditures, by the rate of formation of new families, by the geographic mobility of the population? These are some of the questions now being put by economists; and while none have as yet been answered with precision and some have hardly been answered at all, the rough foundations of an empirical science of consumption are slowly beginning to take shape."

The foundations are indeed rough, but much more has been accomplished than perhaps ninety-nine businessmen in a hundred are aware.

19. COSTS

HOW TO TELL WHERE YOU BREAK EVEN*

Though break-even charts are not usually found in elementary textbooks, they are not a new device but were developed over forty years ago by Professor Walter Rautenstrauch of the Industrial Engineering Department of Columbia University. Handy business tools, they also are a simple means to teach the concepts of constant and variable costs and to remind the student that some businessmen may use another technique than marginal analysis. Break-even charts have their limitations and must be handled with care. These charts are based on data from Rautenstrauch and Villers' The Economics of Industrial Management (*New York, 1949*).

The trouble with business last year was that it couldn't have been better. With a slowdown imminent, apprehensive talk about high break-even points has cropped up in business discussions with disturbing frequency. Businessmen want to know how far their inflated dollar sales can shrink before their profits disappear. To find out, they have set their accountants to compiling elaborate studies of costs and sales. Some of them have discovered what others had long known: that the break-even point can most readily be determined by simple plotting, and that the resultant chart is a handy management tool for a multitude of constructive purposes other than simply finding out where losses begin.

Essentially, the break-even chart is a graphic presentation of the relationship between revenue and expense, projected for all levels of sales (see top of page 98). There is nothing complicated or novel about such a chart. Progressive managements have used this or similar visual aids for years. The break-even chart is no substitute for either detailed accountancy or management judgment.

The basic chart top of page 98 was developed some forty years ago by Professor Walter Rautenstrauch of the Industrial Engineering Department of Columbia University. It is the great granddaddy of the many sales-profit charts in use today, and is, in some respects, superior to them. The 45-degree sales line makes it possible to plot the break-even points for any number of years or months on a single chart, and to compare charts for different companies, products, etc. A prerequisite to the construction of this or any other

break-even chart, however, is a knowledge of which business expenses are constant and which are variable with changes in volume. Once that is known a total-expense line can be drawn for all levels of sales. Few firms customarily break down their costs in this manner, however. Take, for example, the remuneration paid a salesman. Normal accountancy would probably lump his commissions, salary, and bonus together as sales expense. Actually, however, his commission is a variable expense, his salary a constant expense, and his bonus a regulated expense; i.e., although constant in that it is not directly related to sales, it is nevertheless subject to management discretion. The trick of constructing an accurate break-even chart, then, is largely dependent upon proper cost analysis, but that is equally true when the break-even point is computed.

HANDLE WITH CARE

The break-even chart is like a household tape measure. It has many practical uses and yet does not pretend to be microscopically accurate. The total-expense line, for example, is simply a straight line drawn from fixed costs at volume zero through total cost at current volume. No attempt is made at curvilinear refinement because cost figures are themselves mere approximations. Nor can valid deductions be drawn from a break-even chart at volumes widely different from that on which the chart is based. It is important to remember that the chart represents expense at a given moment and under given conditions and that any change in price, wages, *et al.*, will alter the sales-expense relationship. If these limitations are borne in mind, however, the break-even chart can be used to analyze and control costs and to estimate profits under a variety of assumptions.

* From "How To Tell Where You Break Even," February, 1949.

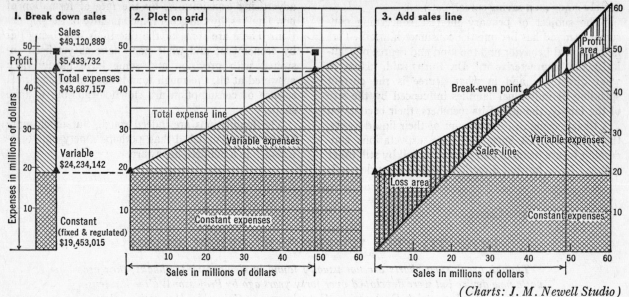

(Charts: J. M. Newell Studio)

The construction of a break-even chart involves three simple steps. Step 1: Expenses that vary directly with volume (materials, sales commissions, etc.) are segregated from constant expenses (real-estate taxes, depreciation, interest, etc.). Step 2: The total expense line is then plotted on a grid with identical horizontal and vertical dollar scales. Step 3: A sales line is superimposed on this grid forming a 45-degree angle with both scales. That this method of plotting the break-even point is accurate is attested by the fact that the computed break-even volume for the company above (an actual firm) was $38.4 million.

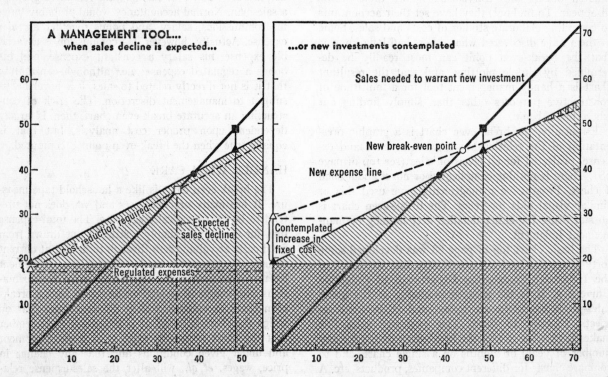

The hypothetical cases above illustrate two of the many ways a break-even chart can be used in management planning. If sales decline $15 million (left) a $4-million loss will result unless costs are cut. If, on the other hand, an investment is contemplated that will increase constant expense by $10 million (right) it can be seen that sales of $60 million are needed to justify the new expense structure.

In the two bottom charts on page 98, the effect of a sales decline or of an additional capital outlay are considered. A decline in sales of $15 million would obviously put the firm into the red unless regulatable expenses (research, promotion, the president's salary, etc.) were cut $4 million. In the other case it is assumed that a contemplated investment will increase constant cost by $10 million but will reduce variable expenses. The chart quickly shows at what volume the new investment becomes profitable. Although these charts (based on data from a book by Rautenstrauch and Villers, *The Economics of Industrial Management*, Funk & Wagnalls) are for an entire company, break-even charts can also be constructed for individual departments, plants, products, or even salesmen.

20. COMPETITION

THE NEW COMPETITION*

How much competition is to be found in the United States economy? According to the analyses and principles presented by economists of the classical school, American business, especially Big Business, does not compete enough and not at all in a socially desirable way. This answer businessmen just cannot understand, for they insist they are always competing. Is the answer to this conflict the fact that American business today is practicing a new kind of competition? This article contrasts the classical competitive model with the "workable" or "effective" competition approach. It suggests that the new competition best answers the crucial question: How well does American business serve the consumer? Reference is made to the views of Galbraith, Adelman, Wilcox, Marshall, Stigler, Arthur Burns, J. M. Clark, Schumpeter, and Griffin.

Here is a nation that is the home and sanctuary of free competitive enterprise, distinguished from all other nations for such determined adherence to the principles of competition that it has written them into the law of the land with constitutional force. Virtually every American businessman, manager or owner, big or small, producer or distributor, uses the word "competition" habitually and usually sincerely in describing American capitalism. So do his employees, and so do editors, journalists, and even labor leaders.

But here also is a nation about whose competitiveness many "objective" and professional observers are very dubious. Certainly the country's economists, the men whose job it is to describe, analyze, and interpret the economy, do not talk of competition as businessmen do. Many seem to deny that the word competition has much relevance in the twentieth-century U.S.A.

In his new *American Capitalism*, Harvard's J. K. Galbraith makes what is perhaps the most sweeping statement so far. He says in effect that there is no competition in the classic sense, and hasn't been for years. Real competition has all but disappeared and oligopoly, or a few big sellers—the "Big Three," "Big Four," and so forth—dominate American markets. The economy is workable because big concentrations of industrial power almost automatically beget "countervailing power"—other concentrations of power organized against one another—which tends to prevent abuse. But the time has come, says Dr. Galbraith, to call an economic fact an economic fact, and to cast out "this preoccupation with competition."

The paradoxes of modern American capitalism are not lost on "realistic" Europeans. Probably few things amuse the sophisticated French businessmen and the cynical German industrialist more than the "romantic" American attempts to demonopolize the Continent. The British, too, are amused. Only last December 15, the London *Economist* chaffed the "evangelical" American businessmen for preaching competition and practicing something else. The Kremlin, of course, harps endlessly on its old, well-worn theme that *all* American business is monopolistic.

If the concept of competition has no relevance today, why does the American businessman stubbornly insist that competition is the heart of the enterprise system? Is he hypocritical or merely naive? Is it possible, on the other hand, that he is right? For the good of the national psyche, for the honor of the national reputation—and last but not least for intelligent administration of the antitrust law—it is time to try to resolve this great paradox of the new American capitalism.

The paradox arises in the fact that American capitalism in the past fifty or sixty years has experienced a profound transformation. It *is* a new capitalism, and the period of change coincides with the rise of the big modern corporation with large aggregations of capital and nationwide markets. This corporation changed the pattern of the critical producing areas of the economy from one of many sellers to one of few sellers and more recently to few buyers. The corporation, moreover, is usually run by paid managers who, in the long-term interest of their company, are forced to be responsible not only to stockholders but also to employees and to consumers.

One result of this change is that the word competition no longer means what it once did. American business today, and particularly Big Business, is practicing a new kind of competition. This competition is not *Fortune's* invention. It has been developing for more than fifty years, and although it is belittled by many

* From "The New Competition," June, 1952.

economists, a growing number of respected ones have espoused it. And most businessmen have a very good idea indeed of what it is.

They know for one thing that the "new competition" has been a stunning success, especially when measured in terms of delivering a standard of living to the consumer. Could "classic" competition have done any better? As businessmen see it, that's a fair question, the only question. They ask to be judged by results, not by theory. If they tend to grow apoplectic when they are discussed in learned papers as "monopolists" or "oligopolists," it is because they *know* the U.S. is competitive.

As buyers and sellers, businessmen recognize this new competition in terms of such things as prices that respond to market pressures, products that are constantly being improved, and choice for the buyers. They apply such standards pragmatically, not only because they are unfamiliar with formal economic thought but because they know all too well how markets change with industries, products, companies, regions, and from year to year or even month to month. This approach is more or less what the new competition amounts to. It is also more or less what modern economists think of when they talk about "workable" competition. M. A. Adelman of M.I.T., for instance, suggests that workable competition exists when non-collusive rivalry occurs with a sufficient number of alternates open to both buyer and seller.

What causes the great paradox is that most of the economists and experts who have until recently shaped the accepted notions of competition do not describe it that way. Competition to them is a way of life that can be defined fairly rigidly. They conceive of competition in terms of the grand old original or classic model of Adam Smith and his followers.

THE GRAND OLD MODEL

Now this model is based on a great and wise principle, verified by the experience of man through the ages and back into the abyss of time—the principle that the peoples of the earth, if they know what's good for them, should never trust their welfare to the discretion of a powerful few. Thus competition is free society's main safeguard against economic injustice. It drives people to produce more rather than less because it enables them to make more money by producing more to sell for less. It tends to make the best use of resources. It is both a regulator and a spur, and its ultimate benefactors are people as consumers.

On these general truths the early British economists reared an ideal superstructure. Its chief characteristic was a market with many sellers turning out practically the same product, and with no seller large enough to have any power to control prices. Competition was assumed to occur by price alone; supply and demand, the impersonal forces of the market, "the hidden hand," automatically regulated the price of everything, including the price of labor. Everybody got no more or less than he deserved, and resources were used with maximum efficiency.

The model was natural and just. It was infinitely superior to socialism in that it recognized the validity of individual incentive. Because it was so comprehensive and fundamental, it became the academic model. When pedagogues expounded capitalism to their pupils, they expounded it in terms of the classic model.

But like many great concepts it was a model of perfection rather than of reality, even in its time. It was set up when no one wielded great economic power. Although the concept of the market and the law of supply and demand retained their validity, the notion that competition was effective only when many sellers competed by price alone gradually lost relevance.

Even in the U.S., the only nation that continued to take the model seriously in the twentieth century, the ideal of many sellers went by the board. Large companies grew up swiftly, both by internal growth and by acquisition and merger. The U.S. antitrust laws, of course, were inspired by and partly based on the classic model. But they at first punished only clear conspiracies and accomplished monopolies. And although the Clayton and its subsidiary acts were passed to *prevent* monopoly by catching it in its "incipiency," confusion and irresolution prevented the new law from being effective until the middle 1930's, and even then it did not reform the economy in its image. It could do nothing about the prorationing of the state commissions, which in effect decides the level of the world's oil prices. It could do relatively little about the price "leadership" of big companies—the judgment of the leader, who posts prices in response to his "feeling" about the market, replaces the impersonal forces of the classic market.

The law, finally, could do nothing about the rise of Big Little Business, Big Agriculture, and Big Labor, which proceeded to use political means to gain what Big Business had gained by political and economic means. They not only emulated but outdid Big Business. All three carried their war to the citadel itself, amending the antitrust laws to exempt themselves from many if not most of the effects of price competition.

The classic economists realized that their model was not working well; the last of the great classicists, Alfred Marshall, made due allowances for the fact that competition in practice was bound to be imperfect. The classicists nevertheless went on preaching and teaching orthodox theory because they believed and still believe it provides them with valid principles for measuring a free, competitive society. Let the U.S. strive for perfect competition, they say in effect, and it will be likely to remain tolerably competitive.

THE PRAGMATIC STANDARD

The new competition is an approach, not a model: it cannot be, or certainly hasn't been, rigidly defined. It does not cast aside the classic model. It simply retains the basic principles and discards as much of the model as is necessary to make it consistent with reality. It has no use for collusion, monopoly, or deliberate restraints of trade. But it puts the consumer's interest ahead of theory, and shuns perfect competition for the sake of perfect competition. It makes allowance for the fact that the American economy has delivered to people the benefits that perfect competition was calculated to give.

Therefore, it does not hold that business, to bring maximum benefit to consumers, must necessarily consist of many small sellers competing by price alone. It does not hold that the rivalry of a few large sellers necessarily means economic injustice. And it does not necessarily think of competition as the impersonal, pervasive force of the classic model, but grants it can be, in the words of Michigan's Clare Griffin, "conscious and personal." It corresponds roughly to the businessman's pragmatic description of competition. And in terms of such a concept, the businessman who talks sincerely of our competitive way of life is right. Just look at our economy today.

To begin with, that economy is too complex to encompass with a few generalizations. It is a matter of considerable doubt, for example, whether a relatively few large companies—"the oligopolists"—do "rule" the nation's prices and markets. Professor George Stigler, author of "The Case Against Big Business" in last month's *Fortune,* is an outstanding classicist, and certainly cannot be accused of partiality to Big Business. But even he estimates that only 20 per cent of the industries he was able to classify with inadequate data were, in 1939, represented by what he defines as unregulated monopoly or oligopoly. It is his thesis that competition, even judged by the classic model, has been increasing, not decreasing, over the years.

Professor Clair Wilcox of Swarthmore also challenges easy assumptions about oligopoly, but from the standpoint that most figures on concentration are irrelevant. "Meaningful conclusions as to the structure of markets," he insists with considerable plausibility, "are not to be obtained until someone devises a product classification that groups goods according to the readiness with which one can be substituted for another."

Therefore he denounces the habit of judging the whole economy in terms of manufacturing, which after all accounts for less than two-fifths of unregulated, non-banking private enterprise. Breaking down the consumer's expenditures, by categories, he finds strong evidence that "oligopoly" does not dominate the market.

Clair Wilcox's emphasis on the consumer is much to the point. The consumer has an immense choice of goods and prices; even in the wilderness he has the mail-order catalogue. American retailing is often highly competitive by almost any standard, sometimes almost by that of the classic model.

Not only do retailers compete briskly, they force manufacturers that supply them to price their products competitively. This is an example of what Mr. Galbraith terms "countervailing power"—the idea that big sellers cannot control markets if buyers are strong enough, nor buyers if sellers are strong enough. Sears, Roebuck and the A & P can buy almost anything at the lowest market prices because they buy so much— just as the motor industry is able to buy steel at a competitive price because it is a big buyer, and labor

unions can sell their members' services at good prices because they are so well organized.

Countervailing power, however, is plainly not a substitute for competition, as Mr. Galbraith seems to imply it is. Without a concept of competition translated into public policy, this power can be a monopolistic force—as it is in Europe, and indeed as it is for the American labor unions that wield power *as* power because they are exempt from antitrust. But countervailing power, plus the competitive principle, does result in delivering to the consumer the benefits that classic competition was presumed to bring.

NOT CLASSIC BUT EFFECTIVE

Many manufacturers, of course, need no direct pressure to be competitive. Certainly most makers of new consumer products don't. The frozen-orange-juice industry (*Fortune,* March) is compelled by circumstances beyond its control to be so competitive it hurts badly. And, of course, garment manufacturers must compete incessantly or go out of business. They do not gang up to fix production or prices. None dominates the market. Their marginal costs often equal—and sometimes exceed—their prices. What keeps them from being an example of classic competition is David Dubinsky and his I.L.G.W.U., which has insulated garmentworkers from the wage market.

And the consumer today certainly enjoys a wonderfully competitive market in appliances, radios, and television sets. Most are made by a fair number of manufacturers, none of whom can control the market, at least not for very long. These durables are today easy to get into (and to fail in, too). Prices are flexible at the retail level, which is where price counts. And they are flexible at the retail level because manufacturers allow for price competition when they set the markup.

Only two years ago, remember, manufacturers were assuring people that they would never again be able to buy a first-line, eight-foot refrigerator for less than $250 or a sixteen-inch television set for less than $350. Today they are both selling at about $150. It is certainly hard to describe as monopolistic and therefore antisocial an economy whose refrigerator industry has sold the astonishing number of 48 million units since 1940; whose radio industry has sold the even more astonishing number of 188 million units since 1922; whose television industry has sold some 18 million units in five years. The competition that made this possible may not have been classically perfect, but who will deny that it has been effective?

This kind of competition, moreover, does not seem destined to wither away but to increase as the nation's productivity increases and the nation's selling apparatus is pressed to get rid of the goods. Buying or countervailing power will surely come into greater play. Retailers will press manufacturers for better buys; manufacturers will press suppliers for cheaper raw materials and components.

Thus the chances are good, unless retailers gang up and legislate sweeping fair-trade laws, that the consumer will continue to buy most of his soft and durable goods, accounting for perhaps 25 per cent of his expenditures, as cheaply as he could were they made and sold under the classic model. (At least no one can demonstrate otherwise.) And although many farm prices are exempt from market forces, the competition of the food chains will doubtless continue to give the consumer a good break on the 30 per cent or so of his income that he spends on food.

THE "OLIGOPOLISTS"

Now what about Big Business itself—the "oligopolistic" unregulated industries like autos, steel, chemicals, cigarettes, rubber, oil, tin cans, and so forth—wherein a few big sellers are said to rule the markets? To begin with, none is describable as a true monopoly. Their prices usually respond to the market; prices may be "sticky" at times but they do move. These industries offer a choice to the buyer (and seller), and they are constantly improving the quality of their products. Many are subject to countervailing power. And all are subject to the pressure of public opinion.

By classic theory, of course, they are presumed to get a higher price for goods than "perfect" competitors. Prices no longer "rule" them; they "rule" prices. But thanks to the American preoccupation with competition, this phenomenon is often inconsequential even when it is true.

Price leadership occasionally takes the form of "dominant firm" leadership—i.e., one or two firms hold the price umbrella steady, regardless of market conditions. Such instances can be—and are—dealt with by antitrust law. But price leadership often is evidence of competition of the new kind. It can be observed as the "barometric" leadership practiced in the oil and rayon industries. "The leader bears the onus of formally recognizing market conditions," an oil-industry spokesman describes it. Eugene Holman, president of the Jersey Co., explains it further: "You paste your price on a wall, but you can't be sure it'll stick." Sometimes the leader's prices don't stick. In 1947, after President Truman's plea to keep prices steady, Esso Standard tried to hold the line as smart public relations. But it could not hold the line, at least for very long.

RULE OR RUIN

Another demonstration of big business' ability to "rule" prices was offered by the motor and steel industries, which after the war held prices considerably below the point where market forces alone would have carried them. The classic argument is that prices should be left to find their own level, not only to encourage more production but to ration what is available "by the purse." But letting prices find their own level, with the restrictions then prevailing, probably would not have resulted in an appreciably greater production. And rationing by the purse, which is theoretically the best way to ration anything, would have created a storm of angry protests from consumers (as the auto dealers' practice of rationing by the purse in fact did).

The motor industry, indeed, could argue without double talk that genuine *competitive* considerations dictated that prices be held. The fundamental purpose

of competition after all is not to throw the economy into a tailspin, but to make it function naturally, to dispense economic justice to the consumer. Classic price competition in motorcars after the war might have meant a precipitous rise followed by an equally precipitous drop, and then perhaps by serious economic disruptions and certainly by economic injustice. The restraint of the motor industry thus seems justified from the short-term view of a competitor seeking public approval and the long-term view of an industry cast in a workably competitive mold.

Whether big business is bigger than it needs to be for efficiency and technical progress is a proposition that can be argued endlessly, but there is little doubt that without modern "oligopoly" much of our immense technical progress would not have occurred. Modern research and development not only demand a lot of money which big companies have; the prospect of making unusually good or "monopoly" profits from research and development before competitors get in the field is what drives big companies to do the research and development.

Thus it can be argued that this incentive, which results from product or "quality" competition, brings society more benefits than classic price competition would have. If the chemical industry, for example, had cut prices to the bone as soon as costs declined, it today might be charging more for its products than it is.

Certainly "quality" and service competition indulged in by big companies cannot be summarily dismissed, as it is in strict classic theory, as a wasteful if cheap substitute for price competition. The plain fact, verified by anyone who compares consumer goods of thirty years ago with those of today, is that quality competition has given him more for his money.

THE UTILITY OF LUXURY

And the plain fact, verified every day by anyone who travels anywhere, eats or drinks in any save the meanest places, or buys anything at retail, is that much service competition is not wasteful unless anything remotely "luxurious" is defined as wasteful. Free delivery and other amenities may add nothing to the national stock of goods. But in a nation whose rising standard of living is measured in terms of rising services, they are an important part of life.

Even in capital-goods industries, anything but an example of classic competition, much real competition is evident as service competition. A small specialty steel company, for example, may quote the same prices as the big companies. But it goes to considerable trouble and expense in tailoring shapes and preparing metal content to the special needs of its customers.

And what about big-business advertising and selling? Many economists say they are economically wasteful methods of bolstering monopoly position and thus excluding potential competitors by differentiating between goods that in fact have little difference. "We may assume," writes Arthur Burns in his *Decline of Competition,* "that sales pressure by one or more firms in an industry has no effect on total demand—it merely shifts demand from one seller to another. . . ."

This might be true in a threadbare society hardly

managing to keep body and soul together. It might also be true in a model society inhabited by clairvoyant manufacturers who always make the right things and by consumers who promptly buy up everything as soon as it is produced. But in this realm of comparative plenty, most people have more money than they need for subsistence, and are "optional" and therefore arbitrary and erratic spenders. Advertising and selling provide the only means of persuading them. And as *Fortune* suggested last April, advertising and selling may provide an important means of keeping over-all consumption up to production, thus helping to prevent oversaving and the consequent deflation.

POWER AND SELF-RESTRAINT

Modern American capitalism, finally, exhibits a kind of long-term drive to behave as if it were competitive even when it is not driven by countervailing power or the impersonal forces of classic competition. It is a fact that businesses often tend to go on expanding sales whether profits are immediately maximized or not. As M. Adelman says of the A & P, it tries not for the largest possible profit over a planned period but for the best possible position at the end of it. "They recognize," says economist J. M. Clark, "that it is bad business to sacrifice future growth to an exorbitant rate of present profit, even if the curves on paper would permit it."

One reason it does so is that it understands the advantages of adjusting itself to public opinion and the moral climate of the times. Big business is more and more run by professional men whose primary aim is to keep their companies strong, and who therefore cannot exploit the rest of the country. As *Fortune* has put it, the American manager "is part of a group that enjoys power only so long as it does not abuse it—in other words, precisely so long as it does not exercise power the way men and groups of men used to [exercise it]."

THE "CREATIVE DESTRUCTION"

Another reason companies take the long view is that they sense or understand that in the U.S. economy no one's place is secure. Research and a free-money market have seen to that. Well-heeled companies, no longer beholden to Wall Street, plow back their earnings and constantly look for new things to get into. No company is safe in a field that is too green, uncrowded, or technically backward. General Motors is not only the largest auto maker; it is the largest refrigerator maker; and because the locomotive industry fell behind the times, G. M.'s Electro-Motive Division is now the largest locomotive maker. Crosley is not only a large refrigerator maker but a large television maker. "Anybody today can make anything," one manufacturer puts it, and it's not much of an exaggeration.

Industrial research, furthermore, is providing hundreds of new products that can substitute for older ones—nylon for silk, aluminum for steel and copper, plastics for leather, wood, metals, etc. The laboratory, today, is the great creator of competition.

No one's place is secure, finally, because the consumer has a great many choices and enough money to indulge the luxury of making them. Thus autos compete with fur coats, television sets with furniture, food with gasoline, and so on all down the line. Any manufacturer who wants to achieve volume must sell at a price that overcomes the competitive pressure of the other dissimilar goods.

On such facts the late Joseph Schumpeter based his notion of the "creative destruction" of capitalism. He argued that actual competition is perhaps less important than the threatened competition of the new technology, the new market, the new product. In the long run, he said, this threat "may enforce behavior very similar to the competitive pattern. It disciplines before it attacks. The businessman feels himself to be in a competitive situation even if he is alone in the field." In the short run Schumpeter noted what we already have digressed upon: precisely because corporations can look forward to good profits for a while, they risk big money for research and technological progress.

Such analysis has been attacked as a plea for letting well enough alone and giving up the fight for a competitive economy—and it is probably true that the country will not stay competitive by itself. But this argument would be valid only if the antitrust laws were not very effective.

"THE BROODING OMNIPRESENCE"

Taking everything together, one of the most important reasons why the U.S. economy is competitive is the "contradictory," "impotent," and yet on the whole profoundly effective body of antitrust laws. They were inspired by and based on the classic model, and their contradictions and failures are those of the model itself. They have won comparatively few victories, and some of these, like the basing-point, Alcoa, and Morton Salt decisions, raise as many difficult questions as they answer.

But the law's greatest achievement is not what it has done, but what its "brooding omnipresence" has induced business to do voluntarily. As the saying goes, it has made the ghost of Senator Sherman an ex officio member of every board of directors in the land. No businessman of consequence makes price, employment, advertising, acquisition, or expansion policies without considering whether or not they will violate the law. "I can't even write to a friend in a competing company," laments one company economist, "and ask him any information pertaining to the business, even if it has appeared in print."

THE ECONOMIC APPROACH

A good case can be made for tightening up some parts of antitrust law and enforcing it more vigorously. But an even better case can be made for the proposition that the law applies the classic model too literally. In general, it lacks an economic approach to what are essentially economic problems. In its preoccupation with "maintaining" competition, as ordained in the various amendments to the Clayton Act, it has tended to produce an opposite result, i.e., to protect competitors from the effects of competition. The recent Alcoa decision has laid it down in effect that business can violate the law merely by growing up to bigness and achieving the *power* to violate the law. And the Federal Trade Commission's stand that identical pricing and "conscious parallelism" are the same as collusion if their consequence is substantially to lessen competition has set a legal basis for prosecuting bona fide competitors.

The concept of the New Competition—"workable" competition—provides not a hard-and-fast definition but an approach to the problem of keeping competition effective. The job of formulating new policies is not easy. But it is not impossible.

Dr. Galbraith, for example, suggests a plausible rule of thumb: let the government encourage countervailing power when that power opposes existing market power, let it even create countervailing power where it is needed; and let it attack market power that is opposed by no countervailing power. As Michael Hoffman of the New York *Times* remarks, that is pretty much what antitrust does now. But Dr. Galbraith's suggestion has merit, and might well be studied by lawyers, prosecutors, judges, and analysts of antitrust policy.

Another and more carefully worked out guide is offered by Clare Griffin in his *"An Economic Approach to Antitrust Problems,"* recently published by the American Enterprise Association. He details five economic performance tests that he thinks should be used in deciding when to prosecute, how to determine penalties, what to legislate, and how to judge. The tests: (1) Is the company or industry efficient? (2) Is it progressive? (3) Does it show a reasonable and socially useful profit pattern—i.e., are its profits the reward of efficiency and progress rather than the result of artificial advantages? (4) Does it allow as much freedom of entry as is consistent with the business? (5) Is it well suited for defense?

Such tests place a heavy responsibility on the discretionary powers of the authorities, and may assume more intelligence and all-around judgment than the authorities possess. But the tests are apt and carefully thought out, and should not be overlooked. They or similar economic tests will have to be applied if antitrust law is to shape competition to benefit the people whom the creators of the classic model themselves intended it to benefit: the consumers.

21. AGRICULTURE

FARM POLICY: A GREAT OPPORTUNITY*

The anomaly of a prosperous American farm community coexisting with huge agricultural surpluses is one of today's major economic issues. To understand the problem and its possible solution, certain facts must be at hand. For example: Who is the farmer? Is agricultural income below that of the non-farm population? How unstable are farm prices? Also a general knowledge of the apparatus of farm controls, here summarized, is important. The inherent difficulties of price supports for farm products are enumerated. Planks for a positive policy are recommended.

It is a hopeful sign that some of the best friends of the American farmer have come to the conclusion that catchall government plans for agriculture are subject to the law of diminishing returns. If one draws away from Washington and goes back to school among economists, one will find all but unanimity of opinion that the sooner the country gets over the idea that there is any one grand panacea for agriculture, the better.

What is necessary and indeed imperative at the present time is to stop designing glittering "programs" and to concentrate on policy. Quite clearly, as argued last month in "Those Prosperous Farmers," present law, with its emphasis on supporting prices, is working very badly, building up huge surpluses in wheat and cotton and increasing rather than decreasing the farmer's fear of disaster. Less observed but equally true is that the underlying pulse beat of agriculture is healthy. The American farm community is not only extraordinarily prosperous but it is also relatively free of debt. It is possessed of an unmatched and spectacular tech-

*From "Farm Policy: A Great Opportunity," July, 1949.

nology that should allow it to compete freely with all comers. If there was an excess of farm population in the thirties, the war served largely to clear that surplus by drawing men and women to the cities. Finally, estimates of total U.S. population have been shifting upward, indicating a strong demand for farm products. In 1938 it was estimated the U.S. population would be 147 million in 1960. But already, a decade ahead of time, the population has grown to over 148 million and is still growing.

All this indicates that American agriculture has a great opportunity to adapt itself to a normal peacetime life, provided, but always provided, that rational policies are pursued. Three propositions would seem to be basic. The first is that agriculture cannot, any more than industry or labor, avoid postwar readjustment and that readjustment should not be confused with depression. The second proposition is that our main effort must be directed not at tinkering with this or that agricultural price but rather with sustaining conditions of high over-all demand in the economy. The third proposition, on which the first two rest, is that American agriculture cannot be looked at as a group or class apart from American society and the market system, which, economically speaking, binds that society together. To do so is to fall for all the fallacies inherent in the philosophy of the socialist or corporate state and to slip unconsciously into planning from the top down, which is wholly futile in its practical applications.

THE MAGNIFICENT DECLINE

The most important development in the history of American agriculture, by all odds, has been the spectacular way its productivity has improved in the past quarter-century. Farm efficiency, lagging for years, has risen faster over the past ten years than the efficiency of the rest of the economy. Thanks to a fertile, progressive technology, the average U.S. farm worker is 110 per cent more productive than he was twenty-five years ago, and so 37 per cent *fewer* farm workers, putting in *fewer* hours, are producing 54 per cent *more* than U. S. agriculture produced twenty-five years ago. Only 13.5 per cent of the nation's population, against 25 per cent in 1930, now lives on the land. What is more, these over-all statistics vastly understate the actual growth in the efficiency and prosperity of U.S. agriculture because they include millions of so-called farms and farmers that are really not part of U.S. commercial agriculture at all. The efficient farms, by contrast, are becoming truly industrial organizations—not in sheer size, and not in market philosophy, but in their approach to investment, technology, and production.

In the next twenty-five years, *Fortune* estimates, U.S. farm production will rise from $34.7 billion to $48.2 billion in constant 1953 dollars, or 39 per cent. Yet the total number of farms will decrease from 5,200,000 to 4,300,000, farm population from 21,900,000 to 17 million, or from 13.5 per cent to only 8 per cent of U.S. population. To put all this another way, the chances are that farm production in 1980 will have more than doubled since 1930, while farm population will have declined by nearly half.

This progress, nowhere so sensational as in the U.S., does create an embarrassment. People in a dynamic economy eat better as their living standards rise, and the value of their food consumption therefore rises somewhat faster than population increases. But even in a dynamic economy the demand for farm products is relatively inelastic—that is, people want only so much of them, and their consumption accordingly does not increase as much as the growth of the economy as a whole. *So agriculture's percentage of national output must decline, and as farmers produce more per hour, the percentage of the population needed on the farm must decline even more.* And so it is and must be with the U.S. Despite agriculture's great progress, it is still only 53 per cent as efficient (in output per man-hour) as the rest of the private economy. If the nation is to continue to progress, American farms must produce more and more with fewer man-hours.

—"The Magnificent Decline of U.S. Farming," June, 1955.

WHO IS THIS FARMER?

For the truth is that agriculture is peculiarly unsuited to central planning. The thing looks feasible only if one forgets that among the 27 million people living on the American land are thousands of capitalists, great and small, each making his own market decisions and existing through those decisions. Farming, we are told, is America's biggest *single* industry and, if we have a taste for aggregates, a case can be made for that. Last year farm cash income topped $31 billion; and the value of America's six million-odd farms and buildings is put at nearly $67 billion. But if we lumped all manufacturing industries together, or even for that matter all the service trades, a similar kind of case for bigness and importance could be made. The point is that there is little to be gained by doing so. No one believes that the interests of the Pittsburgh steel producer are identical with those of the Detroit automobile manufacturer, or that the man who works at a service station has much in common with the man who works in a drugstore. It is only in agriculture, and partly for political reasons, that we assume that every man who owns or works on a farm must be one with every other.

But the assumption breaks down the more it is examined. Even to talk of the American Farmer is at best a convenient shorthand. Who exactly do we mean by this gentleman? Do we mean the big cattleman of Texas who may own 75,000 acres and net $250,000 a year from his beef? Do we mean the Kansas wheat farmer who also turns to large acreage? Do we mean the dairy farmer of Wisconsin or the Northeast? Or the tobacco grower of the Carolinas? Or the cotton operator or the sharecropper of the Delta? Or do we mean just the plain ordinary farmer, found in most of the forty-eight states, who goes in for a little dairying, some hogs, some wheat, some corn, with vegetables and poultry as a profitable sideline? Above all, do we mean the man who sells largely for cash or the family that simply lives off the land? "Much of the confusion regarding agriculture and its problems," Allan Kline of the American Farm Bureau has said, "will disappear if the public will come to an appreciation of the fact that most commercial agriculture is carried on by half of those listed as farmers in the census reports." Secretary Brannan has made this more dramatic. On his estimate about 2 per cent of the nation's farms sell about 25 per cent of its cash crops.

These figures suggest that if we worry about "concentration" in industry we should also worry about concentration in farming. They also throw a rather critical light on the whole operation of price support, since it is only those farmers who produce for cash who benefit *directly* by it. But the complexities do not end here. Large government programs must also elect what crops they are going to favor, and here nature herself rises to confound the issue. Congressmen continue to talk about the nation's six "basic" crops—corn, wheat, cotton, tobacco, rice, and peanuts. But a fertile and generous continent produces not six but hundreds of farm products, including lespedeza, pecans, artichokes, garlic, mint, shallots, avocados, rabbits, pigeons, guinea hens, not to mention the silver fox and the mink.

Even if we are to talk of "basic" products, it has long been recognized that the priorities given in most past farm legislation have little relevance. In order of magnitude the great cash crops of 1948 broke down as follows:

Meat animals	$9,600,000,000
Dairy products	4,500,000,000
Poultry, eggs	3,000,000,000
Food grains (including wheat)	3,000,000,000
Cotton (lint and seed)	2,500,000,000
Feed crops (including corn)	1,900,000,000
Vegetables	1,900,000,000
Fruits and tree nuts	1,200,000,000
Tobacco	1,000,000,000

The list is interesting in the fact that peanuts do not even appear and quite rightly so, since cash sales of peanuts in 1948 amounted to about $220 million. On the other hand, corn is of vastly greater importance than the above figures show, since only a fraction of it is sold for cash, most of it going to feed hogs and other animals. In 1948 the U.S. produced 3.7 billion bushels of corn, which, figured at a loan price of $1.50 per bushel would mean a total value of $5.5 billion. On these figures corn would indeed be "basic," but the whole distinction is fairly arbitrary. The sound and fury coming out of Washington about peanuts and tobacco is in almost inverse ratio to their importance. The healthy sector of the farm economy includes corn, livestock, dairy products, and in the opinion of most students hope for the future lies in further diversification in this direction. Yet cattle, to take a single example, has had nothing done for it support-wise and presumably needs no help at all. And the truck farmer, who sold $1.2 billion worth of vegetables at market prices, is perhaps the best answer to the claim that if the government withholds aid the whole agricultural structure will collapse. What is true is that where government becomes involved in price-support operations, and the greater surpluses become, the more difficult it is to effect retreat. In this matter interference with the price mechanism is not much different from the use of drugs. It is easy to begin. It is much harder to taper off the dosage.

AGRICULTURAL INCOME

This, however, is to anticipate. For the moment let us consider some further aspects of agriculture that are a good deal more debatable. The first concerns farm income. As already noted, the discrepancy between incomes within the farm community is certainly just as great as outside of it. On a per capita basis, however, it is possible to show that farm population receives less than non-farm. The demonstration is made by taking farm cash income and making various additions and subtractions. The additions include wages received by workers who do not own farms, income derived from non-farm sources, and an increment for food produced and used on the farm and for rent. Deduction is made for the farmer's production expenses. The total, which amounted last year to about $25

billion, is then divided by the total number of people living on the land. The per capita net income for 1948 was figured through these abstruse calculations at $909, as against $1,569 for the non-farm population.

This comparison is widely used to show that the farmer must need some form of perpetual assistance, and the leveling of farm and non-farm incomes has been made by Mr. Brannan the ultimate goal of policy. It is a highly questionable goal. At the technical level there is wide dispute as to just what allowance should be made for the benefits that the farmer receives for living on the land. Should we value the eggs he consumes at market prices, for instance, or at prices on the farm, which are apt to be extraordinarily low? What price is to be put on the "intangible benefits" of farming—benefits that are constantly harped on by those who argue that it is a "way of life" to be cherished and preserved? And, in view of all the diversity that exists in farming, can we really argue for a group approach as regards income? If average farm and non-farm incomes are to be leveled, should not the same apply to the wages of carpenters and, say, lawyers, and to the incomes of sharecroppers and government officials?

Moreover, concentration on average income figures tends to obscure rather than point up certain real problems. One reason the per capita income figure is so low is that it covers regions, including the Deep South, where real poverty does exist and cash receipts per family may run down as low as $200 or $300 a year. We must seek to cure this poverty, but we shall not do so just by raising the incomes of all farmers, including the most prosperous ones. Finally and determinatively, we are up against the fact that the farm population is at best a shifting group. At the turn of the century 41.6 per cent of total U.S. population was living on the land. Now the figure is 18.1 per cent. This flow away from the country to the cities has been the mark of all civilization, has made the industrial development of America possible, and is certainly salutary from the point of view of those students who argue that the trouble with farming is that there are too many farmers. We shall scarcely gain through freezing people on the farms by taking wholly arbitrary income goals.

INSTABILITY OF PRICES

The more traditional case for giving agriculture special treatment rests on instability of farm incomes, and more particularly of farm prices, as compared to non-farm. As to incomes, it can certainly be shown that cash receipts from farming have fluctuated widely as the result of both war and depression. Here again, however, one is up against measuring intangibles. Where, seriously, is it best to be in a great depression—on the farm or on the sidewalks? The actual migration of men and women has answered that question rather definitely. Within the secular flow of population, already noted, is a cyclical flow. In times of depression, men and women go back to the land as a haven of refuge. In the last great war boom, despite rising farm incomes, people moved to the factory. From the point of view of society, the refuge afforded by the land in depressions is a limited benefit. Without doubt, however, it intensifies declines in per capita farm income.

Even so comparative fluctuations of real income between farm and city dwellers are subject to wide interpretation.

More obvious, but much less important in welfare terms, has been the performance of farm production and farm prices. Farm output has shown itself far steadier than that of industry, farm prices more volatile, though not necessarily more so than those of metals or other basic commodities selling in world markets. The usual base for figuring farm and non-farm prices are the years of 1910-14, when they were supposed to be in normal relationship. The relationship of prices received by farmers to prices paid by farmers can then be expressed as percentages of "parity"—the 1910-14 base being taken as 100. During World War I all prices in the economy shot up, the prices of farm products going up somewhat faster than the average so that the parity ratio stood at 118 in 1918. Thereafter came a precipitous fall of all prices, with farm commodities leading the way, and the parity ratio averaged 75 in 1921. During the twenties the ratio moved between 80 and 94, only to fall again in the great depression, touching 50 in the bitter days of 1932. Partial recovery then set in, but it was not until the war that the ratio crossed 100, reaching its peak in October of 1946 and then gradually declining. At the present it stands at 104.

The fluctuation of farm prices relative to industrial prices has therefore been real enough, though if we omit the disaster years of 1921 and 1932 it is not so great as often supposed. But admitting the fluctuations, it does not follow that concentration on price stability is the best way of helping the farmer out, or that the fluctuations should be viewed as more than effects of deeper causes. The troubles that agriculture got into in the twenties were magnified by a high debt-income ratio, and the persistence of debt explains to no small degree the farmer's vulnerability in the thirties. The sweep of farm prices upward during the second world war was due in part at least to the fact that the agricultural community, which talks so much about controls, was among the last to accept price ceilings. But beyond all this the whole period studied was one dominated by either war or deep depression. If we assume war as a norm, then agriculture will be on a perpetual spree. If we assume depression as a norm, with wide-scale urban unemployment as in the thirties, then the case is equally bleak. Allowing for relative volatility of farm prices and incomes it still remains true that the farmer's worst enemies have been *general* in nature. We should not frame farm policy on the assumption that the guns are going constantly to boom. Even less should we frame it on the idea that our society is, economically speaking, always going to fall apart.

THE DIFFICULTIES OF CONTROL

Unfortunately these are precisely the assumptions on which most modern farm legislation has been based, with emphasis always gathering on specific class legislation rather than on more general cures. The history is a long one but the general outlines are clear enough. Faced with real distress and open farm revolt in the thirties, the New Deal rather naturally turned to "doing something" about farm prices and in the process found that if prices were propped up, then production in one way or another had to be curtailed through acreage restrictions and marketing quotas. These never cleared Mr. Wallace's ever bursting granary. The war did, and in the war a new doctrine was born. The whole apparatus of price support, born in a depression, was now used in a period of great prosperity to encourage greater production. Price floors were rapidly moved up and extended from the "basics" to over twenty commodities, including pork, poultry, eggs.

The wartime provisions might have automatically lapsed in December, 1948; and, in the opinion of many experts, the greatest single mistake in policy we have made so far was not to have let them die. Instead the Eightieth Congress passed the Hope-Aiken law, which (1) extended the wartime provisions through 1949, (2) provided that in 1950 mandatory supports will be limited to basic crops and all supports will be flexible.

Studying this wavering history, and noting how easily the good doctrine of alleviating distress is perverted into the bad doctrine of indefinite support, sensible men must wonder whether there is really any way to frame sound law. Certainly concentration on price would seem to be dangerous. Not only are the effects of price maintenance highly indirect but we face at the outset the question of criteria. It is all very well to talk of "price floors," but what is the price floor for wheat? Conceivably it might be placed at 70 cents. The more the matter is studied the more one suspects that what is really at issue is not a price floor but a "fair price." But what is a fair price? We may readily admit that average farm prices are more flexible than average industrial prices, owing largely to the fact that the farmer sells in more perfectly competitive markets. This flexibility in itself gives us absolutely no criteria for saying what farm prices should be on the long term. Just as there is no necessary relationship between the price of wheat and cotton over the years, so there is no necessary relationship between the price of wheat and, say, tractors. Monopoly elements in industry may account for tractor prices remaining more rigid in depression than wheat prices. But over a long period the use of the tractor and modern combine will necessarily cut the cost of wheat production, and unless the quality of wheat greatly changes, or demand changes, we should expect a lower average price. All this is taken as elementary within industry. In the past twenty years the price of rayon has fallen 60 per cent and in the past few years the price of penicillin has fallen about 90 per cent. No one argues that this is disastrous. This differential action of prices is taken as normal in a dynamic process of change and growth.

The more familiar arguments against price support are its effects both on demand and production. Demand for many farm products is said to be inelastic, but this is certainly not true of meat, poultry, fruits, and vegetables, where the housewife knows a bargain when she sees one. Even in the great crops, price has more effect on demand than commonly granted. A lower price for wheat would increase its use as feed. Relatively high prices for cotton have made it vulnerable to intense competition from the synthetic fibers and threaten its export still more. In the twenties this country exported an average of 7,500,000 bales of cotton a year. Now exports are running at a rate of 3,500,000 bales. Cotton, too, is probably the great example of where support tends to retard necessary readjustment. It is well recognized that except in the Delta region, where cotton growing is extremely low-cost, hope for higher living standards in the South lies in diversification into timberland, pasture land, and dairying. High supports under cotton have retarded the switch.

Beyond all this lies the ugly problem of controls and enforcement. The place where controls have been most consistently and, in one sense, successfully used is tobacco. Here they have "worked" partly because of peculiarities of the tobacco market. Purchase is dominated by a few large buyers—the great tobacco companies. Production of flue-cured tobacco is confined to a relatively small area—notably the Carolinas, and Georgia, Virginia, Florida, and Alabama. Thus tobacco production is peculiarly adaptable to a kind of cartel arrangement, resembling in some respects the setup in quinine in the interwar years. The cartel, however, is highly vulnerable to technological change and has its own cost. In the Carolinas assured tobacco prices have skyrocketed land values in some cases from $50 to $1,000 an acre. More ominously, land sells almost entirely on the basis of its tobacco allotment, thus putting into the hands of government and large producers wholly arbitrary power.

That power is now extending its sway over other crops. Moreover, as noted last month, all attempts to control acreage and production lead on to fearful dispute between areas. In wheat, producers are already arguing as to whether production in Kansas, or, say, in Colorado should be cut back. In cotton the same kind of argument goes on between the South and newly arrived California with its spectacular mechanization and low costs. In corn, the greatest of all American crops, the whole theory of control and support falls apart. Almost any farmer can grow corn, and as acreage restrictions are put on other crops, more will, to the discomfiture of the corn belt. Even the government's loan program is something of a trick since the great bulk of corn is consumed on farms or sold between farmers at whatever price they may choose. Since most corn is perishable rather than storable, the government carefully limits the quality of corn it will accept under loan by applying "moisture content" restrictions, which in effect limit the amount it will take.

The Apparatus of Farm Controls

In order to understand current debate about farm policy it is necessary to have an elementary grasp of the powers now in the government's hands. These are of two kinds—production controls and price-support operations. To control production farmers are given payments if they plant less "soil depleting" crops, which include wheat, tobacco, cotton, and corn, and acreage allotment programs are worked out for these crops by Washington. If the farmer does not go along with the allotment, he forfeits part of the soil-conservation payment. Moreover, if two-thirds of the producers of a crop agree, the government can invoke "marketing quotas" as well as acreage allotments. Under quotas the farmer can sell only a specified amount of his crop and if he tries to sell more he is penalized by a fine. Compliance with allotments and quotas is also reinforced by the stipulation that only "cooperating" farmers can get the benefit of the government's more direct price-support operations.

These are carried on by the Commodity Credit Corporation, which can affect prices, by buying in the open market, by agreeing to purchase from the farmer at the end of the crop year, and by making loans to farmers or guaranteeing loans made by banks and other institutions. Commodity loans, whether made directly or indirectly, involve no personal risk for the farmer. If the farmer puts his wheat, for instance, under loan, he puts it in storage and can always sell it and pay off the loan if the market rises. At the loan's expiration date, if the loan is not paid off, the government takes the wheat and is responsible for storage. The number of crops the government has had to support has varied over the years. So has the level of support. The level is expressed as a percentage of "parity" —parity being defined as the relationship between prices the farmer receives and the prices he pays for manufactured products in some base period (traditionally 1910-14).

So the list of difficulties goes. Faced with acreage restrictions and artificial prices, farmers plant their rows closer, pour on fertilizer and insecticides, and come up with as large crops as before. The strange case of potatoes, overpublicized as it has been, is still noteworthy for the light it throws on the real task of making any regulation stick. In 1948, when it was acquiring some 400 carloads of potatoes per day at a price of $2.75 per hundredweight, the government tried to sell part of its surplus back to farmers at 25 cents per hundredweight for use solely as livestock feed. To prevent their sale in commercial channels, potatoes were sprayed with a purple dye to identify them. Since the dye rarely covered more than the top potatoes in a sack, farmers fed the colored ones to their livestock, but in some instances resold the rest to truckers at $1.50, thus reaping double payment. The net result of the potato fiasco has been to penalize those who grew them best—the producers of Idaho and Maine. And the case of potatoes, while admittedly something of a freak, suggests the chaos that would ensue were government controls seriously tried with livestock. What the record of controls re-emphasizes is precisely what the complexities of agriculture suggest in the first place. We may be able to plan a little the sickest part of our economy; we cannot plan the healthiest; and the danger is that in concentrating on the sick we hurt the strong.

In framing policy we should distinguish between two major objectives. One is to give the farmer due protection and a storm cellar into which to retreat in case of major disaster. The other is to establish sound working rules for more normal times.

PLANKS FOR A POLICY

In the case of a major disaster the Secretary of Agriculture might require vast discretionary powers such as the Aiken law allows, but these should not be legislated in advance. Moreover, if we are talking disaster the farmer should have and, indeed, potentially has, better protection than anything contemplated in the law. One of the worst features of the thirties, the thing that brought farmers to the road with pitchforks, was eviction from their property. The potential for extending farm credit is now so great that this need never happen again, and in a crisis a moratorium on foreclosures would no doubt be declared. In addition, emergency techniques for expanding demand for farm products have already been tried out and could be rapidly extended—school-lunch programs, and direct subsidization of diets where needed. Fundamentally, however, main reliance would have to be placed on the government's already vast powers to ease credit, to reduce taxes, and to increase spending. As argued in *Fortune* in June ("The Slump"), these are powerful weapons. Nothing in the experience of the 1929 crash indicates that the tide could have been turned by simply propping up this or that price. The collapse was general in nature, and counterattack could have been successful only with much heavier artillery than anything contemplated in present farm legislation.

Meanwhile a major depression of the character of the thirties is certainly not inevitable, and little is gained by acting as if it were. In more normal times the Employment Act of 1946 guarantees that the government will work to maintain tolerably high over-all demand in the economy. With this as a premise, the aim should not be to encourage special supports under farm prices but to trim down the whole complicated structure. Where the government has helped to pile up surplus, as in wheat and cotton, it cannot get rid of its responsibilities overnight. But the direction of policy should be far more unequivocal than in the Aiken law to make reliance on government support increasingly unattractive.

To this end it would seem sensible to stipulate that no crop could be supported in two successive years at the same price. In the second year the price should be lowered by, say, 10 per cent, and in the third year by another 10 per cent—this to go on until a true free-market price emerged, more attractive than anything offered by government. The net result would be that support operations would taper off, and farmers would shape their cultivation plans to their own estimates of real supply and demand conditions. Some grief there would certainly be, but the point is that either there *is* fundamental maladjustment in the crops the government is supporting or there is not. If there is not, there is no need for support. If there is maladjustment, it must be cured, not perpetuated. The principle is that special price programs should be self-liquidating, not self-perpetuating.

As supports were scaled down and eliminated, the amount of money spent by the Commodity Credit Corporation would be reduced and might be employed more constructively. At present the CCC, with a capital of only $100 million, has what amounts to an open drawing account with the Treasury of $4.75 billion. The task force of the Hoover Commission recommended that this setup be changed. The corporation would be capitalized at $3 billion but it would have no borrowing power. Whenever expenditures exceeded income its capital would be impaired and it would have to go back to Congress for appropriations. The capitalization is excessive if one is serious about eliminating controls but the principle is sound. The more the CCC is driven back to Congress for appropriations the more everyone can keep track of what is spent and judge between competing claims.

Once the direction of reducing the powers of Washington was established, new ideas could be tried out and old ones salvaged. The idea of the "ever normal granary," for instance, had an element of merit in it when we remember the effects of the great droughts of the thirties and the chance that seven lean years can always follow seven fat ones. What wrecked the granary idea was its misuse as a price-support measure. A good case can be made for holding a stock of 350 million bushels of wheat—i.e., about half of last year's domestic need—and a certain quantity of corn.

There is also a place for other measures. The government is spending some $200 million per year on soil-conservation measures. Some of it, in the opinion of a good many experts, is wasted but the principle of conserving the soil will stand. There is great need for more agricultural research of all kinds. Finally, there is enormous need for more education. More dollars spent in the South for this purpose might be worth millions, or even billions, thrown away on supporting King Cotton. If the country is really going to attack the problems of poverty and ignorance, it should do so openly and directly.

Whatever is done the farm community will presumably continue to receive considerable sums of money from the taxpayer. The taxpayer will bear that expense if, and only if, the measures undertaken do not cut across the very principles of a free economy. What is suggested here, in summary, is to disentangle two completely different problems, which, when mixed together, lead not to policy but to chaotic and continuous improvisation. In times of real disaster, should they come, the farmer along with every other citizen is pledged the full resources of the federal government to turn the tide. In more normal times he is offered many forms of continuing assistance consistent with market principles. In both cases emphasis on maintaining levels of high demand, rather than rash government action to manipulate prices, is basic.

A POSITIVE PHILOSOPHY

Back in 1945, Professor Joseph S. Davis, director of the Food Research Institute at Stanford University,

California, delivered an address titled "What Kind of an Agriculture Does America Want?" In a time of change and great political pressures his answer is worth recalling today: "America wants an agriculture that earns its way, instead of being continuingly and increasingly dependent on government props, vulnerable to political shifts and forced to accept the accompanying regimentation. It wants an agriculture that, proud of its strength, competes in domestic and foreign markets on the basis of efficiency and fair play, independent of import restrictions and export subsidies. . . . America wants well-tested programs continued and improved, and ill-starred and dangerous programs abandoned or replaced by better ones. America wants genuine, non-political soil conservation, economically achieved. America wants redress of flagrant inequities, wherever they appear, but no truck with guarantees of equality for any individuals, groups, or occupations."

22. SPECULATION

IS THE STOCK MARKET OBSOLETE?*

The New York Stock Exchange is the "nerve center" of American capitalism, but it seems to have suffered partial paralysis in the postwar prosperity period. It is charged here that the stock market, though still a vastly important institution, has become in certain respects "obsolete," and an attempt is made to discover why. Whether this obsolence of stock market is blight or blessing for the nation is discussed.

"How did the market do today?" is a question that is not often heard these days—perhaps because the market has not done anything very spectacular for quite some time. Indeed, while the U.S. has been enjoying the greatest business boom in its history, stock prices have remained notably sluggish. Between May, 1946, when the postwar bull market ended, and March of last year, when momentarily "hard" money atrophied the Eisenhower boomlet, stock prices on the New York Stock Exchange (which accounts for about 75 per cent of all stock transactions in the U.S.) rose less than 25 per cent. In that same period the gross national product rose more than 75 per cent and corporate profits after taxes climbed 60 per cent. Even the modest market rise indicated by Dow-Jones and other "averages" was deceptive. The market, in fact, was even more lethargic than they indicated. It took only a ten per cent decline in the market "averages," between last March and September, to put three out of four stocks listed on the N.Y.S.E. *below* their 1946 prices.

As a result, a lot of people who used to inquire about the market's daily behavior are now inquiring instead "What has happened to Wall Street?" The fact is that a great deal has happened to Wall Street in recent years, and in several important respects the stock market appears to have become obsolete. To be specific, the market has changed or fallen sadly behind the times in at least four distinct areas:

1. The market is no longer a very reliable barometer of business prospects, or even a reliable reflection of current business conditions. Before World War II, what happened to stock prices and the volume of stock transactions was a reasonably good omen of future business trends; turns in stock prices anticipated turns in business 80 per cent of the time before 1939. Since then, however, the market has been a voice in the wilderness of lower Manhattan, unheeded and often off

key. Until 1948, market movements bore no relationship to business trends. The market appears to have regained some of its earlier prescience since 1949—but only superficially. Meanwhile it has provided a distorted picture of current business earnings, dividends, and real worth.

2. The market is no longer the pivotal economic institution and influence it once was. What gave the New York Stock Exchange great influence in the economy before 1939 was the part it played in the New York money market and the fact that the New York money market in turn dominated the credit structure of the U.S. But now that stock trading is a cash rather than a margin proposition, the Exchange is a relatively minor force in the money market.

3. The market has become sadly outmoded in its technology and merchandising techniques. The floor broker, for example, is an anachronism and most of the frenetic bustle on the floor of the Exchange is unnecessary; three automatic punch-card machines, it has been estimated, could accomplish three-fourths of the work presently done by hand and "make markets" faster and more accurately. As for merchandising, the brokers themselves admit that they are chained to their telephones by low commissions and geared to service a particular clientele that is rapidly disappearing.

4. The market is not even equipped with any satisfactory statistical measure of its own performance. The popular market averages and indexes—Dow-Jones, Standard & Poor, etc.—have become so distorted by stock splits or other market developments that their present value is open to question. No single average or index can be taken as an accurate gauge of the market.

All this is not to say that the market no longer serves any useful purpose. On the contrary, the New York Stock Exchange is still vastly important as a market place for the transactions of more than 5,500,000 individuals and 10,000 institutions that own listed shares. It is important, too, as a secondary market, for the 1,084 corporations whose three billion shares of stock

*From "Is The Stock Market Obsolete?" February, 1954.

are traded there. In one respect, it is more important than ever; the market value of the common and preferred shares listed on the N.Y.S.E. last year topped $100 billion. And the fact that the stock market no longer exerts the decisive influence on the nation's money supply is not the sort of obsolescence that needs to be deplored.

A BLUE-CHIP MARKET

The weakness of stock prices in the postwar has been partly obscured by the fact that substantial gains have been recorded by a few stocks, chiefly those of giant corporations. Most people gauge the market by the Dow-Jones averages, Standard & Poor's, or some other index that primarily reflects blue-chip stock prices. Since 1950 most of these indexes have stood well above the 1946 peaks. Last March, for example, Standard & Poor's index of 480 stocks was about 25 per cent above the level of May, 1946, and even in September it was still 15 per cent higher. Since, as in a poker game, the blue chips represent the great bulk of the money invested (the top fifty stocks comprise half the value of all listed shares), it is only logical to ascribe the greatest weight to them in the averages. Yet as a guide to the market fortunes of hundreds of other companies the averages can be very misleading.

Most stock prices are low not only in relation to earlier periods but by most other standards as well. Except for a handful of "growth stocks," most securities are low-priced in relation to present earnings, dividends, and book value. At their peaks last year, for example, the stocks in Standard & Poor's index of industrial prices were selling for only eleven times earnings and yielding an average 5.5 per cent. U.S. Steel was selling at half its book value in late 1953. And as E. T. Weir of National Steel pointed out, the valuation the market placed on his company's stock last year was less than the amount of money National had reinvested out of earnings alone since 1946.

PROFESSIONAL AMATEURS

The caution and investment-mindedness of today's stockholders help explain the extreme "selectivity" that has characterized the market in recent years. Some stock prices have been consistently high and others low, but most have followed a more erratic course. While the blue chips as a group have risen steadily since 1950, the individual stocks accounting for the rise have varied from year to year. Standard Oil (N.J.), for example, rose sharply in 1950 and 1951 but fell in 1952 and 1953; General Electric, on the other hand, has risen steadily since late 1951 and established new post-war highs all through the fall of 1953. And the selectivity has been evident as between industry groups, too; the utility averages, for example, rose steadily while railroad shares (including the blue chips) dropped in price throughout 1953.

PLAYING IT SAFE

In part, these crosscurrents have resulted from the rise of economic forecasting and the fact that people seldom buy or sell on blind tips any more or because "the market" is rising or falling. Investors (and even purchasers who buy for a quick speculative turn) now study the voluminous literature put out by brokers' research departments and by advisory services like Standard & Poor's, Moody's, and United Business Service. There is a growing preference for "security analysis" rather than "market analysis," for individual stocks likely to appreciate in value, irrespective of the trend of the stock averages or of the stock's industry group. When a consensus develops among the stock analysts, trading becomes concentrated in a small number of individual stocks and stock groups, which consequently rise or fall more than the market as a whole.

Even the professional traders have changed their approach. "None of my partners would think of making a purchase or sale without first analyzing the particular company's balance sheet and its industry's trend," the research head of a big brokerage firm recently remarked. "Twenty-five years ago they wouldn't have been caught dead looking at such detailed statistics." By astute analysis of individual companies and industry groups, some traders have managed to make substantial profits even in periods of relative market stability like 1951-53, when the "averages" fluctuated only about 15 per cent.

Another reason for the high degree of selectivity in the market in recent years has been the growth of institutional buying (which last year added an estimated $1.5 billion of new money to the stock market). The research staffs of insurance companies and other large institutional investors are constantly watching industry and company trends, and the institutions switch their holdings in accordance with the analysts' recommendations. Institutional buying is also largely responsible for the strength of the blue chips since 1950. Most pension funds, life-insurance companies, mutual savings banks, and bank trustees are legally restricted to buying from so-called "approved lists" of stocks. The mutual funds, while not so limited, have shown a similar preference for blue chips, perhaps on the thesis Keynes once advanced that "worldly wisdom teaches that it is better for reputation to fail conventionally than to succeed unconventionally."[*]

Institutional buying has not necessarily made the market more rational, however. Indeed, many security analysts think that the institutional investors' preference for blue chips has pushed the price of some stocks unduly high. In consequence, their expected growth for years to come has been discounted while they provide inadequate returns now. The mutual funds are under constant pressure from their sales departments to invest in equities regardless of price levels, since it is hard to convince prospective customers to buy mutual-fund shares if the fund in turn holds the money in government bonds pending a market break. Conversely, any

[*] The term "blue chip," which once referred primarily to the stocks of big corporations with stable earnings, is more frequently applied today to the stocks of leading "growth" companies.

open forecast of an impending bear market might produce a rash of cashing-in of mutual-fund shares that could contribute to a major market break.

CUTTING THE CORD

All the changes that have occurred in the stock market in recent years make it hard to remember that twenty-five years ago the market—and more particularly the N.Y.S.E.—was regarded as the nerve center of U.S. capitalism. Changes in stock prices and trading volume were watched closely as harbingers of business trends. But now that businessmen have available to them a variety of economic statistics—on the gross national product, industrial production, inventories, shipments, new orders, etc.—they pay little attention to the stock market as an economic barometer. Nor does the market have the impact on the economy it once had.

Pre-1929, and to a degree even pre-1939, what happened to stock prices and the volume of trading on the N.Y.S.E. had a very decided effect on business conditions. The most important reason for this was the role the stock market played in the New York money market, which in turn dominated the nation's credit structure. Most stock transactions were on margin, and brokers extended credit to customers (as high as 90 per cent) on the basis of their own borrowings from New York banks. In the late 1920's bank loans to brokers accounted for about a third of all New York bank loans.

Thus the brokers' loan market played approximately the same dominant role in the money market that the Treasury plays now. But the stock market was a highly unsettling influence. Since it competed for funds with other sectors of the economy, a rapid rise in brokers' loans reduced the amount of credit available for ordinary business purposes. Conversely, changes in business activity affected the money market, which in turn affected the stock market. All the great financial panics of the past— and fourteen of sixteen recorded business downturns before World War II—were closely linked or preceded by slumps on the N.Y.S.E.

That umbilical cord has now been cut. The change is most strikingly apparent on the floor of the Exchange: the old "money desk," where New York banks once stationed permanent representatives, now serves as an information booth. Only 25 per cent of N.Y.S.E. transactions are on margin today, and the margin is 50 per cent. (It was 75 per cent until last year.) Brokers' loans, as a result, account for only about one-tenth the volume of New York bank credit now.

The stock market also exerts less influence on consumer spending today than it did before 1930. A rising market used to be a virtual prerequisite to high levels of consumption; the upper-income groups (whose incomes still derive importantly from stock dividends and capital gains) accounted for a much larger share of consumer spending then; and margin trading pyramided their gains or losses. The speculative fever that usually developed when stocks were rising caused spending to expand even faster than incomes (and, conversely, to decline faster when prices dropped). The

redistribution of income since 1929, however, the relative caution of the investing public, and the absence of margin trading have all combined to reduce the market's impact on consumption.

BLIGHT OR BLESSING?

All this would seem to be to the good. The U.S. economy is certainly more stable now than when the market was operating on the cuff, and the stock market itself is less susceptible to violent cycles of boom and bust. But what about the market's influence on economic growth? Has it become obsolescent even as a significant source of capital?

There is a widespread belief, particularly among stock brokers, that the capital market has suffered as a result of the low volume of trading on the N.Y.S.E., and that this has impeded capital formation. Investors, it is said, hesitate to buy new securities now for fear that resale on a "thin" market may involve a loss; corporations, for their part, are deterred from floating new stock issues because stock prices are so low in relation to earnings and net worth. These attitudes are widely believed to have produced a sharp rise in internal financing and a strong preference for debt among those corporations that still use the capital market.

The brokers' concern is not shared by investment bankers, however. On the contrary, underwriters claim they cannot begin to satisfy investors' demands for new securities. "Anyone who says there's a shortage of risk capital can bring his securities to me," observed one investment banker, "and I'll be happy to peddle them for him."

Nor do the statistics indicate any weakening of economic growth or shrinkage in the supply of equity capital. Corporate expenditures for new plant and equipment have averaged almost $22 billion a year since 1945—two and a half times the 1923-29 average —and are expected to top $26 billion during the current "recession" year.

Only one-quarter of these expenditures have been financed via the capital markets, to be sure; net new issues (i.e., new securities less retirements) have been averaging only about $5 billion a year. But the proportion of business expansion and replacements financed through sales of stocks and bonds wasn't much higher in the 1920's when net new issues were about $2.5 billion a year, or less than 30 per cent of total capital outlays by corporations.

MORE EQUITIES THAN EVER

A change of that magnitude hardly indicates a trend away from financing through the capital market. In any event, whether or not a firm goes to the capital market with a new stock or bond issue depends mainly on how fast it is growing; in general, internal funds suffice until capital expenditures by business are increasing more than 3 per cent a year. The need for external funds may be somewhat low right now, as a result of the big increase in depreciation allowances since Korea, but even so a growth of internal financing does not necessarily mean lower capital outlays.

But as a matter of fact the market for equities has

shown little sign of withering away. Although interest payments on bonds are tax deductible, common and preferred stock issues have actually accounted for a slightly larger share—one-third—of net new security issues since 1945 than in the 1920's. In that heyday less than 30 per cent of the money raised on the capital market was in the form of equities.

Nor is there any evidence that small businesses are having a harder time tapping the capital markets now than pre-1929. The popular view that they are usually rests on an exaggerated notion of the number of small businesses that ever financed themselves through the public sale of securities. Indeed it would appear difficult to make any kind of case that the decline in importance of the N.Y.S.E. has had any harmful effect on the capital market or the economy as a whole.

EVERYONE'S OUT OF STEP. . . .

Fundamentally, the job of the N.Y.S.E. has always been to provide an open market for a limited number of well-established securities, in which full publicity is given every transaction. From this standpoint the Exchange has done its job well. Nevertheless, it has fallen sadly behind the times in organization, technology, and merchandising methods, and as a result most Stock Exchange firms have been caught in a squeeze between falling volume and rising costs.

The Stock Exchange, for example, has failed to adapt itself to the requirements of institutional investors, and consequently has lost a large chunk of institutional business to the over-the-counter market. About a twelfth of the trading in the stocks listed on the N.Y.S.E. is now done over-the-counter.

Institutions often find it cheaper and faster to sell over-the-counter than on the floor of the Exchange. Few of the N.Y.S.E. specialists* have sufficient capital to absorb the blocs of 25,000 shares and more in which the institutions generally deal. A sale on the floor of the Exchange, therefore, may take weeks to complete and may drive the price down in the process. On the other hand, a few well-capitalized over-the-counter houses like Blyth & Co., and First Boston Corp. will take the blocs at a firm price and resell them to other institutions. Each institution may save an eighth to a quarter of a point on such transactions.

The Exchange is becoming increasingly concerned about over-the-counter competition, however, and last year doubled the capital requirements for its own specialists and revised trading rules to permit "special transactions" in which the broker or specialist in effect acts as an over-the-counter dealer.

HORSE-AND-BUGGY TECHNOLOGY

More than anything else, however, Wall Street seems to suffer from a lack of imagination and organization. While their old clientele has been shattered by the redistribution of income (there are very few "big traders" any more), most brokerage firms either have not been able to afford to go after new customers or

* Specialists "make markets" on the floor of the Exchange in a limited number of stocks, which they buy and sell for their own accounts or for their "book," or broker's inventory.

have not seemed to want to. The inadequacy of commission rates is only one aspect of the problem; commissions were raised last November and might be adequate to permit profitable brokerage operations if costs could be brought down.

The stock market's technology has changed considerably since World War II, of course. "We couldn't stay in business without the I.B.M. machine," the managing partner of one small firm recently observed; mechanization of his clearing and bookkeeping operations had cut his personnel requirements by two-thirds since 1946 and had eliminated overtime work entirely. Only Merrill Lynch, Pierce, Fenner & Beane has approached full mechanization, but three out of four member firms now use I.B.M. or other electronic systems for clearing and bookkeeping operations.

The Exchange's own *clearing* and *bookkeeping* operations are now almost fully mechanized; sixty clerks and a roomful of I.B.M. machines do the work formerly handled by 400 people. But the *trading process* itself—the heart of the business, after all—hasn't changed in any essential for at least thirty years. Yet most of the floor brokers, clerks, pages, and other personnel on the floor of the Exchange could very well be replaced by electronic machines, too.

Three-fourths of all orders to buy and sell securities are given at or near the market price, and these could be handled more quickly and accurately by electronic card-sorting machines. Three such machines, which would match like data entered on punch cards—e.g., buy and sell orders—could easily handle a two-million-share day. (Unmatched bids and asks would still have to be handled by brokers and specialists, although it is certainly not inconceivable that machines could be devised to handle this job, too.) Orders from out-of-town firms or branch offices could be transmitted directly to the floor of the Exchange, instead of being routed, as at present, through a New York correspondent or home office.

The obstacles are obvious: mechanization is bound to be opposed by the people whose jobs it would jeopardize or abolish. But there is a growing, if guarded, sentiment for the change, especially among managing partners. "I need two floor brokers like I need a hole in the head," one of them recently complained. "There's nothing they can do," he added, "that my chief order clerk can't do better."

HOW CLOSE TO MAIN STREET?

No permanent solution to Wall Street's present difficulties is possible, of course, until it decides how many customers it needs or wants and how it is going to get them. The management of the N.Y.S.E. was somewhat taken aback by the Brookings Institution's discovery last year that only 6,500,000 Americans, representing 4,500,000 families, own shares in publicly held corporations. The Exchange had thought there were perhaps ten million stockholders. In any case, President G. Keith Funston has suggested a market potential of 21 million families and has set as a three-year goal the acquisition of 1,500,000 new share owners.

The Exchange, accordingly, is sponsoring, among

other things, a plan for the installment purchase of stocks, with payments as low as $40 quarterly. The heart of the plan is an I.B.M. system worked out and administered by the N.Y.S.E.'s two odd-lot firms, Carlisle & Jacquelin and De Coppet & Doremus. They will handle all the paper work for the standard odd-lot fee, the full commission going to the broker who makes the sale. Since the commission is now 6 per cent on sales of $100 or less (yielding brokerage firms *more* than the sale of mutual-fund shares), Mr. Funston feels there should be sufficient incentive for aggressive selling.

The Funston plan, despite its publicity, is not entirely new. Eisele & King, Libaire, Stout & Co. had unveiled its own installment-purchase plan, called the Investors Club, some two months before the Funston plan was announced. The plan run by Quinby & Co., a Rochester investment firm, has been handling installment purchases of a few stocks for fifteen years. A few firms are enthusiastic about the new plan, but for the most part Wall Street's enthusiasm has been distinctly tempered: a month after it was announced, only one firm in ten had indicated a desire to participate in the Funston plan.

Some firms apparently feel the mass-class market belongs to the mutual funds. Selling securities to the uninitiated involves a fiduciary responsibility they do not wish to assume. The small investor, in their view, needs diversification and supervision of his investments and he can only get both in an investment trust.

These firms, therefore, are devoting their energies to pushing the sale of mutual-fund shares and to attracting institutional trading accounts. A number of them have become expert in matching institutional buyers and sellers; such "swaps" tend to keep prices firm on the Exchange, and also yield the same broker a commission at each end of the transaction.

The mutual funds, however, are not necessarily the perfect solution for equating fiduciary responsibility and widespread ownership of stock. Selling mutual funds can involve conflicts of interest, too. The S.E.C. has twice indicated its concern over brokerage firms allegedly pushing the sales of particular mutual funds in return for those funds' brokerage business.

CAVEAT EMPTOR?

The Funston plan, however, does raise some fundamental questions of responsibility that the managers of the Exchange have not really faced. If Exchange advertising induces uninformed people to buy stocks— and much of it is directed to that end—does the Exchange bear any responsibility to those people as a result, and what is it? And what would the public reaction be if there were really widespread stock ownership and the market went to pot? And finally, would wider stock ownership indeed constitute "our strongest defense against foreign isms" and "insure the proper functioning of an enlightened capitalistic society," as Mr. Funston suggests?

Some advantages are readily apparent, of course. Wider stock ownership, for example, would induce greater sentiment for the idea of corporate profitability and give more people a direct stake in the preservation of private ownership of enterprise.

On the other hand, the U.S. has done very nicely so far on a relatively narrow base of stock ownership— one far narrower, in fact, than the Brookings study suggested; while 6,500,000 Americans own stock, the top 3 per cent still own approximately 65 per cent of the dollar value of the shares outstanding. Even this, of course, is a far broader private-ownership base than is to be found anywhere else in world history, and millions of other Americans invest in "capitalism" through such buffers as life-insurance companies and banks.

Moreover, it can be argued that dispersion of stock ownership has already tended to divorce corporate ownership from control in the U.S. Even boards of directors, the theoretical representatives of the stockholders, have more and more come under managerial dominance. Further dispersion of stock ownership might only widen the schism and induce even greater managerial autonomy.

THE "BIG SELL"

This is not to say that Wall Street should not push its various sales programs; like any other profit-seeking enterprise, it should, providing it takes into account the public, and consequently its own, long-range interest. The remarkable growth of a firm like Merrill Lynch (which accounts for more than 10 per cent of all Stock Exchange business) suggests that the conflict between salesmanship and fiduciary responsibility can be successfully resolved.

Like any other business, the stock market, from now on, will have to make its bid for more business on the basis of the service it renders. It will be unfortunate if, instead, it tries to identify its own welfare with the survival of capitalism, or to recapture its speculative past, as it sometimes seems intent on doing. Wall Street, after all, was the scapegoat for many of U.S. capitalism's real and fancied ills for over twenty years. The fact that it is no longer the potent influence that it was—a fact that seems to have escaped only Communist propagandists and a few myopic denizens of Wall Street itself—is not a cause for great concern. For even if the stock market has become obsolete in a number of ways, it still performs an essential function and U.S. industry, the basic commodity in which it deals, was never more valuable.

5. Income Distribution

THE RICH MIDDLE-INCOME CLASS*

The central fact about the revolution which has recently transformed the American market has been the rise of the huge new moneyed middle-income class. Today, more than one-third of the nation's family units are in the $4,000 to $7,500 income bracket, a 230 per cent increase since 1929—even after allowing for taxes and price rises. This article converts the usual statistical studies into recognizable people. It establishes who these middle-income receivers are; how they earn their income; in what age groups they cluster; how large their families are; and how many members of the family are working and at what jobs. The article also identifies the families scattered above and below the middle.

Though not a head has been raised aloft on a pike-staff, nor a railway station seized, the U.S. has been for some time now in a revolution. The income explosion of recent years, and the great reshuffling associated with it, have transformed the older American market beyond recognition. This transformation—not to mention the drastic upward revision in living standards—can be construed in no less portentous a word than revolution. It arrived without advance billing, and proceeds without public clamor; it is one of the most quiet and orderly overthrowings of an old established order possible to imagine. Indeed, it seems that most participants in the great event are only dimly aware it has even taken place.

Fortune has been delineating the salient features of the revolution. The central fact about the new American market, it is now clear, is the rise of a huge new moneyed middle-income class; specifically, the burgeoning of family units with cash income after taxes of $4,000 to $7,500.† The size and spending capacity of the group may be inferred from the statistical studies that issue endlessly from the Commerce Department, the Census Bureau, BLS, and FRB. But these nine and twelve-digit statistical aggregates are of little or no help to the marketing men in their problem of identifying the customer. The middle-income group has grown so numerous that one cannot easily generalize about it. The aim of this article is to establish who these middle-income spenders are; how they have been earning their income; what age groups they tend to cluster in; how large their families are; how many members of the family are working, and at what jobs—in short, to convert the statistics into recognizable people. The article, of course, will also identify the families scattered above and below the middle.

CROSSING THE BOUNDARY LINE

The scope of the revolution may be roughly measured in a few data. The number of family units with

*From "The Rich Middle-Income Class," May, 1954.

† A reminder: the term "family units" as used throughout this series includes (1) families of related persons residing together, and (2) individuals, residing alone or with others.

$4,000-to-$7,500 cash income has increased about 50 per cent since 1947, about 80 per cent since 1941, and about 230 per cent since 1929. (Unless otherwise stated, income figures are given after taxes and "after inflation"; 1953 dollars are used throughout.) There are now some 18 million family units in this middle bracket; they comprise more than a third of all units in the country, and receive almost $100 billion cash annually—more than two-fifths of all spendable income. This swelling of the middle-income class is even more remarkable for the fact that it was restrained by two vast special cases: farm families and unattached individuals. For reasons that will be set forth later, these two kinds of family units receive rather low cash income—but they have greater spending power than their cash income would suggest. If only nonfarm families are considered, then the $4,000-to-$7,500 class comprises 43 per cent of the units.

Another perspective: 55 per cent of all nonfarm families now receive more than $4,000 cash income after taxes.

The $4,000 boundary line is not an arbitrary one, for at about this point on the way up the income scale, something happens. At $4,000, quantity changes into quality (to lapse briefly into the Marxian dialectic); the average-sized family is no longer solely preoccupied with obtaining the minimum decencies, for it has money now to spend on the "extras." The over-$4,000 family, instead of merely buying a chicken and cooking it, is apt to demand the conveniences afforded by frozen chicken pie. It is apt to prefer a new car instead of a used one; indeed, the middle-income units by themselves now buy half the nation's new cars. And half its new homes too.

Where did this new middle group come from?

A NATION OF SHOPKEEPERS?

Historically, what has been called the middle class has been composed of small entrepreneurs and property owners, professional men, and highly skilled, self-employed artisans; this is, roughly, the group that on the Continent has been called the petty bourgeoisie and in

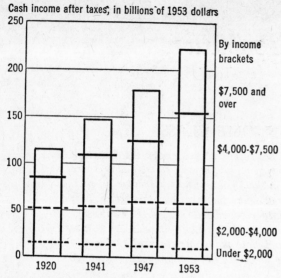

Cash income after taxes, in billions of 1953 dollars

By income brackets

$7,500 and over

$4,000-$7,500

$2,000-$4,000

Under $2,000

1920   1941   1947   1953

(Design: Clifton Line)

THE MARKET IS IN THE MIDDLE

The tremendous swelling in real cash income since 1929 has been accompanied by a steady shift in the *kinds* of incomes Americans receive. Income from pensions and other governmental aid programs, though still only a sliver of the total, has increased sevenfold. Property income—rents, royalties, etc.—dropped sharply, from 18 to 7 per cent of the total, principally because of the impact of taxes on the upper-income brackets. But the wage-and-salary component grew from less than two-thirds in 1929 to almost three-quarters today.

This last change is intimately related to the blooming of the vast $4,000-to-$7,500 group, which now receives 42 per cent of all personal income.

Britain and America the middle class. Now "middle class," of course, does not mean quite the same thing as "middle income"; the former term has always measured social status rather than ability to purchase goods in the market place. But in the U.S., where social mobility has always been greater than in Europe, the two terms have tended to blur together. The blurring was furthered by the fact that for many decades—up until 1929, at any rate—the socially defined middle class tended to be the middle-income class too. It might be supposed, therefore, that the recent middle-income boom is somehow associated with swelling incomes in occupations traditional to the middle class. It might be supposed, but it is not so.

The fact is that, since 1929, there has been a steady decrease in the proportion of personal income deriving from property and from the operations of proprietors. Property income accounted for more than 18 per cent of all cash income in 1929; last year the figure was down to almost 7 per cent. (Again, these figures are after taxes.) The personal income of proprietors fell much less significantly, from 15 per cent of the total to 13 per cent; and even this small drop can be largely accounted for by the declining numbers of farm operators. Nevertheless it is clear, on balance, that the swelling income of the middle group did not derive importantly from growth in the traditional *sources* of middle-class income. The sources of income increasingly are wages and salaries. These now account for three-quarters of all cash income, compared with only two-thirds in 1929.

To be sure, the ranks of the apparently middle-class occupations have increased enormously since 1929. The number of professional men has more than doubled, and the number of managers and proprietors (a group that is "upper class," too, of course) has grown by about 50 per cent. But while these groups have been swelling in numbers, they have been caught in a vast sociological "downgrading." In 1929 the majority of them consisted of businessmen, doctors, lawyers, and other self-employed earners. Today a clear majority—

about 60 per cent—of these 8,500,000 professional and managerial men are salaried. The professional group is now dominated by accountants, engineers, and teachers —by professionals working for somebody else. The managers and proprietors, considered by themselves, embrace some five million men; but only the 2,500,000 proprietors work for themselves. Most of the other "managers" are the bureaucracy, so to speak, of corporate enterprise: the vice presidents, the department heads, the junior executives, and the assistant-assistants. In other words, the traditional middle-class occupations have begun to seem more and more like skilled white-collar jobs.

But there is not even a simple "white-collar" explanation for the burgeoning of the middle-income class. There is often a tendency to make a vague identification between the "middle" class and the white-collar group. The latter does indeed have a middle-class look about it; it is neither rich nor poor, and socially it seems to share many of the values and attitudes of the traditional middle class. The figures, however, suggest otherwise; that is, they suggest that the growth of white-collar jobs has played only a secondary role in the foundation of the $4,000-to-$7,500 group.

To begin with, the white-collar growth is not so great as is commonly supposed. Since 1929 the number of clerical and sales workers has increased from a little under eight million to a little more than eleven million —a rise slightly less rapid than that of total nonfarm employment. The number of salaried professionals and managers has risen more steeply, as we have seen, but the totals involved are not so high; the rise has been from fewer than four million to a little more than seven million. On balance, then, the white-collar revolution one hears so much about has entailed an increase of about, 65 per cent in the jobs involved—vs. a 50 per cent rise in the nonfarm employment.

This 15 per cent differential can be accounted for entirely by the increasing push of women into clerical and sales jobs. Since 1929 their employment in these occupations has gone up from three million to nearly seven million. Their rise in white-collar employment has ample economic consequence, as we shall see; but they have not made the revolution. Women workers plainly do not head very many of the middle-income families.

THE NEW BOURGEOISIE

The fact is that America's booming new middle-income class consists, to a startling extent, of groups hitherto identified as proletarians. This news represents a turn of the historical screw that, before the fact, was portrayed by virtually no one. Marx and Engels had written confidently in the *Communist Manifesto* that "The modern laborer . . . instead of rising with the progress of industry, sinks deeper and deeper below the conditions of existence of his own class. He becomes a pauper, and pauperism develops more rapidly than population and wealth." While this dismal view of capitalism was contested by many economic philosophers, it is hard to name one who was so sanguine as to predict that the "workers," far from sinking into class-conscious misery, would ever merge into the middle—if not the ruling—group.

The figures, nonetheless, are clear. There are, at present, some 15,500,000 nonfarm families with incomes of $4,000-to-$7,500. About 1,400,000 of these families—some 10 per cent—are headed by laborers or service workers. Another 3,500,000 are headed by "operatives," i.e., factory workers (ordinarily semi-skilled), miners, truck drivers, delivery men, etc. Four million more are headed by foremen and by "craftsmen"—the carpenters, electricians, mechanics, etc., who make up the most skilled elements in the labor force. Nine million middle-income families, then—almost 60 per cent of the total—are "workers." Plainly, it is time to change the stereotype of the American middle-income consumer: he is not, and has not been for some years, a small landlord or drugstore proprietor. If any stereotype at all is meaningful, it might be a machinist in Detroit.

The elements in the rise of this "Detroit middle class" are reasonably clear. Aggregate employment of unskilled laborers (sweepers, hod carriers, etc.), service workers, operatives, craftsmen, and foremen rose by eleven million in the years after 1929—an even smaller rise, proportionally, than in the white-collar area. But within this group two things occurred to push up take-home pay. First of all, there was a steady shift to the better-paying jobs; the ratio of semi-skilled to unskilled rose dramatically. While there has been an absolute decline in the number of laborers since 1929 (from 5,300,000 to 4,500,000), the number of operatives rose from seven million to almost 14 million. The most spectacular rise in this category was among women, whose employment as operatives nearly trebled, and who are now about a third of the semi-skilled labor force.

In general, this upward movement within the group has been caused by the increasing mechanization of industry. It seems not so long ago that the rising productivity of industry was regarded as a positive threat to the skilled worker. Charlie Chaplin's *Modern Times* (made in 1935) expressed dramatically the widespread delusion that mass production would slowly grind down the labor force into so many robots. In fact, mechanization first replaces the unskilled laborer; then it expands the number of "technicians," e.g., tool-and-die makers, engineers.

The second booster effect on take-home pay was provided by manufacturing wage rates, which have tended to rise faster than over-all rates. This development, too, must be laid to industry's astounding productivity, which has been increasing, over the long pull, about 3 per cent a year. It is hard to say whether union wage policy has contributed to the disproportionate rise in manufacturing wage rates. The question is a theoretical bed of thorns, and in any case is not entirely relevant. What is relevant is that manufacturing rates (in 1953 dollars) have risen from about 90 cents in 1929 to about $1.80 an hour today; and in most heavy industry the *average* rate is over $2.

The astounding result of all these changes is the metamorphosis of the "worker." *Of 20 million families headed by craftsmen, operatives, laborers, etc., nine million today are in the $4,000-to-$7,500 class, and another two million are in the over-$7,500 class.*

The remaining 40 per cent of the middle-income class is composed of families whose head is doing just about what he might be imagined to do. More than four million $4,000-to-$7,500 families are headed by professionals, proprietors, and managers—nearly half of the families in these occupational groups. Another 2,400,000 are headed by clerical and sales workers, apparently the best situated of these: the bookkeepers, insurance salesmen, advertising salesmen, etc. Finally, there are 100,000 presumably happy family units deriving incomes over $4,000 without working: from rents, royalties, annuities, stocks and bonds.

EVERYBODY WORKS

Thus far, we have been considering only the occupation of the family head in these middle-income units. But now a striking, and somewhat disquieting, fact must be noted about these consumers: *about two-fifths of nonfarm families in the $4,000-to-$7,500 group are there only because somebody besides the family head is working—at least part of the time.* The low-paying occupations are, naturally, the most dependent on supplementary earners: 70 per cent of the 1,400,000 middle-income families headed by laborers and service workers would be under the $4,000 level if the family had no "extra" earners.* But, actually, a substantial proportion of families in all middle-income occupations are dependent on supplementary earners. There are about six million families in the $4,000-to-$7,500 group headed by operatives, clerical workers, and salespeople, but 2,700,000 of these families would drop below

* The other 30 percent, accounting for 400,000 middle-income families, are difficult to identify. The family head undoubtedly works in one of the elite service jobs—for example, as an unusually high-paid waiter, barber, policeman, etc. It is hard to believe that he is ever a laborer.

$4,000 if only the family head were working. Professionals, managers, craftsmen, and foremen do somewhat better in providing for their middle-income families without assistance; some two-thirds of the eight million families have only one breadwinner.

The supplementary earners are important not only to middle-income families, however. Of the 41 million families in the U.S. today, about 17 million have at least one earner in addition to the family head. Some 42 per cent of all families, then, rely in varying degrees on some extra income—a rise from about 36 per cent in 1929.

THE WIVES DID IT

The percentage change is perhaps less signficant than sociological change related to it. In 1929 there were just about as many female supplementary earners as male; today 15 million of the 22 million workers boosting their families' income are women. What has happened is clear enough: The number of extra female earners was swelled by the increasing job opportunities for women in both industrial and white-collar work. The number of extra male earners, meanwhile, was reduced as the age of marriage declined (see "Sixty-Six Million More Americans," *Fortune,* January, 1954). The nation's young men have been moving from the "supplementary" to the "family-head" category.

About five million of the seven million men classified as supplementary earners today are sons of the family head. The women in the group are mostly wives. Some nine million wives worked some time last year, in addition to four million daughters, and two million sisters, cousins, aunts, etc., of the family head. Altogether, the 15 million female supplementary earners account for about two-thirds of the female labor force.

Of the 17 million families with supplementary earners, the great majority—13 million—have just one. But the importance of "extra" workers in boosting family standards is enormous. Almost two-thirds of the families who get this assistance are in a higher income bracket because of it. Two-fifths of the middle-income group would fall below $4,000 without these earnings, and more than half of the top group would fall below $7,500 without them. As these figures suggest, the proportion of families with supplementary earners goes up as income goes up. The moral is not, however, that the family heads who need assistance the least are apt to get it the most. Perhaps the point really is that, to attain the middle and upper-middle status to which they aspire, a great many American families are willing to send more workers out into the labor force. Furthermore this relationship between supplementary earners and family income does not extend indefinitely into the upper-income groups. Somewhere around $15,000 the proportion begins to decline; at the very highest levels—over $25,000—most families have only one earner.

MIDDLE-INCOME VARIETIES

It is clear, then, that the great push past the $4,000

line, and the establishment of the vast new middle-income class, may be substantially accounted for by the supplementary earner. The earnings of these extra workers, however, are characteristically precarious. Sons and daughters leave home to get married; wives quit work to bear children; parents of the family head grow too old to work. Any of these events may precipitate sharp revisions in the family's earnings and living standards. There is, in other words, a great deal of movement into and out of every income class; and though the aggregates in each class may show up roughly the same from one year to the next, the actual families are different. To get some sense of the fluidity of class boundaries, consider a few of the types that recur frequently:

The family head is a young semiskilled worker, a truck driver, earning about $3,500 a year. He has no children and his wife earns another $1,500 working part time as a salesgirl. But since they are planning to have children fairly soon, it would be dangerous for them to try adjusting permanently to a $5,000 living standard. They have little or no savings, and there may even be a sizable installment debt for them to wrestle with. It appears likely that in a year or two they will drop below the $4,000 line, at least temporarily. Eventually, of course, the family may stage a comeback: the wife may return to work when the children are older, the children themselves will begin working, and the earnings of the family head himself will have increased slowly over the years.

The family head is a factory foreman in his fifties, earning $5,000 a year by his own efforts; his wife has stopped working, and his two daughters are already married. His own pay is just about at its peak; however, the family income is lower than it was five years ago, when his wife and daughters were working too. Moreover, the time is approaching when he will have to think about retirement. Though he may have accumulated some savings, he is acutely aware that in another ten years or so his income—to be derived from a pension, social security, perhaps a small annuity— will be substantially less than $5,000. Here, then, is a family passing downward through the middle-income group.

The family head is a junior executive in his late twenties, married with a young child, and earning $5,000. His wife, of course, is not working. Both are college graduates and accustomed to living at a higher level than is afforded by his present income. Both, furthermore, are intensely conscious of the fact that he will very likely be raised over $7,500 in five or ten years. The family is passing upward through the midde.

AWAY FROM HOME

In addition to the 145 million family members in the U.S., there are about 10 million "unattached individuals," i.e., not living with relatives.* They are on the

* Individuals and family members thus account for about 155 million Americans. The remaining five million or so are in the armed forces or in institutions—prisons, hospitals, etc.

whole a low-income group, with a median income of about $1,700. This figure is higher than the median income of all nonfarm family *members* (about $1,500); however, not many of the individuals enjoy the economies that accrue from living together, and so their real living standards are probably lower.

The workers among them tend to earn less than nonfarm family heads. Among the latter, only 11 per cent earn less than $2,000, while among the working individuals the proportion in this bottom class is over 40 per cent. A clue to their low economic status is suggested by their occupations. Almost half are in the bottom occupational groups; they are the low-paid service workers (janitors, messengers, domestic service) and laborers (including farm laborers).

The story of the unattached individuals is not entirely one of grinding poverty, however. Even though their incomes are clustered thickly in the lower brackets, a good many of them are able to live at a fairly decent economic level. The reason is, they are also clustered thickly at the extremes of the working-life cycle. More than two-fifths of these unattached individuals are either over sixty-five or from twenty to twenty-four (compared to only one-sixth of the population as a whole in those age brackets). One may safely assume that the $20-billion income they receive annually is supplemented substantially by their life savings (especially for the elderly) or by gifts from relatives (especially for those starting out in life). Forty per cent of the individuals do not work at all, and their income—from pensions, relief, disability aid, etc.—is inevitably low. But many of these folk are "retired" rather than poverty stricken.

HOW TO LIVE WITHOUT INCOME

The lines separating any income group from those above and below it have been shown to be, for most Americans, remarkably penetrable. But what about the truly poor? Is there not a vast, submerged "one-third of a nation," or at least one-fourth, that remains anchored in poverty? On the whole, no.

We know from Commerce Department data that there are some 12 million family units with cash incomes of less than $2,000. This group does indeed comprise almost a quarter of the nation's family units—a fact that at first glance may shock anyone with pride in his country, and appall most American marketers. The picture is a good deal less appalling however, when a little flesh is larded onto the statistical skeleton.

To begin with, six million of the 12 million family units are not families at all; they are unattached individuals. Their living expenses are not comparable to those of families, and their income often is supplemented by savings and gifts. Another two million of the under $2,000 family units consist of farm families. These too are special, since they receive a great deal of noncash income.

That leaves about four million nonfarm families with cash income below $2,000—not a quarter but a tenth of all the families. This proportion represents a remarkable improvement over 1929, when a third of all nonfarm families were below the $2,000 line. Yet there are no grounds for complacency about the figures; a tenth is still too many.

Most of these four million families are just plain poor, period. And yet even here the statistical aggregates must be interpreted with caution. It is important to remember that the four million nonfarm families who turn up regularly in the under-$2,000 listings *are not all the same families every year*. There is always a great deal of movement into and out of the labor force, not only by part-time and occasional workers, but by regular family bread-winners. During any year about 1,500,000 full-time workers will be sidelined for three months or more by illness, accidents, strikes, etc. A variable number will always be temporarily "between jobs." In other words, an important minority of these urban families consists not of the chronically poor but of over-$2,000 families who "had a bad year."

A final optimistic note about the under-$2,000 family units: About a quarter of that class now consists of Negroes, but Negroes are the fastest-climbing consumers in the American market. Since 1939 the median income of the Negro workers has climbed from 38 to 52 per cent of the median for whites. (These figures are before taxes.) The story of this disproportionate rise is largely one of Negroes deserting southern agriculture for trade and industry. Before the war about 45 per cent of male Negro workers were employed on southern farms; today the proportion is down to 20 per cent. The proportion of Negro men working in manufacturing has gone up, meanwhile, from about a sixth to almost a quarter. If Negroes continue to move from southern farms (and if the industrial expansion of the South continues apace) they should gradually cease to be a large bulge in the lowest economic group.

THE IN-BETWEENERS

Just as the low-income group is not "anchored" at its station in life, neither is the group just above it— the $2,000-to-$4,000 group. This group is a sizable community of 12 million nonfarm families—i.e., a third of all such. On the whole, it is a group pushing upward into the middle-income class, and doing so fairly rapidly.

The vast majority of these families—about eight million of them—are headed by "working-class" types: craftsmen, semi-skilled workers, service workers, and laborers. There are two good reasons for viewing this group as a rising one.

The first is their relative youth; they are the youngest of the four major income classes. About a third of the nonfarm families in the group are headed by men or women under thirty-five versus a quarter for all nonfarm families. It would be forcing the facts to suggest that the $2,000-to-$4,000 class is merely a younger version of the middle-income class, poised to rise as experience and seniority raise its income. Actually, there are important differences between the two classes. The $2,000-to-$4,000 group has more laborers and service workers among its family heads, many fewer craftsmen and foreman; furthermore, the workers in this class appear to be in lower-paying *industries* than those in the middle-income class—e.g., textiles and meat packing, rather than steel and auto. Still, the group will be rising in the next decade. For its wages will be rising with productivity, and more and more of its workers will drop from the ranks of the laborers, elevator operators, delivery boys, etc., who now typify the group. Their families will increasingly find more skilled work—at higher rates.

The second reason for regarding this $2,000-to-$4,000 group as rising is the remarkably low proportion of supplementary earners in the group—almost 33 per cent, as noted above, compared to over 50 per cent in the middle-income group. Now this low proportion may be interpreted in various ways. There are, undoubtedly, some families in the group who have consciously decided not to send their wives or offspring out to work; they have perhaps rated leisure for the wife (if housework can ever be leisurely), or more schooling for the son, higher than added income. But many of these families must be considered another way. Many of them are typified by the young truck driver and his wife described above —or rather, by the couple as it will appear in a year or two. They are, in other words, families that were middle income in the past, and will be again in the future, by reason of supplementary earnings. But right now the wife is home minding the baby.

The supplementary earners also provide a sort of link between the middle-income class and the over $7,500 group. There are approximately five million nonfarm families who receive more than $7,500 cash income after taxes. More than two-thirds of them receive at least some income from supplementary earners. The point may now be made more forcefully: Some 2,700,000 of these families would be down in the $4,000-to-$7,500 group if the family head alone were working. All of the high-income families headed by laborers and service workers would be pushed down to the middle-income class (!) if it were not for supplementary earners.* About five-sixths of the families of craftsmen, foremen, and operatives in this top bracket would also drop to the middle without these extra workers. About half the families of salesmen would be moved down. And even some families headed by managers and professionals are vulnerable; more than a third of them depend for their status on supplementary earners.

THE RICH AND THE VERY RICH

The fact is that the over-$7,500 group is heavily concentrated in an area not very far above the line. Some

*An astonishing but well-verified statistic issued by the Census Bureau reveals that there were in 1953 about 100,000 families headed by laborers—not service workers—with incomes over $7,500. Before deciding against a college education for his son, the reader must visualize the kind of family responsible for such strange data: typically, it would be a large family in which everyone is working on, say, construction projects.

three million of the 5,200,000 families involved are under $10,000, another 1,200,000 families are under $15,000, and still another 800,000 families are under $25,000. Only a very thin upper crust of about 227,000 families have cash incomes after taxes of more than $25,000. (See "The Wonderful, Ordinary Luxury Market," *Fortune*, December, 1953.)

At about the $15,000 level, as suggested earlier, the proportion of families with supplementary earners begins to drop, and the over-$7,500 class loses its sociological ties with the middle-income class. Up to about $15,000, two-thirds of the families have supplementary earners; above $15,000, it is two-fifths. At the same time, predictably, the proportion of income derived from salaries also declines, and the share from partnerships and proprietorships rises steeply—to about 40 per cent of the total. This group in the range just below $25,000 consists of the successful lawyers, doctors, retailers and of some high-salaried executives. The over-$25,000 after-tax families tend more often to be "capitalists"; dividends, interest, rent, etc., become increasingly important. The quarter million families over $25,000 receive about 40 per cent of their income from these "property" sources.

THE ALL-AMERICAN MARKET

The major showcase of America's great income revolution is the vast new class of consumers, however it is defined: as the 35 per cent of all family units in the middle bracket, or the 43 per cent of nonfarm families in the middle, or the 55 per cent of nonfarm families over the $4,000 line. If no depression or war occurs during the next decade, and if U.S. industry continues to exhibit the productivity gains of recent years, this last figure could well grow to around 75 per cent by 1965. At that point, of course, the middle-income group would no longer be the showcase. It would be pretty much the whole show.

But it is clear by now that no definition can contain the "real" middle-income families; they are scattered all over the income spectrum. It is probably safe to say that nearly three-quarters of nonfarm families have tasted the over-$4,000 life at some time, at least for a year or two. In the next decade, most of the families who have had this taste of higher standards should attain them as steady fare.

The figures for income distributions and related matters in this article were prepared especially by and for Fortune. *They analyze, combine, and summarize in one consistent pattern the salient facets of income distribution from data originally published by such agencies as the Brookings Institution, the Federal Reserve Board, the Department of Commerce, the bureaus of Agricultural Economics, Internal Revenue, Labor Statistics, and, particularly, the Bureau of the Census.* Fortune *is indebted to Dr. Paul Boschan of New York, who worked out the complex techniques used in the statistical analysis.*

DO UNIONS RAISE WAGES?*

By DANIEL BELL

This article is a balanced analysis of the arguments and statistical evidence pertaining to some crucial questions concerning unions: What economic role should the union play? What is the impact of unionism on the wage structure? Can the unions be held responsible for the wage-price spiral? Is the union a "thermometer" or "furnace"? Mr. Bell in his presentation has summarized a wealth of technical literature—the writings of economists Sumner Slichter, Milton Friedman, Henry Simons, Charles Lindblom, John Dunlop, Arthur Ross, Albert Rees, and Walter Morton.

Just as fifteen years ago the economists discovered the fact of administered price (the theory of imperfect competition, or oligopoly), so today a new generation of economists is grappling with the problem of administered wages, and seeking to integrate this fact of economic life into general economic analysis. Government wage-fixing during the war dramatized the new situation. Since then, negotiated wage decisions between giant corporations and giant unions, proceeding in a lock-step gait, have set national wage patterns to a degree hitherto unknown in American capitalism. Seemingly, deliberate and coordinated union demands, rather than the market forces of supply and demand, are becoming the determinants of income allocation (as among consumption, savings, and investment), of the price level, mobility between occupations, the rate of technological change, the amplitude of the business cycle, etc. This is the implication, of course, of Sumner Slichter's phrase "laboristic economy." Its consequence, as some have pictured it, is the growth of two tightly organized power blocs, business and labor, which in the competitive grab for the greater share of the national produce will disrupt stable price levels, disorganize markets, and thereby plunge the economy into a wild inflation. The crucial question is whether unionism does in fact bring about these results. Or is it, as Milton Friedman puts it, "simply the thermometer registering the heat rather than the furnace producing the heat"?

The idea that unionism has revolutionary consequences is novel and startling. The historical role of trade unionism, in the traditional Leninist view, was to shore up the capitalist system. Unions gave the worker a stake in a job, thereby draining away the heat and fire that otherwise would go into the revolutionary movement. The late Henry Simons, of the University of Chicago (in an essay entitled "Some Reflections on Syndicalism"), first proposed the idea that the conservative wage-fixing function of trade unionism was actually pushing American society to some form of syndicalist, guild, or corporative society.

Recently the Simons thesis has been skillfully ex-

tended by Professor Charles Lindblom of Yale in his book, *Unions and Capitalism*. He makes two major points. Unionism, says Professor Lindblom, first, by artificially setting wage rates, distorts market patterns and second, by pushing the level of wages, introduces a permanent inflationary bias into the economy and hastens the demise of capitalism. Under "normal" market conditions, union insistence on an above-competitive wage rate pushes up prices to a point where, because of elastic demand, sales fall. As a result production is cut, and unemployment results. Union pressure recedes. Under the existing government-spending policies, however, a constantly high demand is assured so that increased wage pressure is passed along into a constantly ascending price spiral. Consequently the price level is ruptured, havoc is inflicted on rentiers and on saving, and finally the whole economy goes into a mad dance of destruction.

This apocalyptic prophecy has its doubters. Such a leading light of economic orthodoxy as Chicago's Milton Friedman insists that the economic role of unions (as of monopoly in general) tends to be exaggerated. Changes in the wage structure, he argues, operate through changes in demand. Changes in technique, innovations, discovery of new resources, and changes in taste create shifts in demand—and these determine the demand for and supply of labor of various grades and hence changes in wage rates. The only difference is that while these forces once operated indirectly on wage rates, they now work directly through the mediation of the union. Since these wages are negotiated at specific time intervals, forces that would have worked themselves out gradually are abruptly brought to a head, and because of the clash of arms they attract attention. Underneath, however, is the powerful magnet of the market, which lays out the fields of force. Market forces, for example, were responsible for the proportionately equally high wartime rise in the wages of domestic servants and coal miners. The work is dirty, and when jobs open elsewhere labor becomes scarce and wages rise. But the wage movement of the millions of domestic servants rarely is noticed alongside the spectacular strikes in coal.

*From Daniel Bell, "Do Unions Raise Wages?" January, 1951.

INFLUENCE EXAGGERATED

Professor Dunlop of Harvard, arguing from statistical data, asserts further that union influence is overestimated. "If it is contended," he writes, "that unionism has . . . 'distorted' the wage structure of the country and created unemployment, there is a considerable body of evidence to test the validity of this position. Indeed, it is high time that Lindblom, Machlup, Wolman, *et al.*, 'put up or shut up' on the consequences of unionism to *date* for the structure of wage rates in this country. The position that there has been significant distortion and arbitrary movements in the wage structure can be rejected. The data are consistent with the alternative hypothesis that unionism has had little independent influence on the wage structure among bargaining units." He cites the following evidence: (*a*) The geographical wage structure of manufacturing industries did not change to any marked degree in the period 1907-46. (*b*) The occupational wage structure within industries has remained consistent among various regions. (*c*) The wage structure by industries in the years 1923-40 appears to have responded more to changes in productivity and product market conditions than to changes in the extent of union organization. (*d*) The uniformities in the wage structure among the crafts in the building industries (e.g., the relation of a bricklayer's to a plumber's wage) suggest that accidents of union strength are not decisive.

To complicate the argument, Professor Arthur Ross of the University of California states that unionism *has* influenced the wage structure (i.e., the internal distribution of labor's share, as between skilled and unskilled, as between areas, between industries, between occupations, etc.) but that the effect of the total wage level is not inflationary. Anyway, says Professor Ross, in his influential *Trade Union Wage Policy,* an attempt to judge unions by economic criteria is false. Unions cannot be fitted into supply-and-demand theory: they do not control the labor supply, nor do they "maximize" wages in the way classic theory pictures the maximization of profit as the motor force in a capitalist economy. Trade unions, Ross argues, are political institutions operating in an economic environment.

(For the propagandist, the situation is almost ideal. Pay your money and pick your economic theory. A businessman can regard unions as a powerful monopoly, responsible for inflation; or, if unions boast too loud of their power, he can pooh-pooh their role. Similarly unions can claim to be influential and decisive forces, or they can belittle the disruptive effects of their wage bargains.)

What, then, is the impact of unions on wage structure? One of the ideals of classical price theory is that the wage system should distribute labor among occupations and industries so as to effect the best possible allocations according to demand. Such a distribution calls for freely adjustable wage differences which, as Sumner Slichter puts it, (1) equalize the drawbacks of jobs in different occupations, and (2) reflect the different efficiency of different occupations. From this

standpoint, the limited evidence suggests that union "distortion" of the wage structure (i.e., special advantages for particular groups, e.g., the coal miners) is not at all disruptive.

THE FOUR WAGE ROUNDS

The next question is: do unions raise money wage rates in the economy? At first glance this may appear incredibly naive. What else, one asks, have the unions been doing in the four wage rounds since the war? The meaningfulness of the query appears in the alternative: what would have happened to these same money wage rates if the unions had not been present? An unpublished study by Albert Rees of the University of Chicago indicates, for example, that the steelworkers' union did *not* affect the level of wages in basic steel from 1945 to 1948, for wage increases of similar size probably would have been obtained without collective bargaining. The proof of the argument rests on two counts: a comparison of wage movements in steel during a comparable period of non-unionization, the wartime period of 1914 to 1920; and the high demand for steel in the postwar period and the shortage of labor relative to ongoing wage rates. Rees concludes that the negotiated wage decisions were more a reflection of demand and supply than a result of the bargaining process itself. In fact, he implies that collective bargaining may even have delayed wage increases by freezing rates for the period of the contract.

It does not follow that without unions wages would have gone up automatically; some amount of disruption in the labor market would probably have occurred before the steel companies took heed. As wages were held down relative to an increasing demand, the quit rate would have risen, productivity would have fallen, and the corporation, in the bidding for labor, would have been forced to raise wages. By this reasoning a union tends to stabilize an employer's labor force; workers don't run to higher wage opportunities elsewhere, they expect the union to get the comparable wage rise for them.

To a large degree the wage picture in steel can be generalized for the economy as a whole in the last five years. Inflation (or in this instance rising prices) can be a "push" or a "pull" phenomenon. In the postwar years, costs were not the prime force in pushing up prices; prices were pulled up by a market demand that came from the large volume of money in circulation as a result of the government's cheap-money financing power, the hunger for consumer-durable goods, and the expansion of the labor force. In the strongly competitive industries, agriculture, textiles, meat packing, the wage increases were an excuse for price increases that would have come anyway from the heavy demand. In industries such as steel and auto, whose price policies are based on cost plus markup, union demands were the means whereby the heavy inflationary forces in the economy exerted their pressure. Naturally wages, as buying power, constitute a demand factor as well as a cost factor. Between 1945 and 1947, according to Sumner Slichter, increased demand due to wages accounted for about one-half the increase in prices.

What might have happened if the four wage rounds had not materialized; if, that is, the union leaders made the noble sacrifice of refusing to ask for more? The evidence indicates that the *total* amount of spending would not have changed. The composition of the national income would have altered, and with less money going into wages, the price spiral of food and clothing might have slackened sooner. But, on the other side of the coin, corporate outlay for plant and equipment would have increased. And the tremendous demand for consumer-durable goods, autos, refrigerators, etc., would have held up, since these products were bought largely on installment credit. We have become so fascinated with the Keynesian concepts of income-expenditure, declares Professor Walter Morton, that we fail to see that the old-fashioned quantity and velocity theory of money is the simplest and best explanation of the postwar inflation.*

UNION PRESSURE

Without unionism altogether, would the spiral have taken place? The historical evidence (as well as orthodox economic theory) suggests that it would. On the other hand, in the administered-price industries (auto, steel, etc.) it is likely that the effect of unions was to slow the acceleration of the price spiral. Prices—and wages—were held at a point *lower* than they could have gone, because of the fear of sticky wages in a later period of falling prices. The auto industry is a case in point. From 1945 to 1949 the list price for autos was considerably lower than the black-market or "equilibrium" price in a free market. One reason was public relations and fear of political repercussions. Another was the existence of a strong union, for any rise in list prices would immediately be matched by a rise in wages, whereupon the industry would be stuck with a higher permanent wage rate. Thus the fear of wage rigidity narrows the amplitude of the wage pendulum.

Actually, wage earners have much more to lose than has industry during rising prices and inflation. In those periods, the proportion of national income going to business owners and self-employed rises, and the share going to workers drops. In the last decade, because of the consistently high demand, net corporate profits came out ahead of wages in the share of the inflationary income. According to the statistics of the U.S. Chamber of Commerce:

	1939	1948
Wages and salaries	$45.7 billion	$131.2 billion
Net corporate profits ...	5.0 billion	20.3 billion

Thus industry gained—the proportion of profits to wages went from 1:9 in 1939 to 1:6½ in 1948.

What about the pressures of unions when demand slackens? How responsible and resilient is the union leadership then? Some evidence is at hand from the recession at the end of 1947 and 1948. Unions in the men's and women's clothing industry, textile, shoes, and other consumer-goods lines did skip a fourth round when it was apparent that these industries could no longer afford an increase. Even the Communist fur workers' union, as a result of "rotten" business in 1949, agreed to return to the prewar "two-price" system, which meant an 11 per cent reduction in wages during the six-month slack season. An equally significant sign was Reuther's five-year acceptance of the G.M. formula, which meant, concretely, that the union would forgo any effort to push money wage rates up beyond a specified rate of increasing productivity for the industry. In these, as in many other instances, it appears that unions do respond to market conditions and take into account the probable effect of wage demands on the level of employment for their members.

Most of these generalizations are limited to the experiences of the last five years when Big Unionism came into its own. If union pressure tends to be inflationary, it is itself a response to the political temper of a permanent war economy that does not meet its full expenses out of pocket but must instead rely on borrowing and a mortgaging of the future.

INFLUENCE SOCIOLOGICAL

The influence of unionism on American society is largely sociological. Unionism has articulated a security-consciousness felt by the American worker. (The drive for pensions is one manifestation.) Unionism has insisted on a particular egalitarian treatment of the worker, substituting seniority in place of merit systems and an umpire in place of unilaterally operated grievance machinery. It has insisted on equal pay for similar classifications of work, and the wage-rationalization programs initiated by unions in both the steel and the packing industries have created a streamlined structure that managerial leadership itself failed to institute.†

In economic terms, the main impact of unionism would seem to be indirect. The existence of a high wage structure moves management to substitute labor-saving machinery for labor, thus reducing the unit cost of product and, in the long run, raising real wages. In the largest sense, unionism has helped to create a political environment whereby the measures it demands become part of a wider program for the governmental underwriting of social-welfare policies.

---

* "Because we had given up hope of controlling the dammed-up inflation after the war by reducing the quantity of money or lowering its velocity by drastic taxation, we tried to stop the spiral by exhorting and threatening labor and business. As a consequence, the erroneous belief grew that the level of prices is determined by the spiral and primary attention was directed to the wage bargain and to profits rather than to the quantity

of money." "Trade Unionism, Full Employment and Inflation," by Walter A. Morton, *American Economic Review*, March, 1950, perhaps the most provocative of recent discussions of the wage problem.

† At one time, in steel and packing, there were literally thousands of different rates within a plant as a result of wage practices being determined by foremen.

THE FUNCTION OF PROFITS*

By PETER DRUCKER

Peter Drucker, professor of Political Economy at New York University and consultant on management organization and industrial relations, interprets the function of profits in a new way which touches the whole rationale and purpose of the modern industrial enterprise. Classical economic thinking about profits was derived from Ricardo's London stockjobber living in a timeless trading economy of past costs with profits an individual motive. For Drucker, profits are the return for future costs or risks of the modern industrial enterprise. The four major risks discussed are replacement, risk proper, uncertainty, and obsolescence. A basic distinction is made between profitability and profit. Profitability, the more significant and comprehensive term, goes beyond the covering of costs and emphasizes the notion of increased productivity which is the rationale of every industrial enterprise. It might be called "social profit" as distinct from "personal profit," the motive of the individual businessman. Profits in the conventional sense are a rough measure of profitability. However, the average corporate profit account both overstates and understates profitability; it is based on a false time sense; and there are aspects of productivity which are still beyond its reach. The present article was condensed by Peter Drucker from a chapter of his book, The New Society, *(New York, 1950).*

The big industrial enterprise is the dominant or "socially constitutive" organ of everyday life in all industrial countries: the modern corporation in the U.S., the Public Board in Britain, the trust in Russia. Like any other institution, the enterprise must first serve its own survival; this means it must operate at a profit. But this law of its being must be consonant with the aims of the society in which it exists. Many Americans today, both in and out of the labor movement, believe that the aims of society and the corporation's focus on profit are somehow incompatible. This conflict provides the theme of much high-minded palaver: "production for use" versus "production for profit," "pecuniary versus social accounting," "private greed versus public interest," and the like.

I propose to show that the conflict is more literary than real. Profit discharges a function essential to the success if not the survival of any industrial society, and profitability must be the criterion of all responsible business decisions, whether the society is organized along free-enterprise, socialist, fascist, or communist lines. There are serious conflicts within any industrial system, but there is also an overriding harmony, which may be expressed thus:

1. The survival of the corporate enterprise depends on its economic performance; and
2. The overriding demand of society is for economic performance; and
3. The criteria of economic performance, both from society's standpoint and from the standpoint of the survival-seeking corporation, are *cost* and *increased productivity*. Both are measured and expressed by profitability.

*From Peter Drucker, "The Function of Profits," March, 1949.

THE DUTY OF ECONOMIC PERFORMANCE

It is fashionable nowadays to think of the modern corporation as a political rather than an economic institution. So it is; there is even some merit in the claim of ultraprogressive managements that their purpose in life is not to make profits, not even to make goods, but to make people happy. As Dean David of the Harvard Business School puts it, "Business leaders must assume the responsibility for increasing all the human satisfactions of the group with which they are associated." But they will fall the shorter of this aim the more they forget the purpose for which corporate enterprise developed. Its original purpose, and its first duty to society still, is economic performance.

In the discharge of this duty, its first objective must be to preserve intact the productive capacity of the resources entrusted to it. Never mind how it got these resources; consider them—as many managements today consider them—as a public trust. The resources consist of machinery, land, skills, know-how, men, money, and, not least, the productive unit into which these elements are joined. The preservation of these resources is the corporate enterprise's first obligation to itself and to society. If it fails in this, it not only weakens its own power to survive, but impoverishes the whole of society.

To keep its resources intact, the corporation must be able to cover costs out of current production. But "cost" and "current production" are misleading terms. The cost of doing business, for example, by no means covers the cost of staying in business. Industrial production focuses on the future; the loss it seeks to avoid is future loss, the costs to be met from current production are future costs; and one of these future costs is risk.

RICARDO'S IMAGE

If this sounds too simple, compare it with orthodox economic thinking, whether Marxist, liberal, or conservative. All these schools still bear the stamp of Ricardo, who gave orthodox economics its terms, tools, and mood. Ricardo was a London stockjobber, and he built his system in that image. No other vocation could have furnished so pure a model of "economic man in the market." The stockjobber works without employees and without organization. The time element does not enter into his activity. He turns over his entire capital immediately; for the first rule of the stockjobber's profession is to clear the books and liquidate all positions every day. Every morning, therefore, the stockjobber starts business anew, as it were from scratch. Every evening he liquidates his business completely. His is an almost timeless world—very much like the universe of the Newtonian physicists.

In this trading economy all costs are in the past. The surplus of current income over past costs is profit. It is measured by comparing the present income with the past outlay; it is a projection of the present on the past. Its explanation must, therefore, lie in the past. In this traditional system the role of "profit" is not so much a function of production as it is an individual motive.

The structure of a modern industrial economy is radically different from that of a trading economy. In the first place, the economic subject of an industrial economy is not an individual but an enterprise, which means an organization of a great many people and a heavy fixed investment of capital. Second, the economic activity of an industrial economy is not the "trade" taking place in the instant of exchange, but production over a very long period. Neither the organization (the human resources) nor the capital investment (the material resources) is accountably productive in the "here and now" of the present. It will take years before the organization or the investment begins to pay for itself.

This shift in economic facts is beginning to make itself felt in our economic theory. A sure sign is the revival of pre-Ricardian mercantilist ways of thinking with its implicit sanctification of the "going concern." The very idea of a war economy, with its emphasis on "flow" and "bottlenecks," as well as the whole theory of national-income analysis on which our financial and fiscal policies are increasingly based, suggest not Ricardo but the thinking of the eighteenth-century physiocrats whom Adam Smith and Ricardo were supposed to have killed forever. The resemblance between Quesnay's once celebrated *Tableau Economique* and a national-income table is much more than superficial. The mercantilists and the cameralists of the seventeenth century, whom Keynes and others have revived, thought in terms of economic institutions rather than in terms of the "isolated individual in the market." Their institution, however, was the state rather than the enterprise; and their mere revival cannot give us an adequate theory of industrial economics. Though a good deal of prepartory work has been done,* the big job is still ahead.

So far we can state these propositions:

1. Where a trading economy focuses on the past, with difference between past costs and current income a "profit," an industrial economy focuses on the future, with difference between current cost and current production a "premium" for the future costs of staying in business.
2. But the future is always unknown and unknowable, unpredictable and uncertain; hence these future costs are "risks."
3. Coverage of these "risks" of the future out of current production is a law of the industrial enterprise. It is its responsibility toward itself and also toward society. And this coverage can come only out of current production.

FOUR KINDS OF RISK

The future costs of staying in business can be divided into four major risks. They are: replacement, risk proper, uncertainty, and obsolescence. Replacement and obsolescence refer to the industrial process; they affect the organization's capacity to produce physically. Risk proper and uncertainty refer to the industrial product; they affect the organization's capacity to produce economically—that is, to produce something accepted by society as worth its price.

Of the four risks, only one—*replacement*—is calculable in advance. And the fluctuating value of money makes even this calculation inexact (which is why U.S. Steel and others have recently had to set up special inflation reserves). Replacement is also the only one of the four risks that is commonly accepted as a cost by our laws and mores. The tax collector allows it as depreciation, though he is vigilant against its imaginative use. The costs of replacing a good labor force, for example—and a good labor force is the most perishable of all assets—may go well beyond the standard pension plans approved as costs by the Treasury.

Like replacement, *obsolescence* is generally understood as a fact of industrial life and accountants rarely make advance provision for it. General Motors recently set up a special obsolescence reserve, but of the four kinds of risks obsolescence is probably the least calculable in advance. It means simply that the economic life and the physical life of equipment are not necessarily of the same duration. Virtually new equipment may become obsolete through a sudden advance in the art. During the depression millions of dollars worth of steel rolling equipment, although well protected against replacement, were made obsolete almost overnight by the development of the continuous-strip mill.

In contrast with replacement and obsolescence, risk proper and uncertainty (which relate to the product rather than the process) are not considered costs at all, but rather charges against "profit." Nevertheless, they are part of the cost of staying in business.

Risk proper is the cost of management's inability to foresee the economic future of its product. In preindustrial economies the proper risks were mostly

---

* The two best studies were both done more than a quarter of a century ago: Frank H. Knight's *Risk, Uncertainty and Profit*, and Joseph Schumpeter's *Theory of Economic Development*.

physical ones. The husbandman ran the risk of an epidemic among his sheep, the farmer the risk of a hailstorm. What was produced, in other words, was practically always marketable; the only question was whether there would be anything to market. One of the greatest achievements of the mercantile age was the conversion of many of these physical risks into something that could be predicted and provided against. It is no exaggeration to say that without the eighteenth-century development of insurance, which subjected physical risks to the laws of probability, industrial society could never have been born.

RISK AND PLANNING

But in the place of physical risks, the industrial system is subject to genuine economic risks, risks of marketability of the product. Risk proper stems from unforeseeable shifts in demand. It may be a change in fashion or a change to a genuinely improved product. In any case this risk is inherent in any industrial system, not just a free-market economy. For example, that seemingly least competitive of services, the inter-urban streetcar, has in two decades been erased by the automobile from the face of the U.S.

The advocates of a planned economy claim that they can control this risk: i.e., if strawberries and cream are produced, people will eat them and like it. Under unusually favorable circumstances this may be true. Risk proper may be controlled in an industrial economy—whether planned or unplanned—when it operates under extreme scarcity conditions, when any product is eagerly bought at any price, as in Russia since 1917 or in the U.S. from 1945 to 1948. Risk proper may also be controlled in part as long as the planned economy is backward; for then it will confine itself to imitating by and large products and services successfully tried out elsewhere. But if ever a planned economy reaches the stage of technological leadership, it will have the same problem of risk proper in deciding what new products to make and what old ones to continue making. Shifts in demand stemming from fashion are even harder to control than those stemming from real improvement. When the Nazis tried to control the fashion market just before the war, the black market in non-standardized buttons upset all their calculations. As for the next risk—uncertainty—it becomes actually greater under planning, as we shall see.

Uncertainty is the time factor in risk proper. How long must the new product stay in the laboratory, or compete in jeopardy, before it establishes its marketability against the old? This is a new contingency hardly known to pre-industrial producers. The farmer always knew that if he did not have a corn crop by frost time, he would not have a corn crop at all. But an industrial producer, even if he has a sure-fire product, cannot say with certainty when it will be successful. Ever since the development of the polymerization process during World War I, it was clear that natural-rubber tires would someday have a synthetic substitute. The laboratory man-hours piled up, first in Europe and then in the U.S., and the product was good enough for war. But not until a year ago was nature

actually improved upon. This was the result of concentrating on the special purposes for which the synthetic was wanted, and also of the adaptation of low-temperature processes used in oil refining. The date of this solution could not possibly have been predicted in advance. The "bugs" in any new process or product are by definition unforeseeable.

NO TELLING WHEN

The importance of this risk can be seen from the fact that modern research engineers estimate from five to twenty years for the successful development of a new product or process, from laboratory to sales. Indeed, in our larger industrial research laboratories, uncertainty is considered so basic that little attempt is made to focus research directly on the production of a marketable product. Companies like General Electric and the American Telephone Co., as well as the major chemical companies, have gone in for pure research and expect the marketable product to come out as a byproduct; and experience has proved the soundness of this policy of "serendipity."* It is based on the realization that the time factor is so unpredictable and incalculable as to make it more profitable not to try to predict or calculate it at all.

"Uncertainty" usually occurs together with risk proper, and it is difficult in any concrete situation to separate the two. As a concept, however, "uncertainty" has to be kept separate. For one important characteristic of industrial production is that every single advance in productivity increases the "uncertainty" under which production operates.

Such are the four risks faced by each individual enterprise in its battle for survival in a modern industrial economy: replacement, obsolescence, risk proper, uncertainty. The enterprise must cover these risks out of current production as a duty to itself. But the *successful* enterprise also owes two additional duties to the industrial society of which it is a part. And these duties, though they are not so represented in the average balance sheet, are also necessary charges against current production.

THE DRY HOLES

First, the successful enterprise must carry a share of the losses that unsuccessful enterprises will sustain in the future. Just as a productive oil well must pay for the pipe and labor that went into a dry hole, so the surviving company must pay for the economic loss of its competitor's failure. In 1941, for example, about 40 per cent of all American corporate enterprises did not make a profit; they barely covered their replacement costs or lost money.

The dry hole, the competitive failure, are wastes that any individual enterprise may avoid but a society of enterprises cannot. They even perform a necessary function: that of keeping the economy's bowels open. They are nevertheless economic losses, and society must demand correlative gains from its successful enterprises over and above what the successful enterprise needs to provide for its own risks. If they are

---

* The art of finding things by looking the other way.

not provided for, the economy as a whole will shrink.

If all enterprises could be successful—that is, could cover their private risks successfully—there would of course be no need for this additional social premium. But even the Russian planned economy has not been able to make all its enterprises successful. On the contrary, the profit margins in Russian industry—three to five times as great as those of American industry—indicate that planning actually increases the amount of social risk these industries must cover. This is probably because uncertainty is a larger problem in a planned than in an unplanned economy. For the essence of planning is to accept unduly long odds in the bet on timing: the planner bets he will roll not one seven but an unbroken series of sevens. Everything comes to depend on the correct or lucky forecasting of when a new product or process will be successful. Many new developments must reach the stage of success at the same time or the whole plan collapses.

Thus it is not by eliminating competition that the social waste of failure can be avoided. Competition is merely one rather efficient way by which the elements of risk in any changing industrial economy can be explored. These risk factors, not competition as such, cause the social losses of which the successful enterprise must bear a share.

THE SOCIAL BURDEN

Finally, the enterprise must bear—again out of its current production—a share of all those social services that do not pertain to the economic process: schools, churches, hospitals, armies and navies, foundations, zoos, the custodial overhead of the Grand Canyon, what not. It does not concern us here whether these social services are supplied by government or by the enterprise itself, or to what extent they contribute indirectly to productive capacity, or how much of them we can afford. However evaluated, they are a non-economic burden on production, and their cost must therefore come out of a surplus of current production over the enterprise's own replacement cost and risks.

To sum up, the current production of the enterprise must cover:

1. The current costs of doing business,
2. The future costs of staying in business, which are replacement, risk proper, uncertainty, and obsolescence,
3. A share of the future losses of unsuccessful enterprises, and
4. A share of society's non-economic burden.

Only if the enterprise can cover all these costs out of current production will it preserve its own and its society's resources intact. But if the economy is to expand and improve, still more is required.

CHANGE AND PRODUCTIVITY

All societies change; but changes in pre-industrial economies were mostly the result of outside forces. The dramatic changes of history—war, conquest, exploration—caused great dislocation in the use of existing resources. Thus the discovery of America, by shifting the centers of trade from the Mediterranean to the Atlantic, made England and the Netherlands wealthier at the expense of Venice, Genoa, and Augsburg. Dislocations of the same sort followed the Crusades, the great gold discoveries in California, Alaska, etc., the collectivization of Russian agriculture, the total conversion of the English economy after Dunkerque; men and resources were moved into new employment, for good or bad. When economic expansion resulted from these huge dislocations, it was usually an unintended byproduct. The change was physical or political in origin, and did not come out of the economic system itself.

Quite otherwise is the change to which the industrial economy is subject. Now change is self-generated, built in. We must always be either expanding or contracting; increasing our economic resources or using them up. Expansion therefore is the very purpose of the industrial economy, and its imperative need. Lest it contract, society demands of its tool, the industial enterprise, that it increase its productivity. This is the second basic law of the enterprise: the *law of increasing productivity*.

EXPANSION OLD STYLE

Adam Smith, and even more so the classical economists who followed him, knew of only one way to increase economic production. That was the employment of existing resources for the activity they were best fitted for. How to bring about the most economical application of the existing resources was the great problem to which the whole classical tradition from Adam Smith to John Stuart Mill addressed itself. But the resources themselves were considered God-given and unchangeable. Only on this assumption of changelessness can the classical doctrines be understood, above all the free-trade doctrine and that of an automatic, self-adjusting gold standard.

Marx, unlike the classical economists, understood that expansion is not only desirable but necessary to the new industrial economy that was coming into being in his lifetime. But he saw only one possibility of expansion: expansion into new territory. Out of this grew the Marxist theory of "imperialism" as developed by Hobson and Lenin, according to which capitalism in order to expand must enslave. Out of it grew also Henry George's theory of new land as the source of all enrichment and Franz Oppenheimer's theory of conquest as the dynamic principle in history. But even Marx and the Marxists did not believe that expansion was possible for long; indeed they based their prediction of the inevitable collapse of capitalism on their conviction that expansion, while impossible to the capitalist system, was inherently impossible except at somebody's expense.

Fuller and better use of existing resources is still one of the major ways to greater wealth, as is the exploitation of virgin resources. But what is basically new about the industrial system is its power to expand at nobody's expense. The application of technology results in an actual transformation of old and fully utilized resources into bigger and more productive resources.

This expansion is called increased productivity. The way to increase productivity—the only way—is through an improvement in the art by which the same resources employed in the same activity are made capable of producing more. Hence the economy can produce more of the same goods, or it can, without any cut in existing production and without dislocation, shift resources to produce something new.

The industrial system has made this expansion a normal process. We have grown so familiar with it that we underestimate its miraculous nature. Among an infinity of examples, take rayon. The basic chemical processes of this industry were all in use by the middle twenties. Yet with no new chemistry of any significance the output per worker in the rayon industry has multiplied in the past twenty years through innumerable small, anonymous, on-the-site improvements, the total effect of which has been revolutionary.

ARE PROFITS RESPONSIBLE?

This habit of increased productivity is the chief characteristic of the industrial system. In traditional economic terms, how is it obtained? The traditional answer is, by the reinvesting of profits; and the many examples of this process cited before the Flanders Committee show how ingrained is this notion in practical corporate accounting. Yet in theory it is a misleading answer. An increase in productivity does not really come out of profits, which are payments to capital, for the increase does not require new capital at all. In fact it releases capital; its agent is not the capitalist but the innovator. When capital is directly released by increased productivity in the form of repayment or bigger dividends, then profits are the vehicle by which this transfer is made. But if the released capital takes the form of higher wages or lower prices —which may well be the more normal case under competitive conditions—it does not even show up as a profit.

Yet clearly there is a continuing social profit from increased productivity. In this sense *profitability* is the better, more inclusive word. Profit, as understood by accountants, is a crude and inaccurate prototype of the gauge we need to measure profitability. Crude and inaccurate as it is, it is the only approximation that corporate management has.

PROFITS VS. PROFITABILITY

The meaning of profitability may be clarified if we compare it further with profits. The average corporate profit account both understates and overstates profitability; it is based on a false time sense; and there are aspects of productivity that are still beyond its reach.

Profits understate profitability because they fail to include such social dividends as higher wages, lower prices, and contributions to the social burden (the latter are symbolized rather than measured by taxes). Profits overstate profitability because they have to cover risks that are really future costs of staying in business. Except replacement, all these costs are made to appear as profit, which they are not.

Moreover, accounting on an annual or quarterly basis is but a picayune enlargement of the instant or day that was the time unit of Richardo's trading economy. Industrial production neither begins nor ends with the production of a given unit. The farmer's natural unit is the cycle of four seasons. The cattleman's is the two- or three-year reproduction cycle of the herd. What is the natural time unit of industry: the depreciation period of the machine? Or the business cycle? Or even longer? Whatever it may be, the calendar year has long since ceased to make sense as the unit of industrial measurement.

Also the rate of productivity increase, and indeed the measures of risk, are realms of wild surmise to most corporate accountants. The art has not yet yielded the figures needed for determining the optimum rate of change; we have only hunches. Without wishing here to prejudge problems in the nature of capital formation, I will own to a hunch that none of the great industrial economies today operates on so high a rate of profit as Soviet Russia.

PROFITABILITY IS A FUNCTION

The search for the optimum rate of change will of course raise all manner of social and moral questions: how, and by whom, should future risks be covered? How, and to whom, should increased productivity be distributed? The questions of justice involved here, though real, would be much easier to solve if it were no longer necessary to justify or vindicate the enterprise's need for profitability. That should be accepted on functional grounds.

The function of profitability *has nothing to do with the profit motive*. Whether this motive still exists in our society, and what good it does if it does exist, are beside the point. If archangels ran our enterprises, profitability would be the first law of their actions. It is also the dominant consideration of the commissars who run Russia's industries. Profitability has nothing to do with any individual's motives. It is founded in the objective necessities and purposes of industrial production. Nor has profitability anything to do with the legal or political environs. It works the same way whether a labor government disapproves of profits or a capitalist government smiles on them.

Profitability is the whole rationale and purpose of the modern industrial enterprise. It includes the first law of the enterprise—the covering of all costs; and the second law—the law of increased productivity. Profitability is also what society demands, or what it should demand, of the enterprise; for the coverage of future costs and the release of capital for expansion through increased productivity are as important to society as they are to the enterprise.

When this concept is more widely understood, many of the most heated arguments over the role of profits in the U.S. economy will be found to be sterile, if not pointless. The only trouble with profits is that they measure profitability too crudely. Profitability is the lodestar of economic performance, by which the enterprise, in order to serve itself *and* society, must necessarily set its course.

6. International Economics

26. FOREIGN TRADE

"THE DOLLAR CRISIS IN NEW ENGLAND"*

By J. K. GALBRAITH

The brief fable told here teaches in striking form the importance of a free international trade. The six New England states are portrayed as a separate nation having seceded from the Union. The economic problems they encounter reveal the detrimental effects of tariffs, immigration quotas, and exchange restrictions.

An unexpected consequence of the secession of the six New England states was the severe financial crisis experienced by the new commonwealth. It was all the more surprising, for New Englanders had a well-established reputation for caution and prescience in financial matters. The bankers in Boston, the financial capital of the new state, had always handled their own and other people's money with commendable prudence and rectitude and the New England banks, alone, had been unembarrassed by the severe banking crisis some fifteen years earlier. New England had suffered little disorganization and even less physical damage from the second world war, and some caution is called for in comparing the position of New England with that of the European states of the period.

Prior to partition, however, economic conditions in New England had been a cause for some apprehension. A contemporary authority had observed that, although wages in New England were lower than in most other parts of the United States, production per man was frequently even lower. Some branches of the manufacturing industry, on which the area was singularly dependent, were in a precarious position. Partly as a result, New England had been buying more food, raw materials, and other goods from the rest of the country than it had been selling in return. This deficit had been made up by payments received for such services as insurance and private education and from earnings on investments in other parts of the then U.S.†

In spite of the uncertain state of its balance of payments, the New England area never experienced an actual dollar shortage in the prepartition years. Apparently, as manufacturing enterprises found themselves unable to compete with newer and more modern plants in other parts of the country (a condition that had characterized the New England textile industry for many years), they simply closed down. The younger and more energetic workers then migrated to other parts of the country. There were no immigration barriers to stop this movement and by the middle of the twentieth century, travel facilities, though often primitive, were no barrier to the hardy. As a result of this migration, the population of New England had increased less rapidly than that of other sections. In 1880 it had about 8 per cent of the population of the U.S. as a whole and by 1940 only about 6.4 per cent.

In retrospect, it would appear that it was the closing down of inefficient enterprises and the migration of workers that prevented New England from having balance-of-payment problems while it was still part of the U.S. The plants that remained in operation were, inevitably, those with the lowest costs and best management and hence the ones that were best able to maintain or expand their exports to other parts of the U.S. At the same time the closing of inefficient plants and the emigration of workers reduced, relatively speaking, the volume of raw materials, food, and consumers' goods that had to be imported into New England. This crude process had kept New England's imports automatically in balance with her income from exports, services, and investments.

AUSPICIOUS BEGINNING

No nation ever came into existence under circumstances more auspicious than those attending the inauguration of the New England Union on that Arbor Day that has since become a sacred memory of all New Englanders. The facilities of the federal government, including post offices, dams, internal-revenue offices, and the headquarters of the regional soil-conservation service were turned over to the infant republic. The mayor of Boston became the first ambassador to Washington.

Unhappily, financial difficulties followed almost at once. While the principal incentives to the creation of NEU were social and cultural, the founding fathers were aware of the unsatisfactory state of their industries. They took steps to provide modest tariff protection for those in most serious trouble and launched a carefully designed program of industrial rehabilitation. The predecessor state governments, while they could accord minor tax concessions and other subsidies to industrial enterprises, had been generally unable to raise capital on behalf of private industry. The borrowing power of these primitive governments was usually

---

* From J. K. Galbraith, "'The Dollar Crisis in New England,'" April, 1948.

† These and other observations were made in an article entitled *New England's Decline in the American Economy*, by Seymour E. Harris, a distinguished economist of the period, and were published in the *Harvard Business Review* in the spring of 1947, not long before partition. Another important contemporary document bearing on prepartition conditions is a thesis by Penelope Hartland entitled *The Balance of Interregional Payments of New England*.

exhausted in providing needed public works and improvements. For reviving and recapitalizing depressed industries, local officials had been forced to rely mostly on oratory and incantation, which, though greatly used, had never been completely effective.

The men who forgathered at the new capital at Increase, Massachusetts, were under no such handicaps. They had at their disposal the credit resources of a sovereign power. In Wall Street the first bond issues of NEU encountered the then prevailing suspicion of foreign loans but patriotic New Englanders subscribed generously and what remained was readily absorbed by the new central bank. Plans were drawn to recapitalize the cotton-textile, shipping, shoe, and farm woodlot industries, and to modernize the New Haven Railroad. With an adequate supply of public capital to supplement the efforts of private enterprise, chances for success seemed promising.

Partition, unfortunately, made the new commonwealth subject to the tariff of the U.S. Although it received most-favored-nation treatment and quickly negotiated a reciprocal-trade treaty as well as a treaty of friendship, commerce, and navigation with the U.S., products of the NEU entered the latter country at a considerable handicap. New York farmers, after drawing attention to the substandard labor and sanitary conditions in Vermont, were able also to have fresh dairy products from that state excluded from the New York market.

There were other minor sources of irritation in the trade between the two countries. New England, for example, had long been a manufacturer of inexpensive watches, and these cheap timepieces flooded the U.S. market, endangering, it was believed, the watch industry of the latter country. Fortunately, a previous arrangement between the U.S. and Switzerland provided a formula for resolving this problem, and NEU watch manufacturers undertook, voluntarily, to limit their exports to the U.S. Tobacco was also a source of difficulty, for the U.S. Government was then engaged in supporting the price of this product for its own farmers. It was necessary to keep Connecticut tobacco producers from taking advantage of a market that, in the contemporary phrase, was being maintained "at the expense of the American taxpayer." It would be unfortunate, however, were the trade problems of the two countries exaggerated unduly. At this particular period the U.S. was actively engaged in promoting world trade. Its policy, which had been enunciated with great force and clarity, was a source of much encouragement to the manufacturers and exporters of the NEU.

EMIGRATION RESTRICTED

Had it not been that times were good and the labor requirements of the new industrial-rehabilitation program substantial, unemployment in NEU might have been serious. Inevitably there was dislocation in industries that had been accustomed to market their products in the U.S. At the same time the extraordinarily strict immigration quotas established by the U.S. for the NEU effectively prevented workers from the latter area from seeking employment in the U.S.* As it happened, most of the actual suffering was confined to the part of NEU adjacent to New York City. The people of that area had long found employment in New York and many of them had rather specialized talents coupled with an attitude toward manual labor that made it difficult to absorb them into the NEU economy.

The difficulties the new country encountered in selling its products, together with the restraints on emigration, coincided with its growing need for steel, non-ferrous metals, and other raw materials and certain types of machinery for its industrial-rehabilitation program. As a result there was a heavy demand from NEU for U.S. dollars to buy U.S. goods and a considerably more limited demand from the U.S. for NEU dollars to buy New England products. The NEU dollar, for that reason, went to a sharp discount in New York. Fearing a further fall, holders of NEU dollars, bank deposits, and other liquid assets endeavored to convert their money into U.S. dollars and this capital flight added to the instability of the new currency.

The government of the New England Union, although opposed in principle to the step, was forced to institute exchange control to halt the flight of capital. All U.S. dollars earned from exports were turned in to the central bank and these were doled out only for approved imports. In addition U.S. dollar assets in NEU were registered and their transfer out of the country was prohibited.

The government of NEU also curtailed imports of citrus fruits, automobiles, films, alcoholic beverages, and other nonessentials, and it launched a "Buy New England" program that was a model of its kind. The tourist trade was encouraged and unnecessary travel in the U.S. was prohibited.

These steps were not taken without some sacrifice in the standard of living or, indeed, without some criticism from within NEU. At no time, however, did this criticism seriously jeopardize the future of the young country since most of it was directed at the regulations and the manner of their administration—at what a speaker in a much quoted address to a meeting of the New England Council spoke of as "the cancerous red tape and the capricious job holders who are the sole architects of our agony."

The firm measures taken by the government of NEU, criticism notwithstanding, served to arrest the deterioration in the exchange position. It was not possible, however, to eliminate the deficit in the balance of payments entirely. Eventually the assistance of Washington had to be solicited and, after some hesitation, Washington made a series of advances to the young republic. This help proved temporary, for Washington itself was in difficulty after California left the union and Texas reasserted its independence. The Canadians, who provided aid for a time, were always inclined to make their assistance conditional on closer economic cooperation between the secession states.

* Prior to partition, one or two influential U.S. newspapers urged that New Englanders were subject to alien influences and, so were a comparatively non-assimilable group.

U. S. TARIFF*

Today it is generally acknowledged that the United States, as is only fitting for the world's leading creditor nation, must increase its imports. However, this realistic article shows, more is required than lower tariff rates. A solution must be found for the problems of the "invisible tariff" or red-tape entangling custom practices, the even more complex and more potent law of valuation with its five possible criteria, and the almost unlimited number of other hypocritical non-tariff forms of protection. Some interesting insights into United States tariff history are sprinkled throughout the article. A way is suggested how tariff policy may be reformed so that United States imports may be increased.

For the first time in years the U.S. protective tariff is likely to become a national political issue. ECA would like to make it so, and the dismal logic of international events also argues for it. The State Department, after having for fifteen years muffled the issue under the Reciprocal Trade Agreements policy, may at last be forced to take a stand. Procedural reforms in our tariff have been promised the British and Canadians by Secretary Snyder, and their tariff experts are now talking with his. The objective, of course, is to increase U.S. imports as a substitute for the free gifts of tax-payers' dollars without which our enormous postwar export trade could not have been sustained. If the tariff is really a big obstacle to U.S. imports, as all Europeans firmly believe, it is rightly a problem of national concern.

This is a new thing, virtually without precedent in our politics. In the past the tariff has been by turns a sectional issue, a local issue, and (since the thirties) no issue at all. But Americans have never argued it out on grounds of national policy, as the British did when they went for free trade a century ago. We have accepted protectionism as a natural part of "the American system." In the eighties Bryce recorded that there had never been a free-trade party in the U.S., except for a few Republican intellectuals†; and there still isn't. John C. Calhoun, the great low-tariff spokes-man, was a frank sectionalist; he never claimed that low tariffs were good for the North, and the only great national issue he could make of it was the constitutional one on which South Carolina tried to nullify the 1828 "tariff of abominations." Grover Cleveland, who tried to reduce the tariff in 1887, had a very practical reason: an embarrassing revenue surplus, and in blaming the tariff for it he carefully dissociated himself from free-trade principles ("too much like bandying epithets") and proclaimed, "It is a condition which confronts us, not a theory." W. H. Taft also had a practical reason—conservation—for his unsuccessful treaty with Canada, which would have meant free trade in food and lumber: "We have drawn upon our own resources in such

a way to invite attention to their necessary limit." As for Wilson's Underwood Act, which was inaccurately called "the Free Trade Tariff," it was actually sold to Congress as an antitrust act, to stir up big business and "whet American wits"; no serious redivision of labor with other countries was contemplated.

The present Democratic sponsors of the Reciprocal Trade Agreements are often called free traders by high-tariff interests. Senator Malone of Nevada, for instance, calls the act "nothing less than a free-trade act." But the history of the R.T.A. refutes this. Its avowed purpose has been to promote new markets for U.S. exports by tariff concessions that are carefully chosen so as to cause no injury to protected U. S. interests. Its sponsors have believed, or professed to believe, that trade can be enlarged without hurting anybody; and in fifteen years they have neither hurt anybody nor noticeably influenced the quantity or pattern of trade. With the help of a fifteen-year inflation, they have reduced the average level of duties on all U.S. imports from 20 per cent, the all-time high

---

MR. MARX VETOES FREE TRADE

For the first time in many moons, the gospel of Karl Marx was cited approvingly in the halls of the U.S. Senate. The approval was qualified and the area of discussion was limited. Nevertheless, that highly vocal high-tariff man, Senator Malone of Nevada, felt sufficiently impressed with Marx's warnings against the evils of free trade to read into the *Congressional Record* these words from the co-author of the *Communist Manifesto:* "Generally speaking, the protective system in these days is conservative, while the free-trade system works destructively. It breaks up old nationalities and carries antagonism of proletariat and bourgeoisie to the uttermost point."

In citing Marx so respectfully, Senator Malone introduced one stylistic novelty. Throughout, he referred to his source as "Mr. Marx." This is a courtesy that could have been applied by no one but a conservative Republican Senator; in the radical movements, the surname has customarily sufficed.

—"In the Economic Zoo," March, 1952.

---

*From "U. S. Tariff," December, 1949.

† For example, W. G. Sumner. But the protectionists have also had first-rate intellectual support, e.g., Henry Carey, Simon Patten, Alvin Johnson.

to which Smoot-Hawley raised it, to 6 per cent, virtually an all-time low. But this familiar statistic conceals the fact that those U.S. industries which most depend on protection still have all the protection they need, and the additional fact that U.S. imports have steadily lost ground in relation to our domestic trade, from 5 per cent of our national income in 1929-33 to 3 per cent today.

This is one of two reasons why the tariff has been "no issue at all" during R.T.A. The other is that the tariff has been superseded by quotas and other direct controls as the prevailing method by which governments channel trade, a method against which our tariff concessions have made no headway whatever. Tariffs, as a spokesman for the American Tariff League rightly said, are "the fairest and mildest of trade controls." R.T.A.'s Clair Wilcox agrees: "A country which confines trade restrictions to the use of a tariff can be said to be pursuing a liberal trade policy." If there is such a country in the world today, it is not the U.S.

The protective tariff is, however, the *chief* way in which the U.S. controls its trade; and if the size and pattern of that trade is to become a national issue, so will the tariff. Let us therefore examine it. It is not a simple subject.

FIVE THOUSAND DUTIES

The basic U.S. tariff law, which occupies 110,000 words in the *United States Code,* is the ill-famed Smoot-Hawley Act of 1930, the most thoroughly log-rolled and, according to Professor Taussig, the most unnecessary of all the twenty-one major tariffs that we have enacted since the first one on July 4, 1789. This basic law describes over 5,000 articles within fifteen broad categories, prescribing a duty for each; and also contains over fifty pages of special provisions and administrative rules, mostly taken over intact from the 1922 tariff. Although most of the 5,000 duties have been reduced under R.T.A., the Smoot-Hawley rates are untouched, or left very high, on some of America's most important industries, among them woolens, meat, nonferrous metals, rayon, a bewildering variety of cotton specialties, sheet glass, hundreds of finished steel products, most kinds of machinery, and miscellaneous high-skill specialties like optical goods, cameras, film, and surgical instruments. Because of postwar changes in costs, the degree of tariff dependence of such industries is more uncertain than usual, but none of them would want to dispense with protection altogether. The most exorbitant rates of protection are found in a variety of lesser goods, such as peanuts (200 per cent), neutral spirits (162.5 per cent), mesh bags (110 per cent), cigarettes (104.4 per cent), cheap cigarette lighters (110 per cent), and costume jewelry (55 per cent).

Of all U.S. imports, about a third carry a duty of some kind. Raw materials and crude foodstuffs (e.g., bananas, coffee, tea) compose the bulk of the two-thirds of our imports that enter free. Some exorbitant Smoot-Hawley rates have all but disappeared. The duty on whiskey has dropped from $5 a gallon to $1.50. Jeweled watch movements have gone from over 100 per cent to less than 40.

The import tax on raw sugar was 2 cents a pound in 1930 and is now 3/5 cent. But as far as protection is concerned the sugar tax might as well be eliminated altogether, since that purpose is now much more efficiently served by the quota system that has limited our sugar imports since 1934. Watch movements, woolens, and many other products are also subject under R.T.A. to new "tariff quotas," which restore the old prohibitive rates on imports over a given amount.

It is useless to look too far for meanings in the changed level of tariff rates since Smoot-Hawley, or to assign any shifts in trade to any one of them. Since the "escape clause" was written into the Trade Agreements Act in 1947, the Tariff Comission has been empowered to hear complaints from subsequent victims of tariff reduction. Ten* have been filed; in six cases the commission found that an increase in imports either was not attributable to the tariff cut or had done no damage (the other four cases are pending). The Tariff Commission enjoys the confidence of protectionists. Set up in 1916 as part of the drive to "take the tariff out of politics" and put it on a "scientific" basis, it has become the most anonymous body in Washington not through any fault of its own but because of the near impossibility of its assignment, namely, to measure cost-price differences here and abroad and the effect on them of any particular tariff. This quest for tariff certainty (which still goes on, notably by Senator Malone) will always fail for the reason given by Professor Taussig after his lifetime study of tariffs: "The notion that there is one uniform cost abroad and another uniform cost at home, and that comparison between them is a simple matter, probably holds good in no case whatever."

Far more significant than the level of duties is another change in the U.S. tariff. Since 1916, every act and treaty has added new refinements and subdivisions to the classifications of merchandise. This has thrown an increasing burden of work on the customs administrators and made their rulings a matter of the gravest importance to every U.S. importer. Since the basic rules and inbred bias of our customs administration were formed under high protection, the complexity of our tariff is itself a great obstacle to imports. This is the heart of the so-called "invisible tariff," or "administrative protection." Customs practice has become a special branch of the law and also supports a profession of licensed experts in red tape known as customs brokers, who extract a well-earned commission on almost all dutiable imports. A customs lawyer, Benjamin Levett, once wrote, "Let me write the Administrative Act and I care not who writes the rates of duty." That act was written with protection in mind.

THE CODE

In his book, *Through the Customs Maze* (1923), Levett showed how a traveler, sending home a rug that

* Complaining industries: candied marrons, whiskey, spring clothespins, knitted berets, crude oil (independent), California hops, Florida sponges, knit gloves and mittens, rattan and reed products, narcissus bulbs.

he innocently entered as worth the $100 it cost him in Persia, could become liable for $710 worth of customs fines and duties and perhaps a jail sentence besides (if he tried to throw the rug away at customs, he would still owe them $150). The rules which made that theoretically possible in 1923 are mostly in force today, and there is no shortage of current horror stories. Wayne Taylor's mission (ECA and Commerce) to Europe last summer brought home a fresh crop. Because of the predatory inclusiveness of the phrasing of the lace and fringe classifications, for instance, European exporters of fringed rugs pay 45 per cent (it used to be 90 per cent) instead of the 30 per cent called for in the carpet classification. Dutch orchid plants are subject to fumigation, which means they will not bloom for two years and so prevents their export. Cut flowers, on the other hand, arrive by plane only to wither under delays in customs. Boxed candy from the Netherlands was refused admittance because, although the net weight was clearly printed on the label, the appraiser thought the corrugated paper in which each candy was wrapped took up so much space that the appearance of the package was "misleading." English exporters of men's sweaters with appliquéd neckbands were subjected to the embroidery duty (45 per cent) instead the sweater duty (25 per cent). No Dutch bricks are shipped here because each one has to be stamped "Made in Holland." Not many Dutch cigars, either, because the valuation includes the Dutch domestic sales and excise taxes, despite the fact that the exporter does not pay them. An exporter of fine wrapping paper, who had secured a reasonable "advisory" classification from New York customs, found that when he shipped to San Francisco he had to pay the much higher rate on "bible" paper. Many an upholstered chair pays the duty on wool, as do corn plasters; the British claim that a recent shipment of sheep shears was classified as surgical instruments (40 per cent duty); and tires of synthetic rubber are classified under nylon because rubber has been defined as "india rubber" by the Supreme Court. There is not always logic, but there is almost always a precedent and often a binding court decision behind customs rulings. To avoid stretching a word in their voluminous regulations, the appraisers will first subject the usual sample of the import to minute chemical analysis, then the rules to metaphysical analysis, then the importer to character analysis, delay, market missing, and sometimes bankruptcy.

THE PROBLEM OF VALUATION

It is not the appraiser's fault. The complexity of his job is imposed by law, and not only by the laws of classification. Still more complex, and more potent in controlling imports, is the law of valuation. The duties on a large percentage of all imports are based wholly or partly on their value. For this purpose the appraiser has five possible criteria.

First come (1) the *foreign* value and (2) the *export* value. The appraiser must choose whichever is higher. This usually proves to be the foreign value, which is defined by law as the price at which "such or similar" goods are "freely offered for sale" to the *domestic* trade of the country of origin, "in the usual wholesale quantities and in the ordinary course of trade." But this does not always mean what it says; it sometimes means the price of *retail* quantities in a quite extraordinary course of trade. Dutch floor-polishing machines, for instance, have been sold to importers here at $30.15 or less, the same price the Dutch wholesaler pays. But they are valued by customs at $38.73, the price to the Dutch retailer. This is because there is only one wholesaler of this line in the Netherlands. The precedents maintain it is the number of transactions, not the quantity of business, that sometimes determines "the ordinary course of trade." The New York firm of French-Van Breems discovered this via an extra assessment six months after they had imported and sold some polishers here at the lower duty. French-Van Breems should have known better than to use common sense in interpreting a customs law. In recent years complications of this kind, plus foreign price controls, have made "foreign value" more and more meaningless. Moreover, the reasons behind the Supreme Court decision of the nineties that first gave "foreign value" its importance have since been removed by antidumping legislation. Hence "foreign value" today has mostly nuisance value, and ought to be done away with altogether.

Export value comes closer to what the importer really pays for his goods, but it not the same thing. It is the price at which "such or similar" goods are offered to the trade for export to the U.S. This prevents a sharp or lucky importer (and his U.S. customers) from deriving a customs advantage from a below-market purchase. Export market prices are easier for customs men to ascertain than "foreign value," but they are subject to just as much distortion in the coral reef of litigation that is the customs code. For example, "foreign value" usually includes the taxes—excise, consumption, etc.—which are paid by the foreign consumer even if they are remitted to the exporter. But "export value" usually does not include export taxes even though they show up in the U.S. landed price. As R. E. Smith summarizes this wrinkle (in his *Customs Valuation in the United States*), "Under the law an importer is compelled to pay duty on Chinese taxes on someone else's goods that never leave China and is exempt from duty on Chinese taxes on his own goods which he must pay before they can leave the country."

If the foreign and export values are unascertainable, the appraiser must next try (3) "United States value." This starts with the price at which the importer will sell the merchandise here and arrives at its synthetic export value by deducting his assumed costs. In doing so customs uses an 8 per cent ceiling for the importer's assumed profit. In his next alternative, however, which is (4) "cost of production," the appraiser can impute to the foreign manufacturer a 50 per cent profit. Such inconsistencies, in which customs rules abound, are consistently loaded against the importer.

The next type of valuation, (5) "American selling price," applies mainly to certain coal-tar derivatives;

it is unimportant but instructive. It was written into the 1922 act for the special benefit of our infant chemical industry. In effect it enabled Allied Chemical *et al.* to set (via their own domestic selling price) the price at which "similar competitive" German imports would be valued. By this means a duty of 60 per cent concealed an actual price equalization, which, had it been written into the rate instead of into the method of valuation, would at that time have taxed some chemicals at about 2,000 per cent. Our chemical industry's costs are now more competive, but it still enjoys this unique indirect control of its own tariff.

After he has appraised the import, the customs officer finally turns to still another valuation: the *entered* value. This is the importer's own attempt at appraisal on his customs entry; since he naturally sets it as low as he legally can, the appraiser pays it little attention, except for two purposes. If by some hideous mistake, or an abrupt market fluctuation, it should prove higher than the appraiser's valuation, then the importer's overvaluation becomes the dutiable value. But if the opposite is the case, then he has undervalued, and becomes subject to certain penalties and also a presumption of fraud, which if sustained on appeal carries very serious penalties indeed. In other words, the importer is presumed to be a liar unless he is proved a fool, in which case his word is preferred to the customs officer's. The legal source of this presumption is in the phrase "whichever is higher," which runs through the customs code like a refrain.

Hypocrisy, as in the use of "American selling price" for chemicals, has characterized U.S. tariff practice since 1816. After Jefferson's embargo, which gave our textile industry its start, the new duties on cotton and woolen manufactures were made to look less protective than they were by means of the "minimum value" provision, which said that imports worth 4 cents a square yard "shall be taken and deemed to have cost 25 cents per square yard," yielding an actual rate of 520 per cent. Classification by value brackets is still a favored method of obscuring actual rates.

Hypocrisy is also involved in our many non-tariff forms of protection. The protective uses of the sanitary code are moderately well known in the case of Patagonian beef, which is excluded not because it is subject to the Argentine hoof-and-mouth disease but because it is un-American. The protective uses of public morals are best known to our contraceptive industry (no imports allowed). But perhaps the cooniest of these discriminations is that against foreign books in English. They cannot be copyrighted here (although books in other languages can) unless they are manufactured here. This old law, of union inspiration, prevents U.S. membership in the International Copyright Union, keeps most new English titles from finding their audience here, and is a thorn in the side of our book-publishing industry.

Except for exchange control and multiple currencies, there is almost no limit to the protectionist devices Americans have resorted to. Our agriculture has been increasingly divorced from world market prices since 1933; today the government not only pays export subsidies on wheat and any other crop "in surplus," but can impose direct import quotas on large categories of commodities—for example, practically all fats and oils are under quota at this writing. Our synthetic-rubber policy, imposing "mixing requirements" on Akron, is an indirect import quota. Our maritime and airline policies involve not only a protective tariff (50 per cent on non-emergency repairs to U.S. ships or planes in foreign ports) but direct subsidies and indirect protection, as in the requirement that 50 per cent of all ECA shipments must go in U.S. vessels. Our coastwise shipping is protected by a complete embargo. The Treasury also has the extraordinary power—which it has never used—to impose a 10 per cent extra punitive tariff on *any* import arriving here in a foreign vessel.

Another little known form of protection is the Buy American policy legislated into federal (and many state and local) purchases since 1933. The Secretary of Defense and the Bureau of Federal Supply have some discretion under this act if domestic prices are "unreasonable," but they use it only when the differential is more than 25 per cent. Even our stockpiling program, which makes sense only in respect to foreign materials, was carefully subjected by congressional direction to the Buy American Act.

WHAT OF IT?

Foreigners, of course, have even more drastic protective devices of their own. Seventy-seven of the world's eighty-five trading countries now license either all imports, or all foreign exchange, or both. During the six months ending last October 1, forty-two new bilateral barter treaties were added to an already long list. "For every step we take forward [toward freer multilateral trade]," said a State Department official recently, "we slip two backward." As *Fortune* has pointed out (July), the unfortunate ITO charter itself is final evidence that our official trade policy of the last fifteen years has failed to stem the trend toward statist trading and has reached a dead end.

The U.S. tariff, in such a world environment, seems more innocent than ever. Do we really want to change it, and if so why? Old-fashioned as it is, the tariff has nevertheless worked for the U.S. It has played a part, if not a precisely measurable part, in our becoming a rich, busy, and nearly self-sufficient country with the most variegated industry and agriculture in the world. What if we have had to fool each other a bit in the process; what if we have had to pay more for many things than economic theory says they are worth?

Before answering that question, let us look at the condition (not a theory) that now confronts us: a seemingly chronic export surplus, which, if we do not find a way to accept payment for it, will soon cease to deserve the name or the few remaining rights of private international trade. That export surplus leaves us only four ways to balance our international accounts. The first is continued gifts of dollars; the second is foreign investment (Point Four); the third is to let our exports drop toward our import level. Nobody has yet described a feasible combination of these three ways that is adequate to the problem. Everybody in his right mind—including the protectionist American Tariff League—agrees that a fourth way must also be brought into the picture; in short, that the value of U.S. imports must somehow be increased. How should tariff policy be employed to this end?

ADMINISTRATIVE REFORMS

The least controversial way is to cut "the invisible tariff," i.e., without changing the level of rates, to reform customs procedures and so replace the mastiff with a welcome mat. Since most customs procedures are enshrined in court decisions, congressional action is required and will soon be sought. The Interdepartmental committee now working on this is hampered by the fact that the State Department wants to get the reforms as a byproduct of congressional ratification of the ITO charter, which would require many of them. But if ITO is defeated (as it should be), the reforms will still be desirable, and should therefore be pressed independently of ITO. The following are endorsed by most government experts and private trading groups:

1. Eliminate "foreign value" as a basis for appraisal, and use "export value" instead.

2. Give up "entered value" as a contingent basis for assessment, and use appraised value even if lower than entered. The "whichever is high" rule is an archaic device to trap fraudulent undervaluers, dating from the period when customs men and their informers were allowed to split fines.

3. Let customs give more binding rulings. Advisory rulings are not now binding; moreover, customs can now change a classification or a valuation and make it retroactive on imports of a year past. This kind of uncertainty can be reduced, even if never eliminated.

4. Require a prima-facie showing of injury before invoking the Anti-Dumping Act. At present it is invoked more often in fear than in pain, and imposes "countervailing duties" against imports that may be subsidized or may be merely unpopular (it was used against prewar Japan).

There are plenty of other possible administrative reforms. McKinsey & Co., which made a management study for the Treasury two years ago, recommended 150 (including, for example, modern statistical controls instead of a 10 per cent sampling), of which only a few have been adopted. Harry Radcliffe of the National Council of American Importers estimates that procedural reforms would increase our imports by $1 billion a year (about 15 per cent). That would not close the dollar gap, but reforms should be made anyway as a matter of fairness and common sense.

"GET THE LITTLE GUY"—?

After the "invisible tariff" is cut, what about the level of rates? A spreading theory holds that certain protected U.S. industries are dispensable—not worth the international trouble they cause. This is the theory behind the C.I.O.'s consistent support of tariff reduction. Our mass-production industries pay the best wages and are least dependent on the tariff; why, then, should their highly productive workers be made to carry, as consumers and as world citizens, the precarious, lower-paid, and tariff-dependent jobs of American glassblowers, glovers, dollmakers, jewelers, confectioners, potters, watchmakers, greenhouse keepers, and other highly skilled specialty jobs that the Europeans are able and eager to do for us? The argument has its Calhounian overtones, but it appeals to common sense.

In nine small factories in Maine and Vermont work 750 people who can make all the spring clothespins the American market absorbs. Another 850 small farmers (in Senator Smith's movingly diminutive words) "cut the wood for the little plants," and depend greatly on this little income. Comes now an RTA tariff cut from 20 cents to 10 cents a gross, and the Swedes have already seized 30 per cent of the American spring-clothespin market. In fact, the Swedes took it away not only from the New Englanders but from the Mexicans, for whose benefit the tariff cut was supposedly negotiated.

The clothespin industry has won a formal investigation of its plight from the Tariff Commission (something the oil drillers and the distillers failed to get). According to the theory of dispensable industries, the Tariff Commission ought to find better use for its time. The sacrifice of this clothespin market is worth $2 million to Sweden, means cheaper clothespins to the American consumer, and would drive those Maine appleknockers—who would, of course, be helped by the government through their difficult transition—into more productive labor, thus adding to (rather than subtracting from) the real wealth of the U.S.

In so far as this is an orthodox free-trade argument it is unanswerable, but it applies equally well to Eastman Kodak and to cotton farmers. In so far as it makes a distinction between clothespins and other protected products, it involves a basic inequity and a new kind of political favoritism. A selective sacrifice policy could become a kind of reverse logrolling, picking on those industries for de-protection whose congressional representatives are weakest. This would produce a great spectacle—American foreign policy pitted against the spring clothespin—but scarcely a great debate.

NATIONAL DEFENSE

The debate gets better when a protected industry claims to be important to national defense, the argument allowed by Adam Smith himself. Before the House Ways and Means Committee last spring, the eloquent Walter Cenerazzo said that the Swiss treaty is destroying our watch industry. He argued that it takes three to six years to train skilled watchmakers, that they are indispensable to other precision processes in wartime, that the Swiss may be on the wrong side of the next battlefront, and that it is criminal to let any watchmakers, such as Waltham's, lose their skill in some other job. But the President of the Gruen Watch Co., Benjamin Katz, spoiled Cenerazzo's effect by testifying that he, an importer of Swiss watches, is also building a $3-million watch factory on Long Island for which he said he could train the highest skills in six months, that they were no more indispensable to defense than any other precision workers, that the Waltham company, managed as it was, could not have

Protectionists, by the way, used to cite Waltham Watch as an example of how free trade can work havoc on a fine old American company. Waltham was supposed to have been run into the ground because the tariff was reduced on Swiss imports. Well, last year Waltham more than doubled its sales to $5,328,300, increased net earnings fourteen-fold to $163,000, and added some 500 employees to it rolls. There was no change in the tariff on Swiss watches in 1952, but there was a change in Waltham's management. Demon salesman Teviah Sachs, who started his career as an errand boy for a New York jeweler and rose to a top-executive job in Gruen Watch Co., took over as president of the hundred-and-three-year-old company. He sold off a lot of the stale inventory, reorganized the plant, changed merchandising policy, and gunned aggressively for new civilian and defense business. In all this excitement, the energetic Teviah Sachs didn't have much time to fiddle with the tariff problem.

—"Editorial Notes," June, 1953.

been saved by any amount of tariff, that "management is what keeps companies in business," and that Cene-

razzo himself was largely responsible for Waltham's troubles because he had "lulled the Waltham people to sleep with the idea that Swiss competition is all they had to worry about."

The Waltham case illustrates how the national-defense argument for protection can hopelessly becloud the tariff issue. Most of our industries and agriculture —clothespins being one of the few exceptions—have some claim to military usefulness under modern total-war conditions. But the Waltham case is also another proof of Taussig's law, that no particular tariff ever wholly explains any particular business failure or success.

This works both ways: if the experienced Katz, can start a watch factory here under diminishing protection, so European manufacturers can find plenty of markets here despite high tariffs if they wish to go to the managerial trouble. ECA is quite rightly trying as hard to foment aggressive salesmanship on Europe's part as it is to foment tariff reduction on ours. And if tariff reduction should in turn stimulate American salesmanship in American markets, Americans could scarcely lose by that.

Thus the arguments for some kind of tariff reduction are compelling. But to make them effective in political terms is another matter.

28. FOREIGN EXCHANGE

CURRENCY CONVERTIBILITY—NOW*

By MICHAEL A. HEILPERIN

It has been a long time since the world's businessmen could convert pounds into dollars into guilders into cruzeiros into marks; but currency convertibility, a somewhat technical subject, is the key to a healthy international movement of goods and capital. This article explains what convertibility means and distinguishes between the spurious and the real kind, between relaxation and reform. The importance of the free transfer of national currencies is stressed. However, a crucial question arises: Is full convertibility feasible? This introduces the thorny problem of the adequacy of central-bank reserves. The author proposes a bold and farsighted foreign monetary program for the U.S. Reference is made to the views of D. H. Robertson, John H. Williams, Lionel Robbins, and others.

U.S. foreign economic policy, 1945-53, has been a $40-billion disappointment.

It cannot be called an outright failure because the vast sums we have donated abroad have unquestionably contributed some stability, economic and political, to our allies. In several countries, at several times in the past eight years, our dollars did achieve a minimum, negative objective: to prevent chaos. But our dollars have conspicuously failed to create on this side of the Iron Curtain a community of economies capable of balancing their own accounts and paying their own way. All our aid, in short, has failed to create a system of multilateral trade and convertible currencies.

* From Michael A. Heilperin, "Currency Convertibility—Now," September, 1953.

Convertibility is a somewhat technical subject—one of the most portentous technicalities the U.S. businessman and the U.S. politician must deal with. Convertibility is the key to a healthy international movement of goods and capital. The prosperity and indeed the security of the U.S. are deeply involved in the failure to achieve convertibility of the free world's currencies.

The failure is not America's alone, of course. But for a variety of reasons, the *decisive* moves toward freely exchangeable currencies can come only from the U.S. And in the months ahead the U.S. is going to be hearing more and more about its responsibilities and opportunities in this area:

In Washington this month the governors of the International Monetary Fund and the International Bank for Reconstruction and Development will hold their eighth annual meeting. The top monetary-policy makers of fifty-two countries will be waiting to hear whether the Eisenhower Administration has a foreign monetary policy.

As Congress this summer debated foreign-aid funds, it was clear that "donation diplomacy" had just about run its course. But for all its growing distaste for giving the American voters' money to foreigners, Congress has not yet accepted the alternative: a loosening of restrictions on trade, including restrictions on imports into the U.S. When and if Congress is willing to let the free world earn more dollars in this market, it will find that this reform will not really pay off unless accompanied by measures looking toward full convertibility of the free world's currencies.

Now in power in Western Europe—though for how long nobody can say—are governments strongly disposed toward convertibility. In the first five postwar years, and especially at the peak of American aid, much of Western Europe thought it had discovered a new era of monetary knowledge in which it was possible for a country to do what it pleased at home and yet balance its external accounts. It *was* possible—so long as the U.S. donated the extra dollars every year and so long as import quotas and exchange restrictions remained in lavish use. In 1951 the tide began to turn. By the end of 1952 the Continent had returned to the tenets of economic liberalism, hinged on the time-honored belief that a country's external solvency depends on the nature of domestic policies and especially on the avoidance of inflation. (See "Western Europe Rediscovers Money," *Fortune,* September, 1952.) This rediscovery, to which, by the way, the U.S. had made no contribution, opened the doors wide to monetary reconstruction and currency convertibility.

What have we done about it? Very little—either in the closing months of the Truman Administration or in the opening months of the Eisenhower Administration.

What should we do about it? A very great deal indeed. Below, we shall outline some of the elements of an American foreign monetary policy, but first let us be quite sure we know what convertibility is and why it is so important, not only for our allies but for our own national future.

THE OLD FREEDOM

No U. S. businessman in his thirties, forties, or fifties has firsthand knowledge of a world of fully convertible currencies. But there was such a world, before 1914. In those days convertibility in a currency was, as someone has remarked, like virtue in a lady: part of the definition.

Within each country the various currencies were convertible in gold or silver or foreign exchange. Notes issued by the central bank were predominantly backed by precious metals and by bills of trade representing goods in production or goods intransit, rather than by government securities. The volume of circulating media would fluctuate in accordance with the changing volume of trade (as represented by bills of trade rediscounted by the central bank) and the changing position of the country's balance of payments (reflected in the central bank's holdings of precious metals). But fluctuations in the condition of government finances did not have any significant bearing upon monetary circulation.

National currencies, regulated by the semi-automatic system, were freely transferable into other currencies, at their owner's wish, without permit or license. Because under the gold standard each national currency was convertible into gold, its transfer into any other currency could take place at rates fluctuating but mildly around a fixed parity. The question of altering a once-established parity, when a country's economic conditions underwent some fundamental change, was not seriously discussed in those days. But the logic of the system might easily have admitted of such an alteration, provided it was made only in cases of major and fundamental maladjustments and provided it was carried out by mutual consent of the various parties concerned.

The essential feature of a world economy in which currencies are fully convertible is the ensuing freedom of international payments. This means that anybody can spend or invest his money wherever he wants without first obtaining an official license or permit.

The fact that buying power can be transferred from one currency into another at the market rate of exchange without license or permit and without restriction assures the world economy of an almost homogeneous monetary circulation comparable to that which exists inside a country. This means, in particular, that price movements taking place in the various countries are related to one another, that their economic fluctuations are organically connected and largely "synchronized," and that the problems of economic growth and stability are viewed in a worldwide rather than in a purely national perspective. Once this concept prevails, an important safeguard against policies of narrow economic nationalism comes into being.

Freedom of international payments is also—and most importantly so—a condition without which multilateral trade cannot expand and flourish. Exchange control, i.e., the subjection of foreign payments to governmental license and control, tends to favor the bilateral settling of accounts between countries while restricting the aggregate volume of world commerce. If multilateral trade is to flourish, the elimination of exchange controls must be paralleled by the elimination of import quotas. As methods of controlling international economic transactions, exchange controls and import quotas are, of course, intimately related and either of them can serve, up to a point, as a substitute for the other.

RELAXATION VS. REFORM

The basic concept and benefits of convertibility have become obscured, unfortunately, in some of the recent discussions of "practical" policy. Thus Sir Dennis Robertson, one of Britain's foremost academic economists, addressing the Vienna Congress of the International Chamber of Commerce last May, devoted half of his address to the meaning he personally would attach to the word "convertibility." He had been invited, he said, "to discuss the internal and external conditions requisite for the restoration of something called convertibility." If he were to do that in the short time allotted him, he must ask certain preliminary questions: "What exactly is the projected change which we are invited to examine? What persons, who at present are not allowed to do so, are going to be allowed to convert what into what, by what method, on what terms, and for what purposes?" Robertson's answer to these questions resulted in his giving the concept of "convertibility" a very limited scope, indeed. He discussed only the dollar convertibility of the pound sterling and that only for certain purposes. In other words, he devoted his attention to the problem of *relaxing* British exchange control and not to that of restoring *full* convertibility.

Now, from the point of view of an American reflecting upon the future of international economic relations, upon the kind of world economy the U.S. should strive for and the contribution we should be making to its achievement, nothing short of full convertibility will do. This ambitious goal cannot, of course, be reached overnight.

THE AMERICAN STAKE

But only when full convertibility has been won will the American investor be able to invest abroad in full assurance that the sole risks he has to face are the usual business risks and that he is free from arbitrary action by foreign governments, especially those that result from the administration of exchange control; it is only then that the American exporter will be able to develop foreign markets without fear of losing them again through the application of discriminatory quotas or exchange restrictions; it is only then that the American productive system will be able to look upon the entire world as its market in full confidence that the "merit system" prevails and that the principles of free markets and free enterprise are acknowledged and respected.

Full currency convertibility means the restoration of the freedom of payments not only on certain transactions but on all of them, including capital movements. It means the elimination not only of exchange control but also of import quotas. It involves convertibility not on a regional basis alone but over the widest-possible area, i.e., the largest possible part of the non-Soviet world.

It follows that we must be on our guard against semantic abuses; we must reject, in particular, every attempt to apply the term *convertibility* to what is merely a liberalization of exchange control and a limited improvement in the transferability of currencies. We must, similarly, realize that arrangements such as the European Payments Union are not a step toward full convertibility but merely a means of alleviating some of the consequences of inconvertibility. The EPU must of necessity go from crisis to crisis because the network of payments that it is designed to clear is not closed and balanced but open and lopsided. Unless we

set our sights high and keep them so, we can be entirely certain of getting lost on the way.

A CHRONIC SHORTAGE?

The dispute over the feasibility of full convertibility is, in effect, a dispute over whether or not there exists in the world a structural and incurable "dollar shortage." Those who believe that there is a fundamental "dollar shortage" conclude that dollar convertibility cannot be obtained and that sights must be set much lower. Such authorities as the *Economist* of London, Robert Marjolin, the able Frenchman who is Secretary-General of the Organization for European Economic Cooperation (OEEC) in Paris, Professor John H. Williams of Harvard, to name but a few, are convinced, for reasons that are not necessarily the same in each case, that there exists a basic disequilibrium between the American economy and that of the outside world. They are skeptical, to say the least, about the chances of establishing full convertibility and are persuaded that discrimination against American trade will remain an integral part of international economic relations.

This point of view is controverted by other authorities of no lesser rank, such as Professor Lionel Robbins of London, Jacques Rueff, the prominent French economist, Per Jacobsson of the Bank for International Settlements in Basel, and Jacob Viner of Princeton, again to name but a few. It is the view of this latter group of experts that there is no structural disequilibrium in the economy of the free world. They argue that a proper adjustment of exchange rates and the acquisition of sufficient monetary reserves by various countries, coupled with the pursuit of appropriate domestic policies and all-around trade liberalization, would result in an environment favorable to the achievement and maintenance of currency convertibility.

There can be no doubt that inflationary policies, combined with the pegging of exchange rates at artificial levels, have been responsible for a large part of the payment difficulties of the postwar years. Once they have been reversed—and much progress has been made of late in that direction—there is no valid reason why international accounts should not remain in balance for an indefinite time to come, subject only to reversible fluctuations of relatively short duration.

Those economists who believe in a fundamental structural disequilibrium between the dollar and non-dollar areas will dissent from this conclusion. But only if it should develop that great difficulties remain even *after* domestic economics have been made solvent and international transactions and payments freed from crippling restrictions, can the contentions of such pessimists become guides to policy. To follow their advice *now*, to accept trade discrimination as inevitable and convertibility as unattainable, would be an act of sheerest defeatism.

A POLICY FOR THE U.S.

Assuming, then, that convertibility *can* be attained, it is the contention of this article that it must be attained soon if it is to be attained at all. This, in turn, requires that the U.S. Government treat as a matter of real urgency the development of a bold and farsighted foreign monetary policy. Such a program could be divided into three phases:

(1) Achievement of full currency transferability on current account without necessarily eliminating import quota restrictions against dollar goods.

(2) Following as rapidly as possible upon the completion of phase 1: elimination of import quotas and trade discriminations.

(3) Restoration of full freedom to capital movements and elimination of the last vestiges of exchange control. A lengthy period might have to elapse before we could enter this plase, which requires a far more substantial degree of international confidence than now prevails or can be anticipated in the near future.

Here let us examine the critical first phase more closely. The restoration of currency transferability on current account corresponds to what is frequently and mistakenly regarded as *the* convertibility problem. But in order to achieve even this first, limited objective, national inflations must be brought under full control and safeguards adopted against their recurrence; central banks must have adequate reserves in gold or dollars in order to meet temporary payments deficits; and free foreign-exchange markets must be restored.

All of these measures, let it be acknowledged at once, present very difficult practical problems, political and economic. Inflations seem to be politically more acceptable than are the stern financial measures that prevent their continuation or recurrence. Governments now in power in Western Europe have accepted the political handicap of anti-inflationary policies on the assumption that currency convertibility and freer trade will follow within a reasonable time. Should the delays become too great, however, these governments might be swept out of office by popular discontent, thereby jeopardizing not only currency convertibility but the entire system of Western cooperation, political as well as economic.

The discovery of economically correct parities between currencies is as difficult as it is important after nearly two decades of exchange control and "pegged" rates. Foreign-exchange rates must be given enough flexibility to find new equilibrium levels. Thereafter, fluctuations around these new parities should be kept within reasonably narrow limits, albeit less narrow than those that prevailed before 1914. These elements of flexibility will contribute to making future convertibility more secure.

THE CRUCIAL RESERVES

There remains the thorny question of central-bank reserves. No one denies that the reserves of the United Kingdom (representing the sterling area) and of a number of Continental countries are inadequate at the present time. We run into trouble, however, as soon as we try to define "adequate." There is, of course, no clear-cut quantitative definition. Much depends on the success of anti-inflationary policies, on the prompt finding of "correct" foreign-exchange rates, and, most

of all, on the return of public confidence in the various currencies. And the continued unbalance in the foreign payments of the U.S. renders the achievement and maintenance of adequate reserves abroad more difficult. This is why free transferability on current account will have to precede the end of all discrimination against dollar goods.

The future of convertibility will largely depend upon the speed with which the problem of reserves is solved. The year 1952 was one of growing monetary soundness in numerous countries with inconvertible currencies; 1953 has been, in most respects, a year of marking time; 1954 must become the year of improving international liquidity.

There are several theoretical ways in which the countries of the Western world could increase their reserves but most of these are outside the realm of practical policy.

Although a liberalization of U.S. commercial policies must become an integral part of U.S. foreign policy, no large and immediate increase in foreign reserves via dollar earnings is in sight today.

Nor is there much chance of expanding foreign reserves by raising the world price of gold. In theory, and indeed in the light of considerable historical experience, there is much to be said for an increase in the price of gold from $35 an ounce to as much as $70. Many economic authorities argue that much of the economic instability that culminated in the depression of the Thirties could have been avoided if, around 1925, the price of gold had been raised from its 1914 level, thereby acknowledging the depreciation of money in terms of goods that took place in the intervening decade. Today, of course, despite another world war and postwar inflation, the official price of gold is still what Franklin Roosevelt said it should be back in 1933. And the fact is that the U.S. Government and people are now strongly opposed to any "tampering" with gold prices, which makes it unrealistic to look in this direction for any early reinforcements of foreign currency reserves.

A ROLE FOR EPU?

What other solutions are in sight? The European Payments Union or the International Monetary Fund might extend stabilization loans to countries with inadequate reserves, provided, however, there were an increase in their own resources. There are advocates of an expansion of EPU to take in the U.S. and Canada and eventually Latin America, combined with a substantial increase in its resources. Belgium's Foreign Minister, Paul van Zeeland, a monetary expert in his own right, strongly advocates this solution. So does Robert Marjolin of the OEEC. So do some American economists, such as Robert Triffin of Yale University. The weakness of this recommendation is that it would merely perpetuate the use of a crutch instead of achieving the final cure. An important body of financial opinion in Western Europe, especially strong in the Bank for International Settlements in Basel, opposes the perpetuation of EPU and urges a determined effort aimed at full convertibility.

The use of the International Monetary Fund for the purpose of increasing reserves also has strong supporters, especially in Britain. It is known that the British recently sounded out the U.S. Government on the possibility of raising the dollar subscription to the I.M.F. (The response was not encouraging.) Lionel Robbins of the London School of Economics has lent his great prestige to this suggestion while coupling it with recommendations for a major reorganization of the fund's cumbersome management. Officials of the I.M.F. themselves agree that its dollar and gold resources (currently amounting to $3,255,000,000) are insufficient to bring about convertibility, especially since not all of them can be put at the service of Western Europe and the sterling area.

THE BIGGER THE CHEAPER

There remains one final solution to the problem of international liquidity. The U.S. and, to a lesser extent, Canada and Switzerland might extend "convertibility loans" to the central banks of countries with insufficient reserves. This involves the establishment of large "convertibility funds." It is this solution that was advocated last spring by a group of leading authorities brought together by the International Chamber of Commerce and headed by Thomas H. McKittrick of the Chase National Bank.*

In order to create an atmosphere of real confidence these "convertibility funds" would have to be very large. The American fund should, according to advocates of this proposal, run to the order of $10 billion. It is a shock, to be sure, to see such a figure in this context for the first time, but shock is precisely what is needed: the shock of confidence.

The first congressional reaction would doubtless be one of horror. But the "convertibility funds" would be essentially a *guarantee,* rather than expenditures. As is

* The committee included Sir Jeremy Raisman, deputy chairman of Lloyds Bank in London, M. Emmanuel Monick, former Governor of the Bank of France, and Dr. Per Jacobsson, economic adviser of the Bank for International Settlements and one of the most influential monetary thinkers in postwar Europe. The writer served as the committee's *rapporteur.*

the case with every successful guarantee fund, actual drawings against it are likely to be relatively small in relation to its authorized size. Disbursements from a large fund are likely to be smaller not only in relative but also in absolute terms than disbursements from a small fund incapable of reviving confidence.

ALL THE WAY

As things stand now, we may never reach the second and third phase of the full convertibility program, having failed to make any headway with the first. But if the Treasury and Congress take a more imaginative view of our responsibilities, and deal successfully with the first phase of the full convertibility program, they could well deal with the second phase in the life of the present Administration. This second phase, elimination of the international use of import quotas as well as all trade discrimination against dollar goods, is, of course, closely connected with the program of American trade liberalization. Until we are ready to open our doors far more widely to foreign goods than we do at present, we, cannot seriously expect the end of discrimination against dollar goods.

The third and final phase would see the ending of controls on all capital movements. This phase admittedly lies in a more distant future. It presupposes a high degree of international confidence, in political conditions as well as in the stability of the monetary reserves of many countries. The latter must be capable of expanding at a fairly even pace with the growth of international transactions. Finally, certain measures of internal monetary reform will have to be adopted in order to build into the monetary systems of the various countries semiautomatic anti-inflationary devices. This involves a substantial diminution of the role played by government securities in the "backing" of national currencies and a corresponding diminution of the scope of monetary "management."

Only when all this has been accomplished will full convertibility come into being and the world economy be stimulated by the full and free play of private enterprise.

7. Economic Systems and the Future

29. COMMUNISM

HOW BUSINESS GETS DONE IN RUSSIA*

One of the best ways to realize what communism means is to see it in action, and the daily working day of the factory manager is the key to communism in action. Here is the Soviet manager, a man who works feverishly to turn out the goods demanded of him. His operation is chaotic, his production prodigious. Communism's incessant straining of machines, plants, managers, and men to meet present official quotas and its waste of economic effort must inevitably be paid for in reduced future production.

There is a Plan, but the Russian manager does not plan for the future.

There is no making a profit, but the manager is ordered to make profits.

There is no competition, but the manager battles other managers for labor and supplies.

There are socialist goals, but the manager is prodded by motives of money and rank to struggle for personal success.

There is the collective image of "the ideal Soviet man," but the manager operates by himself and watches his colleagues with catlike distrust.

There is "financial discipline," but the manager practices deceptive bookkeeping, irregular banking, and even unscheduled production.

These paradoxes embrace no more than the sober truth concerning the goals of Soviet government and the practices of Soviet business. For all the antlike regimentation that has been fastened upon the Russian people, business under communism is conducted by stratagems, scrambles, dodges, deceits, along with a great deal of hard work.

Witness the Russian joke about the manager trying to hire a chief bookkeeper. He asks each applicant how much is two times two. The first applicant says four, the second says four; and so do the third, fourth, and fifth. Finally a man answers, "What would you like it to be?" and that man gets the job. In the actual workaday life of Soviet executives, this story is worth more than a shelf of books on management and production.

Let there be no mistake about this calculated confusion. It actually encourages tremendous and increasing production. But it also generates increasing economic strain. Whether production will go on increasing in spite of the strain or start collapsing under it is a question of no less import for the free world than for the Communist. And that question is acutely posed in the daily operations of the Russian manager.

THE MANAGER GETS A PLAN

The manager is the key to the practical workings of Soviet business because he heads "a firm." The firm is

* From "How Business Gets Done in Russia," February, 1953.

the basic unit in all sorts of plans—Five-Year Plans, special plans, and particularly yearly and monthly plans, tailored to each firm and called by each manager simply the Plan. Both the Plan and the manager are now known quantities: both are endlessly discussed in Russian newspapers, technical journals, books on management, and even popular novels. This information is supported and supplemented in detail by the experiences of managers who have fled to the West.

The Plan describes precisely what the manager is *supposed* to do. It specifies quantity, quality, and type of production. It dictates working capital together with expenditures for plant and equipment (the economy is run on a money basis) and sets prices.

It prescribes the number of workers, office personnel, and wages. It gives a cash figure for costs and a percentage figure for cost cutting. It schedules the total intake of raw materials and fuels. It even announces ahead of time what profits—planned value of sales minus planned cost of production—shall amount to.

Of the manager it is demanded not only that he fulfill the Plan but that he help make it; in theory, Soviet planning proceeds both from top to bottom and from bottom to top. The economy's basic organization is a starkly vertical chain of command. Under the ruling clique in the Presidium there is a Council of Ministers who oversee all important industrial operations. Under each Minister are a host of intermediate organizations called *glavki*, each of which gets authority directly from its particular Minister and is directly responsible to him. Directly and immediately responsible to the *glavki* are the managers of firms. Responsible in like manner to the managers are the executives who head the various "sectors" of the firm—production, engineering, dispatching, planning, bookkeeping, procurement, construction, and so on. From these men the line of command continues down through the executives who head the various production departments, and on through shop foremen, senior shift foremen, shift foremen, "brigadiers," to the workers themselves. The formal promulgation of a Plan begins with the state planning commission of the Council of Ministers and travels straight down the line.

But under the associated principle of "planning from below" the workers are expected to propose additional speedups, and the men of intermediate rank are to hunt out places where some extra ounce of output can be delivered. The firm's party unit and the union are to discuss ways of rewarding labor less and working it more. And the manager is to take all this information, pull it together, add his own ideas, and come up with new schedules for bettering those of the year before. These schedules are then to go to the *glavk*, the ministry, the central planning commission, and back down the line again.

When the schedules come back, the manager knows the amount of working capital on deposit for him in the State Bank, the exact quantity of materials and fuels scheduled to come into his factories, and—more important than anything else—the exact production that must go out. Compared to this goal, the money profits a manager is supposed to make are relatively trivial, inasmuch as the production goal itself includes a different sort of profit: namely, the difference between what the total economy produces and what it consumes in the producing. Such profit provides the wherewithal for vast plans of expansion. Indeed, the whole planning procedure has a single overriding purpose: the greatest output possible each year.

THE MANAGER GOES TO WORK

But the very emphasis on immediate output makes the practice of Soviet business remarkably different from the theory of it. Consider the career of a postwar manager, S. F. Liputin.* Shortly before the end of the war—he was then thirty-four years old—Liputin became manager of a thousand-man farm-machine firm. Fortunately for him, he followed in the footsteps of five managers who, in the course of a single year, had mismanaged production until it fell below 40 per cent of capacity, and who themselves had either disappeared without trace or been demoted to the ranks. Since future quotas are calculated on the basis of past production, Liputin knew he would have not too difficult a quota to start with, and he resolved not to let his quota be increased rapidly. Everything in his life, he knew, from his need to eat to his desire to educate his children, depended on his meeting the output assigned him. The quota was based on three-shift twenty-four-hour operation with a full labor force, and Liputin knew he was short of labor.

Thus when it came time to "plan from below" he consulted his executives—one at a time since he could not be sure whom he could trust with full knowledge of the plant's capacity—and talked for form's sake with a few high-output workers and the plant party leader. He decided he could soon turn out 100 machines a month. From this figure he subtracted twenty machines to cushion the plant against future quota increases, ten to allow for miscalculations, and twenty to hold out for bargaining purposes. He took his fifty-unit proposal directly to the ministry (bypassing the *glavk*), explaining that the misdirection of his predecessors

*Not the man's real name. Certain unessential details of his experience have also been altered.

cessors had brought equipment and machinery into such serious disrepair that it would take months of heroic effort to meet even this objective.

A week later the ministry proposed a quota of 125 machines. Liputin swore "by the tomb of Lenin" that he had whipped his staff and his workers to tremendous efforts in restoring machinery, that he had driven himself mercilessly, and that as a consequence he would pledge himself to sixty units a month. After several such sessions he managed to settle for an actual quota of eighty.

Meanwhile he sought to get the ministry to establish the lowest possible prices for his raw material and the highest possible prices for his machines. But managers selling raw material and managers buying farm machines were also clamoring their case at the ministry, and the decision favored the side with the most cogent arguments, the most voluble tears, the best connections, and sometimes the most valuable presents. Liputin dipped into the "manager's fund," supposed to be employed for rewards for quota fulfillments, and sent the chief of his procurement sector to buy caviar at the nearest *Gastronome*.

Prices on Liputin's farm machinery were set at a figure not too far out of line, but his working-capital allowance was skimpy, and part of it immediately disappeared to pay for the services of the ministry, which were charged to plant overhead. The chief bookkeeper, however, was skillful, and the plant was solvent in its account at the State Bank, which receives all a firm's income, pays out all its costs. So long as he met production quotas, Liputin could have operated even if his firm had been patently insolvent, but only through continual, time-consuming, and troublesome appeal to the ministry. As it was, the chief bookkeeper put even the manager's fund in order. Inspectors from the party and from the government went over the plants and the books, found no irregularities. A terrific speedup at the end of the month pushed production to eighty units, and Liputin deduced that, so long as the quota was filled and the proper formalities staged, he might be able to keep out of trouble.

THE MANAGER BREAKS THE LAW

Next he addressed himself to his labor problem. Russian labor is not allowed freedom of movement, but it is sometimes traded, sometimes maneuvered. The Soviet manager bargains for it by one means or another when he has not enough of it, hangs onto it as insurance against future shortage even when he has a surplus. Liputin first set about making his plant more attractive to workers. He built a community hall and a nursery, repaired the housing barracks—all part of the plant—at the cost of further depletion of funds and of considerable activity by a *tolkach*, a "pusher," on the local black market. He wangled a side deal for farm-machine repair with a local collective farm, stipulating that payments would have to be made in potatoes. These he promptly added to the factory mess.

Certain that no appeal to the ministry would get him more labor, Liputin now undertook to recruit labor, illegally and on his own hook. He connived with the district party leader for permission to order all persons not working in his factory but still occupying its housing to vacate or go to work for him. Since these people had nowhere else to live, they were able to beg transfers from their employers. Next, Liputin sent several of his senior shift foremen to nearby factories where housing and food were causing grumbling. The foremen's mission was to give workers in these factories tips on how to get the necessary release from their current jobs without getting into trouble. (The trick: do work that is sloppy enough to decrease production, but not so sloppy as to look like sabotage.) Finally, he kept an eye on the needs of other firms, and whenever one of them needed a trained worker or a specialist in oversupply at Liputin's own plant, he traded that worker for others he needed. In one case he even got rid of an overgraded lathe operator, who was receiving higher wages than he was worth, for ten ordinary laborers.

By such strategems, Liputin never failed to meet his quota, even though it rose continually. In fact he regularly produced 120 per cent of it. But he reported only 102 per cent fulfillment. This was enough to give him and his executives—particularly the all-important chief bookkeeper, procurement chief, and "pushers"— a big bonus, to stage an occasional banquet for the workers, and to add extra rubles to some of their pockets. The remainder of the output Liputin treasured as safety insurance against a day when there might be raw-material tie-ups, hard bargaining by some other plant manager, an epidemic of illness, or any one of innumerable and unpredictable emergencies. He hid this output from the eyes of the regular monthly inspectors by keeping the machines partially disassembled and by wining and dining the inspectors. The machines were marked down as "work uncompleted."

All the while Liputin cultivated the *glavk* and the party. When power failed at the plant and he could not cajole the electric firm into restoring it, a call to the district party leader would bring prompt action. When he had to have scarce material not officially available anywhere in the district, the party would sometimes produce it, and if the party could not, the *glavk*, which, after all, depended on Liputin's quotas to meet its own, could frequently call on even broader connections. The *glavk* and the party together smoothed his dealings with the ministry.

ILLEGALITY AND STATISTICS

Party and government inspectors, of course, were constantly asking questions, poking around the plant, searching the books, and demanding information from subordinates about production, shipments, and raw-material receipts. Against the discovery of illegalities, however, Liputin had erected four safeguards: he had maneuvered his subordinates into taking responsibility; he had paid them their regular bonuses; he had kept each one from knowing about what went on in another's department; and, finally, he had met his quota regularly.

At the very time his mind was busy with schemes and fertile of fears, Liputin had to remember two different sets of statistics. The first was the official set turned out by the chief bookkeeper, the hapless fellow who might be imprisoned if the inspectors chose to notice his irregularities. The second was highly informal—it existed only in Liputin's head—but it had to serve in making actual business decisions. Liputin knew very roughly that half his total costs went into labor, material, and fuel, and that the rest went to overhead, including the maintenance of inspectors and agents, known and unknown. Skyhigh overhead is common in Russia, and Liputin was not troubled by it. But he was troubled because, try as he would, he could not arrive even at a rough idea of unit costs.

ULCERS AND ESCAPE

Liputin's firm was relatively small, and his remuneration of 3,500 rubles a month was not great: it was, in fact, only six times higher than the wage of a skilled worker. He was given, however, a three-room apartment, a private kitchen and bath, a servant and a car, plentiful food, and the hope of education for his children. Liputin's only trouble was the strain of worrying, scheming, working a thirteen-hour day, and then attending in the evening party, community, or business meetings three or more times a week. All this had so worn on him that he had developed ulcers and incipient tuberculosis. Liputin applied for sick leave, but his record was too good for him to get it. He was ordered to East Germany as inspector of operations over ten factories. This work he found less exhausting. But he also found it shocking.

In Russia Liputin had done his best for the Plan, never taken graft, and always assumed the superiority of Soviet methods over all others. In East Germany he found a defeated and stripped enemy living in far greater comfort than his own victorious Russia. One day he inspected a factory of the same size and capacity as one he had known in Russia; the Russian plant required an administrative staff of forty-five persons; the German plant used just seven.

Two weeks later Liputin chanced to overhear himself described by a party official at his office as "a worshipper of Western culture"; he had become suspect. The next morning he boarded a streetcar and rode it straight across Berlin, through Potsdammer Platz and into the Western sector. "If I had known," he says today, "how much the economic rewards of management cost, I never would have tried to rise out of the workers' ranks."

THE PRESSURE

No single manager, of course, is typical of all Russian managers, particularly one who has the chance to escape to the West. Scrounging and wheedling, however, are common activities. Why the chasm between the theory of Soviet enterprise and the facts of it? For one thing, Communist dogma requires that every detail of the economy be planned in the light of vast political ends and controlled by suitable laws. But it is very difficult to plan the details of an economy as large as the Russian, particularly when the plans call for breakneck output from each factory and firm. So interrelated are the various firms that one bottleneck in supply or one tie-up in communications, of course, throws many plants completely off schedule.

In practice, bottlenecks and tie-ups are remarkably frequent, raw materials and transportation are often scarce. Were there rigid adherence to all the details of a plan, labor and supply jams could not be unsnarled and production goals could not be achieved. The details, even the laws, consequently, have to be sacrificed to the central objective: output. In effect, planning has to be supplemented with bargaining. The Plan has to become a device for wheedling as much production as possible out of the men who run the plants and work them. The best way to wheedle is to install a one-man boss at the head of each firm and to permit him an *un*certain amount of latitude in maneuvering to meet his quotas. It is also necessary to get young bosses. Few men above forty can stand the strain. To get the greatest production possible, the Communist state puts the manager under very heavy tension and subjects him at one and the same time to pressures of great rewards and drastic punishments.

WHAT PRICE FAILURE?

All managers are encouraged to greater production (and to more deceptive bookkeeping) by a bonus system that pays nothing if a firm falls short of its plan by even 1 per cent, and that pays off at 30 to 100 per cent of regular salary if the plan is fulfilled or overfulfilled. Failure, unreliability, or error, on the other hand, can occasion a staggering change in a manager's circumstances, ranging from a reprimand for slipshod concealment of illegalities to execution for political unreliability. When the trouble is low output, the manager may simply be junked—thrown back to the ranks of the workers or, perhaps, the foremen. The driving end-of-month finish in most Soviet factories—the Russians call it *shturmovshchina*—reflects the difference between getting one's salary doubled and having one's professional career ended.

Some managers are able to escape this more or less permanent crisis by finagling non-managerial jobs in research and development, often work without purpose, and thus without danger. There are also fanatic managers so stirred by participation in mighty works that conviction keeps them in their jobs and drives them to prodigious efforts. And about one manager in a hundred arrives at a state of prominence and comparative tranquillity, in which he does not have to fear anything but the secret police. For such men, "failure" at one job does not mean demotion but transfer to another job and possible promotion to higher rank.

By contrast there are the cases of two managers who (at different times and places) balked at the Communist system and refused outright to do any more work. They were brought to trial and sentenced to five years of forced labor. At the camps they continued to refuse work. They were brought to trial again and sentenced to ten years. They continued to refuse work. They were not brought to trial again. They were shot and their pictures were hung in their factories as warnings.

CALCULATED UNCERTAINTY

Most managers, however, neither act on splendid conviction nor enjoy splendid careers. Uncertainty is a major force in the economic arena within which they operate, and a powerful motive by which they are compelled. They know that they are utterly accountable for fulfilling the ends they are supposed to fulfill, and they do not know whether the means they are forced to use will be held against them. If they violate laws as a means to fulfilling ends, they may be denounced for criminal sabotage and opportunism. If they do not violate laws they may be denounced for "slavishly following tradition."

Managers try to gather "papers for the prosecutor": i.e., a record that might mitigate future punishment. They try to shunt ticklish illegalities to subordinates and to get their signatures on the necessary papers. Compulsion to fulfill the Plan is all the manager shares with his subordinates; otherwise his relationship to them is one of distrust. The subordinates too are trying to cover themselves. Furthermore, their work tends to be routine. The decision-making manager stirs their frustrations and sometimes impels them to an all-or-nothing effort to "get" him and his job. The manager is friendless.

Indeed, the government wants him to be friendless. Long tenure at any one firm might lead to the establishment of friendships and to a concerted effort by the manager and his executives to circumvent all-out production. Successful managers seldom stay at one job more than two years. (Some important firms have been known to use up half a dozen less successful men in one year.)

JOBS, SPECIAL AND SECRET

Worked until mind and body are groggy, shifted here, shifted there, the manager is not even permitted to hold to the Plan as an unceasing verity. There are sometimes secret orders—from the Ministry of Internal Affairs, the MVD, for instance—that require him to drop the Plan altogether, strictly on his own responsibility, of course, in order to do a special job that even the ministry to whom he is responsible knows nothing about.

Other special tasks, and a variety of high-priority operations designed to break bottlenecks or speed defense production, also take precedence over the Plan, and the manager is expected to deal with them without even being told to. To recognize them he has to cram into his mind the general operations of the entire economy, the details of the current five-year plan, and the national importance of the work of his own firm. If he fails to recognize them, he is likely to land in prison.

Meanwhile, the Plan itself is subject to constant change. For one firm, for instance, there were no fewer than sixteen material changes during a six-month period. Production quotas are rarely reduced in the course of a given year, but they are regularly increased —often the manager is notified of a simple "operational correction" in his quota—when raw materials or component parts or fuel or power become less scarce.

Amid these changes and uncertainties the manager must do more than make the right decision; he must make it with political "enthusiasm" and "sincerity." Otherwise he is guilty of the deviation known as "swimming with the stream." In practice, he is expected to swim in all directions at once. About the only way a manager can do this, with unrelenting pressure upon him, is to put pressure upon the men under him and to surround them too with uncertainty.

STALIN IS WAITING

The pressures under which the manager has to struggle lead to frenzied reactions. Consider one day in the life of P. A. Kalganov, thirty-eight, manager of the Zhdanov shipbuilding firm in Leningrad, as reported by a refugee chief engineer who worked under him until transferred to East Germany. The firm normally employs 6,000 workers and builds submarines and ocean-going vessels up to 10,000 tons. Recently, however, 2,000 men have been added to the labor force, and Kalganov has been ordered in the name of Stalin to building nothing but submarines, and those in a quantity he scarcely deems possible.

This firm operates directly under a defense ministry and has practically no financial problems. Books are kept for the sake of form, but operations are not expected to show a profit. Supplies are requisitioned directly from the ministry and submarine handed over to it without concern for prices or costs. Payroll and operating expenses are met by scheduled payments.

Kalganov arrives at his office promptly at 9:00 A.M. Briefed by his business manager on the morning mail, he roughs out answers to the most important letters, orders others relayed to various subordinate executives.

From ten to eleven he talks to the night plant manager, the deputy manager, the chief engineer, the chief mechanic, and the chief of transport. The night plant manager reports that a casting for an engine support, planned to weigh 3,000 pounds, has turned out to weigh 3,500 pounds. Kalganov remembers a hint from an acquaintance in the ministry that there might be a special inspection of the casting department. He immediately summons the responsible personnel.

The casting-department engineer knows, of course, that the molds for the engine support were improperly made. He knows also that there are only seven completed castings and that there should be ten. About this he says nothing. He says that tests have shown the need for additional strength, and therefore additional weight.

The chief design engineer, called on to verify these nonexistent "tests," realizes at once that if he does not verify them there will be trouble for the manager and the chief engineer, neither of whom he dares offend. Were he to offend, they would watch for mistakes of his own—inevitable in the nature of his work—and dispose of him. He not only verifies the tests but signs a brief report on them. After this, the chief engineer is called in, informed about the mistake in weight and given a hint about the forthcoming inspection. Kalganov suggests to him that three units already alongside the drydock should be carried back to the casting department "for tests." The chief engineer at once telephones for three crews of men to move them.

HANDS BEGIN TO SHAKE

From eleven to twelve Kalganov conducts a conference on "dispatching" with the shop chiefs. This has to do with scheduling the flow of supplies and construction so that the weekly production quotas can be met. In the course of this conference, he begins to realize that he is critically short of steel, and that one department has to borrow from another at a waste of time and effort.

Just before twelve he receives word from his deputy that inspectors are going over the casting department in company with the chief engineer. Kalganov judges that problem to be in hand, and spends the next hour telephoning every steel manager he knows to arrange a swap of coal (of which he has purchased a quantity solely for purposes of bargaining) for steel plate. Finally he manages to trade coal for limestone with the manager of a cement plant. He then trades the limestone that a steel manager needs for the plate he needs himself.

While he is concluding this barter, he begins to worry about his financial resources for future deals. Since the ministry pays all his bills directly, he does not have much room for maneuver. He calls in the chief bookkeeper and has him bill the ministry for "experimental work."

Meanwhile the inspectors have counted ten engine mounts in the casting room and have listened to the report on the "tests" that show the need for extra weight. From one to two, Kalganov takes lunch with the inspectors.

From two to four he visits various offices in the city, the *glavk*, the district committee of the party, and a suboffice of his own firm, where he talks with a "pusher" who is trying to round up steel or goods that can be traded for steel.

From four to six he signs important letters and reports, prepared by other executives, to suppliers, the ministry, and various party groups. From time to time he calls in the men who have prepared the reports.

At six he leaves for dinner at home. He talks briefly with his children and gets to work with the evening paper and the *politinformatsia*, the special economic and political briefing sheet that he gets from the ministry and that is supposed to be factual.

From eight to eleven, back at the office, he calls in executives for production conferences, attends a party meeting, and goes over confidential orders with the chief of the secret sector.

From eleven to one he deals with the progress of the housing being completed for the additional two thousand workers. One after the other he talks with his assistants in charge of food, housing, and medical service; with the chief of the OKS, the capital-construction sector; the chief of the personnel sector; the plant's party secretary; and finally the trade-union chairman.

Shortly after one, Kalganov's hands begin to shake. He leaves the office and drives home.

CHAOS IN A BOTTLENECK

Out of the frenzy of activity that possesses the Russian manager there still proceeds an increasing flood of goods. There proceeds very little long-term planning. Whatever is in the mind of the manager, problems of maintenance, repair, and increasing the efficiency of labor are seldom there. The manager lives strictly in the present; his thoughts are too busy to recall the past; his problems are too taxing to permit serious consideration of the future. His tenure at any firm is too short to encourage anything but exploitation of its immediate productive resources. Yet the Russian economy is running fast; it is operating not for the present but some sort of future.

The absence of plans and projections whereby individual firms can anticipate their future growth, their future sources of supply, and their future assets—this is a key fact in the day-in day-out life of Russian business. The economy is a bottleneck economy. All the stratagems and devices of the managers are brought to bear on the bottlenecks as they affect their own plants. All the stratagems and devices of the regime itself are brought to bear on the most critical bottlenecks that affect the economy as a whole. The solutions are strictly *ad hoc:* improvisations thought up to take care of one emergency after another. There is a shortage of vital metal. Suddenly this problem becomes the one great problem; an immense quantity of human effort is discharged upon it, concentrated around it. But by the time that bottleneck is broken, whether in the individual firm or in the whole economy, another bottleneck appears. When it is broken, again there is another, another, another.

The Soviet word for this sort of trouble shooting is the same as the word for the end-of-month rush, *shturmovshchina.* Literally it means an assault on a particular objective.* There is something more involved, however, than the progressive conquest of increasing confusion. There is a type of economic activity that grows by destroying itself.

ECONOMIC CANNIBALISM

The elements of the Soviet economy, after all, are machines, plants, managers, and men. The pressure for maximum immediate output wears out machines and runs down plants. It eats away at the morale and the physical strength—in short, the productivity—of workers. It transforms managers into superexpediters and discards most of them about the time they are

* The terminology of Russian enterprise is replete with the phrases of military tactics.

gaining in managerial experience. Wide managerial experience, in fact, is the monopoly of a small group of top officials, just as experience of day-to-day expediting is the monopoly of the manager and his executives: whence the enormous overhead of Soviet firms.

Soviet economic effort is wasted, of course, to the degree that managers are not allowed to delegate authority and build for the future. It is wasted to the degree that managers produce less than they could, either because they want to protect themselves or because their true capital assets are wearing out. It is wasted to the degree that managers bargain to lower their productivity goals, understate production when high, overstate it when low, and sacrifice quality to quantity.

The reason for this misuse of economic effort is the decision of the Soviet ruling clique to produce as much as possible now in order to create as large an economy as possible *in the near future.* Soviet planning is not a continuing long-range undertaking that seeks to make each firm grow in size and health. Rather it is an incessant transfer of the profits that can be squeezed from existing plants, machines, managers, and men to new plants, new machines.

HOW LONG CAN IT LAST?

In short, today's production is used largely to provide for tomorrow's production that will be used to provide for another and another tomorrow's production. This process hurts first the older firms, but in time all firms grow older. In effect, the Soviet economy attempts to function without heed to obsolescence, and when age finally catches up with it, it will confront a crisis. Obsolescence did not catch up during the last war; lend-lease and the looting of going concerns in Central Europe and Manchuria made up for the destruction of plant, much of it obsolescent, in Russia proper. But as Soviet industry feeds more and more hungrily upon itself, the inevitable confrontation approaches.

There is no way of getting rid of obsolescence by means of purges. The concentrated ruination of the present to provide output for the future must sometime end, either through adoption of rational management, through serious trouble in the economy itself—or through military victory so sweeping that the Russians can exchange a host of wornout factories for new ones.

Meanwhile, Russian business is conducted in an atmosphere of rush and unreality, wherein feverish and pressured managers override today's problems to produce the machinery for a questionable tomorrow.

THE TRANSFORMATION OF AMERICAN CAPITALISM*

American capitalism has changed in the last fifty years. Since the "robber-baron" days of greed and irresponsibility and domination by Wall Street, it has a history of reform from without and within. The present transformation is chiefly a reform by business itself, manifested particularly in the new attitude of "Big Business." One of the chief characteristics of the big modern enterprise is that it is run by the professional manager who is becoming increasingly aware of his responsibilities to society as a whole. However, all sectors of American capitalism have not been transformed; there are still defects.

Nothing demonstrates the strength of the American way of life and the adaptability of the American system better than the transformation of American capitalism. Fifty years ago American capitalism seemed to be what Marx predicted it would be and what all the muckrakers said it was—the inhuman offspring of greed and irresponsibility, committed by its master, Wall Street, to a long life of monopoly. It seemed to provide overwhelming proof of the theory that private ownership could honor no obligation except the obligation to pile up profits. It was, indeed, close to the capitalism that Andrei Vishinsky today keeps on denouncing so laboriously and humorlessly. And it was the capitalism that millions of people abroad and many even at home, to the immense aid and comfort of the Communists, still think American capitalism is.

American capitalism today is actually nothing of the kind. What has happened is that it has changed and developed beyond the ability of the historians to catch up with it; that its transformation, perhaps because people rarely see in perspective what is occurring before their eyes, has escaped the full awareness of even most businessmen; that most of the popular books, the great books even, that have furnished Americans with their stereotypes about capitalism are now obsolete. American capitalism is all-pervasive and intimately bound in with the political system, and it has undergone a vast dispersion of initiative and ownership. What might be called the influence of Main Street has become vastly more important to it than the control of Wall Street, and it has thus been changed into something very different from the capitalism that flourishes in most other lands.

The transformation can best be understood by looking at what has happened to "Big Business," which once was supposed to have controlled the economy from its headquarters in Wall Street. The fact is that Wall Street no longer wields much power over Big Business, which in turn is far from being the most powerful sector of the economy. For economic power boils down to the ability to decide who makes what and who gets what and in what proportions, and business alone no longer decides this. "The class struggle

*From "The Transformation of American Capitalism," February, 1951.

in America," writes Professor Clair Wilcox in the *Harvard Business Review*, "is not a struggle between the proletariat and the bourgeoisie. It is a struggle between functional groups possessing concentrated power—a struggle to control the products of industry." These groups, as Professor Wilcox describes them, are Big Labor, Big Agriculture, Big Little Business, and Big Business. Of them all, Big Business, if only because it is subject to the most pressure, exercises its power with a strong and growing sense of responsibility. Out of the experiment and change of American life, observed by all but comprehended fully by few, capitalism has developed into something that neither Karl Marx nor Adam Smith ever dreamed of.

IT'S EITHER RIGHT OR WRONG

At the bottom of the change is simple morality, which has concerned the U.S. as it has concerned no other great nation in all history. "The American," H.L. Mencken once said, "save in moments of conscious and swiftly lamented deviltry, casts up all ponderable values, including the value even of beauty, in terms of right and wrong." Like the European who described moral indignation as suppressed envy, Mencken scorned it as the mark of the peasant; and the American's capacity for moral indignation *has* resulted in many "uncivilized" excesses like prohibition. But it has also made him the most omnivorous reformer in history. Karl Marx based his philosophy on the fatalistic assumption that what he described as the inherent defects of capitalism are above the will of men to affect them. It has remained for the history of U.S. capitalism, beginning as early as the 1870's, to show that the moral convictions of men can change the course of capitalistic development.

And it would have been strange if a nation that had only recently fought a terrible war over the question of slavery had *not* got indignant about the excesses of its "robber barons." People, of course, do not necessarily rise up voluntarily and act on moral indignation. What is essential is their capacity for it; given a free, lively press and plenty of politicians, the action follows. Action followed in the U.S. because a whole school of commentators, from novelists to reporters, from historians to cartoonists, rose up to expose the financial and industrial scandals of the day. There were the Ida Tarbells and Henry Demarest Lloyds, the Upton Sinclairs, and Frederick Oppers, backed by the Hearsts, McClures, and Munseys. Some were hypocritical and others wholly sincere, but all operated on the effective principle that the public could be fetched by an appeal to its moral standards.

In their zeal the muckrakers paid little attention to the great economic role played by "robber barons" in forming the capital to lay the rails, erect the factories, build the machinery for a new and expanding economy. Naturally the muckrakers were concerned not with amoral economics but with immoral practices. Their pictures of the American economic brigandage of the late nineteenth and early twentieth centuries became stereotypes all over the world—Daniel Drew feeding his cattle salt to make them drink heavily the day before market; Cornelius Vanderbilt bragging how "we busted the hull damn legislature"; foxy Jay Gould, whom Vanderbilt called the smartest man in America, cornering the national gold-coin supply through his White House connections, and systematically and openly robbing the Erie; gelid old John D. Rockefeller perfecting the trust system and eliminating competitors like clay pigeons. Here was the principle of property ownership carried to its absurd conclusion, capitalism gone berserk. But here also was the moral indignation of the American people. Fanned by lurid accounts in the press and by politicians and publicists of almost every persuasion, from Populists to Republicans, it started the transformation of American capitalism.

"A BROODING OMNIPRESENCE"

Popular resentment of the railroad rate making came early, even before the muckraking school was in full swing. The Interstate Commerce Act was passed in 1887. And only three years later there occurred what is probably the most portentous single legislative act in the history of American capitalism: the passage of the Sherman Act against monopolies and combinations "in restraint of trade." Although endorsed by all parties, its birth was inauspicious, and the bill was amended almost to death. Senator John Sherman himself, the story goes, never read the final version. And for several years, under Cleveland and McKinley, the act was used little, and then ineffectively. In 1901 J. P. Morgan disregarded it and put U.S. Steel together. "What looks like a stone wall to a layman," said Mr. Dooley, "is a triumphal arch to a corporation lawyer." But the muckrakers began to make themselves felt. In 1902 Teddy Roosevelt, a man who not only understood the public mind but judged almost everything in terms of righteousness, whipped out the Sherman Act and used it as a "big stick" on what he was the first to call the "malefactors of great wealth." He wielded it so effectively against the Northern Securities Co. that the legislation became a power in American life.

The defects of the Sherman Act were soon and widely recognized. "No law can make a man compete with himself," observed J. P. Morgan characteristically. Others noted the great paradox of the antitrust con-

ception: a strong company that really obeyed the law and competed strenuously would end up as a monopoly, violating the law. Contemplating such contradictions, the "realistic" Europeans abstained from trust busting; they left it to the naive Americans, who in their preoccupation with right and wrong were foolish enough to take so seriously and apply so dogmatically their notions of fairness and justice.

The antitrust law nevertheless acquired stature and authority. However patent its imperfections, however hollow its victories, however vitiated by later acts like Miller-Tydings and Robinson-Patman, it became, in the words of Justice Holmes, "a brooding omnipresence in the sky." Even when businessmen are puzzled and irritated by the letter of the law, they respect its spirit. Even when their lawyers tell them how to get around it, they know they *are* getting around it. There probably is more competition, as competition is now understood and practiced, than there was fifty years ago. The law, in the last analysis, amounts to nothing less than the successful extension of the Anglo-Saxon common law, the basis of the whole English-speaking world's unique liberty, into the realm of business. And its success is among the chief reasons why American business is today so vastly different from European business.

REFORM UNLIMITED

Other reforms came sporadically. The American's moral indignation, naturally enough, did not burn with a steady flame. In good times he tended to overlook violations of his basic notions; in bad times he looked for something to blame things on, and demanded that something be done about them. During the 1920's popular demand for reform was almost nonexistent. For one thing, the scorn of some of the nation's most effective writers made preoccupation with moral issues unfashionable if not ludicrous. For another, business seemed to be doing fine, and seemed to deserve not reform but praise. As the immensely popular *Saturday Evening Post* demonstrated in almost every issue, as Herbert Hoover himself phrased it, "The slogan of progress is changing from the full dinner pail to the full garage."

The catastrophe of depression blasted this dream. The shocked and angry people, seeing their livelihood disappear, put the Right to Life above the other rights. Their natural tendency to blame the bust on those who only yesterday were taking credit for having started an eternal boom was strengthened by revelations such as those of the Pecora congressional investigation into Wall Street financial practices. So they embraced the latter-day Populism of the New Deal, and demanded that something be done. Writers and intellectuals took up the cudgels. Some were merely inclined to condemn what they had for so long contemned, but many tried to find out how and why it had happened, and how to keep it from happening again.

Many of the ensuing reforms survived. Immediately after the Pecora investigation, Congress passed a law divorcing investment banking from deposit banking. And a year later it passed the well-intentioned Securities Exchange Act, which put the Stock Exchange under federal regulation, gave the Federal Reserve Board authority to limit speculative margins, required all officers and stockholders of big companies to report their dealings in their companies' securities, and created the Securities and Exchange Commission to watch over the investment market.

Other attempts at reform were less successful. NRA, for example, went to a well-deserved death. As for the famed Temporary National Economic Committee, much of what it investigated was beside the point by the time it was in print—and not only because of the impending war. Even while the committee was mulling over the power of big business, and the intellectuals were in full cry on the trail of finance capitalism, business initiative had been dispersed among hundreds of enterprises, business power in the aggregate had been largely yielded to the farmers and unions, and Wall Street had ceased to be a valid symbol of great power.

The decline of Wall Street actually began long before the reforms of the New Deal. It began when corporations grew rich and independent. The rights to their profits, of course, were by traditional economics vested in the stockholders. But their managers saw no point in paying, say, $20 a share in dividends on their stock when $10 was enough to sustain the company's credit rating. They also reasoned that it was *they*, and not the stockholders, who were directly responsible for the profits. So they began to hold back on the stockholders and put the money into corporate reserves. As early as 1905 the Santa Fe, under Edward Ripley adopted the policy of a dollar for the stockholder, a dollar for the property. Owen Young of G.E. and others, some years later, further developed the idea of self-capitalization, arguing that the money plowed back would in the long run enhance the stockholder's equity. Whether it did or not, it enabled a large part of business to do its own banking.

THE DECLINE OF WALL STREET

Wall Street did not feel the change at first. In the boom of the 1920's the issue of new securities passed the $500-million-a-year mark, and a rich time was had by all. But even then the bulk of the Street's effort was going into the buying and selling of old issues (and new issues of holding companies that used the money to buy old issues), the promotion of dubious foreign bonds, and the lending of money at, say, 7 per cent for the speculative purchase of stock paying, say, 5 per cent. And even then corporations were putting up to ten times as much money into their reserves as all companies were raising in new stocks and bonds. And the depression hit the Street's new-issue function even harder than it hit the trading function. High income taxes and the growing corporate practice of financing new issues through insurance and trust companies trimmed the new-issue business almost to the vanishing point.

Except as its opinions still influence investment policies, Wall Street today exerts only a fraction of the power it once wielded. Industry now plows back 60 per cent of its profits, as against 30 per cent in the 1920's, and the bulk of money used in capital formation comes from corporate earnings or from internal sources such as depreciation. The largest brokerage house on the Street, accounting for 10 per cent of the stock trading on the Stock Exchange, is Merrill Lynch, Pierce, Fenner & Beane, 90 per cent of whose customers are small-fry out-of-towners.

The House of Morgan is still one of the large commercial banks of the country (its underwriting business was passed over to Morgan Stanley in 1935), with total resources of about $667 million; and the phrase "Morgan Company" still evokes images of the old days when Morgan did direct U.S. business. But the working capital of General Motors, by contrast, is more than $1.6 *billion,* and G.M. not only finances itself but recently loaned money to Jones & Laughlin. As for leadership and control, Robert Young's defiance of Morgan in buying control of the C. & O. years ago was more a feat of derring-do than genuine audacity. And when the "Morgan" directors of Montgomery Ward found themselves disapproving Sewell Avery not long ago, they shortly afterward found themselves resigning. The power and the glory had vanished. The dynamic leadership of the economy had moved to the big corporate offices in midtown New York, Schenectady, Chicago, Pittsburgh, and points west and south. It is indeed hard to believe that only thirty-nine years ago J. P. Morgan, the one-man center of the American business universe, was candidly laying his cards on the table at the Pujo investigation: "I like a little competition, but I like combination better. . . . Without control you cannot do a thing."

THE MANAGERIAL EVOLUTION

One of the two chief characteristics of big modern enterprise is that it is run by hired management. As Berle and Means put it, the power inherent in the control of the "active property"—the plant organization and good will—has superseded the power inherent in "passive property"—the stocks and bonds. Even companies whose owners are managers may be described as management-run. The Ford company, for example, behaves not as an organization solely dedicated to earning the maximum number of dollars for the Ford family, but as an organization dedicated first of all to its own perpetuation and growth.

The other chief characteristic of the big modern enterprise is that management is becoming a profession. This means, to begin with, that a professional manager holds his job primarily because he is good at it. Often he has begun at the bottom and worked his way up by sheer merit. Or more often he has been carefully and even scientifically chosen from a number of bright and appropriately educated young men, put through an executive-training course, and gradually insinuated into the activities for which he shows the most talent. Since even at the top he generally functions as a member of a committee rather than as a final authority, his talents are so well balanced that none of them protrude excessively. He lives on what he makes, and even when he is well paid he doesn't have much left after taxes. Generally he is gregarious, and usually he is not a colossal

The Average Stockholder's 19½ Shares

Readers of free-enterprise advertising doubtless feel familiar with the cloying little scene in which an ordinary American couple, standing on the front steps of their rose-covered cottage, are approached by a kindly mailman bearing a dividend check. The couple look fondly at each other (or the check) and all hands exchange congratulations that they live under a system in which the owners of industry are—gosh, just about everybody.

There happens to be quite a bit of truth in this, but it is very seldom, unfortunately, that the advertising copy really nails down the case. Too many corporations make a great fuss over the fact that their *average* stockholder holds only 19½ shares, approximate market value $1,100, or some such amount. Well, the *average* American is sensible enough to know that isn't the whole story. He rather imagines that a few of the stockholders own many thousands of shares, and many thousands of the stockholders own a few shares. Very probably no one owns 19½ shares. And since it was the corporation that brought up the whole thing in the first place, the reader of the ad might well ask: Who owns just how much?

—"Notes on the Permanent Revolution," August, 1951.

"personality." But if he is not a General MacArthur, neither is he a Mr. Milquetoast. And if he is expected not to give arbitrary orders, he is also expected not to take them. In most well-run big enterprises, an executive is by definition a man who would object officially to a policy decision he disapproved.

More important, the manager is becoming a professional in the sense that like all professional men he has a responsibility to society as a whole. This is not to say that he no longer needs good, old-fashioned business sense. He does, and more than ever. The manager is responsible primarily to his company as a profit-earning mechanism, and current talk about the corporation as a nonprofit institution is more than a little naive. Any self-respecting businessman would rightly suspect a colleague who allowed he was in business not to make money. The modern enterpriser *should* be in business to make money. His ability to make money is the prime measure of his company's efficiency. If it cannot prosper on the service it supplies to society, or if it cannot persuade society to pay it enough to prosper, it does not deserve to stay in business. Moreover, the good, efficient manager *likes* to make money, and it is mainly because he likes to make money that he does a first-rate job. As the Russians have discovered, when the profit motive does not exist it has to be invented.

But the great happy paradox of the profit motive in the American system is that management, precisely because it is in business to make money years on end, cannot concentrate exclusively on making money here and now. To keep on making money years on end, it must, in the words of Frank Abrams, Chairman of the Standard Oil Co. of New Jersey, "conduct the affairs of the enterprise in such a way as to maintain an *equitable and working balance* among the claims of the various directly interested groups—stockholders, employees, customers, and the public at large." Not all pundits have understood this vital point. In his romantic *Managerial Revolution,* for example, James Burnham described the trend accurately enough but conveyed the idea that somehow the corporate manager is destined to become the Western equivalent of a King Farouk or perhaps an unusually favored commissar. The corporate manager neither is, nor is becoming, anything of the kind. He is part of a group that enjoys power only so long as it does not abuse it—in other words, precisely so long as it does not exercise power the way men and groups of men used to.

Thus it is easy to define management's responsibility to the stockholder. Management is no longer occupied exclusively with the interests of the stockholder, who often has become a kind of contingent bondholder rather than a part owner, and who rarely exerts any direct influence on the affairs of the company. But management cannot flagrantly disregard stockholders' interests, at least not for long. As the management of Bethlehem and U.S. Steel know well, stockholders can be a considerable nuisance. Even when widely dispersed, they can be induced to take a point of view by proxy. And on the whole, management is treating the stockholders well—despite "abuses" like the habit of holding annual meetings in some out-of-the-way railway station or in Wilmington, Delaware. Almost any good manager can honestly argue that the growing importance of the hired management and its policy of self-capitalization have been to the benefit of the stockholder. Above all, he can argue that the stockholder's long-term interests lie in letting competent, responsible management build up the company and deal justly with employees, customers, and the public.

Modern management exhibits a sense of responsibility to its employees not only to prevent or anticipate the demands of labor unions but for the simple, obvious, and honest reason that a satisfied, loyal group of employees is at least as much a capital asset as a modern plant or a vital piece of machinery. A few enlightened managers, as a matter of fact, have been taking such an attitude for years. It is now twenty-five years since General Electric, under Owen Young, introduced employee stock-buying plans and the idea of a "cultural" rather than a "living" wage.

Corporations today support a wide variety of material benefits. Some go in for stabilization of employment. ATF Inc., for example, which recently bought into the furniture business, has succeeded in almost eliminating the highly seasonal character of that business. Some companies (Procter & Gamble, Nunn-Bush, Hormel) carry employment stabilization to the point of guaranteeing an annual wage. Others have developed forecasting techniques to anticipate trends and to stabilize employment by leveling out production.

Almost every important company now has a pension plan, or is in the process of getting one. Many, like Sears, Roebuck, combine pensions with savings plans, so that when an employee retires he takes with him a sizable capital sum. Then there is the profit-sharing approach, backed by the newly formed Council of Profit-Sharing Industries (276 members), with annual bonus distributions ranging up to 100 per cent of base wages. Finally, there is the "participation" school, reported in *Fortune* in January, 1950 ("Enterprise for Everyman"). Its purpose is to bring the worker into the enterprise system by giving him a share in productivity decisions and a cut of productivity profits. Since *Fortune's* report, at least a dozen firms, including Stromberg-Carlson of Rochester, New York, have adopted a Scanlon participation plan. There is a growing tendency on the part of blue-chip management to regard a job in its company as a kind of employment package, complete with pensions, savings plans, and numerous "fringe benefits" such as severance pay, maternity leaves, hospitalization and medical insurance.

But material benefits, as Elton Mayo and others have demonstrated, are often not as important as job satisfaction—the feeling of having done a good job, and of having it recognized by people who know what a good job is. Related and equally important is the feeling of participating in the company, of being a kind of partner without, of course, fully being one. The problem of generating these attitudes in the worker—particularly in making him feel his "participation"—is tremendous, and it cannot be solved merely by the resolution to do something about it. In one of the Standard Oil affiliates, for example, management was stumped by a case of group dissatisfaction until the president of the company began to talk to the men informally about some of the problems that were plaguing him and his board. "The men showed an immediate and extraordinary interest, and that gradually revealed the source of their dissatisfaction," recalls Frank Abrams. "They had been 'left out of things.'" The point to be noted here is that not every president could have done that. This president obviously had the "something" it takes to put a man across with his employees. And the gradual cultivation of that something is one of the unfinished tasks ahead of management.

Taking everything together, management has done well by its employees. The problem indeed may be to prevent it from discharging its responsibility to its employees *too* well. For when a company distributes employee benefits that are not compensated by rising productivity, it must in the long run pass the cost increase on to the consumer. Obviously a company *can* be tempted to win employee cooperation easily, and a few producers and a single union can combine to gang up on the public.

THE FINAL RESPONSIBILITY

Thus far, however, it is the modern manager's sense of responsibility to his customer and the general public that gives him his best claim to being progressive. More goods at lower cost (and prices) is the basic principle of American industry, and even companies regarded as anything but socially minded have built themselves upon it. Many a chemical, for example, has been sold at a progressively lower price without the spur of competition, simply to encourage the market. And most modern managers do worry a good deal about the related subjects of prices, monopoly, and competition. Competition has come a long way since the time of Lord Dewar, who cracked that "competition is the life of trade, and competition is the death of profits." The alternatives today are not monopoly or all-out competition. The Darwinian concept of all-out competition has given way to the concept of a pragmatic or "workable" competition, which far from being the death of profits provides, as smart companies know, the soundest way to ensure their survival.

Aside from its value as a foil to antitrust, which can be exaggerated, healthy, workable competition provides a good check on how a company is doing. Take du Pont, which, though almost unique, may well set a precedent. Pursued by the hounds of antitrust (unjustly, it maintains) du Pont spent over a year looking for a competitor willing to put $20 million into a cellophane plant. Having found one in Olin industries, it is building the plant for Olin and supplying the necessary technical assistance. And that is not all. Because du Pont was the only market source for sodium metal, it induced National Distillers to make the stuff. And recently it turned over its nylon patents to the Chemstrand Co.

Other companies have learned that a similar self-discipline is the best price policy in the long run. The recent furor about rolling back the prices of automobiles obscures the fact that the automobile companies had conducted themselves with a notable respect for public opinion. Had they let the law of supply and demand take its course in the sellers' market of the past four or five years they could have priced their cars much higher. Their dealers, it is true, sometimes did extract a premium from eager buyers. But it was the manufacturers' list prices that in the main determined the price level, and the auto makers' refusal to charge what the traffic would bear must be reckoned as an extraordinary example of the transformation of the capitalistic mind.

THE MANAGER AND PUBLIC OPINION

One of the most pressing concerns of almost every large company today is what people are going to think about it. Board meetings often turn into self-examination sessions, with managers defending or explaining their actions as if before accusing judges. At a recent board meeting of a large consumer-goods company, the president rose up and remarked that the foremen had in effect built up a block between management and labor, and that management was mostly at fault. Fully two hours were devoted to soul-searching and discussion. There was also the matter of closing an old mill in a small town. Not only was the specific situation explored thoroughly, but a whole history of other similar cases was brought up. This problem was solved, after a full hour's discussion, by the decision to move a storage plant into the town and so absorb nearly all the displaced employees. As one executive remarked, "At least half our time is taken up with discussing the repercussions of what we propose to do. And this is what the boys who write the books call the managerial revolution."

What may set a new high in business' concern with fundamental values and questions is a current project of Corning Glass Works, which is celebrating its centennial this year. On the premise that "As long as there are men making and operating machines, there will be a humanistic problem as well as a scientific and technological problem in an industrial society," Corning has joined the American Council of Learned Societies in sponsoring a conference on "Living in an Industrial Civilization." The conference, to be held next May at the Corning Glass Center, will be attended by academicians and men of affairs from all over the world, and they will discuss such subjects as the industrial man's creativity, his sense of community, and his confidence in life.

Nothing perhaps is more indicative of the corporation's awareness of its responsibilities than the growth of public-relations activities. Upwards of 4,000 companies now go in for public-relations "programs." Although many of them are hardly more than publicity campaigns, more and more managers understand tolerably well that good business public relations, as *Fortune* has defined it, is good performance publicly appreciated, because adequately communicated. Now the mere comprehension of a moral axiom, as all parents know, does not guarantee its observance. But its constant iteration does make the subject more and more acutely aware of its importance, and thus eventually influences his behavior. As Paul Garrett of G.M. has been saying for years, "Our program is finding out what people like, doing more of it; finding out what people don't like, doing less of it."

HOPE FOR THE FUTURE

All of which should not be interpreted to mean that business is already rolling us down the six-lane, high-speed highway to economic paradise. When this article speaks of modern managers, it speaks of the pace setters, and does not presume to imply that all other managers and all other companies are doing as well. Many still give precedence to the big, quick profit, and incline to regard the stockholder mainly as a convenient personification of that goal, labor as a lamentably sensitive kind of commodity, and the customer as the man who gets rolled. Like many a labor and agricultural leader, they try to increase their share of the national product regardless of their contribution to that product. What Professor Wilcox calls Big (or organized) Little Business, for example, is responsible for or protected by most of the fair-trade laws, licensing systems, local bidding laws, and other legal devices that maintain prices independently of the market.

Big Business, too, has something to answer for. Just how much power it has for example to fix prices and to what extent it uses or abuses that power are right now the subjects of much expert contention. Some economists maintain that "Oligopoly is by all evidence the ruling market form in the modern economy"—i.e., since the nation's corporate assets are concentrated in a relatively few companies, the market is one of a few sellers, who can administer prices. Other economists, attacking the statistics on which such conclusions are based, maintain that only 20 per cent of the national income is provided by unregulated oligopoly, and that an analysis of competition in terms of market realities, which nobody has yet completed, will show that the American economy is becoming more, not less, competitive. It is to be hoped that such an important analysis will be undertaken soon. But whatever its results, it is not likely to reveal that business, socially speaking, has yet attained perfection.

What counts, however, is that the business leaders *are* setting the pace, and *are* being followed. What counts is that the old concept that the owner has a right to use his property just the way he pleases has evolved into the belief that ownership carries social obligations, and that a manager is a trustee not only for the owner but for society as a whole. Such is the Transformation of American Capitalism. In all the world there is no more hopeful economic phenomenon.

31. AUTOMATION

"AUTOMATION": NEWS BEHIND THE NOISE*

By HERBERT SOLOW

There is much talk these days about "automation." The difficulty is that the term's meaning is not clear. Everything from the giant automatic feed-back machine to a gimmick to set up bowling pins has been called "automation." This introduction to a technological article attempts to clarify the term.

It is fine to have a new word coined when one is needed. "Automation" is a new word, fashioned out of an earlier one, "automatization." Whether or not it was needed has become a question. The man who, around 1947, first gave the word wide circulation is Delmar S. Harder, executive vice president of Ford Motor Co.

His intention was modest: he used the word to describe a new step taken by Ford after World War II—mechanization of the handling of workpieces between machines that perform successive tasks. This innovation is achieved by "transfer" machines.

Some of Ford's new "automation" machines are made by Cross Co. of Detroit. Recently that company's Ralph E. Cross exclaimed: "In the interest of

* From Herbert Solow, " 'Automation': News Behinds the Noise," April, 1956.

sanity, I think that automation should be debunked to some extent." Certainly there has been considerable bunk, promotional or otherwise, talked about "automation"; but what is needed even more than debunking is clarification. For, behind a confusion that bothers many besides Mr. Cross, important new things have been happening to industrial technology, including the introduction of new kinds of machines that cut labor costs, raise productivity, increase yield from raw materials, cut design costs, improve products, and even enable industry to do things it never could do before.

Detroit's mechanical transfer of workpieces is one instance of the new achievements. Another is automatic monitoring of instruments in an ammonia plant for more efficient process control . . . A new giant, self-correcting machine controlled by magnetic tape can automatically mill a complete aircraft wing skin . . . Items ranging from small automotive parts to freight cars in a marshaling yard are sorted by new electronic devices with a vast increase over earlier speed and accuracy . . . Electronic weighing devices are helping to produce more uniform mixes for cement and processed foods . . . Many kinds of accounting work have been speeded by electronic computers . . . Computers are also being used for rapid design of high-pressure steam-power piping systems, reinforced-concrete structures, etc.

All these and hundreds of other recent developments—including such modest ones as a gimmick to set up bowling pins and a ferris-wheel sort of rig for easy display of burial caskets—have been called "automation." Some experts construct their definitions of "automation" from the parochial viewpoint of one industry. Some have produced several definitions, with inconsistencies among them. In addition to the definition popular in Detroit (i.e., mechanized transfer of workpieces) and also used by appliance, radio, and TV manufacturers, there are several other common uses of the word.

In one definition the criterion is *machine control by any non-human means*—that is, by another machine or by its product, such as a punched card or magnetic tape. According to another definition, there is no "automation" without *feedback*—feeding information automatically from the end product of a system back into the system to control (regulate, adjust, correct) it. This is sometimes called "closed loop." Computer salesmen and some physicists define "automation" as nothing less than the use of *electronic devices,* more especially digital computers, for their considerable range of purposes. John Diebold, head of a New York management-consultant firm, and some others speak of "automation" as *a philosophy of organizing any work as a system*" in which product design, operations research, control engineering, and management science in general constitute the essential approach to details of equipment and process. Another definition—which is supported by some manufacturers of quite advanced machinery—equates "automation" with *any technological progress;* one of this group, for example, says that "automation" began with Neanderthal man's invention of the club.

The range of definition—Neanderthal club to the giant electronic computer—is considerable. The indiscriminate uses of the word recall the practice of Humpty Dumpty:

"I meant by 'impenetrability' that we've had enough of that subject, and it would be just as well if you'd mention what you mean to do next, as I suppose you don't mean to stop here all the rest of your life."

"That's a great deal to make one word mean," Alice said in a thoughtful tone.

"When I make a word do a lot of work like that," said Humpty Dumpty, *"I always pay it extra."*

The heavy labor of the word "automation" is hardly worth the price, some of which is paid by those who attend the "automation" conferences and round tables that have been erupting all over U.S. industry. The definition problem is acute at all these meetings. Armour Research Foundation's "automation" conference in February of this year had as a principal purpose to "stabilize thinking." This involved more defining, but whether stability has resulted may be doubted. The American Standards Association now has a committee busy defining. Meanwhile, people are brought together to discuss "automation" who have quite disparate interests and seem often to confuse each other's thinking. Hardheaded men who are supposed to believe that time is money throw away a lot of time on this sort of thing.

Another part of the price of overworking the word "automation" is paid by society in general. However exciting the technological news, the excitement over the word is greater. Fans of "automation" have been anticipating an early return to the Garden of Eden, where man got his living without a sweaty brow. In other quarters, phobias are born. A Detroit public-opinion poll has reflected intense fear that mass unemployment will be caused by "automation." Such a fear helped to inspire congressional hearings on "automation" last fall. The resulting report declared it to be "clearly wrong to dismiss automation as nothing more than an extension of mechanization," and voiced vague forebodings. In February the International Confederation of Free Trade Unions anxiously asked the United Nations to forecast the "economic and social repercussions" of "automation."

Many people talk of a "second industrial revolution." It may be questioned, however, whether anything that is being called "automation" has a higher significance than did the introduction of interchangeable parts, the assembly line, or continuous-flow methods in producing chemicals. Each of those gave impetus to the revolution that James Watt began by inventing the self-powered engine in 1788. Indeed, Watt himself invented not only the steam engine but its flyball governor, an information-gathering, feedback control mechanism similar in purpose to all other feedback mechanisms. The plain fact is that the industrial revolution never stops revolving. It is a permanent revolution, and even the most novel items thus far realized in the range of what is called "automation" are part of that continuing process.

In reality, none of the major definitions now circulating refers to anything that cannot be covered by the word mechanization—that is, replacement of men by machines. What complicates mechanization concepts today and has let "automation" into the language without clear meaning is, apparently, one fact. Two human functions are theoretically replaceable—the providing of energy and the handling of information. Mechanization has long been replacing the first, and now it is replacing the second at an impressive rate.

Yet mechanization still embraces all "automation" phenomena. Mr. Diebold—who thought up the word "automation" independently of Mr. Harder—has wondered whether it is headed for the junk pile.

AUTOMATION—SOCIALLY DESIRABLE?

For its last question of the day Fortune *asked: "How much weight should industry give to the social desirability of the Automatic Factory?" Almost without exception Round Table members feared that most workers would view the emergence of the Automatic Factory as a threat to their security.*

The comments of Mr. Hitchings, manager of Ford's economic-analysis department, were typical.

MR. HITCHINGS: I think a better selling job has to be done on the social desirability of increased mechanization, because even though many people accept the idea that well, yes, it is a good thing to have increased productivity, they always point to the particular situation and say, "Well, that is bad, because you displace labor in that particular spot."

MR. JAEGER: I don't think we are consciously trying to ease the burden of our workers, nor consciously trying to improve their standard of living. These things take care of themselves. They have a feedback of their own that closes the loop automatically. I don't think that it is the part, nor can it be the part, of industry to try to plan the social aspects of this thing.

Professor Riesman, the Round Table's sociologist, surprised some of his listeners by supporting Mr. Jaeger.

PROF. RIESMAN: I have a feeling that it is a kind of grandiosity for each trade to worry about the social consequences of its work. Journalists are inclined to be awfully pious about how effective they are. Social scientists worry about manipulation before they have any cause to worry, because they aren't that good. Engineers worry about the consequences of their achievements.

I think of the Rust brothers who used to worry about their cotton picker in the early 1930's. It turned out that some of the people displaced by it are working in the Boeing plant in Wichita. It was senseless to worry. It wasn't their job.

He didn't mean, however, that sociologists might not be entitled to worry about the consequences of the Automatic Factory.

PROF. RIESMAN: I am interested in leisure, and the feeling of many Americans that leisure is a threat, a problem, burden, or hazard, rather than as man has thought for centuries, a clear gain—and I have somehow the feeling that this fear of leisure may be one of the factors holding back further automatization.

My second interest is in work itself as an emotional hazard for men and women which can be relieved by automatization. I think, for instance, of a study by William Whyte (not *Fortune's*) of the crying waitress —why waitresses cry, caught as they are between irascible customers and even more irascible cooks.

When I see an Automat, I would like to bow down and salaam to it as a blessing, because it gets rid of the crying waitress, only qualified by my feeling that there may be some waitresses with a vested interest in their miseries, and I think the problem of the Automatic Factory and transition to it is that of taking care of those with a vested interest in their deformities, such as a masochistic need to work too hard.

I am also thinking of the one institution in our society where automatism has moved very fast, namely the home, and where we have a whole cadre of unemployed people, namely children. We are bringing up, it seems to me, a generation of people who lack the industriousness and work-mindedness of the present generation. The development of the Automatic Factory is salutory if only to keep the level of production rising to meet the growing population's growing needs.

Of the technically trained people at the Round Table, only Dr. Brown and Mr. Leaver seemed deeply concerned about social consequences.

DR. BROWN: My view about the whole field of automatism is that it is a subject whose far-reaching implications almost no one has grasped. Correctly applied, it will cause a change in Western living habits and attitudes toward work that will dwarf the effects of the Industrial Revolution. My hope is that because of what I think is our greater awareness of human values, we can find a way to reap the vast benefits of automatism without incurring too many of its serious penalties.

—"A *Fortune* Roundtable: The Automatic Factory," October, 1953.